Élites, Intellectuals, and Consensus

CORNELL INTERNATIONAL INDUSTRIAL
AND LABOR RELATIONS REPORT — *NO. 7*

PUBLISHED BY

New York State School of Industrial and Labor Relations
A Contract College of the State University of New York
at Cornell University

Labor Unions and National Politics in Italian Industrial Plants
by Maurice F. Neufeld   *(out of print)*

American Labor and the International Labor Movement, 1940 to 1953
by John P. Windmuller   *(out of print)*

Jobs and Workers in India
by Oscar A. Ornati   *(out of print)*

Contemporary Collective Bargaining in Seven Countries
Adolf Sturmthal, Editor   *(out of print)*

Italy: School for Awakening Countries
by Maurice F. Neufeld   600 pp. $9.00 cloth

Poor Countries and Authoritarian Rule
by Maurice F. Neufeld   256 pp. $5.00 cloth

Élites, Intellectuals, and Consensus: Chile
by James O. Morris   312 pp. $6.00 cloth

ÉLITES, INTELLECTUALS, AND CONSENSUS

*A Study of the Social Question and
the Industrial Relations System in Chile*

By JAMES O. MORRIS

*Associate Professor, New York State
School of Industrial and Labor Relations*

NEW YORK STATE SCHOOL OF
INDUSTRIAL AND LABOR RELATIONS
CORNELL UNIVERSITY, ITHACA, NEW YORK
1966

Copyright © 1966 by Cornell University

Library of Congress Catalog Card Number: 66–65151

Price: $6.00

ORDER FROM

Distribution Center, New York State School
of Industrial and Labor Relations,
Cornell University, Ithaca, New York

PRINTED IN THE UNITED STATES OF AMERICA
W. F. HUMPHREY PRESS, INC., GENEVA, NEW YORK

For my parents:

OSHEL C. *and* ELVA M. MORRIS

Preface

SOME of the research which eventually found its way into this book was begun in 1958 when I was a Fulbright fellow at the University of Chile in Santiago. My work continued after I returned to Chile with my family in late 1959 and, as Chief of Party in a Cornell University — University of Chile labor relations project, remained in Santiago until the middle of 1962. During these years, through subsequent visits to Chile, and in stays of several weeks or months in other countries of the area, I believe I have come to know Latin America in more than a superficial way. Since 1963 I have offered a graduate course on "Industrial Relations in Latin America" in the New York State School of Industrial and Labor Relations at Cornell and have been a member of Cornell's Latin American Program Committee.

The complete first draft of the manuscript was read and commented on by several colleagues and fellow "Latin Americanists": Professors Leonard P. Adams (Cornell), Tom E. Davis (Cornell), John J. Johnson (Stanford), and Henry A. Landsberger (Cornell). A second draft, considerably revised and expanded (three new chapters), was read and commented on by Professor Fredrick B. Pike (University of Pennsylvania). In addition, single chapters were read and commented on by Professor Victor Alba (University of Kansas lecturer, 1966) and Professor William V. D'Antonio (Notre Dame). This final product is hopefully superior to all antecedent versions. I willingly acknowledge the debt I owe my critics in this regard.

PREFACE

Many Chilean friends and former colleagues in the University of Chile provided valuable assistance in data collection and interpretation. For this, I wish to express my special thanks to Moisés Poblete Troncoso and William Thayer Arteaga, and also to Alberto Armstrong Verdugo, Jorge Barría Serón, and Carlos Salazar Umaña. The papers of several of my students in the University of Chile have been most useful, particularly in the writing of Chapter 1, and credit is given them by name in the footnotes to that chapter.

Many of my research notes were typed in Spanish by Miss Patricia Elbo (now Mrs. Patricia Elbo de Jurgensen) whose many kindnesses will always remain a pleasant memory. My Cornell secretary, Mrs. Mary Turner, typed the manuscript in all its versions, and her diligence and speed never cease to surpise and please me. During "peak" periods she was assisted by Miss Nancy Doty and Mrs. Karen Wright, whose cheerful cooperation I am now pleased to acknowledge. Finally, for very careful editorial work which has greatly improved the readability of the manuscript, I recognize and thank Miss Frances P. Eagan and Mrs. Mary Jo Powell.

In a broader sense, I am indebted to the University of Chile, and particularly to the Institute of Business Administration (INSORA) of the Faculty of Economic Sciences, for institutional support during the period research was in progress. For this support, I would like to express my appreciation to Juan Gomez Millas, then Rector of the University, to Luis Escobar Cerda, then Dean of the Faculty of Economic Sciences, to Ricardo Saenz, Juan Iampaglia Sgubin, and Jorge Ide Kindermann, who served as Directors of INSORA during my assignment in Chile, and also to Roberto Oyaneder Casanova, Chief of INSORA's Department of Industrial Relations.

Had the Agency for International Development not conceived the idea for and then financially supported the university labor relations project, my research would probably not have been completed in this form. The AID/Chile labor officer at that time, Irving G. Tragen, who continues to be a warm personal friend, was without a doubt the key AID man.

The support my own institution gave to the project, and then gave to me personally after my return to Ithaca, has similarly been crucial to the present publication. To former Deans of the School, Martin P. Catherwood and John W. McConnell, and to our present Dean, David G. Moore, I therefore express my genuine gratitude. Finally, and in recognition of the hard fact that no manuscript becomes a book unless a publisher so decides, a simple thank-you to Professor Leonard P. Adams (the School's Director of Research and Publications) who considered this manuscript worthy of publication.

The book is being published in a Spanish edition by the Editorial del Pacífico in Santiago, Chile.

J.O.M.

Ithaca, New York
June 27, 1966

Contents

Introduction

THIS book is a study of the genesis and the first fourteen years of development of the legal industrial relations system in Chile. Although an introductory chapter on the present-day status of ideology and the industrial relations system is included, the book essentially covers the period from about 1900, when the "social question" first attracted national attention, to 1938, when the Popular Front won the presidency and the consolidation of the legal industrial relations system was assured. This system was actually enacted in 1924, after more than two decades of intellectual ferment and political debate, and at that time consisted of seven laws dealing with the following subjects: (1) blue-collar labor contracts (individual and collective); (2) sickness, invalidity, and accident insurance; (3) reform of a previously enacted law on work accidents; (4) conciliation and arbitration; (5) unions; (6) cooperatives; and (7) white-collar labor contracts. These laws underwent only minor change before they were brought together with other labor laws in 1931 to produce the first labor code in the Western Hemisphere.

By the end of the 1930's a great many legal unions were in existence, tens of thousands of laboring men and women were enrolled in them, conciliation boards were hearing a growing number of "collective conflicts," and a labor court system was in operation. Moreover, national union leaders were, regardless of politics or ideology (anarchists excepted), supporting the government-sponsored system. This support of

Socialists, Communists, Radicals, Liberals, and Conservatives alike among the union leadership cadre, and the electoral victory of the Popular Front (dominated by the Radicals and Socialists and supported by the Communists), were key elements in the consolidation of the legal industrial relations system. Later events have not altered the main outlines of the system and, for this reason, 1938 is a convenient year with which to end this study of the origins of the industrial relations system in Chile.

As an historian, the writer's first purpose is simply to provide as fair and complete an account as possible of the establishment of the industrial relations system. If this history is worthy of the name, it should, like any true history, help illuminate the present and make it more understandable. There are also, in the writer's opinion, some things about present-day industrial relations practices, structures, and behavior patterns in Chile that can hardly be understood at all, and cannot be wisely amended, without knowledge in depth of the origins of the system.

However, too great an emphasis in historical writing on the utilitarian value of history to those grappling with the still unresolved problems of life can distort the true meaning of the past. History can serve the present by providing lessons from past experience, but it cannot be *made* to do so without risking loss of its intrinsic "own" meaning. This is no lapse into a sterile rationale of "history for history's sake" but is rather a recognition of the fullness of the historical approach and a self-warning not to limit its reach either to current problem-solving or to an isolated account of now forgotten events.

The second purpose of the study is to single out the intellectuals, show the extent of their contribution to the development of the legal industrial relations system, and analyze this contribution within the generalized context of intellectual behavior in Latin America and, to a lesser extent, in the more advanced nations of the West. Special attention to the intellectuals is believed justifiable because of their crucial role in labor law development in Chile. Their part was crucial not so much because of the vast social protest literature that poured from pen and press in the opening decades of the twentieth century as because of the politically active part a few intellectuals played in the debates on, and the actual drafting of, labor legislation proposals. Also, the constructive role of student thesis writers in combing the labor relations literature of advanced countries for ideas and solutions adaptable to Chile's problems is certainly impressive to a North American observer and is not, one suspects, fully appreciated even in Chile. The general view of the university student as political activist in Latin America seems to be that of a stereotyped street demonstrator, "hot-head," striker against defenseless professors and hapless administrators, one who seldom shows a sense of civic responsibility. Two or three generations ago the National University student in Santiago showed other qualities.

The third and final purpose of the study is to provide a psychosocial analysis of the failure of Chilean élites to avoid the ideological division of their society and to resolve the "social question" by means of the 1924 laws. In other words, the history of the origins of the industrial relations system in Chile reveals that in the early stages of industrialization the urban and mining labor movements became alienated from society. As anarchists, socialists, and communists, labor leaders declared a revolutionary intention to upset the social system and assume power in the name of the working classes.

This loss of consensus continues to characterize Chile today. Loss of consensus is also observable in other Latin American countries like Argentina and Brazil and in countries elsewhere in the world, including Europe. It can cause chronic political instability or reduction of efficiency in the economic system, and it can also terminate in successful revolution. It is, therefore, appropriate to ask why consensus disappeared in Chile during the transition from an overwhelmingly agrarian society to one with important urban and industrial sectors.

The writer confesses to having no special analytical tools with which to provide scientific answers in social analysis of this kind. Explanation is based on historical evidence from the minds and mouths of Chilean writers and politicians and on intuition. It is hoped there will be some insights in this study of interest to others working on this exciting topic of consensus in society.

In Part I, consisting of three chapters, the aim is to develop each of the three purposes or themes of the study well enough, in their informational and conceptual content, to lend clarity and comprehension to their further development in the chapters which follow. The historical theme will largely explain itself as the study proceeds, and Chapter 1 can, therefore, be brief. It consists of an explanation of concepts and a glimpse at current ideologies and the present industrial relations system in Chile. Chapter 2 opens up the subject of the intellectuals in Latin America and in Chile, and Chapter 3 attempts to define consensus and provide some general thoughts, including those of other writers, on its presence or absence in society.

Part II, the heart of the study, contains five chapters (nos. 4–8). Chapter 4, "The Social Question," establishes the broad historical background one needs in order to understand the nature and significance of the industrial relations system established in 1924. It presents material on economic development, the labor force, worker organizations, labor-employer relations, and political parties. Chapters 5 and 6, "The Conservative Project and the Intellectuals" and "The Liberal Alliance Project and the Intellectuals," describe the genesis of the élite labor relations proposals with emphasis on the intellectual role. Chapter 7, "The Élite Opposition," identifies and evaluates the opposition to labor reform legislation among key agricultural and business organizations and the Roman Catholic Church. Chapter 8, "Crisis in the Congress," is the story of the labor proposals in the Congress, a five-year period (1919–1924) of debate, maneuvering, political rivalries, and constitutional crisis which finally ended in military intervention.

Part III has two chapters, the first of which — Chapter 9, "Unanticipated Consequences" — tells how a revolutionary labor movement accepted the legal industrial relations system and eventually consolidated its hold on that system through the instrument of Popular Front government. This chapter covers the period 1924–1938. The final chapter brings together the major findings of the study and provides a commentary on the present status of consensus in Chile.

PART I

PART 1

CHAPTER 1

Chile Today:
Ideological Division and the
Industrial Relations System

WHAT is the meaning of "industrial relations system"? Who is responsible for formation of the industrial relations system and when does this formation take place? Answers to these questions must first be provided if a description of the present industrial relations system in Chile is to be at all meaningful.

The concept of the industrial relations system is borrowed from the writings of the Inter-University Study of Labor Problems in Economic Development. The major theoretical contribution of this project is Clark Kerr, John T. Dunlop, Frederick H. Harbison, and Charles A. Myers, *Industrialism and Industrial Man* (1960). These writers explain, first of all, that industrial relations systems are created in the industrialization process. They all contain important similarities and, at the same time, reflect important differences. Thus, all industrial relations systems involve three parties: workers, managers, and the state. All systems serve the three major functions of "defining power and authority relationships [among the parties], controlling worker protest, and establishing a complex of rules" for the workplace and the work community. Their differences derive from the different times, cultures, and stages of economic development during or in which they are started. They also derive from the different élites who command

1

industrializing societies and who have "different visions and programs for the emerging industrial relations systems."[1]

An especially acute observation of *Industrialism and Industrial Man* is that the essential form and content of the industrial relations system are "crystallized by the leading élite at a relatively early stage" of industrialization. Moreover, the system is likely to retain these characteristics permanently so long as democratic processes are respected. Only a revolutionary upheaval can alter the fundamental character of an established industrial relations system.[2] The observation applies quite accurately to the industrial relations system in Chile which, today, is the same in most essentials as it was at its inception in 1924. The saying "past is prologue," although often belied by events, is a trustworthy guide in this instance. That is why a history of the origins of the industrial relations system in Chile illuminates and makes more understandable the present situation of labor-management-state relations.

However, a refinement is now in order. This study has already been referred to as treating the origins of the *legal* industrial relations system in Chile. Politically speaking, the legal industrial relations system is assuredly the most important part of the total system, although, in terms of numbers, more workers and employers may be out of it than in it, at least with regard to such important matters as unions and resort to the government conciliation boards. The legal industrial relations system embraces the seven laws passed in 1924 (the core of the system) and all subsequent labor legislation. It includes all worker organizations established in conformity with these laws and incorporated by the government (granted *personalidad jurídica*). It also includes all workers, not necessarily members of legally recognized unions, and employers who have recourse to government-supervised collective bargaining and dispute settlement machinery (a series of general and special conciliation and arbitration boards) and to the labor courts. Finally, it includes all workers and employers affected by national legislation on individual contract terms, social security, and similar protective legislation.

Within the legal industrial relations system described above, emphasis in this study is on the first two functions outlined by Kerr and his associates; namely, those of defining power and authority relationships

[1]Clark Kerr, John T. Dunlop, Frederick H. Harbison, and Charles A. Myers, *Industrialism and Industrial Man* (Cambridge, Mass.: Harvard University Press, 1960), pp. 234–235.

[2]*Ibid.*, p. 235.

2

and controlling worker protest, rather than on the web of rules in shop, factory, and work community. Issues of power and protest are considered to be the more "difficult" ones and, depending on how they are handled, the ones which are more apt readily to reveal the psychology of the system, the security or insecurity of the power élite, and whether the system will last or operate efficiently. Unions, collective bargaining, strikes, ideology, and conciliation and arbitration boards are the kinds of phenomena which receive most attention. In a word, it is the basic political import of the legal industrial relations system which is of greatest concern. That one should elect to speak of a legal industrial relations system with strong political biases should not occasion surprise where, in a country and in the area of the world it represents, so much is said to be "politicized."

If the major characteristics of the industrial relations system are determined at an early stage of industrialization by the leading élite, then it follows that industrial relations "are not discrete phenomena in society; they are, by and large, determinate results rather than determining forces."[3] Important determining forces are the élites, five in number: the dynastic élite, the middle class, revolutionary intellectuals, colonial administrators, and nationalist leaders. Who are the members of an élite? They are the leaders of the industrialization process. "These leaders vary from one society to another, but they include the political leaders, industrial organization builders, top military officers, associated intellectuals, and sometimes leaders of labor organizations."[4]

The different strategies by which these five élites seek "to order the surrounding society in a consistent and compatible fashion" determine the different routes they take to industrialization and, consequently, the industrial relations systems peculiar to these routes. The élites and their routes are ideals "and, as such, no individual historical case corresponds fully to any one of them. But most individual cases may be understood better in relation to one of these types."[5]

Actually, there were two élites vying for power in Chile during the period under study, and they developed two comprehensive labor bills. These were the dynastic élite and the middle-class élite. The former is identified here as the "aristocratic-Catholic" élite rather than as the dynastic élite because this terminology more accurately describes the traditional power group in Chile (rural landowners and the Catholic Church hierarchy). It must be made clear now, and it must be kept in

[3]*Ibid.*, p. 1.
[4]*Ibid.*, n., p. 8.
[5]*Ibid.*, pp. 50, 51.

mind throughout this study, that the two Chilean élites were neither always neatly separate nor uniformly antagonistic groups. To a limited but necessary extent (i.e., necessary for analysis), they are ideal types even in the case study environment of Chile. Important individuals and political groups sometimes identified with the "wrong" élite; rural elements sometimes supported the middle-class élite, and powerful urban politicians sometimes lined up with the aristocratic-Catholic élite. Moreover, the two élite labor bills had the common objective of preserving the existing social system, although they contained significant differences of policy, form, and detail.

The Chilean industrial relations system cannot, therefore, be effectively studied in isolation. To know that system, one first needs to know something of the thoughts and anxieties of the élite groups who fashioned it. Hopefully, this strategic power relationship is given the consideration it merits throughout this book.

I

The present industrial relations system in Chile reflects the larger play of contending élites and competing political parties. At the national level, as distinct from the level of a particular industry or plant, the industrial relations system reflects (1) the ideological division which has characterized Chilean society for almost two generations; (2) strong multiparty influence in, if not control of, strategic labor organizations; (3) a heavy government role in prescribing and enforcing the rules which guide, and in many instances stipulate, labor-management-state relations; (4) marked employer paternalism, which is as much a psychological as a material phenomenon; and (5) a relatively weak union or worker role in rule making and enforcement.

On the broader issues of élites and parties, the two élites identified above still exist in Chile today, but the balance of power has shifted markedly in favor of the middle class, and, as a consequence, the traditional aristocratic-Catholic group (with a much diminished identification with the Catholic Church) has lost even a veto power in the Congress. In addition, a revolutionary alliance of Communists and Socialists, the Popular Action Front (FRAP), now offers strong opposition to middle-class and traditional elements.

The six major political parties fall roughly into the three élite categories pertinent to Chile, although there is some straddling and although the élites and the political parties are not, of course, mutually inclusive groups. In the aristocratic-Catholic élite, there is the Conservative party, badly mauled in recent elections, and perhaps most Liberal party elements. In the middle-class élite, one can place a section of the Liberal party, the Radicals, and the Christian Democrats. In the revolutionary left are the Socialist and Communist parties, united for many years in the FRAP coalition. The Christian Democratic party might also be placed here since it proclaims "Revolution in Freedom" and, as one observer notes, is "far to the left" on the political spectrum as compared with the Christian Democratic parties of Europe.[6] Part of the left-wing of the Radical party might be added to fill out the revolutionary élite. Depending on where one wishes to put the Christian Democratic party, either the middle class or the revolutionary left is divided against itself in Chile, since that party has little in common with either the Radicals or the FRAP. Other parties, some of them splinter groups, appear from time to time, generally on the left, but they have little persistent impact on the national scene.

This array of political parties is ideologically divisive in Chile not because it constitutes a multiparty as distinct from a two-party system (multiparty systems can operate effectively in consensus societies) nor solely because it reflects competing ideologies. It is divisive because the parties reflect competing ideologies *and* are electorally strong and persistent contenders for power. The term "ideology" is used in this study to mean an internally consistent body of thought based on such a concept of man and such an arrangement of social institutions that it differs in important ways from some other ideology. Ideology thus refers to a more or less total system of thought like fascism, democracy, Christian democracy, socialism, communism, and anarchism. Some of these ideologies can sometimes be compatible or partially compatible with one another depending upon circumstances of country, political leadership, traditions, and local adaptations of a particular theoretical model. An illustration from Chile itself is the FRAP coalition of socialists and communists, unique in the world today and paralleled in recent experience only by the now defunct alliance of Nenni socialists and communists in Italy. Party differences in a stable democracy like the United States on such current issues as federal versus state control, foreign versus domestic spending, and civil rights are not considered

[6]See Ernst Halperin, *Nationalism and Communism in Chile* (Cambridge, Mass.: M.I.T. Press, 1965), p. 178. Landsberger *et al.* also note that the Christian Democratic party in Chile is "a distinctly leftist group in favor of basic change." See Henry A. Landsberger, Manuel Barrera, and Abel Toro, "The Chilean Labor Union Leader: A Preliminary Report on His Background and Attitudes," *Industrial and Labor Relations Review*, vol. 17, April 1964, p. 417.

to represent ideological disagreements. They could theoretically become such, and, on a regional rather than a political party basis, one might concede that there is at this moment ideological division in the United States on the matter of Negro citizenship. However, ideological division on this one issue is not tantamount to a generalized national instability or to loss of national consensus.

Chile is considered to fulfill the first requirement of ideological division: namely, the presence of competing and, in significant measure, incompatible ideologies. It is true, as Kalman H. Silvert has written, that all groups in Chile are agreed upon the need for industrialization and that "respect for constitutional form and political legality is so profound that even revolutionary leftists promise to follow constitutional methods in their political tactics." One can question, however, whether these areas of agreement constitute a "grander consensus" among "real policy differences."[7] Another approach, offered as a general theory of industrialization, states that it is the existence of alternative routes to industrialization and the contending élites who advocate and pursue these routes that differentiate societies and divide the present world.[8] In other words, if division occurs it is precisely at the level of route choice rather than at the level of whether or not to industrialize. Agreement upon constitutional methods is certainly necessary to establish consensus in a democratic society, but a second major requirement is agreement on ideology. The two are obviously related, but, in a democracy, it is possible for political dissidents to respect constitutional methods up to a point (e.g., perhaps up to the moment of power seizure itself) with no deep, sincere, or permanent commitment to democratic values or ideals. Circumspect behavior while one is an "out" is one thing; another test, perhaps more demanding, is whether the "out," upon gaining power, is able and willing to respect *his* opposition.

To put the matter a little differently, it can be said that the use of revolutionary means (i.e., violence in whatever form) in the struggle for power is not a necessary condition of ideological division (although such means may indeed be present and may sharpen conflict in some ideologically divided societies). In his recent study of the Chilean left, Ernst Halperin declares categorically that nowhere in Latin America, including Chile which has one of the strongest and best organized

[7] Kalman H. Silvert, *The Conflict Society: Reaction and Revolution in Latin America* (New Orleans, La.: Hauser Press, 1961), pp. 51–52 and Kalman H. Silvert, *Chile: Yesterday and Today* (New York: Holt, Rinehart and Winston, 1965), p. 86.

[8] Kerr *et al.*, *Industrialism and Industrial Man*, pp. 50, 51.

6

Communist parties in the hemisphere, does communism have a "vigorous revolutionary tradition." By that he means there is no "ruthless determination to seize power at all costs" and that, quite to the contrary, Communist parties are content to play the political game "co-operating both with dictators and with democrats in return for small benefits." On the other hand, the Chilean Socialist party is strongly antiparliamentarian and prefers to seek power from a narrow, working-class base. Regardless of the absence of revolutionary means, however, Halperin acknowledges the totalitarian and antidemocratic objectives of the FRAP coalition. With reference to the electoral program of the FRAP in the 1964 presidential election, he judges its reforms as "so sweeping that they could certainly not be implemented within the framework of Chile's existing democratic institutions." His general conclusion is that the FRAP "had in mind a revolution similar to that carried out by Castro." Moreover, whenever the communists in Latin America have come to enjoy at least a share of political power (as in Cuba, Guatemala in 1954, and in Chile briefly during 1946–1947), "their totalitarianism has at once become manifest in their behavior toward both allies and opponents."[9] In the longer view, it may make little difference, therefore, whether an extremist movement violates democratic institutions in its drive for power or whether these institutions are respected in the drive but violated after power has been won. What price democracy? What price respect for constitutionalism? In the absence of thorough agreement upon ideology, use of democratic means may have no lasting significance.

Regarding the second test of ideological division, that ideologies be strong in some measurable sense (e.g., national election results) and persistent contenders for power, it is well known that the FRAP candidate lost the 1958 presidential election by the slimmest of margins to a conservative businessman politician. In the most recent presidential election (1964), the Christian Democratic candidate won a sweeping

[9]Halperin, *Nationalism and Communism in Chile*, pp. 13–14, 42, 140–141, 142–143. Halperin also notes that in 1964 the FRAP was fearful that the "right" in Chile would not permit the FRAP presidential candidate (Salvador Allende) to assume office if elected. He quotes a FRAP spokesman as saying that "no one has the right to entertain illusions as to the attitude of the reactionaries in the event of their defeat in 1964; some sectors might sincerely accept it, but others are already preparing to prevent it without any half measures. At present the Republican Militia is being clandestinely organized, and in the armed forces they are eliminating without inhibitions every officer who manifests a progressive mentality or, because of his disciplined attitude, is considered a danger to the perpetuation of the oligarchic system." *Ibid.*, pp. 151–152.

7

victory (56 percent of the vote), although the FRAP polled nearly a million votes (39 percent) out of the two-and-a-half million cast. That the FRAP lost more heavily in the cities, where it should have been strongest, than in the rural and mining districts has been interpreted as a failure of the extremist message.[10] Whether or not the year 1964 will ultimately go down in Chilean history as a great ideological turning point, the fact remains that up to now the left has been very strong, strong enough to constitute a divisive force.

Party representation in the Congress shows the full spread of competing ideologies. As of March 1966 the 45 seats in the Senate were held as follows: Christian Democrats 13, Radicals 9, Socialists 7, Liberals 5, Communists 5, and Conservatives 2. The remaining four seats were held by representatives of two small left-wing parties and two independents. The right-wing and right-of-center parties (Conservatives, Liberals, and Radicals) thus held 36 percent of the seats, the Christian Democrats 29 percent, and the FRAP 27 percent. As one would expect, the distribution was more favorable to the "popular" parties in the Chamber of Deputies. Out of 147 seats, the Christian Democrats held 82, the Radicals 19, Communists 18, Socialists 15, Liberals 6, and Conservatives 3. Three other seats were held by a single left-wing party and one seat was vacant. The comparable percentage distribution was: right-wing and right-of-center parties 19 percent, Christian Democrats 56 percent, and the FRAP 22 percent.[11] Probably not since the last century has a single party held a clear majority of seats in either house of Congress. Ideological division, as represented in the Chamber of Deputies, may therefore be weaker today than it has been for many years.

Present congressional strength of the several parties tells nothing about the persistence of ideological division in Chile. The Conservative, Liberal, and Radical parties all date from the last century, and, in coalitions of varying membership, they have dominated the Congress, controlled cabinets, and placed their leaders in the highest political office in the land. The Communist party (1921) has been a factor of importance in Chilean politics "longer and more consistently" than any other similar party in Latin America. With the exception of the late 1930's, when the Socialist party was the chief spokesman for labor, the Communist party has been "the principle political force among

[10]*Ibid.*, pp. 195–196, 218–222, 238.

[11]"Distribución de los Miembros del Senado y de la Cámara de Diputados por Partido, al 2 de Marzo de 1966," tabular data provided by Alberto Armstrong Verdugo.

the country's workers."[12] Since the 1920's it has elected representatives to both houses of the Congress and has achieved official recognition in one presidential cabinet. Most of the party's electoral successes have, however, been at the communal or municipal level. Today it is considered one of the four strongest communists parties in Latin America (the other three being those of Cuba, Brazil, and Venezuela).[13]

The Socialist party (1933) has always had a sizeable contingent in the Congress. It shared power with the Radicals during the short-lived Popular Front (1938–1941) and boasts a number of ex-ministers of state. Despite its loss of working-class leadership to the Communists, it is an "almost equally strong" party and is "intellectually extremely lively."[14] The Christian Democratic party has emerged slowly over the last thirty years. Whether it can effectively organize and retain its recent burst of membership growth remains for the future to tell.

II

The ideological division in the nation at large, as reflected in national politics, is carried into the labor movement through the "union departments" (national, regional, and local) of all six major parties. Party activists in the unions set up cells (Communists), brigades (Socialists), fronts (Christian Democrats), or other political groups in local, regional, and national labor organizations. These same activists are the gears which synchronize the political groups in the unions with the union departments of the parties. The party objective is to control or influence the decisions and activities of the infiltrated union body.[15]

The major requirement for membership in the party side of this structure is loyalty and a history of service to the party. A candidate must also be or have been a union leader.[16] Workers therefore come to the union department of the party primarily as Christian Democrats,

[12]Robert J. Alexander, *Communism in Latin America* (New Brunswick, N.J.: Rutgers University Press, 1957), p. 177.

[13]Martin C. Needler, *Latin American Politics in Perspective* (Princeton, N.J.: Princeton University Press, 1963), p. 106.

[14]Halperin, *Nationalism and Communism in Chile*, pp. 22–23.

[15]Jorge Barría Serón, *Trayectoria y estructura del movimiento sindical chileno, 1946–1962* (Santiago: INSORA, 1963), pp. 326–327 and Fernando González Labbe, "El Departamento Sindical del Partido Demócrata Cristiano," a student paper presented to the writer's seminar in the University of Chile in 1961.

[16]The Radical party prescribes five to ten years of party membership as a requirement for holding office at the various levels of its union department structure. Mabel Bullemore, "Departamento Sindical del Partido Radical," student paper presented to the writer's seminar in the University of Chile in 1961.

9

Socialists, Radicals, Communists, etc., rather than primarily as union leaders. The major objective, from the party standpoint, is to have labor serve the party politically rather than to have the party serve labor technically (or politically). Some success in both areas is, however, clearly necessary to permanency and to effective operation.

Through direct structural tie-in with the labor movement, and particularly with the rank-and-file work force in factory, shop, office, and mine (sometimes even where there is no local union in existence), the party hopes to gain members and votes in local, provincial, and national elections. A party or coalition may call upon the unions it controls to support its program if it is in power at the executive level and/or has a proadministration delegation in the national Congress. Conversely, if the party or coalition is not in power and opposes the government, it may ask the unions it controls to fight the government's program. In either case, resort is to strikes, marches, demonstrations before the Congress, and the like, or to abstention from such tactics. Finally, the party may expect its union adherents to make the kinds of alignments within the labor movement at large which are believed most in accord with the party's immediate and long-range goals. Several times within the last half dozen years, for example, the Radicals and Christian Democrats have changed their attitude toward participation in congresses of the Single Central of Chilean Workers (CUT) and toward representation in its executive council.

An unusual system of voting, prescribed in the Labor Code, probably tends to exaggerate ideological division and "politicization" within individual local unions. The law requires that every legal union elect an executive board of five members. Every worker is entitled to one vote for each position on the board, or two votes if he has had a minimum of three years service in the plant. Any worker's votes, whether five or ten, can be "saved" and placed on only one candidate for office (or on only two candidates, or three, etc.). This system of multiple votes and "cumulative" voting encourages great play on politics and emphasizes the rewards of party discipline. It also tends to perpetuate political minorities.

To illustrate, in the 1958 election of the executive board of the Pacific Steel Company industrial union, 20,460 votes were cast as follows: Communists, 4,800 votes for 2 candidates; anarchists, 6,060 votes for 2 candidates; Radicals, 1,800 votes for 2 candidates; Christian Democrats, 6,600 votes for 10 candidates (they were split at that time and presented 2 slates of 5 members each); 1,200 other party and independent votes for 5 or 6 candidates. The results are not self-evident from these figures, but the Communists elected 2 board members, the anarchists 2, and the Christian Democrats only one.[17] Thus, the Communists, with 23 percent of the votes, elected 40 percent of the board; the anarchists, with 30 percent of the votes, elected 40 percent of the board; and the Christian Democrats, with 32 percent of the votes, elected 20 percent of the board.

While the labor movement in Chile would undoubtedly be politically divided in the absence of this voting system, the division might be less marked and would, in any case, occur more between unions than within them, if the present system were changed in favor of a straight majority vote on each board position. Such a change would have been easier to accomplish forty years ago when the labor laws were under discussion, when the traditional parties were stronger, and when the leftist parties were weak or nonexistent, than it is likely to be today. Today, the older parties are on the whole weaker, yet are stronger in the country at large than they are in the labor movement, and take a defensive attitude toward cumulative voting which gives them some hope of minority representation in the country's unions. All of which raises the intriguing questions of why multiple, cumulative voting was adopted in the first place and whether the political consequences were anticipated by the legislators of the 1920's. Something will be said on these matters as the story unfolds in later chapters.

Let it be made very clear at this point that political party influence in, or control of, unions in Chile is not a simplistic, unchallenged, and uncomplicated mechanical process. Infiltration of the labor movement is not pursued with equal vigor, centralized discipline, and success by all parties; its consequences are not felt evenly at all levels of union structure; and it is not the only force, nor necessarily the most important one, at work in the labor movement. Most of the daily and routine functions of local unions are probably not much affected by "politicization"; the party apparatus is simply not big enough to become involved in more than a few union or labor-management problems; and party leaders lack the expertise to deal with a great variety of industries and their special characteristics. In other words, there is a broad area of union-management-state relations, still to be described, which is substantially free of partisan political concern.

Moreover, there is also a reverse pressure of union upon party which varies in strength and general significance from party to party and from union to union. Some unions seek and get important financial, tech-

[17]Statistics provided the writer by the personnel director of the company in 1958.

11

nical, and political assistance from party leaders; the party has a national structure, more effective than the union's, which reaches into government agencies, the Congress, and perhaps even into the Cabinet and the office of the President. Legal aid, strike support, educational programs, and unemployment and convention funds may be underwritten by the party. At crucial moments, however, and especially at the confederation and national union levels rather than at the local level, major decisions involving union activities are reached on the basis of political criteria. The party collects its *quid pro quo*. Workers with some voice in party circles may be the ones who get elected, some key strikes are called primarily for strategic party reasons, and major splits or unity moves are determined by overriding political objectives.[18] A convenient summary of this subject is provided by Robert J. Alexander who calls attention to "the exceedingly political atmosphere which surrounds Chilean trade unionism." "The parties," he continues,

> ...are constantly seeking to get control of the unions, and very frequently a leading trade unionist will also be a figure of importance in a political party. Representatives of labor sit in important government bodies, either in an elective or appointive capacity, and they have a good deal to say about government policy; but they usually speak more as members of the particular party to which they belong than as trade-union representatives.
> As a result of this situation, Socialist, Communist, Christian Democratic, or Radical labor leaders, as politicians must continue to talk and think in terms of the diametrically opposed interest of the working and employing classes, which is the stock in trade of their respective parties. Failure to do so will get a trade-union leader in difficulties with his political group upon whose support he depends. This situation is intensified by the traditional division of Chilean political opinion into "left" and "right" — and labor leaders must at all costs be on the "left." It is only when the current political line of his party veers toward "national unity" that the labor leader can let down his guard, so to speak.[19]

Nowhere in the labor movement is political influence or control more obvious than in the major trade union center, the Single Central of Chilean Workers (CUT). Most organized blue-collar workers are affiliated with, or are under the spell of, the CUT, though a rival Na-

[18]The best structural study of the union departments is Emilio Morgado Valenzuela, "Departamentos Sindicales de Seis Partidos Políticos Chilenos," term paper presented to the writer's class at Cornell in 1964.

[19]Robert J. Alexander, *Labor Relations in Argentina, Brazil, and Chile* (New York: McGraw-Hill, 1962), p. 306.

CHILE TODAY

tional Confederation of Workers (CNT) is also active. The CNT, composed largely of anarchists and independents who once were counted among the members of a unified CUT, goes unnoticed and seemingly has little prospect of growth. The CUT, on the other hand, regularly claims hundreds of thousands of working-class adherents. Although neither the CUT membership nor, in a broader political sense, the CUT "following" can be precisely stated with assurance of accuracy, there is little question that it is the dominant labor confederation in the country.

Dominant, however, does not mean all-powerful. As a union organization, the CUT is weak in the extreme. It has little control over affiliated local, national, and provincial unions, and what centralized authority it does have derives from similarity of party allegiance among leaders at various levels in the structure and not from economic strength or statutory grants of authority as such. In other words, as Victor Alba has pointed out, CUT decisions are made "in negotiations with the parties rather than by the official leadership of the unions."[20] Jorge Barría refers to this situation as the "ideological polarization" of the labor movement, and he sees the CUT conflict with the state and its own internal division as "a great problem not only for the workers but for the entire society."[21]

At the Fourth Congress of the CUT, held in Santiago in 1965, there were in attendance more than two thousand delegates representing six political tendencies. Forty-two percent were Communists; 33 percent Socialists; 9 percent Christian Democrats; 5 percent Radicals; anarchists and "ex-Trotskyites" of the Revolutionary Leftist Movement each 1 percent; and another 8 percent were independents or were unidentified with respect to political or ideological loyalty.

This line-up of delegates represents changes of both position and relative voting strength as compared with previous years. However, because some groups have not regularly participated in CUT congresses and because the number of independents and non-voters has been so large and variable (5 to 32 percent), it is not meaningful to make a detailed analysis of the delegate composition of these congresses, but the data are strong enough to support these general conclusions: (1) the Communists and Socialists are far and away the two strongest groups, and, with the exception of the Constituent Congress

[20]Victor Alba, *Historia del movimiento obrero en América Latina* (México: Libreros Mexicanos Unidos, 1964), pp. 383–384.

[21]Barría, *Trayectoria y estructura del movimiento sindical chileno*, pp. 320, 348–349.

13

(1953), the Communists have enjoyed a clear lead over all the rest; (2) most anarchists withdrew from the CUT in 1957, so they are somewhat stronger in the country than their current CUT representation would indicate, though they have probably weakened in recent years; (3) Radical strength has tended to remain rather stable; and (4) the Christian Democrats have apparently about tripled their strength, although they remain a distant third behind the Socialists.

The Christian Democratic showing in the 1965 CUT Congress understated their following by about half. In three previous congresses they accounted for from 15 to 18 percent of the delegates. In 1965 they split regarding participation in the Congress, one group refusing to send delegates.

Moreover, the Communists and Socialists could not agree on how to handle the Christian Democratic faction and the Radicals in attendance at the 1965 Congress. The Communists preferred a broad appeal to all groups in a unified CUT and the allocation of seats in the National Executive Committee according to a prearranged formula. The Socialists, on the other hand, favored a narrow policy (as they traditionally have) and the election of council members in strict accordance with voting strength and CUT statutes. They were strong enough to force the issue to elections. The Christian Democrats and the Radicals thereupon abstained from voting. Consequently, the elected council was made up only of Communists (12) and Socialists (9). In previous years Christian Democrats and Radicals have had as many as four to eight council members between them. It can also be noted that the Radicals, weak to begin with, were divided into two groups at the Congress, one of which looked to the FRAP for leadership.[22]

CUT principles and program have always been revolutionary in purpose and Marxist in ideology. Changes have been made over the years in efforts to preserve unity and satisfy Radical and Christian Democratic minorities, but the essence of CUT's declared platform is about the same today as in 1953 when CUT was founded. In its 1962 "Declaration of Principles," the CUT stated that

> The social injustice and misery which oppress the national majority have as their cause the chronic incapacity of the capitalist regime which, based on private property in land and the instruments and means of production, divides society into antagonistic classes—workers and employers, exploited and exploiters.

[22]Jorge Barría Serón, "Informe Provisorio sobre el IV Congreso CUT," March 11, 1966. See also Barría, *Trayectoria y estructura del movimiento sindical chileno*, pp. 332–346.

14

To confront and defeat the workers' enemies, the CUT proposed action based on "the principles of class" to win "the total emancipation of the workers."[23]

At its most recent convention (1965), the CUT approved resolutions calling for general and complete disarmament, destruction of nuclear arms, diplomatic and commercial relations with all countries of the world, unity of Latin American workers in a regional organization, support of the Cuban and Dominican peoples against foreign intervention and imperialist sabotage, and the reunification of Vietnam on the basis of proposals advanced by the Viet Cong and the government of North Korea. It called for an end to the "sacking" of natural resources by national and international trusts and monopolies, for rupture of relations with the International Monetary Fund, and for repudiation of the Alliance for Progress. The CUT rejected "educational and cultural imperialism" and "spy operations" like Project Camelot, and, finally, called for termination of the United States - Chile military pact and for the dismantling of all foreign military bases in Latin America.[24]

At the same time as the CUT has maintained a militant and revolutionary ideological position, its actual behavior has become more reformistic or constitutional. Existing on an almost constant fare of threatened or real general strikes, twenty-four hour strikes, marches, and demonstrations in its first years, a disastrous general strike in January 1956 dictated a new and somewhat quieter era. Harassed by continuous, severe inflation, plagued by bitter internal conflicts, and routed in some industries by antiunion employers, workers lost interest in militant action and the CUT was forced to trim its sails.[25] Yet it is still a left-wing organization, out of harmony with social institutions as they are now constituted, and claims to speak for the Chilean working class.

A recent sample of opinion from 231 local industrial union presidents (representing the three major industrial centers of Santiago, Valparaíso, and Concepción) tends to confirm CUT leftism as a genuine expression of organized labor's political preference. Asked which of the several parties was doing most for the working class, 43 percent of these presidents selected the FRAP coalition, 23 percent the Christian Democrats, and only 9 percent the Radicals. Another 19 percent in-

[23]Barría, *Trayectoria y estructura del movimiento sindical chileno*, "Declaracion de Principios de la Central Unica de Trabajadores de Chile," pp. 383–385.
[24]*El Mercurio*, August 30, 1965.
[25]For a good description of the CUT's history, see Barría, *Trayectoria y estructura del movimiento sindical chileno*, especially chaps. 3 and 7.

sisted that none of the parties "really cared for the working class."[26] This group undoubtedly included many anarchists, traditionally hostile to organized authority and to government.

In response to a related query on social change, 34 percent of the local union leaders declared in favor of the "immediate and total" restructuring of social institutions, 44 percent wanted such radical change "not long delayed," and only 22 percent favored gradual, evolutionary change. The authors of this opinion study emphasize that these responses are "rather general expressions of attitude; they tell us little about behavior, whether revolutionary or otherwise." They go on to conclude, however, that "even though it be at the attitudinal level only, these figures show an intense rejection of the present [social] system."[27]

How has this profound and tragic alienation of the organized labor movement come about? What are the historical origins in Chilean society of the contemporary communist-socialist dominated CUT?

III

While the labor movement is internally divided among several ideological currents and while, externally, it reflects a largely leftist political isolation from the rest of society, there is a complex web of legal rules whose effect, theoretically, should be to homogenize the labor movement and labor relations and make them distinctly subservient to and dependent upon the state. In fact, this is not only theoretically the case but, to an appreciable degree, state regulation has had the above effects. What we are dealing with then is a paradox — an atomized, weak, and controlled labor movement from the economic or functional point of view existing side by side with a powerful political labor movement capable of running and, to date, nearly electing the President of the Republic. Moreover, all of this is taking place in a democratic country whose private institutions, including those identified with industrial relations, have never been juggled with the gross demagoguery or authoritarian self-interest associated with other Latin American republics. Comparisons, revealing this difference, can be made with Argentina (Perón), Brazil (Vargas), or Venezuela (Pérez Jiménez), to cite only a few of the more familiar instances.

The areas and impact of state regulation will now be summarized,

[26]Landsberger *et al.*, "The Chilean Labor Union Leader," *Industrial and Labor Relations Review*, vol. 17, April 1964, pp. 417–418.
[27]*Ibid.*, p. 418.

but it is appropriate first to put three questions: (1) Did the Chilean élite groups of two generations ago expect to prevent labor extremism through tight state controls? (2) If they did, and if they failed, how safe is the generalization that, because labor movements can be controlled and because labor protest tends to decline, the chief labor problem in industrializing societies is "not the handling of labor protest, but the structuring of the labor force"?[28] (3) How does one explain and account for the strength and persistence of labor extremism which has grown, rather than diminished, since government controls were established?

Chilean labor laws stipulate a wide range of working conditions, specify the permissible forms of labor organization, regulate the internal affairs of unions, and specify and regulate the forms and conduct of labor-management relations. Outwardly, the total result is a government role in the industrial relations system quite different from and larger than the role of government in other Western countries like the United States, Canada, and Great Britain. That the government does not fully play out its role or zealously enforce the labor laws makes reality different from appearance, but the contrast with other countries is still meaningful. Besides, what the government does not do in accordance with its legal right is made up for, in small part at least, by the extralegal intrusion of the political parties.

In the area of working conditions (or the "individual contract" in Latin American terminology), the government determines many things that would in some other countries be collectively bargained by union and management representatives or determined by market forces, such as vacations, work holidays, dismissal procedures and payments, family allowances, and the "vital salary" for white-collar workers. There are also special laws for particular occupations or industries which stipulate special treatment or conditions for the workers concerned — laws for the copper, maritime, and agricultural workers and for domestic servants and white-collar employees.

The invidious legal distinction between white- and blue-collar workers has, in the minds of many people, divided and weakened the working class, perpetuated a dislike for manual labor, and, moreover, instilled among blue-collar workers a sense of inferiority quite contrary to the values of "equality," "pride in work," "achievement," and "practicality" associated with dynamic societies. For psychological as well as economic reasons, groups of blue-collar workers regularly petition a government classification board for change to white-collar status.

[28]Kerr *et al., Industrialism and Industrial Man*, pp. 7–8, 30, 228–233.

Bus drivers, taxi drivers, railroad engineers, and others have become white-collar workers overnight. A top executive in one of Chile's major industrial plants told the writer that his labor troubles would vanish if he could, as he said he was personally willing to do, shift all his blue-collar workers to the white-collar category! The subject has aroused much controversy in Chile and, as Alexander has pointed out, the tendency in recent years has been to reduce the economic differences between the two groups.[29] This may eventually also change the nature of the present psychological distinction between them. However, noneconomic differences are also present in the law (e.g., the two groups are not allowed to belong to the same local union), and the elimination of these differences may be more difficult to achieve.

IV

Regarding unions and their internal affairs, the law allows either local industrial unions *(sindicatos industriales)* for blue-collar workers or local craft unions *(sindicatos profesionales)* for particular occupational or skill groups of blue-collar workers or for white-collar workers. Local unions can form national unions *(federaciones* or *confederaciones)*, but only the national craft unions are conceded the right to defend the economic interests of their members, i.e., to bargain with employers or represent workers in the conciliation and arbitration boards and the labor courts. Bargaining for the industrial unions, which enroll two-thirds of all legal unionists, is restricted to the level of the single enterprise. There are exceptions in law (e.g., copper workers bargain on a company-wide basis) and in practice (the shoe and leather workers, sugar workers, and maritime workers have developed a species of industry-wide bargaining). Why is the labor movement functionally atomized in this way by government fiat rather than allowed to find, in the free play of market and power forces, appropriate administrative and bargaining structures?

The law does not permit unions to pay their officers either on a full-time or part-time basis. Most union leaders work all day in plant or office and are expected to tend to union affairs in the evenings. If practice makes perfect, it is no cause for wonder that Chilean trade union leaders are not perfect. This limitation is even said to be "a great handicap to the development of a democratic trade-union movement in Chile."[30] Only candidates for union office and the five elected officers

---

[29]Alexander, *Labor Relations in Argentina, Brazil, and Chile*, p. 269.
[30]*Ibid.*, pp. 292–293. Alexander draws this conclusion because he says the Com-

are adequately protected against arbitrary discharge. The rank and file have such protection *(fuero)* only during a collective conflict, and officers lose it six months after expiration of their term.

Union income and expenditures are subject to close regulation and periodic scrutiny by Ministry of Labor officials. Only ridiculously small amounts of cash can be kept in the union treasury, the rest must be deposited in the nearest state savings bank, and all checks in excess of an exceedingly small amount must be countersigned by the labor inspector of the zone. Industrial unions derive most of their income from a state-imposed compulsory profit-sharing system, and tripartite committees are charged with administering these funds. No unions are permitted to build up strike funds, but this prohibition is sometimes ignored, and strike funds are also raised on an emergency basis through membership collections, donations from parties or individuals, and the like.[31]

Procedures and conditions for establishing unions as legal bodies and for dissolving them are detailed in the law, and, in either case, the state's discretion is very broad. It is not merely a matter of public registration, as in the French system, or of closing the books on inactive unions. Although strong, active unions have seldom been dissolved, it is more difficult to say whether the state has used its powers to prevent an undesirable union from coming into existence in the first place.

There are some 600 local industrial unions in Chile and about 850 craft locals. With allowance for dual membership, there are some 200,-000 workers in these unions. However, this is not the country's total effective union strength because public employees (including railroad workers) are permitted to form "associations" which, although formally denied the right to negotiate and strike, perform these functions admirably. Their representation brings total union strength to about 336,530, and this figure still does not include the membership of a small and indeterminate number of "free" unions, for the most part under anarchist leadership, which are totally outside the legal industrial relations system. It is estimated that about 18 percent of the non-agricultural labor force is effectively organized, far below union organization rates in more advanced countries.[32]

---

munist party capitalizes on the restrictions of the law by paying some of its activists so they can devote their time to union affairs.

[31]The only study of local union income and expenditures in Chile is James O. Morris y Roberto Oyaneder C., *Afiliación y finanzas sindicales en Chile, 1932–1959* (Santiago: Editorial Universitaria, 1962).

[32]See *ibid.*, pp. 26–34.

19

V

One of the first things about labor relations to strike the attention of an outsider in Chile is the psychology of conflict which envelops the bargaining process. In Chile the entire bargaining period is known as the period of "collective conflict," in contrast to U.S. use of "labor dispute" or "work stoppage" to signify only what happens *after* direct negotiations have failed. The collective conflict begins in Chile the moment the union presents new demands to the employer and continues until there is a solution or a strike.

Generally speaking, there is little direct bargaining between the parties, and, technically, very few collective agreements are ever signed. The law allows five days for direct negotiations (subject to extension by mutual consent of the parties) and the conflict then enters a compulsory conciliation process lasting fifteen days. Most agreements are reached in conciliation. Tripartite conciliation boards operate on a regional basis throughout the country and a few have jurisdiction in specific, major industries. Compulsory conciliation may be considered as "government-supervised collective bargaining." Arbitration is voluntary and, if either party declines, the union is free to call a strike (subject to proper timing, a membership vote, etc.)

The conciliation or bargaining system has not been carefully analyzed to date, but indications are that it is effective enough for those who use it. However, perhaps half of all organized workers may not be covered by collective agreements. Only 57 percent of organized workers in the populous, highly industrialized province of Santiago presented demands to the conciliation boards in 1959, and petitions involving 9 percent of these workers were shelved. Although in both of these circumstances (i.e., no use of the conciliation process or shelved petitions) informal agreements may have been reached between the parties and not subsequently registered with the conciliation boards, it is likely that many "social-purpose" and company-dominated unions never sought an agreement and that, in other cases, employer hostility prevented discussions. One source suggests that employers are indeed at fault, particularly with regard to shelved petitions. They could ignore the technical defects of petitions rather than take advantage of them to terminate bargaining if they had a more constructive and responsible attitude toward unions and the sharing of authority.[33]

Most conflicts which reach the conciliation boards are resolved in the conciliation process, however, and the conclusion seems justified

[33]Alberto Armstrong Verdugo, *El proceso de negociación colectiva en Chile* (Santiago: INSORA, 1964), pp. 7–8, 17–26.

that "the machinery for negotiating collective agreements works reasonably well, perhaps as well as is possible in view of the exceedingly political nature of the trade unions and the political considerations which go into the solution of any important labor dispute" in the country.[34] Frequently the political pressures are so great that hearings before the conciliation boards are only legal formalities, the real negotiations taking place elsewhere.

Strikes can be serious in terms both of number and man-days lost, and illegal strikes have been known to outnumber the legal ones. Thus, in 1962 in the province of Santiago alone, there were 667 strikes involving 113,998 workers (equivalent to the total organized labor force of the province). Over a million man-days of work were lost. All but 97 of these strikes were illegal, and the illegal ones accounted for 55 percent of total man-days lost.[35] Apparently only a few of these strikes took place during conciliation. They arose mostly in the absence of a written agreement or because of postcontract misunderstandings. As a rule, there is no formal grievance machinery at the plant level in Chile, and the labor court procedure is cumbersome and time consuming. Given these facts, and the further fact that a legal strike can occur only after the conciliation process has been exhausted, it is hardly surprising that illegal strikes count so heavily in the total. Moreover, most illegal strikes are neither prosecuted by management nor punished by the government. Whether they are political or economic, effective or ineffective, are other matters but their classification as "illegal" has, apparently in the overwhelming majority of cases, little practical effect on labor-management-state relations.

Indeed, one can speculate that a good part of the reason why the legal industrial relations system works with an acceptable minimum of efficiency is that the government does not enforce it uniformly or inflexibly or manipulate it outrageously for political advantage. Workers not organized in legal unions are often permitted access to the conciliation and arbitration boards, unions are seldom dissolved except for inactivity, agreements are not nullified even though they have in fact been negotiated at the industry level, illegal strikes are infrequently punished.

The system also works, however, because workers and employers accept each other to a surprising degree. Twenty-five percent of 231 local union presidents whose opinions were sampled described their union's relations with management as "very good," 48 percent consid-

[34]Alexander, *Labor Relations in Argentina, Brazil, and Chile*, p. 320.
[35]Alberto Armstrong Verdugo, *Las huelgas en Chile en 1962: su magnitud y causas,* tésis (Santiago: Universidad de Chile, 1964), pp. 29–30, 77.

ered these relations "more good than bad," 23 percent "more bad than good," and only 3 percent thought they were "very bad." A companion study of 61 personnel administrators revealed even greater acceptance of the union on management's part. Responding to the identical question, 62 percent considered relations with their industrial union to be "very good," 33 percent said these relations were "more good than bad," only 5 percent said "more bad than good," and none thought relations were "very bad."[36] So we return, emphatically, to the paradox.

When writers say the Chilean worker is "essentially docile and easily pushed or led"[37] or, similarly, that he is "modest, long-suffering, and patient,"[38] they are apparently talking about the worker in the plant or at home, the worker as wage earner or as family head. The worker at the polls, in the streets, or in the Congress is a revolutionary — confident, extreme, and no longer patient.

The paradox is not unique to Chile. An even more striking example comes from Japan. The authoritarian tradition in Japanese industry, accentuated by thoroughgoing employer paternalism and lifetime employment of workers, "generates strong feelings of subordination, obligation, loyalty, and gratitude on the part of the workers." Resentment rarely breaks through the surface of industrial life; it is suppressed and then carried over into the political arena. "There, with a total absence of personal ties and obligations between the participants, the class war bursts forth again and again in compounded bitterness." In politics "the unions show a militant, doctrinaire, extremist face...which many individual employers rarely see."[39] The major trade union center in Japan (Sōhyō) is closely allied to the Japan Socialist party. This paradox of attitudes and behavior is not a mere curiosity. It means there is no fundamental consensus in Japanese society or in the Japanese industrial relations system. Nor can there be "as long as the ideology of Japan's major labor organization is hostile to the prevailing social and economic order."[40] While supporting the latter declaration, the writer

[36]Henry A. Landsberger y Raúl Dastres M., *La situación actual y el pensamiento del administrador de personal chileno* (Santiago: INSORA, 1964), p. 34.

[37]Alexander, *Labor Relations in Argentina, Brazil, and Chile*, p. 246.

[38]Landsberger et al., "The Chilean Labor Union Leader," *Industrial and Labor Relations Review*, vol. 17, April 1964, p. 409.

[39]Alice H. Cook, *An Introduction to Japanese Trade Unionism* (Ithaca, N.Y.: New York State School of Industrial and Labor Relations, Cornell University, 1966), pp. 4, 8, 16, 89–92.

[40]John P. Windmuller, "Model Industrial Relations Systems," Reprint No. 151, New York State School of Industrial and Labor Relations, Cornell University, 1963, pp. 6–7.

does not wish to imply that Sōhyō in Japan (any more than the CUT in Chile) is necessarily to be held responsible for its country's ideological division.

Is the paradox in Chile real or only apparent? Is political extremism the conspiracy of a well-disciplined leadership minority not truly representative of its following?[41] Is political extremism expressive of a psychological need to disagree which may characterize Chileans as a whole and which may, therefore, render conventional political categories largely meaningless?[42] Or does the worker really accept much of the present industrial relations system and, at the same time, reject the over-all social structure? Perhaps there is some validity in an affirmative response to each of these questions, but, in the context of Chilean history, the writer finds much to support the notion of a genuinely divided society. Chile has not always had a multiparty system representing most of the ideological spectrum. Communist labor leaders accepted the legal industrial relations system in the 1920's, both to get out of it what immediate economic gains they could and to stay in the race for long-run political victory. They, later the Socialists, and now the Christian Democrats have carried the bulk of the organized working class with them.

[41]With respect at least to the Communists, this would appear to be Alexander's position. He argues that the large number of well-paid, well-disciplined Communists in the labor movement is one reason why they control many unions "in spite of the fact that their rank-and-file support is quite limited." This is difficult to challenge in the absence of data on union elections and in the further absence of a definition of "quite limited." In any case, the writer believes that the conspiracy doctrine has been overworked and that when the Socialists and Communists can elect 27 percent of Chile's Senators, 22 percent of its Deputies, and poll nearly a million votes in a presidential election, their political following, as distinct from their rank-and-file union support, is not limited. For Alexander's views, see Alexander, *Labor Relations in Argentina, Brazil, and Chile*, pp. 292–293 and *Communism in Latin America*, p. 177.

[42]Dealing primarily with the subject of inflation in Chile, Albert O. Hirschman suggests that "various social groups maintain and prize an attitude and phraseology of unbending opposition and hostility: they coexist, but are anxious to avoid *overt agreement* and compromise." Under these social and attitudinal circumstances, "the degree of harmony and consensus existing in the society" is greater than outward appearances would seem to make it. The writer feels that it would be difficult, however, to explain Chile's ideological spectrum primarily on this basis, or on this basis alone. See Hirschman, *Journeys toward Progress; Studies of Economic Policy-Making in Latin America* (New York: The Twentieth Century Fund, 1963), pp. 208–209.

CHAPTER 2

The Intellectuals

WHO ARE the intellectuals in Latin America? Historically, how have they performed? What is their role in the twentieth century? Generally, how do they compare with other intellectuals in the West? Do the findings of this study with respect to the Chilean intellectuals conform to or depart from the perceived nature of the intellectual in Latin America and in the larger West? These are ambitious questions in a controversial field which, as Karl Mannheim pointed out years ago, lacks both systematic and comprehensive treatment.[1] The lack of comprehensiveness was only in part resolved by the appearance of George B. de Huszar's, ed., *The Intellectuals* (1960), and there is still no widely accepted sociology of the intellectuals.

To the extent that this study concerns the intellectuals, the objective is modest indeed: there will be an attempt to summarize, very briefly, thinking on a few major points such as the functional limits or size and the social position of the intellectual population in Latin America, the class origins and identifications of the intellectuals, and their relative political significance within élite groups and society. The results, which must admittedly be imperfect given the relative neglect of the subject,

[1]See the Introduction to George B. de Huszar, ed., *The Intellectuals* (Glencoe, Ill.: The Free Press, 1960), p. 3.

24

will be studied against the empirical findings of this study of the role of intellectuals in the origins of the industrial relations system in Chile to see what, if anything, has been added to our knowledge about intellectuals.

I

If there are no systematic or comprehensive works on modern intellectuals in general, there are hardly any of any kind on intellectuals in Latin America. Only recently has a literature on Latin American intellectuals begun to emerge (in both Spanish and English), and it is of uneven quality. An excellent small piece by Fred P. Ellison entitled "The Writer" (1964) contains seventy-eight footnotes, some with multiple source references but of these only a few appear to deal in any breadth at all with intellectuals throughout the area; they deal, rather, with limited groups of intellectuals in individual Latin American countries.[2] Ellison's synthesis is therefore a real contribution.

Ellison appears to rely on traditional Western concepts, raised even higher by Latin American artistic expectations, for his exacting standard of intellectuality. His intellectual is "the writer as creator of *belles lettres,* be he poet, novelist, dramatist, or essayist." The essayist, he adds, "may include philosophers, educators, historians, political writers, journalists, and others not ordinarily associated with *belles lettres,* provided they have literary style — that is, a way of writing that pretends to beauty. Stylistic distinction is highly valued in Latin America."[3] Note the severity of this definition when measured against Edward Shils' description of the "modern intellectuals" of the new, underdeveloped states of Africa and Asia. These modern intellectuals are "all [those] persons with an *advanced modern education* and the intellectual concerns and skills ordinarily associated with it." Conceding that this definition is "less selective or discriminating" than "we would use to designate the intellectuals in the more advanced countries," Shils explains that it is "only an acknowledgement of the smaller degree of internal differentiation which has until now prevailed within the educated class in the new states, and the greater disjunction which marks that class off from the other sections of the society."[4]

[2]See Fred P. Ellison, "The Writer," chap. 3, pp. 79–100, in John J. Johnson, ed., *Continuity and Change in Latin America* (Stanford, Calif.: Stanford University Press, 1964).

[3]*Ibid.,* p. 79.

[4]Edward Shils, "The Intellectuals in the Political Development of the New States," *World Politics,* vol. 12, April 1960, p. 332.

The Latin American countries, independent for a hundred and fifty years, with a massive Western, as well as an often rich indigenous, heritage and with proud, genteel upper classes cannot be pressed neatly into the mold of the newly independent states. But neither, one suspects, can they be pressed into the mold of the advanced and highly differentiated Western world. They lie somewhere between, and this may affect the rigor with which we define their intellectuals. Moreover, if we wish to emphasize the public influence and political leadership of the intellectuals rather than the intrinsic artistic merit or beauty of literary production, both the size and quality of the intellectual population are altered. Everything, therefore, depends upon one's definition of the intellectuals, and, as Shils implies, a universal, standard concept may not be possible due to varying conditions of time and space.

A highly important reason for *generosity* in defining the intellectuals in emerging areas is to take into account their articulate and politically active students. "No consideration of the intellectual class in under-developed countries," says Shils, "can disregard the university students. In advanced countries, students are not regarded as *ex officio* intellectuals; in underdeveloped countries, they are." They are because they are a significant part of a tiny minority gaining a modern education and participating in social and political affairs of national import.[5]

Very little attention has been given the university student as intellectual in Latin America, despite the fact that he is, and always has been, the embryo of a tiny educated élite. This apparently unusual situation may be due to the fact, largely unappreciated outside the area, that the political awakening of the Latin American university student is a phenomenon only of this century. Although the causes of the awakening run deep and are apparently related to the break-up of traditional societies and the emergence of the middle sectors, it can be dated from the Córdoba (Argentina) Reform of 1918 which has since swept over much of South and Central America, Mexico, and the Caribbean.

In one of three chapters on Latin American "Intellectuals and Their Inquietudes," Kalman H. Silvert discusses Chilean university students, and he has also written on "The University Student" in John J. Johnson's, ed., *Continuity and Change in Latin America*. Pertinent to the theme of the student as intellectual are Silvert's statistics indicating that only 1 percent of the population over 15 years of age in Latin America attends an institution of higher learning and that, in the specific case of Chile, an educational leader, only about 1.5 percent of

[5]*Ibid.*, pp. 336–337.

its young people between the ages of 17 and 25 enroll in the National University, the biggest institution of higher learning in the country. Moreover, Silvert sees the Córdoba Reform of 1918 as "a declaration of academic independence and political intent" by university students who were determined to change the university's role from the traditional one of preparing "an élite which can work its political will outside of the institution" to the modern one of utilizing the university as "a tool of directed social change" or nation-building.[6] Indeed, the findings of this study indicate that Chilean university thesis writers were making important contributions to thinking on the "social question" in that country during the two decades preceding the Córdoba Reform.

While Silvert clearly brings the university student into the intellectual category, he is careful to point out that not all university students can be so classified. "To be counted in this prestigious company," he qualifies, "the individual must manipulate ideas of a philosophical nature and communicate them in artistic fashion."[7] There is something of a return here to the standard of literary excellence suggested by Ellison, but Silvert apparently sees the student as a notable constituent of the intellectual group nevertheless.

The social origins of Latin American intellectuals are, today, largely middle class. A sizeable number still come from the aristocracy, and a few are beginning to come from humble families. Thus, Alvaro Mendoza Diez, a Mexican sociologist writing about professionals and intellectuals in Latin America, says the proportion of those groups coming from the high class is considerably less than that from the middle class and that only a small number have lower class origins.[8] An Uruguayan writer, Carlos M. Rama, believes Latin American intellectuals are "supra-class," since they include elements from all classes, but he agrees that their origins are primarily urban middle class.[9] American writers confirm these views. William S. Stokes, for example, identifies the intellectuals as "an important element, frequently the most important, in the upper-middle classes which govern everywhere in Latin Amer-

[6]Kalman H. Silvert, chap. 8 "The University Student," pp. 207–209 and 217, in Johnson, ed., *Continuity and Change in Latin America;* and Silvert, *Conflict Society,* pp. 165–166.

[7]Silvert, *Conflict Society,* p. 142.

[8]Alvaro Mendoza Diez, *La revolución de los profesionales e intelectuales en Latinoamérica* (México: Universidad Nacional Autónoma, 1962), pp. 85–91.

[9]Carlos M. Rama, *Los intelectuales y la política,* (Montevideo: Ediciones Nuestro Tiempo, 1962), pp. 5–6.

ica."[10] Silvert sees their social origins "invariably rooted in middle or upper classes."[11] The apparent concentration of Latin American intellectuals in the upper, and particularly the middle, sectors may vary somewhat from the social origins of their European counterparts who, according to Mannheim, are "recruited from an increasingly inclusive area of social life."[12]

More interesting and more complex than the social origins of the intellectuals are their class or group identifications which, in Latin America, show some pattern of change over time. Intellectuals were everywhere aligned with the colonial aristocracies during the independence movements of the early nineteenth century. In many countries this alignment was maintained for decades, or even into the twentieth century (e.g., Brazil), due in part to the intellectuals' dependence upon this élite for employment and patronage. The emergence of the middle sectors toward the end of the 1800's introduced greater freedom of intellectual criticism and social identification. Today intellectuals in Latin America are widely believed to be leftist-oriented in ideology and political action (i.e., identified with the "masses" or the middle and working classes), and only in very rare cases are they said to identify with traditional groups.[13]

There is a tendency, therefore, for some writers to believe that over long periods of time Latin American intellectuals attach themselves more to some élites or groups in society than to others. This is not inconsistent with the observation of Clark Kerr and his associates that intellectuals throughout the world "are inherently socially unattached *on any permanent basis* in the struggle for supremacy in organizing industrializing societies. Both the politically minded intellectuals and the generals often can and do align themselves with one and now with another élite and its strategy. . . . They wear coats of many colors."[14]

[10]William S. Stokes, "The *Pensadores* of Latin America," p. 422 in de Huszar, ed., *Intellectuals.*

[11]Silvert, *Conflict Society,* p. 143.

[12]This apparent difference has already been pointed out by both Silvert and Ellison. See *ibid.,* pp. 142–143 and Ellison, "The Writer," p. 82.

[13]For this historical reference, see especially John J. Johnson, *Political Change in Latin America: The Emergence of the Middle Sectors,* (Stanford, Calif.: Stanford University Press, 1958), pp. 1, 15–18, 23–26, 43, and 180–181. See also *New York Times,* August 8, 1965; Ellison, "The Writer," pp. 83, 89–90; and Silvert, *Conflict Society,* p. 143. In apparent disagreement with the writer's generalization on current intellectual alignments is J. Erlijman, *La función social de los intelectuales* (Buenos Aires: Editorial Bibliográfica Omeba, 1962), pp. 18–19, 34–35, 100, 175, 189.

[14]Kerr *et al.,* pp. 70–74. Italics added.

28

Nor is there any conflict with Mannheim's earlier finding that "un-attached intellectuals" (situated between classes but not forming a middle class) "are to be found in the course of history in all camps."[15]

Yet one can repeat that at any given time (perhaps lasting several decades) intellectuals may be *largely attached* to a particular class or group. This hypothesis, based on the generalizations applicable to Latin America cited above, is also supported by statements on the current political behavior of North American intellectuals. Thus R. Joseph Monsen and Mark W. Cannon call attention to "the mounting evidence of a left-of-center political consensus among a great majority of an opinion-forming élite group of artists, journalists, and academicians, especially social scientists."[16] In the U.S. environment, this leftist consensus is more likely to identify intellectuals as forming a class or group of their own than to identify them with the working class, and particularly with the labor movement which has lost much of its liberal appeal.

As a refinement of the class or group identifications of the intellectuals, Kerr *et al.* remark, analyzing in terms of the power élite, that the tasks of the intellectuals are not always performed in close alliance with this élite.

> In some cases, particularly in the early development of industrialization, intellectuals may be alienated from the emerging industrial society. Historically, they have frequently been in the forefront of protest movements against the excesses of the new industrialization. In middle-class industrializing countries, they have joined with the emerging labor movements in opposing or protesting particular consequences of the industrial society, as did the Fabian Socialists in Britain, or the Socialist parties in Europe.[17]

Similarly, Joseph A. Shumpeter has argued that

> capitalist evolution produces a labor movement which obviously is not the creation of the intellectual group. But it is not surprising that such an opportunity and the intellectual demiurge should find each other. Labor never craved intellectual leadership but intellectuals invaded labor politics.[18]

[15]See Karl Mannheim, "The Sociological Problem of the 'Intelligentsia,'" p. 64 in de Huszar, ed., *Intellectuals.*

[16]R. Joseph Monsen, Jr. and Mark W. Cannon, *The Makers of Public Policy: American Power Groups and their Ideologies* (New York: McGraw-Hill, 1965), pp. 180–184.

[17]Kerr *et al., Industrialism and Industrial Man,* p. 85.

[18]Joseph A. Shumpeter, "The Sociology of the Intellectuals," p. 77 in de Huszar, ed., *Intellectuals.*

Intellectuals can therefore be the close allies of an élite or they can be the leaders of protest and reform, those who try to prod the powerful into new social action. In the ideological division which afflicts many societies today, they can even be basically opposed to an established élite and seek the conquest of power through revolution. The revolutionary role of intellectuals is described below.

As an introduction to his remarks on the Mexican intellectuals, Octavio Paz explains that he will not tell of their artistic creations — their poetry, their novels, their plays — but rather of certain of their attitudes. "Their books and other writings," he says astonishingly, "are of lesser significance than their public influence and their political actions"![19] Ellison has similarly, but not so pointedly, noted that while the employment of many Latin American writers has nothing to do with politics, "political import, reforming zeal, and the pursuit of social objectives are fundamental characteristics of Latin American literature." And he also states the opposite circumstance that "though literature itself may have little direct connection with political power, literary men may have a great deal."[20] Silvert agrees that most Latin American intellectuals of note "have concerned themselves deeply with social problems and ethics, and many have been profoundly involved in the sometimes harsh play of party and even revolutionary politics."[21] Whether as political activist or manipulator of socially significant ideas, therefore, the Latin American intellectual is characteristically politically involved in an important way. He is expected to engage in polemic, he is looked up to for political guidance, and this has been true, in varying degrees and with understandable exceptions of time and place, for more than one hundred and fifty years.

In the colonial period, Spain and Portugal limited intellectual participation in government, but intellectuals took the lead in the independence movements at the opening of the nineteenth century. Inexperienced in the art of politics and government, they, as political leaders, are said to have acted more often on abstractions than on tested strategies. After independence, they were thrown out of power by the generals and, although many of them continued to participate in government as bureaucrats "justifying, refining, and administering the

[19]Octavio Paz, *The Labyrinth of Solitude: Life and Thought in Mexico,* translated by Lysander Kemp (New York: Grove Press, 1961), pp. 151–152.
[20]Ellison, "The Writer," pp. 83, 90–91.
[21]Silvert, *Conflict Society,* p. 142.

30

policies formulated by *caudillos*,"[22] an impressive number rose to the pinnacle of political power.

One list, said to be incomplete, indicates that some thirty writers served as presidents of their countries in the nineteenth and early twentieth centuries. The political history of Argentina "bulges with the names of intellectuals who have made good as major political figures; more intellectuals than military men have been presidents of the country if we discount the intellectuals who have worn the uniform to complete their role as universal men."[23] Other intellectuals of the last century, from lesser vantage points, "supported progressive constitutional regimes, opposed the usurpation of power by force, and advocated the extension of social and political liberties. A few rightists...justified conservative or authoritarian governments. The political role of writers was a great one."[24]

High social prestige, public esteem, and political involvement continue to describe the role of the intellectual today throughout Latin America. Let us listen to four commentators:

> *Stokes:* Among those with status, dignity, and influence in the community, few rank higher...than the...intellectuals....In politics the *doctor* and *general*...compete with each other for control of government.[25]
>
> *Ellison:* In government positions of great responsibility and trust, one finds distinguished poets, novelists, and essayists.[26]
>
> *Wyatt MacGaffey* and *Clifford R. Barnett:* The intellectual is potentially a hero in Cuban culture. Typically, he is a poet and orator exhorting and inspiring a mass audience....The greatest intellectual achievements have usually been associated with insurgent political movements.[27]

Why is the intellectual such a powerful figure, so near the apex of the social and political pyramid in Latin America? It is always difficult in social explanation to get at original causes, but those who have been troubled by this question seem to agree that the first obvious answer is that learning itself has high value in the Latin American culture. The learned élite, because they are learned and not for other standards of ability and accomplishment that might be invoked, are

---

[22]See Johnston, *Political Change in Latin America*, pp. 15–18, 180–181.
[23]Silvert, *Conflict Society*, pp. 178–179.
[24]Ellison, "The Writer," p. 89.
[25]Stokes, "The *Pensadores* of Latin America," p. 422.
[26]Ellison, "The Writer," p. 86.
[27]Wyatt MacGaffey and Clifford R. Barnett, *Cuba, Its People, Its Society, Its Culture* (New Haven, Conn.: Hraf Press, 1962), p. 211.

31

raised to the loftiest cultural and political positions. That this sometimes leads to disaster (according to outside standards of "firmness,"
"efficiency," etc.) does not, or has not yet, altered the pattern. Stokes
summarizes this "prointellectual" ambient of Latin America in three
points:

> (1) higher education...has maximum status in the community; (2)
> learning is...regarded as a value in itself...; (3) the symbols of edu-
> cation are...passionately sought....The high status of titles such as
> doctor..., Lic. (licentiate, lawyer), Ing. (engineer), and Arq. (archi-
> tect) is seen in the excessive use of the symbols. Everyone has his call-
> ing card with whatever symbol of status he can claim ostentatiously
> displayed. Letters are signed with the title added. Name plates for
> homes and apartments display the information. Men are careful to
> address each other in the ceremonial fashion.[28]

That today's intellectuals in Latin America may be largely leftist-
oriented suggests participation in revolutionary politics. This participation has taken the form of leadership and collaboration in the two
major nationalist revolutions of the area (Mexico and Bolivia) and in
the communist or fidelista revolution in Cuba. It has also placed some
intellectuals in some countries in the exposed and sometimes risky
role of opposition to constituted governments — e.g., Communist and
Socialist intellectuals in Chile and many intellectuals in present-day
Brazil and Argentina.

Calling attention to a common Western view of intellectuals as the
"formulators of the group conscience," Alvaro Mendoza Diez believes
this inadequate in Latin America where, he says, intellectuals "are also
the performers and executors of these formulations of group conscience.
Acting as political leaders, the doctores place themselves at the head
of the popular masses and lead them to the conquest of power." Writing before the recent disintegration of the Bolivian MNR (National
Revolutionary Movement), he pointed to Bolivia as the favored place
to study this phenomenon "because in no other Latin American revolutionary movement has there been such a high degree of participation
by the doctores."[29] Maldonado Denis traces the political commitment
of the intellectual to industrialization and to the rise of modern capitalism which has intensified the social and economic criticism of the

[28]Stokes, "The Pensadores of Latin America," pp. 424–425. See also Mendoza Diez,
La revolución de los profesionales e intelectuales en Latinoamérica, pp. 85–91 and
Ellison, "The Writer," p. 88.

[29]Mendoza Diez, La revolución de los profesionales e intelectuales en Latinoamérica, pp. 55–57, 154.

intellectuals and drawn them into "conflict with the most powerful groups of a society."[30]

What may happen to the intellectuals once the revolutionary victory is won is succinctly stated for Mexico, by Octavio Paz:

> Once the military phase of the Revolution had ended, many young intellectuals who had not been able to participate in it, because of their age or for other reasons, now began to work with the revolutionary governments. The intellectuals became the secret or public advisors of the illiterate generals, the labor or peasant leaders, the political bosses. It was an immense task and everything had to be improvised. The poets studied economics; the jurists, sociology; the novelists, international law or pedagogy or agronomy. Except for the painters — who were supported in the best possible manner, by being given public walls to cover with murals — all of the intelligentsia was enlisted for specific and immediate ends: legal projects, governmental plans, confidential missions, educational work, the founding of schools and agrarian banks, etc. The diplomatic service, foreign trade, public administration, all opened their doors to an intelligentsia that came from the middle class. Within a short time the country possessed a considerable group of technicians and experts, thanks to the new professional schools and the opportunity to study abroad. Their participation in the work of government has made it possible to continue the efforts that were initiated by the first revolutionaries. . . .

Paz adds, however, that not all Mexican intellectuals lend their talents to the revolutionary government — "some of them have withdrawn from government service to found opposition groups or parties."[31]

As a vocal and prestigious opposition group, intellectuals are likely in some countries to forfeit public employment, or worse still, to be thrown into jail or to be exiled, actions which they label "cultural terrorism." Such has been the fate of intellectuals in Brazil and Argentina in recent months.[32] While many Cuban intellectuals have supported the Castro movement through all its vicissitudes, many others have gone into voluntary exile or, remaining at home, have found their freedom to criticize curtailed. Intellectual opposition to a revolutionary movement which has achieved power is not tolerated.[33]

Intellectual leadership is nothing new in the sociology of revolution, for intellectuals have led in all the major revolutions of modern his-

[30]Maldonado Denis, "El Intelectual Latinoamericano y la Política," chap. 5, pp. 52–53 in Rama, Los intelectuales y la política.

[31]Paz, Labyrinth of Solitude, pp. 157–158, 159.

[32]See the New York Times, August 8, 1965.

[33]See José Antonio Portuondo, "Los Intelectuales y la Revolución," Cuba Socialista, vol. 4, June 1964, pp. 51–64.

tory, including the American, the French, and the Russian.[34] However, the present revolutionary commitment of some intellectuals in Latin America does serve to dramatize a long-standing political sensitivity of intellectuals in general in the area south of the Rio Grande. This is a significant point which perhaps distinguishes the Latin American intellectual from his North American or European counterpart. Octavio Paz seems to say as much in concluding that the Mexican intellectual "is very different from...the European intellectual. In Europe and the United States, the intellectual has been deprived of power. He lives in exile, so far as the state is concerned, and wields his influence from outside the government, with criticism as his principle mission. In Mexico, the intellectual's mission is political action."[35] Shils, in speaking of the new states of Asia and Africa, asserts that their gestation, birth, and continuing life "are in large measure the work of intellectuals. In no state-formations in all of human history have intellectuals played such a role as they have in these events of the present century." In contrast, he finds that the politics of the West in modern times "have never been a preserve of the intellectuals."[36] An analogy between the new states and those of Latin America would, again, not be completely accurate, for politics in Latin America do not belong wholly to the intellectuals as a special preserve, but their political role would seem to be a more direct and more persistent one than that of other Western intellectuals. Addressing himself apparently only to European and North American intellectuals, Shumpeter asserts that "intellectuals rarely enter professional politics and still more rarely conquer responsible office."[37] However true that observation may be for Europe and the United States, and however much the situation may now seem to be changing, especially in the United States, it does not describe accurately or completely the intellectual in Latin America.

[34]In de Huszar, ed., *Intellectuals,* see Merle Curti, "Intellectuals and the Founding Fathers," pp. 28–31; Alexis de Tocqueville, "How towards the Middle of the Eighteenth Century Men of Letters Took the Lead in Politics and the Consequences of this New Development," pp. 11–18; and Hugh Seton-Watson, "The Russian Intellectuals," pp. 41–50.

[35]Paz, *Labyrinth of Solitude,* p. 159. In a significant addendum, Paz reveals great personal concern over the role of the intelligentsia in modern Mexico. "Has it not ceased to be an intelligentsia?" he asks; "That is, has it not renounced its proper role as the critical conscience of its people?"

[36]Shils, "The Intellectuals in the Political Development of the New States," *World Politics,* vol. 12, April 1960, pp. 329–330.

[37]Shumpeter, "The Sociology of the Intellectuals," p. 78 in de Huszar, ed., *Intellectuals.*

II

With this general (but not universal or complete) background on the intellectuals, a more useful analysis of the role of intellectuals in the genesis of the industrial relations system in Chile is possible. Were they allies of the power élite or were they revolutionaries? If they were allies, did they wear coats of many colors and attach themselves to different élites within the power group? Did they behave like a loyal opposition and align themselves with organized labor? Were they leaders who took the initiative in efforts to translate social protest into legislative action? If so, did their effective influence stem exclusively from high status as intellectuals, in the pattern of the French *ideologues,* or were they also working politicians, in the pattern of many Latin American intellectuals and the intellectuals of the American and English revolutionary periods? In sum, in what ways and to what degree is the Chilean industrial relations system the work of intellectuals?

The findings of this study suggest that intellectuals were indispensable innovators in the development of the Chilean industrial relations system. Without them it is unlikely that either the aristocratic-Catholic or the middle-class élites would have constructed a comprehensive industrial relations system. Strong elements in both of these élites were opposed to anything that went beyond palliatives such as Sunday rest and sanitation laws and regulation of the sale of alcoholic beverages. Among these elements were such powerful bodies as the National Agricultural Society, the Catholic Church, and the Labor Association (a mixed group of large landholders and businessmen).

Opposition to thoroughgoing reform, especially to unions, conciliation, arbitration, minimum wages, and the eight-hour day, was so strong that reform was never achieved through the normal democratic process. Major labor bills were presented to the Congress in 1919 (by the Conservative party, chief political representative of the aristocratic-Catholic élite) and in 1921 (by the Liberal Alliance, a coalition of the middle-class), but during several years of parliamentary maneuvering and debate nothing was passed. Political rivalries and a critical power struggle between the élites (centered largely on the parliamentary versus the presidential system of government and on the church-state relationship) confused and complicated the labor reform issue and encouraged the military to intervene in 1924. One of the first acts of the military was to force the Congress to approve all pending labor bills. The resulting industrial relations system was a combination of the two élite proposals, and this accounts in part for the relative inefficiency of the system today, although philosophically the proposals reflected a common desire to subordinate the working classes and to control their organizations and leaders.

Thus in Chile the intellectuals (along with the generals) were the accidental architects of the legal industrial relations system. Moreover, several key intellectuals played their leadership role as political activists — that is, as party leaders, Deputies, Senators, and high-ranking bureaucrats. They helped commit their parties to a reform position on the social question, they drafted legislation, and they presented it to and fought for it in the Congress. They were, on a rather minor key, philosopher-kings in an area of the world well known for the high social and political status it has at times bestowed upon its poets, writers, and other literati. In Chile, therefore, the intellectuals were something more than servants of the power élite and more than leaders of protest, although they were not revolutionaries.

The relatively small number of Chilean intellectuals who furthered the development of an industrial relations system were not a single, unified group by either organization, social class, political party affiliation, intellectual type and reform role, or ideology. There were, for example, no "Intellectuals for Social Reform" or any similar organization, and the intellectuals never met in a body to define goals or map a strategy. They came from all classes with the exception of the working class and from all parties with the exception of the Socialist Workers' party. By types they were poets, journalists, political writers, social philosophers, lawyers, political economists, and university professors and students who taught and wrote about the social question. They fell into three major groups in terms of their institutional or career identifications: a university group, independent professional writers, and political activists.

The largest group, although not the most significant one, was that of the university professors and students. While the professors were the stable and persistent element in this group, the students, caught up in a university reform movement, made their contribution in association with that movement, and, for the most part, did not continue a major reform interest after leaving the university. A second group, much smaller in size, was composed of those established writers, principally poets and journalists, who responded to their own growing middle-class publics and whose interest was to arouse popular sympathy for a change in the living and working conditions of the common people, especially in the nitrate *pampas* of the "Great North." They traveled alone or with parliamentary investigating committees and then later, in the daily press and other media, told the truth of what they saw in a poignant spirit seldom found in the official reports themselves. The third and most crucial group was composed of those intellectuals who took the political initiative and, as active party members, or Deputies, or Senators, helped develop attitudes and specific legislative proposals designed to accomplish their reform objectives. There is some overlapping among these three groups, and in key instances it is possible to trace an intellectual from thesis writer, to Deputy, to Senator, and to membership on the Joint Committee on Social Legislation of the Congress, and, thus, near the pinnacle of political power as it bears upon our discussion of the development of the industrial relations system in Chile.

The university group of intellectuals deserves to be identified further because, although not judged to be the most crucial of the three, it was probably the second in importance, was organized around a single institution, and has therefore left a more accessible record for description. Moreover, the involvement of a university group in the genesis of social and labor legislation illustrates so well the strong link between intellectualism and politics in Chile that it not only permits but requires more detailed explanation.

The university intellectuals centered in the Faculty of Law and Political Sciences of the University of Chile. Even though many student theses took their inspiration from the moral principles of Christianity and were based upon the Catholic social philosophy as expressed in *Rerum Novarum,* they were written by University of Chile students rather than by students of the Catholic University of Santiago, the second university in size in the country. The reason for this is apparently that the Catholic Church hierarchy in Chile did not yet (at the turn of the century and for a couple of decades thereafter) wish to encourage discussion of the social or labor question.[38] In addition, as Silvert points out, the state universities of Latin America, generally, "attract the innovators — and thus the nationalists — in much greater measure than such schools as the Catholic University of Chile or the Javeriana (Jesuit University) in Colombia."[39]

Although there were a few theses written on social and labor topics

[38]See below pp. 193–197.

[39]Silvert, "The University Student," p. 224. The Catholic University of Chile was founded by a decree signed June 21, 1888. Its Faculty of Law was one of the first two faculties to begin classes in 1889. The date of its founding did not therefore have anything to do with its failure to arouse student interest in the social question. The University was in operation at the very beginning of the social question in Chile.

prior to 1902, it was in that year that the curriculum of the Faculty of Law and Political Sciences first included formal courses in this general area, forerunners of the present chair of Labor Law. Political and Social Economics and Industrial and Agricultural Law were both added to the curriculum at that time,[40] and many of the theses on the "social question" published in succeeding years were undoubtedly influenced by these courses and the professors who taught them.[41]

Between 1898 and 1924 at least seventy graduates of the Faculty wrote their theses on labor and social subjects. Most of the original work at this level was done by 1915, and the relatively few theses written after that date generally added little that was new. Most of the seventy or more theses were studies of labor legislation in the advanced countries, and they covered a wide range of subjects: unionism, minimum wages, length of the work day, labor inspection and labor statistics, the labor contract, unemployment, strikes, white-collar workers, work accidents, social security, women and child labor, housing, arbitration, conciliation, and labor courts. Some of the theses were merely descriptive, others took a point of view and tried to determine what foreign practices would work best in Chile.

That the continued flow of these theses over the years was the result of a conscious and purposeful effort is probably verified by an event which took place in the Faculty in 1908. In that year the Faculty chose the "labor contract" as the theme of its biennial literary competition and invited contributions from outside as well as from within the University of Chile. The purpose in selecting the labor theme was, the Faculty said, "to prepare public opinion for social legislation along lines already adopted in the advanced countries of the world."[42] The competition was won by Pedro Luis González, Professor Extraordinary of Social and Political Economy of the University of Chile and, at that time, also president of the Society for Factory Development.

Students in the Faculty were also aware of their leadership position with respect to the social issues of the day. One law student, writing in

[40]Political Economy was established as a separate course in 1872. To be precise, therefore, Social Economy was the new part of the offering.

[41]In a general curriculum reform of 1924 Political Economy was again established as a separate course, Industrial and Agricultural Law was eliminated, and a new course was added called Social Economy and Labor Legislation. In 1933 Industrial and Agricultural Law was reintroduced into the curriculum, and the following year the Labor Law content of the course was taken out and set up as an independent offering, as it continues to be at present.

[42]*Boletín de la Sociedad de Fomento Fabril*, vol. 24, June–September 1912, pp. 854–855.

1907, believed that the course on Industrial and Agricultural Law represented great progress in the social studies area because it would awaken his generation to the importance of social questions and would develop a body of useful social doctrine. "The spirit of criticism," he said, "has taken a practical turn giving rise to the comparative study of labor law and contributing efficaciously to the future reform of common law."[43] A contemporary, who became a titled professor in the Faculty in 1915, wrote an entire thesis on *The Social Problem and the Teaching of Law* in which he pled for a new juridical-ethical concept which would break the monopoly of the rich and powerful over the legal system and facilitate legislation in the interests of the poor and the weak. Law students and lawyers had to take the initiative in such a movement, he urged, the students as reformers or propagandists (presumably in part through the writing of theses) and the lawyers as participants in the day-to-day struggle for change. The Faculty of Law and Political Sciences of the University of Chile seemed to realize the deficiencies of its own teaching program and methods to further the movement, according to this writer, and was making slow progress toward reform. Courses had been added, examinations were being changed to stimulate the search for truth and the serious observation of social phenomena, and now new and more liberal teachers were needed.[44] We will return to the university group of intellectuals further on and evaluate their influence upon the development of the two major reform bills to come before the Congress.

There was only one important ideological difference among the intellectuals, which centered upon Catholicism, and they were separated, on this basis, roughly into two groups. These groups, generally, though not always, coincide with the two élites already mentioned, namely the aristocratic-Catholic and the middle-class. The aristocratic-Catholic élite in Chile, composed essentially of the landed aristocracy and the Catholic Church hierarchy, was represented politically by the Conservative party, the minority wing of the Liberal party, and other party and splinter groups which operated, in the period under discussion, as a coalition called the National Union. The middle-class élite was composed of industrialists, professional people, and the government bureaucracy, and was represented by the Radical party, the majority wing of the Liberal party, and other lesser important groups.

[43]Eduardo Pantaleon Fontecilla, *La reforma legislativa y política y nuestra cuestión social* (Santiago: Imprenta Chile, 1907), p. 34.

[44]Robinson Hermansen Vergara, *El problema social y la enseñanza del derecho* (Santiago: Imprenta Barcelona, 1907).

They also acted in a coalition, known as the Liberal Alliance. The reader has already been alerted to the fact that these groups were not rigidly exclusive, one from another, and that they were not divided, by philosophy, on all fundamental social issues. There was no unmitigated rural-urban confrontation, the *hacendados* and the Church on one side and the urban burgeoisie on the other. The blending of points of view in the two élites and the shifting about of individuals and groups between them will be mentioned later, as specific occasions arise.

Our analysis of the importance of the intellectuals in the development of the Chilean industrial relations system turns most decisively on their roles in the immediate origins and the congressional history of the two comprehensive labor proposals developed by the élites and ultimately enacted into law. This kind of analytical structure means that the most essential breakdown of the intellectuals will be into the two élite camps rather than into the three functional groups of university, professional, and "political leader" intellectuals. There are disadvantages to this approach (e.g., the university group in particular will have to be discussed twice) but, over all, organization will be more effective and more insightful.

There was no identifiable revolutionary point of view on the social question either among the university group, the professional writers, or the political activists. No legislative project was developed or supported by such an élite. Only one or two thesis writers appear to have accepted a mildly socialist position, and it is difficult to distinguish them from the others. The difference, if any, is in their choice of language and in the harshness of their criticism rather than in their solutions. Moisés Bernales Zañartu, for example, stated that the interests of workers and employers were antagonistic, and he credited socialism with all the major labor reforms in the world up to that time. Yet he too stayed within the evolutionary reform approach of legislative change and did not advocate a social revolution.[45]

Why was this so? In the first place, the explanation is not that the intellectuals were unfamiliar with leftist literature. Such literature was available in Chile from the mid-nineteenth century on — much of it in Spanish, although translation was not always required for intellectual consumption. Indeed, Chilean intellectuals knew the writings of Marx, Engels, Bakunin, Bebel, Kropotkin, Faure, and others, recognized that solutions to the social question fell into the two general

[45]Moisés Bernales Zañartu, *Estudio sobre la legislación del trabajo* (Santiago: Imprenta Claret, 1913).

categories of reform (or class cooperation) and revolution (or class struggle), and deliberately chose the reform approach. For some of them, interest in the social question came as much from their fright at the possibility of a general worker uprising and other extremist solutions as from an idealistic or humane concern for the status and treatment of the Chilean worker. This selfish approach, and correlative lack of spiritual identification with the working class, affected the content of their proposals and is evident today in the nature of the Chilean industrial relations system.

What then can be said? For one thing, intellectuals with a revolutionary bias would have had virtually no political base at that time. Peasants were still tightly held in a semifeudal agricultural system and copied the conservative voting habits of their masters. With the exception of the nitrate workers, there were no large agglomerations of industrial workers in the country and a sizeable industrial labor force did not begin to emerge until the 1930's. Workers in the towns and cities were led by the printers, shoemakers, and other skilled groups who were independent and individualistic in behavior, anarchist in ideology, and therefore opposed to organized politics and government.

Second, there has been a tradition of working-class leadership of unions and popular political parties in Chile, perhaps weaker today than at the turn of the century, which has at times and to some degree limited the role of the intellectual in leftist movements. The first avowedly socialist political party in Chile, for example, was founded in 1912 by Luis Emilio Recabarren, a printer and father of the Chilean labor movement. Although he formally converted the party and the Chilean trade union center into Communist organizations after the Bolshevik Revolution, his ideological thinking was confused and he remained heavily influenced by anarchist notions throughout his life. As an elected member of the Chamber of Deputies he fought against both the Conservative and Liberal Alliance labor bills and, as a substitute, supported an unworkable scheme of unmistakable anarchist orientation which was never debated.

Finally, the middle sectors were only beginning to emerge in the last two decades of the nineteenth century, they sought political power in their own right (although often with working-class support), and their aspirations in terms of the symbols and emoluments of status tended to identify them with the upper rather than with the lower classes. The intellectuals, who were probably found predominately in the middle sectors, seem to have followed middle-sector norms.

41

This overwhelming reform orientation of the intellectuals in Chile did not begin to change appreciably until the 1930's with the formation of a new and more successful Socialist party and the growth in vigor and prestige of the Communists. Fredrick B. Pike has also noted, with respect to communism, that "in the 1930's [it] became increasingly a movement of Chilean intellectuals" after having been dominated for years by labor elements.[46] However, by the 1930's an industrial relations system, centered in a code of national labor laws, was already operative. The revolutionary intellectuals therefore arrived late in Chile and, faced with a modern structure of labor-management relations, have since had a somewhat more difficult time of extending their influence than perhaps would otherwise have been the case.

[46]Fredrick B. Pike, *Chile and the United States, 1880–1962* (Notre Dame, Ind.: University of Notre Dame Press, 1963), p. 203.

CHAPTER 3

Consensus

ALMOST twenty years ago Louis Wirth, in his presidential address to
the American Sociological Association, chose to speak on consensus
because he regarded the study of consensus as the central task of sociology. The "mark of any society is the capacity of its members to understand one another and to act in concert toward common objectives
and under common norms" and, therefore, "the analysis of consensus
rightly constitutes the focus of sociological investigation." It also "provides an approach...to the problems of the contemporary world."[1]
Not all sociologists agreed then, or agree today, that the study of consensus is really as critical as Wirth considered it to be. Nevertheless,
there is a growing and important literature bearing on the subject.

Many disciplines (e.g., sociology, political science, history, psychology,
economics) have become involved in this area of social analysis, each
generally making a contribution from a particular analytical starting
point or frame of reference. Sociologists tend to talk about "common
norms" and "social integration"; political scientists about "political
socialization," "political legitimacy," or "civic integration"; psychologists about "common orientations"; and economists about "stability"

[1] Louis Wirth, "Consensus and Mass Communication," *American Sociological Review*, vol. 13, February 1948, p. 2.

and the satisfaction of material comforts. Less reliant on a single discipline and its jargon are the political sociologists, historians, and generalists (whose broad social interpretation is boundless, in the disciplinary sense).

Not all studies of consensus are, however, at the macrolevel of mass society which concerned Wirth, and which concerns this writer. Many sociologists study consensus in small groups (e.g., the family); some political scientists and administrators are interested in the decision-making process in business and government; psychologists study the interpersonal processes through which consensus is achieved, modified, or maintained in all kinds and sizes of human collectivities; and economists and industrial relations experts may be interested in bargaining theory and harmony in the workplace.

Moreover, not all thinking or writing on the subject of consensus actually employs the term or even deliberately focuses on the area of analysis it represents, all of which means that consensus is not nearly so tightly defined and universally recognized a research area as may have been implied up to this point. At the level of society, the term probably means more to sociologists, political sociologists, and political scientists than to anyone else. American scholars tend to think of consensus in terms of content (the attitudes and values that make it up, the relationships and institutions that articulate it), process (how it is effected and maintained), and deviant behavior in a single, stabilized society (i.e., the United States). There is less consideration of it as a cross-cultural phenomenon and in terms of *why* it is achieved democratically in some societies, by revolution in others, and seemingly never or only very slowly or at great social cost in still others. Psychological studies of consensus achievement or consensus loss in the open laboratories of the developing countries offer a great challenge.

What is consensus? Can it be achieved or strengthened through selection of appropriate political institutions? How is consensus related to economic development and social reform? Why is it especially acute during the transition from a traditional agrarian society to a modern, industrialized one? What evidence is there of consensus loss in Chile, in particular, and when and why did this loss occur? Some material relevant to the latter question has already been presented, and a fuller response will be sought throughout this study. Regarding the former questions, the writer views his task as essentially that of providing a preliminary social-psychological analysis of consensus, drawing in part on pertinent literature and, for the rest, on almost a decade of observation and study of the developing societies of Latin America.

I

Robin Williams has identified four minimal conditions for the achievement and maintenance of "social integration." There must be a sharing of "normative orientations," social structures to link these common values and to insulate disruptive tendencies, mutual dependence through the division of labor, and agreement on the rules to be followed in pursuing interests. The latter includes "the acquiescence of losers in political elections." The sociological explanation of integration must center in this area of "the sharing of a common culture." "This," Williams concludes, "is a hard-won insight in the history of thought about society and its importance must be given every possible emphasis." Neither the rationalistic notion of the "social contract" nor the political notion of balanced power systems tells us much about the ultimate congruent forces in society.[2] A somewhat similar listing of the major dimensions of social integration has appeared in a more recent study of social problems in American society. Authors of this study go on to explain that the sharing of common values provides the members of society with "a common orientation — a common world view."[3]

The four conditions or dimensions of social integration (i.e., consensus) can apparently be reduced to two, with a consequent sharpening of analysis. Williams himself seems to do this in speaking of integration as (1) the sharing of normative orientations which, to become an effective cohesive force, requires (2) the existence of "highly specific processes" which "cannot be taken for granted as belonging to the nature of human association."[4] William V. D'Antonio also sees a fundamental consensus in society as consisting of two propositions: "a basic ideological commitment about man's ends, his nature, his potential, and how his potential should and can be fulfilled" and "the rules for running the political game." In a democratic society the latter rules assure that differences will not be resolved through resort to violence; opposition groups or parties are made legitimate and both the "ins" and the "outs" abide by the rules.[5] As suggested in the first chapter,

[2]Robin M. Williams, Jr., *American Society: A Sociological Interpretation,* 2nd ed. rev. (New York: Alfred A. Knopf, 1960), p. 550.

[3]Russell R. Dynes, Alfred C. Clarke, Simon Dinitz, and Iwao Ishino, *Social Problems: Dissensus and Deviation in an Industrial Society* (New York: Oxford University Press, 1964), p. 375.

[4]Williams, *American Society,* p. 545.

[5]William V. D'Antonio, "Democracy and Religion in Latin America," chap. 13, p. 259, in William V. D'Antonio and Fredrick B. Pike, eds., *Religion, Revolution,*

however, a revolutionary group which achieves power through the democratic process may then ignore the rules and substitute both new rules and a new ideology. Respect only for some of the rules or part of the democratic process is not, therefore, the equivalent of a democratic consensus nor is it sufficient to produce consensus. In a democracy both orderly political procedures and normative consensus must be present. As stated before, the two are closely linked; in the absence of hypocrisy, loyalty to the rules must embody a commitment to the democratic philosophy (e.g., status equality, individual initiative and responsibility, the rule of law, etc.).

Each of these dimensions (norms and procedures or structures) is important, but the first appears to be in the order of an "original cause." Principal concern in this chapter is at the moment with the first, or "normative consensus." Later, something will also be said about the second, particularly as it relates to politics and to two-party versus multiparty systems.

There is tremendous variation in the nature and complexity of norms among societies. In other words, while agreement on norms may produce consensus within a society, norms themselves can also distinguish one society from another. Societies, in turn, can be grouped into democracies and totalitarian states or into traditional societies and industrialized nations for the purpose of making more general normative comparisons. The vast literature in these societal groupings certainly reveals striking differences in what are regarded as the proper relations of man to man, of man to his government, of men to women, parents to children, and of all citizens to the external world.

Williams has listed and described at great length fifteen "major value-orientations" present in American culture. (Attitudes and values of traditional societies are discussed in Section III of this chapter.) Included in his extensive discussion are equality, freedom, democracy, individual personality, humanitarian mores, achievement and success, activity and work, efficiency and practicality, progress, and science and secular rationality. With understandable trepidation, he suggests the following still more general synthesis of American value-orientations:

> 1. American culture is organized around the attempt at *active mastery* rather than *passive acceptance*. Into this dimension falls the low tolerance of frustration; the refusal to accept ascetic renunciation; the positive encouragement of desire; the stress on power; the approval of ego-assertion, and so on.

and Reform; New Forces for Change in Latin America (New York: Frederick A. Praeger, 1964).

2. It tends to be interested in the *external world* of things and events, of the palpable and immediate, rather than in the inner experience of meaning and effect. Its genius is manipulative rather than contemplative.

3. Its world-view tends to be *open* rather than closed: it emphasizes change, flux, movement; its central personality types are adaptive, accessible, outgoing and assimilative.

4. In wide historical and comparative perspective, the culture places its primary faith in *rationalism* as opposed to *traditionalism;* it de-emphasizes the past, orients strongly to the future, does not accept things just because they have been done before.

5. Closely related to the above, is the dimension of *orderliness* rather than unsystematic *ad hoc* acceptance of transitory experience. (This emphasis is most marked in the urban middle classes.)

6. With conspicuous deviations, a main theme is a *universalistic* rather than a *particularistic* ethic.

7. In interpersonal relations, the weight of the value system is on the side of *"horizontal"* rather than *"vertical"* emphases: peer-relations, not superordinate-subordinate relations; equality rather than hierarchy.

8. Subject to increased strains and modifications, the received culture emphasizes *individual personality* rather than group identity and responsibility.[6]

Running through both his extensive discussion of individual normative orientations and his synthesis is the suggestion that the American is, above all, a dignified individual who is life-oriented. Individual dignity or equality is the basis for mutual respect, mutual trust, and the desire and need to delegate responsibility to others. Life orientation means the here and now is important — not death, the grave, and the hereafter. Life is a challenge; it is purposeful; and it not only can but *must* be made better for those we leave behind.

These themes of individual dignity and equality and a life-orientation recur again and again in the thoughts of those who have tried to reach that small inner truth of democracy and the democratic personality. Seymour Martin Lipset expresses it as the "American Creed" of equality and opportunity. He writes that the " 'other-directedness' of Americans, the flattery, the use of first names among people who hardly know each other. . . , the elaborate efforts to avoid hurting the feelings of others, all reflect the fact that deeply rooted in our values is the mandate that all men should respect one another." Moreover, the observations of foreign visitors "continue to support the contention that the two emphases, on equality (respect for others) and achieve-

[6]Williams, *American Society,* pp. 415–470.

ment (competition), are clearly linked together in the United States."[7] Achievement in life demands a sensitive orientation toward others, because one cannot achieve alone. As we become ever more equalitarian, we "become more concerned with the opinions of others, and therefore more democratic and more American in the Tocquevillian sense."[8]

Gabriel Almond and Sidney Verba are acutely aware of the need for "social trust" and "a sense of identity with one's fellow citizens" if a society is to develop a "common political identity" or a "common affective commitment to the political system." An ability to trust and identify with others makes it possible for the citizens of a democratic society to turn power over to a political élite. The same social attitudes discourage political fragmentation and the involvement of the ordinary citizen in unstabilizing mass movements. "These norms," they conclude, "place a limit on politics."[9]

Almond and Verba believe that some symbolic event, like the Mexican Revolution, may be necessary to produce a permeating sense of trust in society. While this may be true, such a result would seem to depend, in a much more elementary sense, on a developing faith in the individual, his dignity, his independence, his equality with all others. Wirth was convinced, for example, that Americans had found the road to consensus "through the idea of cultural pluralism, which is another expression for the toleration of differences"; he then added that the essential residue of democracy is "the freedom and dignity of every personality."[10]

The thinking of William V. D'Antonio and Howard Ehrlich also leads to an ultimate fixation on human equality and a realistic life orientation as the essence of democratic values. "A fundamental belief underlying the practice of democracy is," they say, "that every individual is deserving of respect by the simple fact of his humanity. Respect on this level is not a matter of achievement. It is a fact of social existence....It entails the corollary belief that the end of group participation is the welfare of the individual." Again, "every man must

[7]Seymour Martin Lipset, *The First New Nation: The United States in Historical and Comparative Perspective* (New York: Basic Books, Inc., 1963), p. 318.

[8]Seymour Martin Lipset, *Political Man: The Social Bases of Politics* (New York: Doubleday and Company, 1960), p. 412.

[9]Gabriel A. Almond and Sidney Verba, *The Civic Culture: Political Attitudes and Democracy in Five Nations* (Princeton, N.J.: Princeton University Press, 1963), pp. 490, 503–505.

[10]Wirth, "Consensus and Mass Communication," *American Sociological Review*, vol. 13, February 1948, pp. 9, 13.

be concerned about the well-being of his fellow man if the democratic society is to be anything more than a privilege for a small élite. This concern requires the recognition that the well-being is not foreknown or foreordained, but is to be established via freedom and equality of opportunity for all." The high value of achievement in American society is "probably closely related to the fact that Americans tend to see other people as human beings like themselves."[11]

Whatever the norms in any society may be, they are learned not inherited. They are not innate ethnic or racial characteristics. Normative behavior is learned through group experience, in families and other social institutions. Yet those who learn and later transmit norms seldom realize their behavior has social meaning. Parents transmit norms "every time they remind their children that they should do *this* and not *that*."[12] Neither normative consensus nor individual conformity is static or automatic. They can be maintained "only by incessant effort and active social evaluation" — in the absence of which entire institutional systems may collapse.[13] As Wirth put it, normative consensus is not only agreement but also "the established habit of intercommunication, of discussion, debate, negotiation and compromise." Consensus becomes "the mind" of society, a social sensorium which keeps organized social life effective and going.[14]

How much agreement is necessary to establish consensus? Certainly complete agreement cannot be expected anywhere. All societies have their criminals, the mentally ill, social non-conformists, and "cranks" — the deviants and the dissenters. Moreover, a degree of "dissensus" or cleavage is not only unavoidable, but, in a democracy, is required for the maintenance of social stability. There must be "struggle over ruling positions, challenges to parties in power, and shifts of parties in office." Trade unions and managements are at times in normative conflict yet unions "help to integrate their members in the larger body politic and give them a basis for loyalty to the system."[15] Legitimate cleavage therefore contributes to social integration. Some dissensus makes for consensus; it keeps the social mind alert.

[11]William V. D'Antonio and Howard J. Ehrlich, "Democracy in America: Retrospect and Prospect," chap. 5, p. 130, in D'Antonio and Ehrlich, eds., *Power and Democracy in America* (Notre Dame, Ind.: University of Notre Dame Press, 1961); and D'Antonio, "Democracy and Religion in Latin America," pp. 245, 253–254.

[12]Dynes *et al.*, *Social Problems*, p. 5. Italics added.

[13]Williams, *American Society*, pp. 376, 378.

[14]Wirth, "Consensus and Mass Communication," *American Sociological Review*, vol. 13, February 1948, pp. 4, 9–10.

[15]Lipset, *Political Man*, pp. 21–22.

It is not possible to specify the amount of agreement needed for consensus, nor is it possible to state with precision the limits within which dissensus can be tolerated. However, it is difficult to believe that these limits can extend "up to the point of 'clear and present danger' which threatens the life of the society itself."[16] Any society so threatened must function at a very low and precarious level of consensus, and "low consensus" is confusing, if not contradictory, terminology. For a society to be considered stable or "in consensus," there must be reasonable agreement on the significant norms, which rules out any internal threat to the very existence of constituted society.

Consensus has been firmly established in city-states, empires, kingdoms, and feudal manors. It is found in traditional societies of the present day and in modern industrialized societies. It can therefore characterize small, simply organized, and relatively static societies or large, highly differentiated, and dynamic ones. Any society that has achieved consensus is largely barren of internal ideological conflict, although social change may cause some of the old norms to lose their cohesive power and require that new ones be learned. Consensus is therefore a dynamic concept both in the sense that old norms must be revalidated from generation to generation and in the sense that, in societies experiencing change, new norms must constantly be learned, if consensus is to be maintained.

That disrupting ideological conflict is largely absent in the United States and some European democracies has been contended for many years. Roberto Michels noted in 1927 that in the United States the Democrats and Republicans "are at present almost devoid of theoretical or programmatical differences, so that they can both address themselves to the electorate without any 'ballast' of differentiating ideas."[17] The theory of a pragmatic democratic ideology shared by the two parties has recently been tested and confirmed in one Indiana community.[18] Furthermore, Lipset, Shils, and others have called attention to the end of ideology in many Western democracies.[19] Within the

[16]Wirth, "Consensus and Mass Communication," *American Sociological Review*, vol. 13, February 1948, pp. 9–10.

[17]Roberto Michels, "Some Reflections on the Sociological Character of Political Parties," *American Political Science Review*, vol. 21, November 1927, p. 765.

[18]See William V. D'Antonio, "Community Leadership in An Economic Crisis: Testing Ground for Ideological Cleavage," *American Journal of Sociology*, vol. 71, May 1966, pp. 688–700.

[19]For example, see chap. 13, "The End of Ideology?" in Lipset, *Political Man*. Lipset lists a number of additional sources bearing on this subject.

context of their élite typology and the industrialization process, the authors of *Industrialism and Industrial Man* have proposed that once an industrializing élite anywhere gets the "acceptance" of society, i.e., once consensus is achieved, "the society becomes internally largely ideologically barren, for there no longer is a basic conflict over the strategic approach to industrial society."[20]

Perhaps this state of ideological barrenness prevails today in countries like the United States, England, Sweden, Israel, Egypt, Mexico, the Soviet Union, and China. In the sense in which ideology has already been defined in this study, it is apparent that these societies are essentially united on an ideological basis and are in no danger of internal collapse. Important ideological conflict may exist between societies in consensus (i.e., the basis of the cold war) but not within them. To be emphasized and discussed in detail further on, however, is the fact that there are also societies today with serious internal conflicts, societies which have not yet achieved consensus. Chile belongs in this second category and, for this reason, analysis will later concentrate on the special circumstances of historical and social environment which appear to be associated with internal conflict.

It is important to notice, as implied above, that consensus can be achieved in a totalitarian system as well as in a democracy. In other words, it can be a revolutionary as well as an evolutionary phenomenon. In the former case, to explain an apparent contradiction, the establishment of consensus may consist of two essential steps or stages which can overlap: (1) violent elimination of the key opposition, through the revolution itself and subsequent political assassination, and (2) the mass re-education of the populace. While the second stage may not be the most crucial strategically, it is the most positive in actually integrating and stabilizing the new society. The achievement of consensus by this route is not devoid of consent (in the second stage), for the young people accept and learn the new philosophy and its values and are unaware that there may be workable, perhaps even superior, alternatives.

As a matter of fact, the revolutionary route not only exists but it has in the past half century been traveled by more people than any other. Probably more people who enjoy consensus in the world today have achieved it through violence than through democratic means. One need point only to Russia and her several satellites, and to China, Mexico, and Egypt. This does not mean that the revolutionary route

[20]Kerr *et al., Industrialism and Industrial Man,* p. 76.

is good (or evil), nor, necessarily, that it has been an inevitable experience. It simply puts the matter in perspective and raises the kinds of questions which, if answered, may make democracy a more viable and satisfactory route for present and future generations than it has been in the past.

II

If consensus is reasonable agreement on significant norms articulated with appropriate social structures or processes, then it is essentially a psychological phenomenon — a social mind-set. To borrow from psychology, one might explain consensus as the psychological integration of the personality of society. An attitude, or a set of attitudes, cannot be quantified or expressed in political terms. Consensus cannot be said to exist only in democracies or in all democracies, only in societies with a two-party political system, or in all countries with more than five hundred dollars annual per capita income or a rising real-wage trend. Yet the goodness or meanness in us, our empathy or narrow focus on self, our range of affection can be expressed or revealed in politics, economics, the industrial relations system, race and ethnic relations, religion, etc. There may be an association between distinctive patterns in these areas and the presence or absence of consensus, but the causal explanation is likely to reside in those underlying ideas about man, his nature, and his mortality which appear to govern behavior. In this section a few comments, largely in the form of a selection and summary of pertinent literature, will be made on consensus and its relationship to the political system, to economic development, and to the industrial relations system.

In a stable democracy each of the political parties (or a single party, in a democratic one-party state) generally represents a fair cross-section of the population and its many interest groups. The dissenters are found in all parties, although there may be more of them in one than in another. Cleavage is weak enough and is dispersed so evenly among largely unrelated issues as to discourage the organization or growth of important rival parties. In other words, the dissenters share enough of the major norms to prevent their alienation in any basic sense. They are neither driven together into the same party nor are they separated into narrow, conflictive parties which promote only their own selfish interests. Be it emphasized that this is not a matter of structure as such or of some political wise men manipulating structure in such a way as to isolate the dissenters from one another. It is a question of political structure reflecting normative consensus in society. People who see the world and one another through substantially the same eyes are able to organize themselves institutionally with reasonable efficiency. "Correct" political structures can strengthen consensus but they cannot produce it.

As Lipset has pointed out, a two-party system would seem to be a more adequate political response to normative consensus than a multiparty system. The narrower the political base, the narrower the normative appeal is likely to be. Multiple parties may therefore mean unstabilizing competition or unmanageable conflict. A society so organized may be expressing internal conflict rather than internal agreement; conflict may be organized, not consensus. However, this is not necessarily the case and there are instances of successful multiparty systems (Switzerland and Sweden) just as there are instances of unsuccessful two-party systems (South Africa and Colombia). Yet, in countries like France and Germany (during the Weimar Republic), "where a low level of effectiveness and legitimacy weakens the foundations of democracy, constitutional factors encouraging the growth of many parties further reduce the chances that the system will survive."[21]

Similar argumentation can be presented with respect to geographic as opposed to proportional representation in elective bodies and with respect to federalism versus a unitary state. Geographic representation and federalism may permit optimum cross-cutting cleavage in an integrated society or, on the other hand, they can exacerbate conflict in a divided society. Lipset is probably correct in suggesting that these variations in the political system are not so important as those derived from other aspects of the social structure, such as the way a nation handles the religious question, adult suffrage, and distribution of the national income.[22] At the same time, however, even these more basic structural variations are meaningfully related to differences in norms, particularly as they are found in élite groups from one society to another.

The representative character of political parties, in the sense of a broad appeal to diverse groups, is nevertheless a useful test of social integration, even though it may not explain such integration. Another test, vastly more simple to apply, though not so reliable, is respect for election results. If the procedure for passing on power (i.e., elections in a democracy) operates reasonably well over a long period of time,

[21]Lipset, *Political Man*, p. 92. See also, Lipset, *The First New Nation*, pp. 308–309, 312.

[22]Lipset, *Political Man*, pp. 83–90.

there is circumstantial evidence of consensus. Elections "fit" where there is respect for the dignity and equality of the individual, tolerance of opposing views, and a genuine willingness to share authority with others. When attitudes of this magnitude are present, the likelihood that an influential group or a complete "class" of the population might be alienated is remote. Yet the test is not foolproof. In Chile there have been only two deviations from the electoral process in the last seventy-five years, but, notwithstanding this fact, the country is ideologically divided.

A third test is the historical one of how a nation, at the moment in consensus, handles the "entry into politics" question. Are new groups conceded the vote? Are they absorbed into the existing parties? Are they allowed to participate in the legitimate political system but only after they have established their own new parties? Is the élite able to maintain consensus during periods of marked economic and social change, or is there consensus loss and perhaps revolution? Easy access to the system and, ideally, absorption into the existing parties "tend to win the loyalty of the new groups to the system, and they in turn can permit the old dominating strata to maintain their own status."[23] Contrary policies (e.g., denial of access to the system or forcing new groups into independent political action) can encourage radical political movements and perhaps bring about a revolutionary situation. Such consequences are not the result of a wrong answer to a political science question at a critical point in a nation's history. Rather, they derive from the dynamic nature of consensus and the failure to adapt normative behavior to situations of gradual or rapid economic and social change. Further analysis of this normative crisis follows in Section III.

As the above discussion implies, consensus is fundamentally a human value involving attitudes and relationships among people and not a political abstraction like democracy or federalism. Neither is it, in any absolute sense, an economic or material value. There is no critical minimum growth rate, no critical minimum increase in per capita income, and no critical minimum increase in real wages which, if reached, will assure consensus and stability and, if not reached, will destroy consensus and lead to social upheaval. However, this kind of thinking certainly underlies much of the foreign policy planning of the Western world and, in particular, provides a chief stimulus and justification for the generous foreign-aid programs of the United States. It is also a line of analysis more naturally pursued by economists than

[23]*Ibid.*, pp. 33, 79–80.

by representatives of most other disciplines. One of the most recent concise examples of it comes from the article "Why the American Labor Movement Is Not Socialist" by Walter Galenson. Galenson suggests that during the formative years of the American labor movement real wages in manufacturing increased at the rate of about 2 percent a year and that the annual increase has persisted, although at a perhaps somewhat slower rate and with the exception of only a few depression years, ever since. He draws the following conclusion:

> One of the greatest sources of tension in the modern world is the disparity between the material aspirations of people in underdeveloped nations and the capabilities of their economies. Economic stagnation is not necessarily inconsistent with political stability until the onset of industrialization creates a large class of people who become dissatisfied with their standard of life and who are able to develop organizational means of protest. We have not yet established the rate of economic advance necessary to prevent undermining of confidence in a prevailing social order. But it is perfectly clear that for the United States, at least, this rate was achieved.[24]

To be sure, Galenson speaks of a rate "necessary," and not of a rate "sufficient," to prevent social chaos. However, it is subject to question whether, even in this context, rate of growth is the crucial variable. Income distribution (which clearly involves morality as well as economics) may be more important. Discussion of this significant matter of income distribution is continued below.

One of Peru's foremost sociologists has argued, from an implicit Marxist viewpoint, that the industrialization process creates antagonistic classes of employers and workers. Theoretically, he sees two alternatives open to the workers in industrial societies: they can adopt "a simple pressure-group policy" as they have done in the United States or they can adopt "a revolutionary program for the transformation of social structure." A choice really does not exist in practice, however, because only dynamically prosperous societies can nurture economic unionism. In poor, developing societies workers recognize their class destiny and form revolutionary political parties.[25]

But are the poorest societies really the ones that fail to develop consensus and are sometimes destroyed? An industrializing society

[24]Walter Galenson, "Why the American Labor Movement Is Not Socialist," Reprint No. 168, Institute of Industrial Relations, University of California (Berkeley), 1961, p. 10.
[25]José Mejía Valera, "Los Sindicatos Como Grupos de Presión," *Revista de Sociología* (Universidad Nacional Mayor de San Marcos), vol. 1, no. 1, July-December 1964, pp. 6, 12, 16–17.

usually relies principally upon the wage incentive to recruit workers. Peasants migrate to the cities because factory employment is more remunerative and allows a higher standard of living than rural employment. Yet the same peasants may shortly become revolutionaries. They may even go considerably beyond the point of initial economic advantage accrued in the transition from rural to urban life before they revolt or support a successful revolution. With Cuba in mind, Simon G. Hanson cautions against the expectation that "higher living standards in themselves make for smoother political relations." At the time of the Castro revolution "Cuban per capita income was high among Latin American incomes, twice that anywhere in Africa, four times the Asian average."[26] Moreover, if workers revolt successfully under nationalist leaders or revolutionary intellectuals, they may forego an immediate emphasis upon consumption in favor of establishing their country's economic independence from powerful neighbors. They may agree not to push wage demands at all or at least not beyond the capacity of the firm. This has occurred in Mexico, although self-restraint with respect to wage demands has been relaxing there in recent years. On the other hand, some countries (Italy, France, Japan) remain ideologically divided despite many years of economic growth and their classification as advanced industrial nations. Finally, and at the opposite extreme, there are conditions under which stable poverty in a society can fix a conservative outlook among the masses.[27]

Yet there is an economic context within which consensus or the lack of it can be better understood. Apparently there is some evidence to show that the degree of inequality in income distribution is positively correlated with political radicalism in the lower classes — i.e., the greater the gap between the rich and the poor, the more extreme the political demands of the oppressed are likely to be.[28] This observation implies a feeling among the lower classes that they deserve a better life than the present system provides, and it likewise implies that they are sufficiently independent to rebel and fight for change on the political battlefield.

[26]Simon G. Hanson, "The Economic Difficulties of Social Reform in Latin America," chap. 10, p. 190, in D'Antonio and Pike, eds., *Religion, Revolution, and Reform.*
[27]See Lipset, *Political Man,* p. 63.
[28]Speaking of working-class political parties, Lipset states as fact that "the form which these political parties take in poorer countries is more extremist and radical than it is in wealthier ones." He believes this is "probably more related to the greater degree of inequality in such countries than to the fact that their poor are actually poorer in absolute terms." *Ibid.,* pp. 63–64.

CONSENSUS

In most Latin American cities and towns, a trip through the *barrio alto* (high-class residential district) is enough to convince any worker that the income gap is colossal. He does not need to read about it, understand statistics, or see movies from the United States. If he is filled with resentment, as many workers become sooner or later, he is probably reacting not only to material inequality but also to human inequality, both within his own range of personal experience. The overlay of élite feelings of superiority, and a correlative degradation of the lower classes, is oppressively heavy in most of Latin America. While it has been asserted that a large income gap produces the attitudes associated with human inequality,[29] one can also speculate that the reverse may be closer to the truth. It is the élite, the already wealthy, who must decide that raising the material conditions of the masses through industrialization is a worthwhile goal. They must identify with the needs of the lower classes in the pursuit of economic progress. This kind of empathy, of genuine affection and concern for others, of determination to achieve social justice cannot flow generously from those who do not count human dignity and equality and the independence of each soul among their values. If one considers himself superior, does this not justify the unequal status quo?

The familiar debate as to whether economic development can be successful without social reform therefore needs a third dimension — namely, the role of consensus. It has previously been noted that some nations, now considered to be industrialized, cannot claim the ideological support and loyalty of key groups of their citizens. Lack of consensus is, in these nations at least, no bar to substantial economic progress. It can still be maintained, however, that "a distinctive consensus which relates individuals and groups to each other and provides a common body of ideas, beliefs, and value judgments" is necessary if an industrial society is to reach "its fullest development."[30] A dynamic, maturing consensus would seem to be even more critical to the achievement of social reform in a nation bent upon entering the egalitarian world of industrialization. Every social advance of any significance

[29]On this point, Lipset makes the following observation: "The political values and style of the upper class, too, are related to national income. The poorer a country and the lower the absolute standard of living of the lower classes, the greater the pressure on the upper strata to treat the lower as vulgar, innately inferior, a lower caste beyond the pale of human society. The sharp difference in the style of living between those at the top and those at the bottom makes this psychologically necessary." *Ibid.*, p. 66.

[30]Kerr *et al.*, *Industrialism and Industrial Man*, pp. 42, 64.

(e.g., tax reform, land redistribution, effective industrial conciliation schemes) requires a deliberate act of faith in others, respect for their equal rights, and a concession of power and authority to them.

To agree that real economic development is difficult or impossible without social reform (and not everyone so agrees of course) does not make either social reform or economic development any the easier. In fact, while perhaps raising the ultimate prospects of gain, it would probably slow short-run achievement in most countries. Especially when the existing consensual state is predominantly that of a traditional society, with its superior-inferior value system and superordinate-subordinate class and personal relationships, demand for social reform is likely to meet stiff resistance. And there, in the opinion of this writer, is a normative problem of considerable moment. For the most part, the problem has been overlooked or confused with the more concrete issues of social reform itself. It needs to be removed from the latter context and recognized as a separate, though certainly not an unrelated, area of developmental and social analysis.[31]

A mature industrial relations system in a democracy is usually characterized by the general acceptance of unions, union leaders, strikes, collective bargaining, and written agreements. Such a system also posits the full faith of all parties (workers, employers, and the government) and of society at large in an evolutionary political experience. In other words, there is consensus within the industrial relations system as well as in society as a whole. Arthur M. Ross and Paul T. Hartman have put it this way: "Compromise is the essence of collective bargaining, not merely in the sense that particular bargaining issues are compromised, but in the more fundamental sense that the bargaining system itself represents a settlement of the basic power issues between Labor and Capital." They see such a settlement as present in the United States and the Northern European countries but, so far as the

---

[31]On this point, Asoka Mehta has declared that "as much thought needs to be given to the democratic techniques of evolving political consensus as is currently being given to the techniques of economic planning, because the latter cannot succeed without the former." Quoted in Bruce H. Millen, *The Political Role of Labor in Developing Countries* (Washington: The Brookings Institution, 1963), p. 41. Roger Vekemans insists that there can be neither economic development nor social reform in Latin America without a "cultural mutation," by which he means the economic, social, and cultural integration of Latin America "into an Atlantic solidarity." See Roger E. Vekemans, S.J., "Economic Development, Social Change, and Cultural Mutation in Latin America," chap. 7 in D'Antonio and Pike, eds., *Religion, Revolution, and Reform*. As brought out earlier, Almond and Verba are inclined to rely on some symbolic event, perhaps a revolution, to bring civic integration.

rest of the developed world is concerned, not in Italy, France, or Japan. In the latter countries, a *modus vivendi* has not developed between labor and management. "In the absence of an effective collective bargaining system, the strike has not come into its own as a trial of economic strength. Instead the strike takes the form of a brief, massive gesture of protest and expression of political radicalism." As for the emerging countries, Ross and Hartman do not see the Western experience of evolution through industrial conflict to "basic compromise" as a likely pattern. There are too many ways for government to control or suppress unions in areas lacking strong democratic traditions. Unions, and employers also, may eventually demand a democratic voice, but, so far, "there is little evidence to this effect."[32]

The authors of *Industrialism and Industrial Man* approach the subject of labor-management compromise somewhat differently, although their general conclusion is the same: major unrest in the developing nations is unlikely. They believe that a consensus develops and worker protest declines as industrialization proceeds. There is a "peaking of protest" in the early stages of industrialization, and the peak may not be very high or very difficult to control. Control of labor movements is more common today than in the past, and the central impact of worker protest is "glacial" and toward a greater constitutional sharing of power among the actors (i.e., toward pluralism). Cases of revolutionary transformation are exceptional and, indeed, only two of the five élites they identify, the revolutionary intellectuals and the nationalist leaders, can count on worker protest as a key to power. "These revolutionary transformations with the aid of labor protest can occur in some places (the taking over of power from a dynastic élite or a colonial régime) and also only at some times — those turning points in history when social change is made possible by the decay of an old system — and then only when such decay is made more evident by the effects of depression or of war." Therefore, the authors of *Industrialism and Industrial Man* conclude, "not the handling of labor protest, but the structuring of the labor force is *the* labor problem in economic development."[33] Their belief in the evolutionary development of consensus as a by-product of industrialization itself and their desire to view revolution as a clear exception to the rule of democracy in the

[32]Arthur M. Ross and Paul T. Hartman, *Changing Patterns of Industrial Conflict* (New York: John Wiley and Sons, 1960), pp. 38, 174, 176–177. For added support of the contention that consensus is absent in Italy, France, and Japan, see Millen, *Political Role of Labor in Developing Countries*, pp. 38–40.

[33]Kerr *et al., Industrialism and Industrial Man*, pp. 7, 8, 30, 228–229.

world undoubtedly explain why they give little emphasis to the phenomenon of consensus. It will come eventually in a democracy and only in a few exceptional cases will it be established through violence.

While accepting the analysis of both studies cited above, the point should be made again that Latin America, in this matter just as with studies of the intellectuals, does not support such analysis as well perhaps as Africa and Asia. The culture of Latin America is largely Western, labor movements have a long and violent history in several of the leading countries of the area, and consensus has either not developed very completely in many of them or has followed a successful revolution. In the former category are Argentina, Brazil, and Venezuela, as well as Chile, and in the latter are Mexico and perhaps Cuba.[34] In addition, even if basic conflict be granted the status of an exception, it is still very important indeed in both the industrialized (Italy, France, Japan) and industrializing nations.

To summarize, it would be helpful in assessing the consensual state of a society to know: (1) whether the political party or parties enjoy cross-sectional support among all major interest groups or whether they represent the ideological spectrum, (2) what the degree of income inequality is between the upper and lower classes, and (3) whether the working class has reached an understanding with government and employers or whether there is a labor movement ideologically at odds with the power élite. Actually, however, ideological competition in politics and the labor movement represents an advanced stage of goal disintegration in society and only institutionalizes a loss of consensus already suffered. Such competition is an outward manifestation of conflict, a way of organizing or giving meaning to feelings already in existence

[34]D'Antonio is not convinced that Mexico has yet achieved a stable consensus. He believes that "consensus is still in jeopardy in Mexico because substantial proportions of the society are not finding their aspirations met by the social reality." He asks, "How long will the Mexican people continue to accept the mystique of the revolution? Can the revolution in fact meet the aspirations of this rapidly growing population?" Letter, William V. D'Antonio to James O. Morris, May 23, 1966. Perhaps his doubt is justified. Individual countries are difficult to assess in the absence of deep immersion in their histories, and this writer is not an expert on Mexico. William Ebenstein has previously called attention to the difficulties involved in defining "the balance of democratic versus undemocratic habits and traditions" in many borderline countries. While he is concerned with predicting violence versus peaceful change rather than with determining the presence or absence of consensus, his warning that "every prediction is a question of investigating each particular situation rather than of applying preconceived universal laws of development" is deserving of much respect. William Ebenstein, *Today's ISMS*, 4th ed. (Englewood Cliffs, N. J.: Prentice-Hall, Inc., 1964), p. 13.

and previously expressed in other ways (e.g., industrial warfare, violent demonstrations, spontaneous riots, and simple lack of respect for leaders or for employers as a class).

The crisis for consensus appears to come when an agricultural or traditional society begins to disintegrate and a new consensus based upon the egalitarianism of the industrial society is required. Normative strains may become so generalized and so acute throughout the social structure as to terminate consensus and thrust competing ideologies into the forefront of national life. In the drive toward an industrial society, it is therefore not enough to ask who, among the five industrializing élites, leads the march, what is the purpose of the march, and how the march is organized.[35] A fourth decisive question is this: Why is the march sometimes contested and sometimes not? A meaningful answer to this question can begin with a comparative analysis of the values, attitudes, and structures of traditional and democratic societies.

III

What are the élite values and attitudes in traditional societies? How do the workers respond to them? What is the impact of industrialization upon both élite and worker attitudes in such societies? It is universally recognized that traditional societies are likely to be class-ridden; they may also nurture important racial, ethnic, linguistic, and religious differences. Each of these phenomena may complicate the transitional process and make the peaceful achievement of a new consensus an elusive, if not impossible, goal.

With respect to values, an authoritative and appropriate initial comment is that of Eduardo Frei, Chile's current Christian Democratic President, who compares rural Latin America with the United States and its westward movement of the nineteenth century. His emphasis is on the values of equality and inequality in human relations, although he does not enter upon an analysis of the striking differences he finds in the two societies:

> In the drive of the people of the United States toward the West, we observe a great advancing mass of farmers and immigrants with an ingrained spirit of equality and of adventure, each one seeking a piece of land. Latin America is different. It is a continent with a foreordained distribution, where only a few men are lords of the land, dominating those who serve and work for them. In exchange, the lords give the people protection and security. When the *patrón*

[35]Kerr *et al., Industrialism and Industrial Man,* p. 49.

61

is good there are good chances for a happy life. When the *patrón* is not good, everyone suffers. But it is the happiness or the suffering of a man dependent: He is given a home, food, sometimes money; religious "missions" sometimes visit his area; his health is looked after. He is in a sense one of the family, but subordinated and at a great distance from the *patrón*.[36]

In a brief but insightful article titled "The Behavior of the Chilean Upper Class," Tomás Moulian insinuates a beginning analysis of the peasant's blind confidence in the person of the *patrón* whom, according to Moulian, he always considers "a father." Perhaps, Moulian suggests, the psychological root of the peasant's dependence is his dramatic need to be relieved "of the exercise of freedom." Thus, he not only derives material security from living in the shadow of the *patrón* but his "need for protection and orientation" is also satisfied. The *patrón* rewards peasant loyalty with tenderness, with personal concern expressed in a thousand small ways: becoming godfather to a child, attending family celebrations of great solemnity, caring for the sick.[37] The Moulian contribution, is however, incomplete and one-sided. It says nothing of the *patron's* reciprocal need to have dependents for whom he can care.

A vastly more serious psychological study of traditional society is that of Everett E. Hagen. As part of an even broader personality theory of social change, Hagen develops a most interesting explanation of the authoritarian hierarchy of traditional societies. His system rests upon an anxiety theory of behavior. New situations produce both anxiety and pleasure in people, and generally more of the former than of the latter. In traditional societies both the simple folk and the élite classes feel greater anxiety in new situations than people anywhere else. Their anxiety is fear of the physical world all around them. This he expresses in a number of ways and with different turns of phrase: "a perception of uncontrollable forces around them that restrict and dominate their lives," "great unknown forces," "life seems dominated by forces beyond their control," disease and early death are among the "forces that seem arbitrary and capricious," "a perception of the world as arbitrary, capricious, not amenable to analysis, as consisting of phenomena not related by a cause-and-effect network," "the caprice of the

---

[36]Eduardo Frei Montalva, "Paternalism, Pluralism, and Christian Democratic Reform Movements in Latin America," chap. 1, p. 33, in D'Antonio and Pike, eds., *Religion, Revolution, and Reform.*

[37]Tomás Moulian, "La Conducta de la Clase 'Alta' Chilena," *Panoramas*, año 3, no. 15, May–June 1965, p. 56.

world is not accidental but the play of willful powers far greater" than theirs.

In an emotional environment of such acute anxiety, anxiety does not produce creativity as it does elsewhere. Rather, the great need is to avoid anxiety or relieve it through reliance on precedent in facing problems and reliance on a hierarchical authority system for making decisions. Decision by the proper authority is, by definition, right; there is no need to face problems realistically or with curiosity or to seek new ways of doing things. Satisfaction in yielding to superiors and in dominating inferiors is characteristic of peasant and élite personalities in traditional societies everywhere. Finally, the "lines of dependence extend upward to the spiritual powers to whom the members of the society appeal for protection against the physical forces; in the appeal they gain relief from their anxieties."

Hagen does not employ the term "consensus," but he does observe that the lower classes are not held in grinding misery by force. He sees "great stability" of social structure in traditional societies. Both the lower classes and the élite accept the hierarchical structure of authority and power. Since the élite member does not come to his privileged position through individual achievement, he is forced to believe he is superior to those of humble origin. He cannot share authority with his subordinates because to do so would be an admission of their equality and would raise a question as to the rightness of élite status.[38]

Hagen's theoretical system is important and explains a great deal. Explanation terminates, however, in the identification of a very general anxiety about the world as a dangerous place in which to live. Why, in traditional societies, is the world considered dangerous, capricious, beyond human ken, and controlled by unknown forces? Why, in modern societies, is the world considered a generally safe place in which to live, knowable and subject to increasing domination by the human mind?

As a preliminary and very speculative matter, this writer suggests, as a possibly fruitful area of analysis, the maturation process as it occurs in individuals, families, and ultimately in society as a whole. Further, the hypothesis asserts a direct bearing of death or death-related attitudes on individual, family, and social maturity. The basic norms and values of individuals and societies are reflective of variations in these two closely identified areas. Of course, use of the terms "mature," "ma-

[38]Everett E. Hagen, *On the Theory of Social Change; How Economic Growth Begins* (Homewood, Ill.: The Dorsey Press, Inc., 1962), Part II "Personality and the Stability of Traditional Societies," pp. 55–182.

turity," "immature," and "immaturity" will not please everyone. Yet this terminology is certainly part of the acceptable and even indispensable jargon of psychology and psychoanalysis and is also in common use wherever individuals are evaluated, hired, considered for promotion, or just "typed" among friends. It is not considered farfetched to believe that societies, as well as individuals and families, can be meaningfully characterized and studied from this emotional viewpoint. With apologies to those who may yet be offended and with apologies, too, for the largely intuitive content of his thoughts, the writer offers the following analysis of behavior in traditional and industrializing societies.[39]

Some individuals, and the families of which they are a part, never realize their full growth potential emotionally; they are "underdeveloped," to borrow a term from economics, throughout their lives. If they are numerous and politically powerful, they may determine the character of society as a whole. Key figures in these individual and family situations of underdevelopment are parents. Maturity is learned through a demonstration and training process, and children cannot easily surpass the level of their parents, especially if the latter are their constant and most respected teachers. Key figures in the case of societies as a whole are the élite groups who control them. Immature family leadership can produce rebellious children as they grow older; immature élites can produce an ideologically divided society as economic growth occurs.

In a traditional society, the old class (dynasty in Japan or the aristocratic-Catholic élite in Chile, for example) is strong and either leads the march to industrialization (Japan) or shares leadership in some way with the new middle class (Chile). When the old class is strong, its ideas, beliefs, and values dilute the ideal liberalism of the middle class, and the latter élite behaves socially and culturally much like an aristocracy. The ideal middle-class attitudes of openness, competitiveness, and reliance upon ability to get ahead may exist in very imperfect form, because a class, like an individual, learns much from its elders, and the imperfect or outdated things it learns cannot always be unlearned in a single generation.

A traditional society of the type described is patriarchal and its existence and perpetuation depend upon the social subjection of the masses to the power élite. This subjection is rationalized as the triumph

[39]Much of the material in the following pages has been reproduced, with the permission of the publisher, from James O. Morris, "Consensus, Ideology, and Labor Relations," *Journal of Inter-American Studies*, vol. 7, July 1965, pp. 301–315.

of a superior class over an inferior class, and it is maintained by an emphasis upon the old and respected values, social statics, and the rigidity of statutory law and legal codes. The upper classes are thus afflicted with a kind of refined immaturity. They monopolize politics, education, culture, and wealth, believe they do because they are biologically superior to the "low classes," and are easily able to convince an unlettered peasantry that this is true. Religion can be an aid to the process of persuasion (and of self-deceit) if the upper classes care to emphasize "the providential inequality of man." An ignorant peasantry can be and is treated like a juvenile mass. The bridge between the élite and the peasantry is an autocratic authority system and a compassionate father-son love which requires and expects only obedience of the peasant. Peasants are the children of the *patrón* or master who cares for them and their offspring for as long as he and they live. He feels obligated to do so, and his title of *patrón* or *patrono*, or some other derivative of the word "father," is highly significant in social meaning. If there are both formal and familiar forms of "you" in the language, the upper and middle classes invariably use the familiar when addressing workers, just as they do when addressing children. Each large farm or plantation is an extended family, and society as a whole can be characterized as a "family-state."

Workers (peasants and servants) in a traditional society, as yet unchallenged by industrialization, learn, and are permitted to learn, only the most elementary human response, which is obedience. Obedience can be learned and accepted only where there is love and a close personal relationship, and successful institutions of all kinds which rely primarily upon an interaction of command and obedience are successful because they permit both physical and emotional closeness. The medieval fief, for example, was successful not because the lord was strong but because he was a loving father, and this gave strength and permanence to medieval society as a whole. The same can be said of the family, of the Church, or of the Chilean *fundo*, or large farm, especially one whose owner is not an absentee. When the *fundo* owner addresses his *inquilino*, or semi-serf, with the familiar *"tu,"* he identifies the *inquilino* as his obedient child, and the *inquilino* responds willingly if he is "good" and senses the love which he has been taught is his reward for obedience. (Love in the sense it is being used in this paragraph is the compassionate love between individuals and groups in a status hierarchy and not the full expression of love as status equality which is discussed below, p. 72.)

Indeed, the ideal *inquilino* reveres his master, is totally dependent upon him for the necessities and comforts of life, and looks to him for wise counsel and succor in all the crises he must face. Open defiance, the use of discretionary judgment, or any encouragement of *inquilino* independence would sooner or later crumble the structure of the traditional society. The aristocracy, or part of it, may therefore rationalize that members of the "low class" are incapable of discharging the greater responsibilities required of workers in an egalitarian, industrialized nation. At the same time, however, the aristocracy, or that part of it which is weak, may take the precaution, through its representatives in the government and its church allies, of deliberately discouraging anything that would directly (e.g., unions or formal public education) or indirectly (e.g., industrialization) threaten their position and the status quo. Such a position betrays both their weakness and their rationalization.

To summarize, some of the key values and attitudes of a traditional society are status inequality, fear of the outside world, authoritarianism and paternalism, compassionate love, and obedience. Consensus in such a society is unsophisticated and elementary. Authority patterns, in the sense of a uniform downward flow of communications, are so deeply ingrained that only a minimum or slow development of individuals and institutions takes place. When a major change, such as industrialization, is suddenly introduced into this kind of society neither the authoritarians nor the new industrial working class are prepared to meet, in a fully responsible way, the new and higher demands of a more mature and complex society. At the same time, such a major change also affects the old working class and patterns of authority in agriculture, particularly on those farms whose owners have become absentees. Peasant uprisings and land seizures may occur, and the traditional relationship of love and respect, command and obedience between farm owner or administrator and peasant may be generally shaken.

A closed mind with regard to change and the gradual surrender of special privilege and power may therefore exhibit personal or class immaturity and can prevent the democratic development of a new consensus in society and result in chronic instability or national disaster. The results are not unlike those which would occur if a parent refused to educate his children for adult life and, in this sense, refused to give them up. They might never marry, thus extinguishing the family, or they might turn against themselves or the parent in a moment of truth. Inability to surrender power democratically is contrary to the essence of the Western ideal and, to a lesser extent, of Western achievement.

At a more fundamental (and perhaps even more speculative) level, the static, authoritarian, and superior attitudes held by the élite in a traditional society may be traceable to a primitive form of death fear. Man has not always recognized death as an inevitable experience for every individual; furthermore, the consideration of death as the probable total annihilation of the human personality is a very recent development. Jacques Choron believes the death problem has two aspects: "mastery of the fear of dying [i.e., the act of dying itself] and the neutralization or refutation of the seemingly unavoidable conclusion that our brief sojourn under the sun is a senseless joke, an absurd tragicomedy."[40]

A necessary antecedent of the discovery of death is the emergence of the linear concept of time, what the philosophers and historians call "man's awareness of himself" in time or man's growing self-consciousness in history.[41] Primitive man lived in an "eternal present" and his behavior was governed by "the myth of eternal repetition" (belief that every important event can be traced back to an archetype), or by a concept of cyclical time. He defended himself, to the utmost of his powers, "against all the novelty and irreversibility which history entails." He abolished time, history, his own individuality. In a profound and challenging study of archaic systems, Mircea Eliade concludes that they are chiefly significant for their "abolition of concrete time, and hence their anti-historical intent." Eliade continues:

> This refusal to preserve the memory of the past, even of the immediate past, seems to us to betoken a particular anthropology. We refer to archaic man's refusal to accept himself as a historical being, his refusal to grant value to memory and hence to the unusual events (i.e., events without an archetypal model) that in fact constitute concrete duration....Carried to their extreme, all the rites and all the behavior patterns that we have so far mentioned would be comprised in the following statement: "If we pay no attention to it, time does not exist"....Like the mystic, like the religious man in general, the primitive lives in a continual present.

Far from being aware of himself as a unique and independent being capable of making history, primitive or prehistoric man "sees himself as real only to the extent that he ceases to be himself...and is satisfied

---

[40]Jacques Choron, *Death and Western Thought* (New York: Collier Books, 1963), pp. 22–27.

[41]For example, see Erich Kahler, *The Meaning of History* (New York: George Braziller, 1964), pp. 27–30, and Edward Hallet Carr, *What Is History?* (New York: Alfred A. Knopf, 1962), pp. 178–179.

with imitating and repeating the gestures of others."[42] Such an impersonal and mythical time-consciousness allows death to be known only as an organic phenomenon.

In Eliade's use of the "terror of history" and the "abolition" of time is the strong implication that primitive man must have repressed a fear of movement, a fear of death. In any event, Choron sees an inescapable link between the evolving concept of linear time and the appearance of death as a real and acknowledged personal threat.[43]

Of singular importance to the theme now being developed is Eliade's assertion that even today, and even in sectors of the most advanced nations, humanity is not entirely converted to historicism. The defense against history, says Eliade, "continued to prevail in the world down to a time very close to our own and...still continues to console the agricultural (traditional) societies of Europe, ...to say nothing of the other continents." As a consequence of their obstinate adherence to an antihistorical position, these traditional societies are "exposed to the violent attacks of all revolutionary ideologies." It is, above all, the élites of these societies "that are confronted with the problem, since they alone are forced, and with increasing rigor, to take cognizance of their historical situation."[44]

How élites handle the problem of death may determine the way they see the time-space relationship, the value they place on living and human accomplishment, and the importance and the dignity they confer upon every individual in their midst. It has been said that to credit belief in eternity, and its individualization as immortality, is, in an ultimate sense, a denial of time. Such a belief diminishes the importance of temporal existence and experiences, which are seen less in depth than as a straight path toward the beginning of eternity. Life acquires only a slight spatial quality; one loves it little and is not disposed to make it much better for either his contemporaries or his progeny. Contrarily, if death is seen and accepted as the end rather than as the doorway to another beginning, then life takes on a profound and complicated significance. The "attention to time is translated into an absorption in space, and every detail of change is noted and treasured....Death turns us toward life and forces us to admire or cherish it (even though we despair of it as well)."[45] This circumstance, in turn,

[42]Mircea Eliade, *The Myth of the Eternal Return* (New York: Pantheon Books, Inc., 1949), pp. 34–37, 85–86.

[43]Choron, *Death and Western Thought*, p. 25.

[44]Eliade, *Myth of the Eternal Return*, pp. 141–154.

[45]Frederick J. Hoffman, "Mortality and Modern Literature," chap. 9, pp. 136–137, in Herman Feifel, ed., *The Meaning of Death* (New York: McGraw-Hill, 1959).

"has, in large measure, been responsible for many of the advances of our science, medicine, and technology."[46] Perhaps it also turns people outward toward one another and enlarges the range of interpersonal respect, affection, and empathy, for death can no longer be looked upon as the "great equalizer." Contrarily, an élite failure to relinquish primitive death attitudes may be at the heart of the consensual problem which occurs as industrialization begins and new groups seeking respect and equality emerge.

In a unique study of attitudes toward death in more than two hundred normal and mentally ill persons, Herman Feifel places the "psychologic maturity" of the individual highest among five factors which apparently determine one's reaction to death. Human maturity "brings along with it a recognition of limit, which is a notable advance in self-knowledge. In a certain sense, the willingness to die appears as a necessary condition of life." In the absence of a willingness to give onself up, every risk, every new commitment, every step beyond the secure present (e.g., leaving the home, breaking office routine, "losing one's guard in sleep") may seem foolhardy. Feifel, who in addition to his own study brought together seventeen essays by other writers on the meaning of death, concludes that a dominant *leitmotiv* of the entire book is that "life is not genuinely our own until we can renounce it," until we learn to grapple honestly with the idea of death. This conclusion, he is certain, "has implications not only for the individual but for society as well."[47]

A few scholars have studied death attitudes in children, and it is apparent that from an initial view of life as an "eternal present,"

---

[46]Herman Feifel, "Attitudes toward Death in Some Normal and Mentally Ill Populations," chap. 8, pp. 124–125, in Feifel, ed., *Meaning of Death*.

[47]*Ibid.*, pp. xvii-xviii, 115, 116, 124–125. Many persons have reflected on the relative importance of the fear of death among anxieties in general and, while this subject need not detain us here, a brief summary of some of these views, as Feifel interprets them, can be presented: "Some investigators hold that fear of death is a universal reaction and that no one is free from it. Freud, for instance, postulates the presence of an unconscious death wish in people which he connects with certain tendencies to self-destruction. We have only to think of sports like bobsledding and bullfighting, the behavior of the confirmed alcoholic or addict, the tubercular patient leaving the hospital against medical advice, etc. Melanie Klein believes fear of death to be at the root of all persecutory ideas and so indirectly of all anxiety. Paul Tillich, the theologian, whose influence has made itself felt in American psychiatry, bases his theory of anxiety on the ontological statement that man is finite, or subject to non-being. Others feel that time has meaning for us only because we realize we have to die. Stekel went so far as to express the hypothesis that every fear we have is ultimately a fear of death." *Ibid.*, pp. 114–115. See also Jacques Choron, *Modern Man and Mortality* (New York: The Macmillan Company, 1964), pp. 130–131.

children, by their ninth or tenth year, are aware of the inevitability of death.[48] The childhood of the individual is thus quite similar to the childhood of man as a genus.[49] There is little doubt that family environment and parental attitudes have much to do with the view of death a child forms, and with his adjustment to it as well.

A possible association between death fear and the extreme anxiety (fear of "great unknown forces") which Hagen observes in traditional societies now suggests itself. The association was made explicit by Wilhelm Stekel many years ago when he described fear as "the expectation of the Unknown." Humanity, he continued, fears only the new, "and *death* is for us the absolutely new and unknown."[50] Perhaps the meaning of death in traditional societies is related to their slow movement, their undifferentiated and sparse social organization (i.e., lack of spatial quality to time), their resistance to change, and their comfortable reliance on the impersonal hierarchy and an orientation to the past for the resolution of anxiety-producing current events.

With specific regard to time consciousness in traditional Latin America, Roger Vekemans has this highly significant commentary:

> ...he [the Latin American] is oriented essentially toward transcendency, or, in the case of time, toward eternity. It is difficult for him to conceive time as a specific element of the historic process; it is lacking in value, and especially in money value, in the Anglo-Saxon concept. Therefore, it is something that can be wasted without producing deleterious effects on Latin American life. Essentially, the Latin American transcendentalizes the profane world, and, by making it eternal, he deprives it of temporality.[51]

The clock is one of the most perfect death symbols because it marks every minute and hour of the inexorable flow of time; perhaps the *mañana* attitude so commonly associated with Latin America has far deeper meaning than that usually ascribed to it (i.e., Latin Americans are "easygoing" by nature, they lack a long history of industrialization and the discipline it imposes, etc.).

Paraphrasing Patrick Romanell (*Making of the Mexican Mind*), Pike depicts Anglo-Saxon culture as pervaded by the epic sense of life while the Iberian world is essentially tragic. The difference is useful in interpreting broad social and political characteristics as well as per-

[48]For example, see Maria H. Nagy, "The Child's View of Death," chap. 6 in Feifel, ed., *Meaning of Death*.

[49]See Kahler, *Meaning of History*, pp. 27–28.

[50]Quoted in Choron, *Modern Man and Mortality*, p. 130.

[51]Vekemans, "Economic Development, Social Change, and Cultural Mutation in Latin America," p. 139.

70

sonality variations. At the level of intercultural generalization, Pike
sees

> ...life in the epic-conscious United States...[as] worth-while because
> of the opportunities it presents man *and* his institutions to conquer
> the environment and master physical nature....
>
> Like the human hero, revered political institutions, in the epic out-
> look, are expected to assume heroic proportions, propelling the
> country they govern ever upwards towards a life which is physically
> more comfortable for the vast majority. The thought of failure and
> collapse of institutions is avoided as assiduously as the thought of the
> failure and death of individuals: "Life is real, and life is earnest, and
> the grave is not its goal."
>
> Latin Americans would ask, concerning the author of these lines,
> as Ernest Hemingway has asked in *Death in the Afternoon:* "And
> where did they bury him; and what became of the reality and the
> earnestness?" The Hemingway approach would strike a favorable
> response among Latin Americans because they have tended to possess
> the tragic sense of life. They cannot believe that a man, a political
> régime or an institution can overcome all outer obstacles for an in-
> definite period. They think more of the inevitable failure and death
> of all things human. The highest goal of a person or a government
> is to overcome inner weakness, and thus be ready to die in honor.
> Men, governments and institutions pass away to make way for new
> endeavors. It would not be natural for them to impede this natural
> course of events.[52]

Pike realizes that these generalizations are not universally valid in
Latin America; one must distinguish between Portuguese America and
Spanish America, between the nineteenth century and today, and between the cities and the countryside. Yet enough of the tragic sense
remains to evoke the cross-cultural comparison.

Élite values in the traditional societies of Latin America may therefore have a common denominator in death attitudes. Belief in élite
superiority, authoritarianism, paternalism,. an orientation toward the
past, and a desire to maintain the status quo may be evidence of an
unwillingness to accept realistically the fact of linear movement (i.e.,
death) in all natural cycles, including, and quite especially, that of
human life itself. By doing nothing new and surrounding oneself with
life-long dependents, one can cling tragically to youth and to life. To
educate one's peasants (at least in a non-religious school) or to share
authority with them would be like giving up your children, your
privileged position over them, and, in the last analysis, your own
security and the larger security of the static social structure itself.

[52]Pike, *Freedom and Reform in Latin America*, pp. 39–41.

Different values (e.g., belief in human equality, a life orientation, acceptance of change, belief in individual achievement and social progress, a willingness to share, to give up, deliberately to risk loss) may be necessary to avoid ideological division as the forces of modernization are generated. If the élite clings tenaciously to the old value system in the industrializing process, consensus loss may result.

How, in somewhat more specific terms, can consensus loss occur? How can one interpret worker resort to anarchism and Marxism-Leninism within the normative and consensual framework of this chapter? All or part of the old élite who perpetuate old values and structural relations and those members of the new middle class who identify with them in the industrialization process give up as little authority as they can to the new industrial workers. They persist in efforts to "take care" of them in the factory, shop, and mine through a maze of paternalistic programs. If they are strongly influenced by organized religion, they may believe that their obligation "to care" is moral. They try to keep the workers apolitical by buying their votes (if they are forced to concede adult male suffrage) and by making little effort to affiliate them to the established political parties; they may favor legal unions under the employer's control or that of the state; and they may propose the "solution" of industrial conflict through the compulsory conciliation or arbitration of disputes. They recognize industrial society as a challenge to their accustomed one-way communication pattern, to their authoritarian role in a static society where the master forever enjoys the comfort and security of being surrounded with his "children." They do not understand, or wish to understand, that the compassionate love of farm owner for peasant cannot be transferred, with much hope of long or permanent survival, to the impersonal, independent, and non-family atmosphere of the factory. Nor do they understand, or wish to understand, that there is a greater love than that of compassion, based upon mutual respect among all adults, which must be encouraged in any maturing family. Such love is painful to both parent and child because it requires a breaking away, a sacrifice of the security that most of us derive from having dependents or being dependent. Yet it is also a superior challenge for it is that little area of the heart from whence springs so much of human dignity, human greatness, and our upward march.

Employers imbued with the attitudes and values of a traditional society try to re-establish the harmony they see in nature and in the rural "family" community. They tend to resent worker efforts to engage them in discussion about wages and other working conditions and, most of all, they resent strikes as the ultimate indication of the workers' lack of appreciation for all the things they have done for them. If bargaining is engaged in at all, it is likely to be handled through a third party (perhaps a judge or public functionary), and the system may operate through "conciliation boards" or "labor courts." An employer, a member of the "superior class," finds it difficult to deal directly with those whose obedience he has heretofore unreservedly commanded. Conciliation under government auspices may be compulsory because the élite tends to view compulsion as the only way to get agreement out of workers whose power to reason is believed limited. This view may persist despite years of ineffective operation of the system and the collection of statistics which show large numbers of illegal strikes, perhaps more illegal than legal ones. Actually, a firm resolve to bring greater understanding to industrial relations and a mutual acceptance of the parties, i.e., consensus, is the only "solution" to industrial conflict and even this does not necessarily and should not necessarily eliminate disagreement and strikes.

How do workers, free but emotionally unprepared for freedom, react to continuing treatment as unequals? The early industrial and mining labor force in traditional societies is drawn from the rural areas. These unlettered workers find both unaccustomed freedom and responsibility in factory life, in the anonymity of the city, and even, though to a lesser degree, in paternalistic mining camps if such are present. They are freer in the sense that they live on wages which they can spend as they please, owe the *patrón* nothing other than their own labor, and, in the cities if not in the mining camps, live away from the employer's premises. At the same time, however, they are subject to a tighter work discipline than ever before and to a new autocratic authority system which, by the impersonal nature of industrial life itself, is not and cannot be tempered with the same affection which makes obedience almost second nature to the peasant. They are, in reality, like children turned out at a tender age, emotionally immature, ignorant of the ways of the world, and with no one to turn to other than hundreds more just like themselves.

Childish rebellion is the first, the easiest, and most natural way for such workers to express their independence, their sudden resentment, and their new egos. Anarchism symbolizes the most complete and most irresponsible of all worker rebellions for it denies all authority, all discipline, and all duties and respects no leaders, not even its own. It is destructive, sulking, akin to fantasy, and can be understood by the simplest and most underdeveloped minds. It is not unnatural or accidental that the first unions in many countries have been anarchistic.

Marxist-Leninist rebellions are of a somewhat higher order than anarchist ones. They require of their leaders and their followers a degree of sophistication as well as a deep sense of injustice, resentment, and hopelessness vis-à-vis existing society in order to achieve success. Sophisticated leaders cannot teach unlettered followers the "ideological truth" of Marxism-Leninism, for the minds of the latter simply cannot grasp the full meaning of the "historical class struggle," "dialectical materialism," "exploitation," the labor theory of value, social structure, etc. It is even more obvious that unsophisticated leaders cannot make an intellectual and, in this sense, "ideological" appeal to the unlettered. In either of these two situations (sophisticated leaders and unlettered workers or unsophisticated leaders and unlettered workers) the only appeal that is effective is an emotional one. Its effectiveness depends on the degree to which real injustice, worker resentment, and hopelessness are present in the existing society. One might summarize these two propositions thus: in areas where literacy rates are low or justification for worker resentment is high, the most effective Marxist-Leninist appeal to the masses is an emotional rather than an intellectual one. It is precisely that which makes rebellions in these areas so dangerous, so violent, and sometimes so successful. It is easy for the childish mind of an unlettered worker, who for the first time feels neglected, unwanted, and perhaps exploited, to hate, to shout, and to support violence. For this kind of worker, Marxism-Leninism is a kind of juvenile delinquency. The old society may in some cases deserve it, because it may have tried to monopolize adulthood and the exercise of responsibility and authority which goes with it.

Even the most mature Marxism-Leninism is, at best, ideological adolescence. There are essentially two reasons for this. The first, and by far the most important, is that this ideology is deterministic and thus denies the possibility of man's rational intervention and ability to exert creative influence over the nature and direction of change.[53] In

---

[53]Ebenstein has called attention to the experience of autocratic government in Germany as the probable source of the determinism of Hegel and Marx. "In an environment of mental and political enslavement," he continues, "man is prone to think of himself as being small and helpless, and his emotional pattern will find philosophical expression in determinism. Such a philosophy assures him that his own helplessness is not a personal misfortune, but a principle of world order." Ebenstein, *Today's ISMS*, p. 24.

its application, Marxism-Leninism has been characterized by an autocratic and patriarchal arrangement of institutions within society and of government itself. This has occurred despite the fact that the theory of Marxism-Leninism is at least neutral on the matter of centralization versus decentralization and may even look toward an eventual decentralization of institutions. In practice, however, the people who are attracted to it believe in centralization for emotional reasons, are not yet self-reliant, and cannot govern themselves. In other words, there are many more children among them, emotionally speaking, than there are adults. As William Ebenstein has noted, "the totalitarian system, whether communist or fascist, appeals to people who, for whatever personal reasons, look for the father-child relationship, for security in dependence."[54]

The second reason for the ideological adolescence of Marxism-Leninism is that its dialectic is not in essence scientific, in the sense that it appeals to the mind, but rather it is passionate and appeals to the emotions. The historical class struggle which Marx's dialectic supposedly revealed came from a schizophrenic mind capable of understanding and exploiting only the two extremes of tyranny and rebellion.[55] Both are immature and both are irrational and unscientific. The capacity to understand and to pursue evolution through democracy, which requires a continuous voluntary sharing of authority with others, is a higher capacity than that needed to grasp hate and to establish political paternalism. It is surely no cause for wonder that revolutionary socialism has established itself only in backward and agricultural societies (Russia, China, Cuba, for example) and not in industrialized ones. Marx predicted the contrary, and it was the erroneous and emotional concept of the class struggle and the inevitable proletarian revolution which misled him. Some form of centralized and perhaps even autocratic government may be necessary for a time in new nations emerging from primitive and tribal organizational patterns and in those industrializing societies which try foolishly to cling

[54]*Ibid.*, pp. 106–107.

[55]This conclusion is also partly implied in the following remarks of Lipset: "To Marx a complex society could be characterized either by constant conflict (even if suppressed) *or* by consensus, but not by a combination of the two. He saw conflict and consensus as alternatives rather than as divergent tendencies that could be balanced. On the one hand, he projected consensus, harmony, and integration into the communist future (and to some degree into the communist past); on the other hand, he saw conflict and absolutism as the great fact of history in the epoch between ancient primitive communism and the coming success of the proletarian revolution." Lipset, *Political Man*, p. 24.

to old class relationships. In the latter case, at least, such a development is not inevitable and results more from *social* exploitation than *economic* exploitation. Socialism, communism, and capitalism are all pretty meaningless labels. The crux of the matter is best put by a question: What societies are mature enough to govern themselves democratically through time and which are the immature ones that require compulsion and patriarchal arrangements?

From this it follows that poor or "capitalist" societies are not necessarily the ones that spawn radical solutions but, rather, the immature are the ones that do so. And the burden of immaturity rests primarily upon the élite. Rebellion may be carefully nurtured and at times financed by international communism, but the latter does not produce the conditions for rebellion. While elimination or neutralization of such support might make some difference, it cannot change élite attitudes or make workers loyal to the present social order. Whether they become willing partners in society, or overthrow it, or remain alienated and sullen bystanders depends squarely upon the power élite.

The power élite must, in a short span of time, be willing to change centuries-old attitudes and values. Ultimately, such changes reduce to a voluntary sharing of power with others. A failure of élite leadership in this respect can cause consensus loss, bring violence and competing ideologies, and, perhaps, terminate in revolution.

PART II

CHAPTER 4

The Social Question

IF THE "social question" had not appeared in Chile in the 1880's, and greatly deepened in the three following decades, there would have been no need for a social and legislative reform movement of the kind that got under way in these years. Likewise, there would have been no need for the ambitious industrial relations system established by the government in 1924. Moreover, it is unlikely there would have appeared any really significant ideological opposition to the power élite — an anarchist and Marxist labor opposition which refused to accept the legal industrial relations system as an ultimate answer to the "social question." This opposition was so extreme and strong that it pointed to a loss of consensus in Chile.

The "social question," therefore, has very broad meaning and refers to all the social, labor, and ideological consequences of emerging industrialization and urbanization: a new labor force dependent upon the wage system; the appearance of worker housing, health, and sanitation problems of growing acuteness; the formation of organizations to defend the interests of the new "working class"; strikes and street demonstrations; perhaps armed clashes between workers and police or the military; and some popularity of radical ideas and radical leadership among the workers.

In addition to being a broad term, the "social question" also has a definite historical or time connotation. It refers to an *early* period of social tension, worker protest, and intellectual ferment which commences with industrialization itself. In Chile this early period lasted about four decades — from the mid-1880's to the mid-1920's. During these forty years intellectuals, politicians, and articulate employers debated, lectured, and wrote on the "social question," or somewhat more narrowly, on the "worker question" or "worker problem." The index to parliamentary debates included the "social question" as an entry, and newspaper editorials, magazine articles, books and pamphlets often carried the term in their titles.

This social or worker question abounds in the literature of many other Latin-American countries where it describes the same early concern for the social and labor consequences of economic development. To give only a few titles: in Argentina, Ernesto Quesada wrote *La Iglesia Católica y la cuestión social* (1895) and *La cuestión obrera y su estudio universitario* (1907); in Brazil, Gustavo de Lacerda wrote *O problema operario no Brasil* (1901); Luís Miró Quesada contributed *La cuestión obrera en Perú* (1904); Carlos Loveira studied "El Problema Obrero en Cuba" (1919); and, in Colombia, a special Committee on Social Subjects and Worker Questions developed *Proyectos de leyes sobre asuntos sociales y cuestiones obreras* (1936).

It would appear that the "social question" was not, however, a literary invention of Latin America but rather a concept which originated among the intellectuals and reformers of Europe. It stands to reason, in any case, that since Europe experienced urbanization and factory development earlier than Latin America, her literature should reflect an earlier concern for the social consequences of such change. Thus, in 1872 Paul Leroy-Beaulieu published his *La question ouvrière au XIX siècle*. This and other works of Leroy-Beaulieu, a progressive economist of the liberal school, were well known in Chile and perhaps in other Latin American countries. Two other French writers produced *Question sociale. Le sublime ou le travailleur comme il est en 1870 et ce qu'il peut être* and *Le code civil et la question ouvrière* (1886). An especially intriguing study published in Madrid by a Spanish writer is titled *Estudios sobre la Isla de Cuba. La cuestión social* (1866). Even though written about Cuba (which certainly had no urban or industrial sector to speak of in 1866!), the book probably reflects a terminology then in vogue in Spain and other European countries. Other studies from Madrid include two books by Gumersindo Azcárate: *Los deberes de la riqueza. Estudios económicos y sociales* and *Resumen de un de-*

bate sobre el problema social, published in 1876 and 1881; and Adolfo Posada's *Socialismo y reforma social* (1904). In Germany, Heinrich Herkner contributed *Die soziale Reform als Gebot des wirtschaftlichen Fortschrittes* (1891) and *Die Arbeiterfrage. Eine Einführung* (1894), and Ludwig Stein wrote *Das Ideal des ewigen Friedens und die soziale Frage* (1896). Between 1891 and 1904 Henry de B. Gibbins edited sixteen volumes under the general title, *Social Questions of Today,* dealing with such topics as the shorter work day, the unemployed, housing, and women's work in Great Britain.

Gradually, as the labor force becomes structured along more definite and predictable lines, as measures and procedures are introduced to handle conflict situations, and as individual social problems are isolated and some public or private effort to ameliorate them begins, the all-inclusive term "social question" falls out of regular, persistent use and perhaps also changes in meaning. The literature becomes more specific, reflecting a definition of issues and a growing complexity of organizational and communications patterns, and begins to deal with separate aspects of the former social question such as unemployment, hours, wages, union structural types, social security, and working-class politics. The social question had hardly become a talking point in Chile before the process of differentiation set in, but it remained an important focus of debate and writing until the 1920's and the enactment of Chile's first serious social and industrial relations laws.

In fact, as already implied, books on the social question (or the social or worker problem) continued to be written after the 1920's but, one must add, not with the same regularity nor in the same sense of national urgency. One must also concede that for the disaffected anarchist and Marxist opposition the social question continues in Chile even today. Since this opposition remains so significant as to constitute consensus loss, the social question can be said still to affect the well-being of the country as a whole. However, it is no longer known as the "social question" (a bourgeois term?) but, in the Marxian preference, as the "class struggle." By the same token, it has shed the purely Chilean character of its earlier period, and is generally viewed on the world stage as part of the East-West ideological struggle.

In the pre-1924 period, the social question was given credence by members of the aristocratic-Catholic and middle-class élites, some of whom recognized it as a warning of major malfunction in society. Their answer was the 1924 legislation, and, while this legislation was not to remain forever definitive or complete as their response to the labor problems of an industrializing society, it was comprehensive enough to draw the curtain on the social question as most of them saw it. The continuing post-1924 social question is for the most part an ideological one, given credence by new leftist political parties and trade unions who do not accept reform legislation as an ultimate solution at all but who advocate a revolutionary alteration of Chilean society in the name of the new "popular" classes.

Why this disaster occurred in Chile is a major concern of this study. The social question did not have to terminate in consensus loss. Industrialization does not lead inevitably to ideologically divided societies. It is not primarily, and certainly not exclusively, an economic equation.

This chapter is a statement of the social question. It is historical and briefly surveys, in turn, working conditions, early worker organizations, industrial relations (especially strikes), politics, and the labor movement. Only passing reference is made to worker housing, health, sanitation, and similar matters which are part of the social question, to be sure, but are not of the same priority as more "difficult" issues like unions, strikes, and working-class politics. Since the social question arose as a by-product of economic change and the formation of an industrial labor force, these two subjects are sketched first as background. The reader is warned, however, that in this sketch there is no pretense at providing a finished or thorough economic history of the four decades (1880's to 1920's) covered most intensively in the chapter.

I

Throughout the entire length of its history up to almost the middle of the present century, Chile was an overwhelmingly agricultural and mining country. Factory development, stimulated by special governmental incentives and the influx of foreign capital, began on a very small scale in the years after Chile won her independence from Spain. The pace of industrialization quickened toward the end of the nineteenth century, as exemplified by the establishment of the private Society for Factory Development (1883) and the creation of a Ministry of Industry and Public Works. Chile did not, however, begin to build an industrial sector of major importance until the world-wide depression of the 1930's taught her the consequences of extreme dependence on the importation of manufactured goods. Serious planning for economic development on a national scale then got under way with the creation and financing of the government Development Corporation (1939). As already explained, however, this chapter is not concerned with the 1930's and after but, rather, with the forty years which preceded the social and labor legislation of the 1920's.

Even as regards mining, Chile had little activity until the termination of the significant little War of the Pacific (1879–1881) which added to her territory the large and mineral-rich northern provinces of Tarapacá and Antofagasta. With the help of British, and later American, capital, nitrate mining quickly rose to bonanza proportions, and many believed that the tremendous deposits of natural nitrate in the desert *pampa* of the "Great North" were an inexhaustible source of monopoly wealth which would keep Chile forever among the most privileged of nations. The British historian, Francis J. G. Maitland, remarked just before the outbreak of World War I that "the fear that Chile will lose her world's monopoly of nitrate, through that commodity being manufactured artificially, is so remote that it may be banished."[1] In the short period of a half dozen years, the fear at which he scoffed had become, for Chile, a dreadful reality. The axis powers, cut off from their source of nitrates which were critical to the making of explosives, perfected a process for their artificial manufacture. After the war, the world market for natural nitrates sagged and, were it not for the sheer good fortune of having had equally abundant copper deposits to exploit, Chile might well have suffered a sharp and prolonged depression with untold social consequences. As it was, copper soon replaced nitrate as the primary source of foreign exchange and government revenues.

The economic, political, and social backbone of the nation, in terms of its contribution to national income and its influence over government and social values, was agriculture. From the beginning, agriculture in Chile was based upon the exploitation of latifundia through a semimedieval *inquilino* system. The rich and deep alluvial deposits in the central valley make that area among the most fertile in the entire world, and conquest of the land and some, but not all, of its Indian inhabitants by white men led quite naturally to the *inquilino* system. On the expansive grape, grain, and cattle *fundos*, the *hacendado* or owner became a virtual lord who provided his *inquilinos* with a hut and a little land, cared for them when they were ill or too old to work, and was godfather to all their children. The *inquilino*, in turn, obeyed and revered his master, lived and died on his land, and passed his children on to him, or his heir, or a neighboring *hacendado*. Legally

[1]Francis J. G. Maitland, *Chile: Its Land and People* (London: Francis Griffiths, 1914), p. 109.

he was free, but in practice he was tied to the land. The *hacendado,* on the other hand, was literally the lord and master of all he surveyed. He controlled the government, and he molded society in his own image.

The total population of Chile grew from 2,500,000 in 1875 to 4,300,-000 in 1930, and, although there was a marked trend toward urbanization during this period, the population was still rural at the latter date. In 1875 the population was 73 percent rural (i.e., lived in communities of less than 1,000 inhabitants), and then dropped noticeably to 62 percent in 1890, 57 percent in 1907, and 51 percent in 1930. The predominant rural mix of the population coincides with the predominant influence of agriculture and the landed aristocracy just noted, but, at the same time, the relative growth of the urban sector points to important developments in mining, commerce, and industry and to the appearance of a significant middle-class élite and an industrial labor force. These developments, in turn, challenged the freewheeling leadership of the aristocratic-Catholic élite and at the same time gave rise to the social question.

In addition to the lucrative nitrate production already mentioned, which was of commanding importance in the economy as a whole, the flurry of new economic activity in the late nineteenth and early twentieth centuries embraced coal mining, railroad building and operation, new commercial and banking ventures, port and shipping businesses, and a surge of small shop and factory undertakings. Much of this new economic complex was derived from, dependent upon, or ancillary to nitrate production, but some of it was also part of a more general development pattern. In the former category were shops and factories that began to turn out heavy mining and railroad equipment, such as locomotives, cars, engines, rails, bridge structures, and nitrate crushing machines. In the latter were a variety of enterprises dependent upon agriculture, such as grain and textile mills, shoe and leather goods and printing establishments, food-processing plants, and bottle and glass factories. In the short period from 1908 to 1918, the number of factories and shops increased by almost 60 percent, and at the latter date there were an estimated 8,229 such undertakings in the country.[2] Agriculture was still the dominant economic activity, and, insofar as non-agricultural pursuits are concerned, the typical production unit was the small shop. The largest capital concentrations were undoubtedly in mining, railroads, and port facilities.

[2]Pedro Luis González, *Chile industrial* (Santiago: Imprenta Universo, 1921), pp. 4–5, 43.

Labor-force data for our period are practically nonexistent and, to the extent they are available, provide only rough estimates. They show a twenty-fold increase in nitrate employment from 2,840 in 1880 to 56,961 in 1918. At the latter date there were also an estimated 33,123 railroad workers and some 80,000 employees in manufacturing.[3] The total for these three groups in 1918 was about 170,000, and the principal groups not included in this figure are the dock workers, coal and copper miners, commercial and bank employees, the government bureaucracy, and, of course, agricultural workers. The total active population (roughly equivalent to the "total labor force" in U.S. terminology) in 1920 is estimated at 1,355,000 persons, or about 36.2 percent of the total population.[4] Although these population, business, and labor-force data are not wholly reliable, they do show the growing importance of manufacturing and nitrate employment and the trend toward urbanization in the total population.

The largest single source of supply for the new urban labor force was the *fundo*. The *inquilinos* were easily accessible to the major urban centers of Santiago, Valparaíso, and Concepción and their low skills were in demand in the mines and factories and on the docks. The nitrate companies of the far north resorted to a special recruiting system in order to tap the central valley labor supply, and this system, called the *enganche* (literally, "the hook"), led to considerable abuse. The recruiting agents or "hookers" were actually free of company control, although the companies did encourage and support their activities, and they received a fee for each recruit delivered and hired. Since they were possessed of the normal desire to increase their income and since their responsibility ended with delivery, they sometimes misled or lied to *inquilinos* about conditions in the *pampa* in order to recruit them. Through ignorance and poor communication with nitrate management, they also sometimes delivered their recruits when the world nitrate market was off, production was down, and no jobs were available. In either case, what would normally have been a very difficult matter of adjustment for the *inquilino,* was made even more difficult for him.

[3]See *ibid.*, pp. 4–5, 43 and Hernán Ramírez Necochea, *Historia del movimiento obrero en Chile, siglo XIX* (Santiago: Talleres Gráficos Lautaro, 1956), pp. 73–74, 190.
[4]See Marto A. Ballesteros and Tom E. Davis, "The Growth of Output and Employment in Basic Sectors of the Chilean Economy, 1908–1957," *Economic Development and Cultural Change*, vol. 11, January 1963, Table 13, p. 176 and Carlos Keller R., *La eterna crisis chilena* (Santiago, 1931), p. 293. The total population figure came from the latter source; the percentage of active to total population from the former.

However, the *inquilino* supply was not alone adequate to fill all the labor requirements of the new employing groups, especially their need for skilled workers, and the *hacendados,* in turn, became alarmed over what they called the "depopulation" of the countryside. This led both groups, through the Society for Factory Development and the National Agricultural Society, to search for ways of dealing with the problem, and they proposed both indirect and direct solutions. The indirect were: regulation of the sale of alcoholic beverages and reduction of the extremely high death rate. Believing that drunkenness disabled thousands of workers every week and explained the strong pattern of absenteeism on Mondays, they sought to make more effective use of the present labor supply by, in effect, preventing workers from drinking. Chile's birth rate was high (38 per 1,000 population in 1913) but her death rate was believed to be among the highest in the world (31 per 1,000) and infant mortality was terrifying (304 per 1,000). Since there was more emigration than immigration, there was a net loss of population from these movements which, coupled with the high death rate, reduced population growth to only 1 to 1.5 percent yearly. Health and sanitation programs would, it was thought, save an estimated 50,000 to 60,000 lives per year through reduction of the death rate.[5]

But neither of these indirect measures would necessarily meet the need for skilled craftsmen, and population growth through improvement of the death rate was, in addition, a long-range matter. Direct and immediate redress was, therefore, sought through a government-financed program of "selected immigration." Between 1895 and 1912 more than 30,000 workers, most of them skilled, were brought into the country from northern Italy and Spain. Some of them did not stay long, crossing the border into Argentina where they found a more congenial all-white labor force and better jobs, but enough of them remained to have an effect upon the leadership and anarchist ideology of the emerging labor movement.[6]

[5]"Acta de la Sesíon del Consejo Directivo del 16 de Noviembre de 1906," *Boletín de la Sociedad de Fomento Fabril,* vol. 23, Dec. 1, 1906, p. 781; "La Sociedad durante 30 Años," *ibid.,* vol. 30, Oct. 1, 1913, p. 919; *ibid.,* vol. 30, Nov. 1, 1913, pp. 1007–1010; *Boletín de la Sociedad Nacional de Agricultura,* vol. 43, June 15, 1912, pp. 332–335; vol. 44, Aug. 15, 1913, pp. 477–480; vol. 44, Sept. 15, 1913, pp. 593–594; vol. 45, May 15, 1914, pp. 271–273; vol. 45, Aug. 15, 1914, pp. 454–457.

[6]For immigration data by years from 1895 through 1912, see Teodorindo Parada Zapata, *Algunas consideraciones sobre inmigración* (Santiago: Imprenta El Globo, 1913), pp. 10–11.

II

Working and living conditions in Chile during the forty years under study were, compared with the experience of other industrializing countries, not so inferior, but, by the same test, neither were they salutary or benign. Total daily hours of labor often reached twelve or fourteen and, in sweated trades like textiles, sometimes went to sixteen. Children over eleven were legally eligible to work and many did, although statistics are lacking. A member of the right-wing Conservative party declared in 1921 that he had visited many countries, had studied their workers, and had concluded that the Chilean worker was running far behind in general economic condition. The Argentine worker in particular was much better off than his Chilean counterpart. He had a better home, ate better, and dressed better. The reason for the difference was principally the low wages paid in Chile. In addition, however, he thought there was excessive speculation in the marketing of foodstuffs in Chile and an inequitable railroad rate structure, both of which tended unjustifiably to raise consumer food prices.[7] Because of the labor shortage, wages tended to rise up to the end of World War I, and wages in the nitrate fields were, during the boom, considerably higher than anywhere else in the country.

In the nitrate and coal-mining communities, employers paid the wage bill in tokens or truck rather than money. Either way, the system was inherently subject to abuse. The employer could put his own value on truck and he could put his own prices on the staples he sold in the company store. The president of the Society for Factory Development candidly explained that the mining employer did not sell merchandise as a service to his workers but considered the company store a profit-making venture. "He pays the worker his wage with one hand and then takes it back with the other, largely through the company store or the truck system."[8] That company store prices were excessively high is demonstrated by the fact that merchants in communities removed from the workplace generally accepted tokens only at a discount. Also wages were frequently paid in taverns and stores, where the worker was in debt for credit purchases, and deductions were made as part of the wage settlement. Pay days were not always close or regular, the worker sometimes having to go two or three months without income.

[7]Partido Conservador, *Convención del partido conservador de 1921, actas* (Santiago, 1921), pp. 122–123.
[8]Pedro Luis González, *El contrato del trabajo* (Santiago: Imprenta Universo, 1912), pp. 39–40.

Working conditions in the nitrate mines of the north drew the attention of everyone — intellectuals as well as the rising young leadership of the labor movement. The nitrate operation was dramatic for a number of reasons, each of which helps explain its drawing power. The nitrate companies were the biggest and most important in the country; their capital investments were heavy, their work force large, and their earnings and taxes incredibly high. They were, in addition, foreign-owned, and this made them a natural target of the right, the left, and all that was in between. They were investigated by select parliamentary committees who trekked to the far north on three separate occasions in the space of fifteen years. For sheer drama, perhaps nothing could match the natural geographic setting and unusual climatic conditions of the northern *pampa*. A dry, flat, endless, and uninhabited desert expanse hundreds of miles and several exhausting travel days away from the lush central valley, it was by comparison a little Chilean hell which devoured huge daily quantities of human labor and gave up little for the soul in return. Assessments of company-provided working and living conditions vary, but these conditions do not seem to have differed greatly from those which prevailed elsewhere in the country. Gambling, drinking, prostitution, and political radicalism all flourished, but this was due as much or more to the psychological consequences of isolation, distance, and the barrenness of the land as to the companies' wage and other economic and social policies.

The country at large experienced a steady and substantial inflation during the period under study which is said to have greatly reduced the real income of the working class. Real-wage series are totally absent, but those who have commented upon the inflation nevertheless agree that real wages declined. On the other hand, who, if anyone, was responsible for the inflation and what their motives may have been have recently become disputed subjects.

According to data developed by Albert O. Hirschman, prices increased almost ninefold between 1880 and 1920.[9] As he observes, inflation is a highly political as well as a highly technical problem and, consequently, one can expect commentators to seek to assign responsibility for it or, in the language he uses, one can expect the search for a "villain." Use of this term may cause one to suspect that Hirschman

[9]Hirschman, *Journeys toward Progress*, p. 160. Hirschman gives percentage increases in prices by decades. The ninefold increase cited above is calculated from his data.

himself prefers a technical to a political explanation, but, whatever the accuracy of this suspicion, it is a fact, to be demonstrated shortly, that he explains the Chilean inflation of 1879–1925 largely on technical grounds.

For more than fifty years, however, both Chilean and American observers of the Chilean inflation traced that inflation to the landowners who, they charged, deliberately cheapened the currency in order to pay off their own mortgage debts. Some of these observers also noted the adverse effect of the inflation on worker well-being. One of the earliest Chilean commentators was Alejandro Venegas who, in 1909, named the landowners as the only economic group which had up to that time profited from the paper-money régime inaugurated in 1878. Eternally in debt, "they found themselves in a most favorable position: their products were sold in England against gold while they settled their accounts here in depreciated money. *This prosperity of the landowners which originated in the unbridled issues of paper-money has been the source of all our calamities.*"[10]

Writing just a few years later, Edward Ross also found that the landed oligarchs deliberately perpetuated the paper-money régime. In language reminiscent of Venegas, he reasoned that the *"hacendado* sells his product in Europe for gold and the lower the rate of exchange the more he gets for it in Chilean currency." These depreciating pesos, of which he regularly got more, were as good as ever for paying off his fixed mortgage debt at home. What is more, added Ross, "farm wages do not rise to the same degree as the *peso* depreciates, so that he makes a profit off his *inquilinos,* who have not the dimmest idea why every year it is harder to make both ends meet."[11]

This explanation of the inflation was given classic statement in 1931 by Frank W. Fetter *(Monetary Inflation in Chile),* although the inflation and its consequences have continued to concern writers up to the present time. Addressing himself briefly to the impact of rising prices on wages in the opening years of the century, Fetter said that "the working classes, faced with rising prices, and gradually emerging from a condition of semi-serfdom, were striking for increased wages, and were developing a class-conscious labor movement." He concluded that "rising prices were an important element in the increasing social friction in Chile, and after 1904 references to the labor problem and its

[10]See *ibid.,* p. 168, n. 3 for the above-quoted translation of a passage from Alejandro Venegas, *Cartas al Excelentísimo Señor Don Pedro Montt* (Valparaíso, 1909), p. 41.

[11]Edward A. Ross, *South of Panama* (New York: Century, 1915), p. 373.

relations to the monetary problem are found in almost every [parliamentary] debate on paper money."[12]

If Venegas, perhaps overgenerously, attributed all of Chile's "calamities" to the inflation, Archibald MacLeish *(Fortune, 1938)*, like Fetter, believed that at least "the Chilean social problem" was its legacy. That problem was created "largely by the monetary shortsightedness... of the *hacendados*...who, unique among the conservatives of history, depressed the value of their own currency by unnecessary paper issues." The result was "a slowly and cruelly rising cost of living which finally drove the [nitrate] workers of Iquique into a bloodily suppressed revolt in 1907" and created "an undernourished, miserable, and discontented people who needed only the crisis created by the collapse of nitrate [after World War I] to threaten open revolt."[13]

A less sweeping but equally critical indictment of the landowners was added by John Reese Stevenson in his study, *The Chilean Popular Front.* Stevenson was certain that inflation was an "exploitive technique of the oligarchs." They depressed the currency and maintained wages at the same level while receiving more pesos themselves for goods sold abroad. Currency depreciation was in reality therefore "a means of paying the middle and laboring classes smaller real wages and denying them anything like their proportionate share in the national prosperity."[14]

Citing Fetter as his authority, Tom E. Davis has recently concluded that the years 1879–1925 constituted "an amazing period of virtually undisguised use of political power by conservative governments in their own narrowly conceived, short-run, economic self-interest."[15]

Hirschman *(Journeys toward Progress, 1963)* and Fredrick B. Pike *(Chile and the United States, 1963)* have each attempted a reassessment. Hirschman, granting that the theory of landowner responsibility for the inflation was attractive to those politicians and intellectuals who were hostile to the oligarchy and granting that the middle and working classes became convinced that paper money was "a capitalist plot," nevertheless asks "Were they correct?" He doesn't think so, and, while his evidence is not definitive, it is intriguing as far as it goes. He

[12]Frank W. Fetter, *Monetary Inflation in Chile* (Princeton, N.J.: Princeton University Press, 1931), p. 122.

[13]"South America III: Chile," *Fortune,* vol. 17, May 1938, p. 148.

[14]John Reese Stevenson, *The Chilean Popular Front* (Philadelphia: University of Pennsylvania Press, 1942), p. 25.

[15]Tom E. Davis, "Eight Decades of Inflation in Chile, 1879–1925; A Political Interpretation," *The Journal of Political Economy,* vol. 71, August 1963, p. 389.

begins with the suspension of specie payments in 1878, which he argues had nothing to do with mortgages or European trips but "is quite adequately explained by a number of specific difficulties." Unfortunately, he doesn't say what these difficulties were and adds only the comment that suspension was "one of those lapses from virtue which would have been short-lived...had it not been necessary to postpone restoration of convertibility time and again, first with the War of the Pacific...and then because of the Chilean Civil War of 1891."

He appears to stand on firmer ground in his assertion that the landowners were the key elements behind the short-lived restoration of a metallic standard in 1895. When the experiment proved unworkable after only three years ("probably one of the most disastrous monetary operations of all time"), unconvertibility was again declared. Turning to the years 1905–1907, "the heyday of pre-World War I inflation," Hirschman finds the inflationary cause in "the vigorous business boom ...that got underway...and led to sudden and strong demands for finance on the part of firms and individuals." He adds, "Of course, the complete failure of the authorities to exercise some control...still requires some explanation. But it is best accounted for by the peculiar political structure which the country had given itself after the Civil War, with its weakened presidential powers and its eternally and rapidly rotating cabinets."

Finally, he cites the strengthening of the Chilean peso during World War I (its value, measured against hard currency, increased 70 percent from 1916 to mid-1918) and concludes that "if monetary policy had been conducted in the interests of the debt-ridden landowners, such a rise would have been prevented."[16]

Pike also finds the "plot theory" inadequate. Much of the new mortgage indebtedness of the 1890's he finds was incurred by "humble frontier settlers in the area south of Concepción." His major argument, however, is that "by 1898 the landowning aristocracy of Chile had, as a single group, probably already lost the power to foist a paper-money scheme upon the country. Wealth and power by this time had shifted dramatically toward the cities, and although the landowners still had a veto power they would have encountered grave difficulty in imposing their interests upon opposing urban sectors."[17] This political assessment seems to precipitate the fall of the oligarchy by some twenty to twenty-two years. Conservative party control, through the National

[16]Hirschman, *Journeys toward Progress*, pp. 169–175.
[17]Pike, *Chile and the United States, 1880–1962*, pp. 101–102.

Coalition, of both houses of Congress and the presidency until 1918–1920 gave the oligarchy a dominating role in national life during most of the parliamentary period.[18]

While the Hirschman and Pike analyses restrict the validity of previous thinking on the inflation of 1879–1925, they do not undermine it. There is need for more detailed research on such crucial matters as the extent of the landowners' mortgage debt, the timing and frequency of borrowing and repayment, and the history of income distribution during the period. Indeed, there is need to look more carefully at congressional debates and especially at private letters and documents to see what the landowners themselves said about monetary policy and the reasons for their views.

Whatever the verdict may ultimately be with respect to the role of the landowners in the inflation, however, no one has yet questioned the belief that the inflation caused real wages to drop. Perhaps this belief will be refined if extensive wage data for the period are ever gathered (i.e., workers in some skill areas or in some industries may not have lost any real income, or may not have lost as much as other workers).

In any case, it is not necessary to prove either a selfish or an exploitive interest on the part of landowners in order to link inflation with the social question. The decisive fact is that some intellectuals, politicians, and labor leaders *thought* the landowner thesis was true and were greatly stimulated by this thought to achieve far-reaching reforms. Even in the absence of a "villain" psychology, moreover, one can agree

[18]The views of several students of Chilean politics support this conclusion. Silvert refers to the years 1891–1920 as the "reign of the oligarchy." Halperin concludes that "during the three decades of untrammeled parliamentarian rule that followed the revolution of 1891 the oligarchy dominated the scene." Alexander states that the election of Arturo Alessandri in 1920 "marked the end of the uncontested rule of the country by the old landholding aristocracy which had dominated the nation since independence." Johnson adds that the 1918 parliamentary victory of the Liberal Alliance "started the middle sector leadership on its way to political preeminence." After Alessandri's victory in 1920, Johnson continues, the landed aristocracy still offered "a tenacious opposition through its ability...to exploit the apportionment of seats in the Senate in favor of the agrarian interests." This veto power, however, came to an end in 1938 with the victory of the Popular Front. Silvert agrees that agricultural interests have lost their veto power but are nevertheless "still [1963] strongly represented in government." See Silvert, *Conflict Society*, pp. 50–60; Halperin, *Nationalism and Communism in Chile*, p. 30; Alexander, *Labor Relations in Argentina, Brazil, and Chile*, p. 255; and Johnson, *Political Change in Latin America*, pp. 66–78. For further information on the parliamentary régime, see chap. 6 of this study, "The Liberal Alliance Project and the Intellectuals."

with Hirschman that persistent inflation itself "will arouse or strengthen demands for basic social and economic reforms."[19] This is not to say, so far as this writer is concerned, that "for want of a technical nail, the kingdom can be lost." Disastrous inflation must, in many instances, be complicated by narrow-minded social attitudes. Pike hits the mark in saying that "hard money would not have cured Chile's social problem — not unless the attitudes of the aristocracy had been fundamentally changed. Basically, what caused the nations' social ills was the inability or unwillingness of the upper classes and their middle-class allies to comprehend the inevitable consequences of the simultaneously worsening plight and rising expectations of the lower classes."[20]

At the same time as real worker income may have been declining in the decades before the 1920's, the income of the upper classes is said to have increased, not only through the mechanism of inflation but also through the repeal of almost all internal taxes, the latter having been made possible by the growth of foreign trade and the resulting increased revenue from exports, especially nitrates. In effect, according to some writers, nitrate wealth was not used to launch major development programs but was used instead to justify a virtual end to internal tax support of the government and to support conspicuous consumption in the upper classes. By 1900 over 90 percent of the public revenues were derived from export taxes and the only remaining internal direct taxes were on documents, seals, and newspapers.[21] Chile became "a sort of elegant remittance man among the nations of the earth. Year in and year out she received her average royalty of $25,000,000 from the nitrate fields largely operated by foreigners," and this income relieved the wealthy of taxes and at the same time provided the foreign exchange with which to import most of the manufactured goods they felt the country needed.[22] Among these wealthy there grew up "an excessive taste for luxury which consumes all fortunes. Everyone tries to surpass the other in the sumptuousness of his home, the magnificence of his furniture, and the splendor and cost of his carriage.... Parties, music, dancing, and banquets are the sole preoccupation of the lucky and privileged."[23] While these accounts may be overdrawn, they con-

[19]Hirschman, Journeys toward Progress, p. 216.
[20]Pike, Chile and the United States, p. 103.
[21]Julio César Jobet, Ensayo crítico del desarrollo económico-social de Chile (Santiago: Editorial Universitaria, 1955), pp. 67–68.
[22]"South America III: Chile," Fortune, vol. 17, May 1938, pp. 75–76. See also Ross, South of Panama, p. 370.
[23]Guillermo Rossel Silva, De la necesidad de legislar sobre el trabajo (Santiago: Imprenta Cervantes), 1906, p. 8.

tain some truth, and the spirit they portray has not by any means disappeared from the Chilean scene even today.

After World War I the Chilean economy absorbed a calamitous shock. Loss of the American war-stimulated market for nitrates and the entrance of artificial fertilizers on the world market had an immediate impact in Chile. Recovery came gradually, but at the nadir of the depression in 1922 some 47,000 nitrate workers and thousands of others in copper and coal mining were jobless. A wave of unrest and capital-labor conflict rolled through the economy with consequences for this story which are detailed later in the chapter.

III

As in so many countries, the first worker organizations in Chile were mutual benefit societies, and they date from the middle of the nineteenth century. They were exclusively worker-interested organizations whose purposes were to pool resources for the aid of members, and perhaps their families, who were unemployed or ill and to pay the funeral expenses of deceased members. Employer-interested and/or society-interested worker organizations (that is, those whose principal objectives were to change in some way the workers' relationship to the employer or to society at large) did not appear until the 1880's and 1890's, and there was no labor movement until the turn of the century. Moreover, the two types of worker organizations, the worker-interested and the employer- and/or society-interested, did not always arise as separate and unconnected units but, rather, a metamorphic process sometimes slowly or suddenly changed the former into the latter.

The first mutual benefit society was founded in 1853 by the typographers of Santiago. Most of those which followed were also set up by the skilled or artisan class of workers, such as the shoemakers, bakers, wagon builders, railroad engineers and firemen, but some of the unskilled, such as the dock workers, also organized benefit societies. Regional movements among these societies got underway in the 1880's, and in 1916 a permanent national confederation, the Workers' Social Congress, was established. A much smaller Catholic Federation of Societies of the National Union was also successfully organized.

The number of local societies and the size of their aggregate memberships are difficult to determine because the only data available are government statistics which give the number of corporate organizations in existence at a given time, but do not separate genuine mutual benefit societies from other worker organizations that may have achieved corporate status under the beneficiary provisions of the Civil Code. Moreover, there were many mutual benefit societies which never sought, and were therefore never granted, corporate status. Finally, membership figures for mutual benefit societies have become hopelessly confused with the estimates of trade union membership made by students of the labor movement. It is in part for this reason that we have provided some detail on the mutual benefit societies. Government figures indicate that there were 13 such societies with corporate status in 1870, 240 in 1900, 433 in 1910, and 600 in 1925. Membership data are almost useless, not only because one cannot be sure what they represent, but also because there are often contradictory data for the same year or contradictory years for the same data. To cap it off, this maze of confusion is sometimes the product of the same author in different publications. There are figures which show some consistency, however, and these indicate that there were 65,000 organized workers in 1910, 92,000 in 1913, 200,000 in 1921, 150,000 in 1923, and 204,000 in 1925. The reliability of these figures is anybody's guess, but they are probably inflated and they undoubtedly include a large proportion of mutual benefit society membership.[24]

A change in the spirit and purpose of worker organization became noticeable in the 1880's, when for the first time riots and demonstrations against price rises and strikes for the improvement of wages were reported.[25] Not until the following decade, however, did workers begin deliberately to erect unions to protect their interests or to protest against the emerging industrial society. These early organizations went by a variety of names which many writers have repeated but no one has tried to explain in any detail. The first ones were called "unions for the protection of labor" and, while one writer has tried hard to give

[24]See Rand School of Social Science, *The American Labor Year Book, 1916* (New York: The Rand School of Social Science), p. 233; 1925, p. 314; "Membership of Trade Unions during the Years 1921 to 1926," *International Labour Review*, September 1927, p. 394; Moisés Poblete Troncoso, "Labor Organizations in Chile," *Monthly Labor Review*, vol. 28, February 1929, p. 88; Moisés Poblete Troncoso, *El movimiento obrero latinoamericano* (México: Fondo de Cultura Económica, 1946), pp. 122–123; Ramírez, *Historia del movimiento obrero en Chile*, pp. 167, 256, 266; and Francisco Walker Linares, *Nociones elementales de derecho del trabajo*, quinta edición refundida (Santiago: Editorial Nascimento, 1957), p. 489.

[25]See, for example, Robert J. Alexander, *Organized Labor in Latin America* (New York: The Free Press, 1965), p. 85; Alba, *Historia del movimiento obrero en América Latina*, pp. 376–377; and Ramírez, *Historia del movimiento obrero en Chile*, pp. 282–293.

them a Marxist pedigree,[26] there is not yet convincing evidence that they were anything other than their name implies — organizations to protect workers in their job relationship. One of their objectives was to defeat a government-proposed antistrike bill in 1892 and, while the bill was not passed, it is not clear that the unions were in any degree responsible for this result. They apparently were largely the creation of one man, and they do not appear to have survived for any appreciable length of time.

In the same decade, anarchist unions called "resistance societies" were set up and, while few of them demonstrated real strength or long-term stability, this type of union remained the predominant form of organization among the artisans, shop workers, and dock hands of Santiago, Valparaíso, and Antofagasta well into the twentieth century. They eventually formed the basis for the organization of the Chilean branch of the Industrial Workers of the World. A third major union type, the *mancomunal* or "fellowship," seems to date from the early 1900's and was most popular in the north among the nitrate workers. Its existence was as ephemeral as that of the resistance society, for it seldom lasted much beyond the strike which it was set up to prosecute. Ideologically, it appears to have been a mongrel, with varying strains of anarchism, socialism, and purely economic and beneficial aims. The *mancomunal* was the base upon which Luis Emilio Recabarren built the nascent labor movement, and it became a principal pillar of the first trade union center in Chile, the Federation of Chilean Workers (FOCH), which was actually set up in 1909 as a mutual benefit society.

The history of the FOCH and Recabarren's leadership of it will be taken up shortly as part of a broader description of the events which institutionalized the loss of consensus in Chilean society and erected a positive challenge to the traditional leadership and philosophy of that society. Attention now turns to a brief account of labor-management relations up to the 1920's and of the more overt indications (i.e., violent strikes) of an absence of consensus in an emerging industrial nation.

IV

Throughout the entire period of this study up to the passage of the labor laws in 1924, there was apparently little accommodation between employers and organized workers. The president of the Society for Factory Development wrote in 1912 that there were no collective agree-

[26]See Ramírez, *Historia del movimiento obrero en Chile*, pp. 261–263.

ments in the country, that all agreements were individual, and that all of these, with the exception of a few involving imported workers, were verbal. He said that most employers did not want to have anything to do with unions.[27] A government commission, after visiting the nitrate region in 1919, reported that "the contract is always individual and verbal. Collective contracts or written contracts are absolutely unknown."[28] A university law student, who in 1920 wrote his degree thesis on the labor contract, confirmed the total absence of collective or written agreements in the country and offered an explanation of the employer's opposition to accommodation with the union. The employer, he said, considered that only he would be firmly committed by a contractual relationship, that the union could be bankrupt at the moment when compliance with the terms of an agreement was demanded. Besides, the employer believed that new union members would not respect the terms of a contract negotiated for them by the union before they joined the work force. Finally, employers really did not believe that unions were interested in anything other than "rebellion, strikes, disorder, violence, and revolution."[29] To put it simply, the employer did not want to deal with unions and he preferred and needed, because of his own weaknesses, to take care of "his" workers, in the pattern of the *hacendado-inquilino* relationship, and to monopolize authority in the new industrial world.

Since they did not accept the principle of unionism, employers, the government, and the power élite of Chilean society, in general, found themselves in conflict with union leaders. Their attitude also forced the unions to engage in only those activities they could initiate unilaterally, particularly strikes. Strikes were sometimes the end result of a planned strategy which included the development of demands and their presentation to the employer. More often they were spontaneous acts of desperation. A highly significant few were from the start, or developed into, scenes of death and destruction. These were the outward and visible signs of deep discontent in society, of lack of consensus, and, for the workers, they were also protests against the employing class and against society. Perhaps there is no violence, in potential so passionate and so cruel, as that which may take place when the uneducated find themselves rejected.

[27]González, *El contrato del trabajo*, pp. 19, 28–29.
[28]Quoted in *Boletín de la Oficina del Trabajo*, no. 12, 1919, p. 176.
[29]Daniel Arriagada Contreras, *El contrato de trabajo* (Santiago: Imprenta Nacional, 1920), pp. 33, 44–45, 47–48.

Labor leaders were generally considered agitators, parasites, trouble-makers. Once so identified, they sometimes found it difficult to get a job or to keep one, for they ran the risk of being discharged and placed on an employer's blacklist. While they often conducted strikes, strikes themselves were illegal, were considered crimes, and were punishable under the penal code. Strike leaders could be jailed for interfering with the right of others to work, and, although they were not always so prosecuted, they were often fired as part of the process of reestablish-ing "harmony" in the workplace. Strike demands were sometimes won and, while employers never made concessions in writing and never recognized the union, such successes were a tribute to the use of con-certed action and can indeed be said to have involved an elementary form of accommodation.[30]

The earliest strikes in Chile, which date from the 1880's, took place among the skilled workers of the cities, the dock workers, and railroad construction gangs. They appear to have been purely economic strikes, directed against a single employer or group of employers, and although, allegedly, more of them were lost than won, they were relatively peace-ful experiences.[31] By the following decade, however, thousands of newly recruited peasants swelled the ranks of the nitrate labor force and inflation had begun to erode real wages seriously. Moreover, in 1890, the year of the first big strike in the nitrate region, there was great political tension in the country and a general atmosphere of unrest which eased restraints and encouraged the expression of griev-ances. This political tension was to result the following year in a brief but bloody revolution between the partisans of a parliamentary form of government and the defenders of a strong executive, but in 1890 its major effect was to weaken the ties of obedience and discipline in society and to stimulate industrial conflict. In July of that year, a strike began among the port workers of Iquique and spread rapidly through-out the province of Tarapacá, eventually involving some ten thousand workers. This was the first general uprising in Chilean labor history, and, by the time the military brought the situation under control, an estimated ten to fifteen nitrate workers had been killed and about a hundred had been wounded. The strike wave spread south from Tara-

[30]See *ibid.*, pp. 44–45; Bernales Zañartu, *Estudio sobre la legislación del trabajo*, p. 24; Luis Malaquías Concha S., *Sobre la dictación de un código del trabajo y de la previsión social* (Santiago: Imprenta Cervantes, 1907), pp. 7–8; *Nación*, June 10, 1919; Poblete, *El movimiento obrero latinoamericano*, pp. 126–127; Senado, *Boletín de las Sesiones Extraordinarias en 1920–1921*, I, p. 496.

[31]Ramírez, *Historia del movimiento obrero en Chile*, pp. 282–289.

97

pacá, reached as far as the coal fields of Lota and Coronel, and touched all the major industrial and port centers in between. In the decade of the 1890's, some three hundred "conflicts" have been counted.[32]

It was only in the first decade of the new century, however, that the outbreaks of violence occurred which made the country conscious of the "social question" and set intellectuals and others to work searching for solutions to it. The major port city of Valparaíso was paralyzed for several weeks in 1903 by a dock strike which, in the course of one single destructive day, ran the entire course from peaceful marching, stone-throwing, rioting and burning, to armed conflict. Workers put the torch to one of the principal maritime buildings in the center of town and untold numbers were killed and wounded in engagements with the police and naval squads. A retired admiral was finally called in to arbitrate the differences between the dock hands and the steamship lines, a precedent-setting "first" in the history of labor relations in Chile.[33] Two years later the workers of Santiago protested the taxing of beef imported from Argentina, and matters quickly got so far out of hand that for two full days the city was taken over completely by roving, looting mobs. Police and the army regained control and restored order, and in the process left two to four hundred dead and wounded in the streets. Writing in 1915, Ross described the Santiago riots in these terms:

> Even a decade ago the temper of the people was so ugly that once, when the troops were absent at manoeuvres, a fearsome mob of three thousand persons, that seemed to spring from the gutter like the Paris revolutionaries of the Faubourg Saint Antoine, marched about Santiago destroying property. Nothing but the desperate exertions of the mounted police, who, by remaining in the saddle forty-eight hours, were able to keep the rioters within certain bounds, prevented the burning and sacking of the city. The soldiers were brought back as soon as possible and four hundred persons were shot down. The gilded youth of the Capital, who as an emergency measure had been armed, amused themselves by plotting sans-culottes.[34]

In 1906 the terrible sequence was repeated in Antofagasta and this

---

[32]Ibid., pp. 293–314. See also César Jobet, Ensayo crítico del desarrollo económico-social de Chile, pp. 101–102.

[33]Jorge Gustavo Silva, Nuestra evolución político-social (1900–1930) (Santiago: Imprenta Nascimento, 1931), pp. 16–20, 68–69; Poblete, El movimiento obrero latinoamericano, p. 125; La Nación, June 10, 1919.

[34]Ross, South of Panama, pp. 375–376. See also César Jobet, Ensayo crítico del desarrollo económico-social de Chile, p. 137, and Poblete, El movimiento obrero latinoamericano, p. 125.

time, according to one source, the dead numbered a hundred and fifty and the wounded were double that score.[35]

The blackest and most tragic of all the episodes of violence in Chile, and one which for sheer brutality it would be hard to match anywhere, was the Iquique massacre of 1907. Rebelling against inflation, the token system, the company store, and the lack of protective screens in the nitrate-dissolving ovens, the workers struck and demanded that amends be made in the form of a written agreement. There was relative calm for several days and then, as an American writer has graphically recorded,

> ...one morning, suddenly, 20,000 strikers from the *oficinas* on the arid pampas came pouring over the yellow sand bluffs down into Iquique, and took possession of the city. Houses were barricaded, and the city was left in the hands of a cruel mob. There were no troops on hand to cope with the situation. As subsequent events showed, the leading citizens were marked for death, and the city was to be fired simultaneously in many different places. At this critical moment soldiers were hurriedly despatched by steamer to Iquique, led by an officer of determination — and Chilean soldiers are good fighters. The rioters were maneuvered into a city square where they were massed about a church. Ineffectual efforts were made to induce them to disperse. Instead the leaders of the mob only responded by more fiery speeches. The military sent word that they would fire at 4 o'clock, if the rioters had not then dispersed. This was received with derisive cheers, when 4 o'clock came and no shot was fired. The officer then took out his watch and gave them five minutes in which to withdraw. At five minutes past four the whir of the mitrailleuse began. Piles of dead and dying were heaped up in a moment. Two hundred were killed and three hundred wounded; and the rest fled up the sand bluffs and were lost to sight on the pampas.[36]

A worker delegation from one of the nitrate companies which had been struck later told a congressional investigating committee that "in five minutes of fire and butchery the authorities had worked greater havoc on the morality and patriotism of the workers than had been accomplished in the previous half century by the systematic propaganda of a thousand anarchists."[37]

The violent signs of social cleavage, in the form of industrial battles, general strikes, riots, and antimilitary demonstrations, practically dis-

[35]Fanny Simon, "Recabarren," unpublished book manuscript, pp. 64–67.

[36]J. Lawrence Laughlin, "The Strike at Iquique," *The Journal of Political Economy*, vol. 17, January–December 1909, p. 643.

[37]Paraphrased from a quotation in Juan Enrique Concha, *Conferencias sobre economía social* (Santiago: Imprenta Chile, 1918), pp. 150–151.

appeared for more than a decade after 1907, and it was not until after World War I that they returned. Serious postwar unemployment compounded the inflationary and psychosocial dislocations of the emerging industrial society in Chile, and the result was a repetition of the bloody clashes of the early 1900's. In January 1919 there was a general strike in the far southern province of Magallanes; before the year was out, two more general strikes were held elsewhere in the country and a hunger march took place in Santiago in which an estimated one hundred thousand persons participated. The following year was marred by a raid on the premises of the Students' Federation in Santiago, the abolition of the corporate status of that body, a second general strike in Magallanes, and another in the capital. In 1921 unemployed nitrate workers of the San Gregorio plant in Antofagasta "clashed with the military guards and defeated them, killing several soldiers and later assassinating Daniel Janes, manager of the plant. The workmen lost over thirty men killed and wounded in the encounter, but took possession of the plant, from which they were finally driven by reinforcements of troops."[38] Several long and violent strikes also crippled the coal industry in the postwar years. In sum, in the relatively short span of thirty years (1890 to the 1920's), industrial violence had rocked the country from end to end and the blood of those who rebelled lay in the desert, the streets, and on the barren and windswept plains of the south.

V

Outbursts of physical violence were only the most elementary and most savage expressions of consensus loss in industrializing Chile. Moreover, one cannot necessarily tell from violence alone how broad or serious social cleavage may be and, indeed, whether a loss of consensus has occurred. Other measures of consensus loss, applicable in a democracy, are (1) the breakdown of the two-party system and/or the appearance of strong revolutionary political parties and (2) the organization of a predominantly Marxist and/or anarchist labor movement. A word or two about each of these matters follows.

Chile developed the two-party system after her independence from Spain in the early nineteenth century, and this system continued to operate unchallenged for more than fifty years thereafter. At first the parties were really only loosely organized groups called the *pipiolos* and the *pelucones,* and formal political parties did not come until

[38]"Chile," *Current History,* vol. 13, March 1921, p. 545.

later. The *pipiolos* stood for federalism in government and liberalism in economics, and the revolutionary spirit of the time favored their domination until the early 1830's. The *pelucones,* who advocated centralized government and a strong executive, close ties between church and state, and the retention of colonial agricultural institutions, successfully established their philosophy in the Constitution of 1833. Then in the following decade the *pipiolos,* who were the leading men of commerce, finance, and mining, set up the Liberal party, and in 1856 the *pelucones,* who were the great *fundo* owners and the influential men of the Catholic Church, organized the Conservative party.

Neither of these parties of the oligarchy found it possible to absorb sufficient numbers of the new groups which were emerging politically in the course of slow change (e.g., workers, public servants, professionals) to prevent the development of strong new parties. Moreover, the new members they did absorb came to adopt the values and attitudes of the traditional leading elements. However unconsciously, the Liberals and the Conservatives apparently preferred to maximize political power in the defense of selfish interests and to accept political rivalry rather than surrender some of their own power in the interests of a larger consensus. The divisive consequences of these nineteenth century developments are painfully evident in Chile today.

Some members of the aristocracy, Conservatives and Liberals alike, were sufficiently fearful of change and of losing some power to new political groups that they came to favor a policy of weak national government as a means of delaying an alteration of social structure. When they were unchallenged in power, they stood for strong government; when they felt their narrow base weakening in a more complex society, they could not gracefully initiate an expansion and a compromise with new social forces. They chose rather to seek a peculiarly weak form of parliamentary government which they could manipulate to maintain the status quo and which no one else could use to change it.[39] This approach to government, which was of course supported by many other Chileans for high-minded reasons of political idealism and greater individual freedom, led to the bloody revolution of 1891 and, thirty-three years later, to a military takeover of the country and the restoration of a strong executive. With regard at least to the narrow-

[39]Silvert describes the crisis in these terms: "The ideological division in the Chilean policy group came to a head in 1891 over the question of whether a strong executive was to control the aristocracy as represented in Congress, or whether the latter was to continue to hold the national situation in *status quo* so far as possible." Silvert, *Conflict Society,* p. 56.

minded defenders of the status quo, it would have been wiser to have given in gracefully. In the end, society lost, through inefficient use of more than three decades of time, an unsurpassed opportunity to speed economic development and to create a new political and social consensus. The "parliamentary régime" (1891–1924) in Chile is, in some respects, an unnecessary monument to class rigidity and social statics.

The two-party system faced no serious threat until the 1870's, although the source of this threat, the Radical party, was founded in 1863. Radical party organizers were largely dissident Liberals who resented domination of the country by the central valley landholders around Santiago and the influence of the Church in secular affairs. The new party represented disaffected landholders of the south, the petit-bourgoisie, white-collar groups, masons, some artisans, and later became especially identified with the proliferating state bureaucracy. It won a ministerial post in the Administration of President Federico Errázuriz in 1875, advanced rapidly thereafter, and became a bitter antagonist of the Conservative party. During the parliamentary era, the Radical party was the chief member of the Liberal Alliance coalition which vied for control of the government with the National Union coalition dominated by the Conservatives.

Given the unwillingness of the old established parties to absorb large numbers of the new groups emerging, it was to be expected that a second new party would be founded upon the extension of the suffrage to all adult males in 1884. Just three years later the Democratic party was set up with an appeal to the lower middle-class, artisans, and the growing number of factory workers. The Democrats adopted a non-Marxist platform which committed them to seek the improvement of the social, economic, and political conditions of the people through nonviolent, gradual reform. For many years they were associated with the cooperative movement in Chile, the development of mutual benefit societies, and the advocacy of social legislation. Despite the generally mild, reformistic nature of the party, it did contain a number of utopians, socialists, and anarchists who sought to control or disrupt party organization. The result was serious internal factionalism and splinter movements. Although the party enjoyed some growth and even achieved Cabinet recognition in 1916, it was by that time on the decline and had moved to the right in the political spectrum. If one can properly call the Democratic party the first "leftist" or popular party in Chile, it is equally true that it was not a party of the workingman in the same sense or degree as the Socialist and Communist parties of a later day.

102

Although the Democratic party was weakened by its own internal strains, it also encountered opposition from established authority. In 1894, 1897, and 1901 the party elected one Deputy to the Congress and he was seated without incident each time. In 1906, however, when six Democrats won elections, government leaders denied three of them their seats on grounds of election irregularities. One of the hapless Democrats was Luis Emilio Recabarren who had been elected by the nitrate workers of the north. In his case, the election was held again, won again, he was charged with election fraud again, and denied a seat in the Chamber of Deputies. His presence there, as the rising young leader of labor and architect of the *mancomunales,* was feared by the upper classes. One way to deny the existence of a social question was to remove him from sight. As one Deputy concluded, after reciting Recabarren's past as a labor leader,

> ...if there were no basis in law for expelling Mr. Recabarren from the Chamber, it would be necessary to do it for reasons of high morality and for others which are linked with the happiness and dignity of the people, for we cannot allow the ideas of social dissolution propounded by Mr. Recabarren to be represented in the Chamber.[40]

The social and political thinking of Recabarren was a medley of democracy, anarchism, and evolutionary socialism. For one who does not see beyond the labels, he could be considered only an ideologically confused and emotionally unstable worker. He was both and eventually took his own life, but he was also an uneducated, rejected, and resentful rebel who found some security and self-expression in all three of the philosophies just mentioned. In democracy, he found dignity as an individual in a society which looked down upon the worker and manual labor; in anarchism, he found the most complete expression of his rebellion; in socialism, he found both emotional appeal and organized thought, the latter of which his training and experience as a printer made it possible for him to comprehend.

[40]Quoted in César Jobet, *Ensayo crítico del desarrollo económico-social de Chile,* p. 142. For further information on the Democratic party, see Ramírez, *Historia del movimiento obrero en Chile,* pp. 215–216, 225, 226–250 and Simon, "Recabarren," pp. 73–74, 87, 90–91, 93, 143. It should also be mentioned that a popular political movement known as the "Society for Equality" preceded the Democratic party by more than three decades. It is frequently said to have been the first workers' organization in Chile and the forerunner of popular political parties. See Gabriel Sanhueza, *Santiago Arcos, comunista, millonario y calavera* (Santiago: Editorial del Pacífico, 1956); César Jobet, *Ensayo crítico del desarrollo económico-social de Chile,* pp. 37–39; Tulio Lagos V., *Bosquejo histórico del movimiento obrero en Chile* (Santiago, 1947), pp. 12–16; Poblete, *El movimiento obrero latinoamericano,* p. 121.

After the sharp disappointment of his election experience, Recabarren spent three years abroad in Argentina and western Europe. In Spain he met Pablo Iglesias, the outstanding socialist and labor leader of that country, and he may even have met Lenin in Belgium.[41] By the time he returned to Chile, he was convinced that the only way to fight "capitalist exploitation" was through militant trade unions and a socialist political party. However, his socialism was still at this time, and so remained until the end of his life, "more of the heart than of the mind" and "was larded over with romantic and anarchist notions."[42] Nevertheless, Recabarren himself thought that he was essentially a socialist, and in 1912 he converted the Democratic party organization in Iquique into the Socialist Workers' party. Although the party held a national convention in 1915, it remained largely a regional organization with its chief strength centered in the nitrate provinces of the north. In 1921 the party made a sudden impact on the national consciousness when it placed two men, including Recabarren, in the Chamber of Deputies. Later in the same year, Recabarren, in a move which had been several years in the making, abandoned the evolutionary Socialist Workers' party and set up in its stead the revolutionary Communist party of Chile. By the same act, he and his fellow Deputy became the first Chilean Communists to sit in the national Congress. In 1923 Recabarren traveled to Soviet Russia and then wrote glowingly about the trip in a book called *Worker and Peasant Russia: Something of What I Saw in a Visit to Moscow*. In the second fifty years of the Republic, the two-party system and consensus gave way to the multiparty system and ideological division.

It goes without saying that the parliamentary system itself, as it operated in Chile, tended to splinter the parties, augment the role of strong leaders, and rely upon coalitions to effect some stability and continuity in government. While this system certainly, therefore, deepened political factionalism, it did not cause the disintegration of the two-party system. Indeed, as we have already seen, the parliamentary system was, for some members of the oligarchy, a defensive response to the deepening social crisis. It was the social crisis, not the parliamentary system, which brought forth the Radicals and the Democrats before

[41]Stewart Cole Blasier has said that "Lenin refers...to a Chilean attending a meeting of the Bureau of the Socialist International in Brussels in 1909. Probably, this Chilean was Recabarren who is known to have been traveling in Europe at this time." Blasier, "The Cuban and Chilean Communist Parties," (Ann Arbor, Mich.: University Microfilms, 1956), pp. 131–132.

[42]Simon, "Recabarren," p. 93.

1891 and which also explains the Socialist Workers' party and the Communist party of the post-1891 period. The parliamentary system was thus, from one point of view and with respect to some members of the oligarchy, a consequence not a cause of ideological competition in Chilean politics.

VI

Challenges to the unity and centralized authoritarianism of the old *fundo* society became evident not only in the realignment of old and the creation of new political forces but also in the appearance of a labor movement at odds with the leadership and goals of that society. In contrast to the obedient and submissive *inquilino,* the new worker of the industrial and mining labor force was independent and rebellious and came to believe that the only way he could gain acceptance was through the reordering of society. To be sure, there were dissenters from this pattern, workers who continued to think largely in terms of fraternity and mutual aid, and there were also different degrees and forms of rebellion (e.g., anarchism, mild socialism, revolutionary socialism, and communism). Yet the dominant tone was a discordant one which symbolized a failure to readjust normative behavior and to maintain consensus in the difficult transition from a semifeudal agricultural society to an industrializing one.

We have already mentioned the early appearance of anarchist "resistance societies," the hybrid *mancomunal* which reflected the personality of Recabarren, and the Federation of Chilean Workers (FOCH). While the FOCH is always dated from 1909, it had no constitution until the following year and held its first convention only in 1911. Moreover, it was established by a small group of railroad workers for the limited purpose of restoring wages which had been unilaterally reduced by railroad management. Succeeding in this objective, the workers decided to make the FOCH a permanent organization and to incorporate it as a mutual benefit society under the provisions of the Civil Code. Corporate status was achieved in 1911, shortly after the founding convention, and this year would, therefore, seem to mark the real beginning of the FOCH as a permanent body. As the coordinating center for a number of affiliated mutual benefit societies, the FOCH espoused a variety of insurance, social, and cultural programs. It was also interested in relations at the enterprise level, but emphasized harmony and the arbitration of differences and declared against strikes. Organizers of the FOCH "were good Catholics, pro-government,

105

and the idea of the class struggle and of a radical transformation of society was foreign to their thinking."[43]

In the course of ten short years, however, the FOCH was converted to revolutionary Marxism and became the trade union arm of the Communist party in Chile. The change was sudden and its chief architect was Recabarren, whose political party activities have already been detailed. He was not an original founder of the FOCH and indeed, for several years, opposed and ridiculed the organization as the "lickspittle of the priests" and the "myrmidon of the bourgeoise." By 1916, however, he had decided to infiltrate and capture the FOCH and use it to further the aims of the few but growing numbers of *mancomunales* and the Socialist Workers' party. His organizing success was concentrated in, but not limited to, the northern part of the country where printers, bakers, foundry workers, copper miners, and longshoremen, as well as nitrate workers, had set up unions. These he encouraged to affiliate with the FOCH, and their representation at the FOCH's second convention in 1917 was probably responsible for a marked change in the spirit and pronouncements of the organization. A new militancy was expressed in the endorsement of strike action as a legitimate weapon in dealings with employers, and the FOCH also for the first time explicitly invited all workers in the country to join without regard to religion, politics, nationality, or sex. The government responded to these changes by withdrawing the FOCH's charter and canceling its status as a legally incorporated association.[44]

In the meantime, Recabarren had gone to Argentina (he did not participate in the 1917 convention), and he was in Buenos Aires at the time of the Bolshevik Revolution. He immediately forsook evolutionary socialism for communism and became an ardent backer of the Soviet régime. On December 26, 1917, Recabarren wrote to his friends and followers in Chile that the Bolsheviks had freed Russia "of all despotisms and that the utopian dreams of these so-called crazy socialists had become...not only a reality but the source of all progress and human happiness. Militarism no longer existed in Russia; in its place was 'a people in arms who will not allow itself to be cheated of its con-

[43]*Ibid.*, pp. 120–121.

[44]*Ibid.*, pp. 127–130; César Jobet, *Ensayo crítico del desarrollo económico-social de Chile*, p. 144; and Poblete, *El movimiento obrero latinoamericano*, p. 130. It should be explained that the FOCH was actually known as the "Grand Federation of Chilean Workers" until 1917 when, as part of Recabarren's thorough reorganization efforts, the "Grand" was dropped.

106

quests obtained at such great danger and sorrow.' "[45] Recabarren was perhaps also influenced by the success of the Mexican Revolution and its 1917 constitution,[46] but when the time came to choose between them he opted without qualification for the Soviet model.

Now a self-proclaimed communist, Recabarren bent himself to the task of consolidating his hold on the FOCH and committing that body to the new philosophy. He called and chaired the FOCH convention of 1919 which was attended by some one hundred delegates representing seventy-three organizations. The convention declared a new faith in Marxism and the class struggle, pledged the abolition of capitalism and the wage system, and adopted the red flag as the FOCH emblem. New slogans were "In Unity There is Strength" and "The Emancipation of the Working Classes Must Be the Work of the Workers Themselves."[47] To be sure, there was no special meaning to these developments in so far as the international alignment of the FOCH is concerned. A decision on this matter was made two years later at the historic Rancagua convention.

The presidential election of 1920 and the triumph of Arturo Alessandri Palma as the candidate of the Liberal Alliance coalition temporarily slowed the extreme leftist trend in politics and labor. Had the Alessandri Administration been more successful politically and had the rural oligarchy accepted the full significance of his election victory, it is possible that FOCH extremism might never have been consolidated as the ideological conviction of most organized blue-collar workers in Chile. Although Alessandri drew his principal strength from the upper-middle and middle classes, many workingmen voted for him, even those of Antofagasta which was a major center of FOCH strength. A Chilean reporter has warmly and sympathetically described how workers "were seen to step up to the candidate touring the country and to embrace him with tears in their eyes, when all the intercourse between the common people and our former presidents had been limited to the traditional offering of a toast in the course of the army parade during the national holidays."[48] Recabarren himself decided not to contest the presidency in 1920 in return for Liberal Alliance support of Social-

---

[45]Quoted from Simon, "Recabarren," p. 166–167.

[46]Stevenson, The Chilean Popular Front, p. 28.

[47]Poblete, El movimiento obrero latinoamericano, pp. 131–132 and Simon, "Recabarren," pp. 138–141.

[48]Ernesto Montenegro, "Chile's First Middle-Class President," Current History, vol. 13, December 1920, pp. 400–401.

ist Workers' party candidates, including himself, in the congressional elections of the following year.

The decisions of 1920 were, however, only tactical ones for Recabarren and his lieutenants, and they had no faith in either the desire or the ability of Alessandri to accomplish fundamental social and political reform. Recabarren spent two hundred days in jail in 1920 on charges of sedition, and the postwar years were, the reader will recall, generally ones of great tension, sharp unemployment, and civil strife. The election was no sooner over than both the Socialist Workers' party and the FOCH began to prepare for an alignment with international communism. The alignment was not free of obstacles in either its political party or union aspects because the sudden shifts Recabarren had made in his own thinking were not equally easy for others to make. Moreover, a significant number of FOCH members had always been supporters of the Democratic party rather than of the Socialist Workers' party, and others, incongruous as it may seem, remained wedded to anarchism or anarchosyndicalism. To these workers, maintenance of both the political and union status quo seemed a desirable objective. Any effort to define and adopt a discriminatory international policy would necessarily raise domestic political and union issues and result in the drawing of sharper lines among the heterogeneous elements in the FOCH. In other words, hitherto internal and compatible differences would become incompatible and lead to schism.

The initial reaction of the FOCH was a rebuff for Recabarren. A meeting of FOCH regional councils in November 1920 rejected the idea of a new political party. The delegates did, however, agree to begin to discuss FOCH affiliation to the Third or Communist International and to resolve this matter at the Rancagua convention in 1921. In December 1920 the Socialist Workers' party met in convention and, faced with the FOCH's negative stand, could agree only to debate the question of affiliation to the Third International at a subsequent convention to be held immediately after the FOCH conclave at Rancagua. Recabarren was certain in his own mind that the party would choose to affiliate and would willingly accept Lenin's twenty-one points as a condition of affiliation. He was less certain of what the FOCH would do, but he was nevertheless optimistic. In January 1921 the party organ, *El Socialista*, carried this answer from Recabarren to the question: Where are we going?

> We are now going toward the Third International; we are truly going toward the future "fatherland" of Socialism, the one which belongs to all men and women. We are going there and in front may go a

more powerful body: the FOCH. She may even precede us, for in her runs our Communist blood.[40]

Apparently Recabarren had determined to deliver the Socialist Workers' party to the Third International regardless of the outcome of FOCH debate on affiliation.

Six months before the FOCH met in convention at Rancagua in December 1921, the Third International met in Moscow and created a separate structure for labor organizations. Henceforth, the latter would belong to the Red International of Labor Unions (RILU) and political organizations would continue their affiliation with the Third International. This policy innovation, adopted at the behest of the French delegates whose syndicalist tendency probably explains their desire for structural independence from political parties, altered the affiliation question in Chile. The net result of the change was to favor the FOCH's affiliation with the RILU on two counts. The first was the fact that there were also syndicalists in Chile who would have objected to joining the Third International but who could identify with a labor organization like the RILU. In the second place, now that a separate entity existed for unions, there was greater pressure on the FOCH to join and a greater need on Recabarren's part to have the FOCH join. Unionists could not use the mixed political-union nature of the old Third International as an excuse to avoid the issue of affiliation, and Recabarren could no longer, if he ever did, consider the possibility of a single (party) affiliation from Chile as satisfying the needs of both the party and the FOCH. The issue had thus become focused more sharply and the consequences of any action taken were likely to be more profound. A negative decision by the FOCH would be a greater blow to the leadership of Recabarren, and a positive decision was certain to have immediate schismatic results.

Given his desire for RILU affiliation, Recabarren played his hand well at Rancagua. He forced the Democrats, a significant source of opposition, to leave the convention shortly after it opened. This he accomplished by allowing the matter of FOCH electoral support for Democratic party candidates to come to a vote. Contrary to the wishes of almost one third of the delegates, the convention decided (the vote was 77 to 33) not to negotiate any electoral pact with the Democratic party. The FOCH paper, *La Federación Obrera,* explained that the Democratic party was reformist and willing to work with bourgeois governments, while the FOCH favored "the total emancipation of the

[40]Quoted from Simon, "Recabarren," pp. 168–171.

producing class."[50] *El Socialista* added that partisans of the Democratic party got up and left the convention after the vote and that "with this step the line between the reformists and the revolutionaries has been drawn."[51]

With the Democrats gone, it was easier, though still not free of important controversy, to make the RILU alignment. The railroad workers, represented by FOCH General-Secretary Enrique Diaz Vera, the anarchists, and a fuzzy group of indefinable leftists were against the move. Diaz Vera thought that RILU affiliation was premature, and he proposed that debate be postponed until the next FOCH convention, but the motion was lost (74 to 46, which again shows a very large opposition). At this point, Recabarren shrewdly presented to the delegates the Argentine communist Juan Grecco. Grecco advised that it was necessary to fight in order to destroy capitalism, and he exhorted the workers to destroy the present régime in Chile and to join the international struggle being waged by the Soviet Union. He had full confidence in the FOCH convention, he said, "for from it will come the orientation which will shorten the distance and the time required to reach the goal so anxiously sought by the world proletariat."[52] When the question was then called on joining the Red International of Labor Unions, the delegates favored it by the vote of 107 to 12.[53] Although the negative vote was small, one source estimates that it represented 40 percent of the total FOCH membership.[54] Immediately after the FOCH convention adjourned, the Socialist Workers' party convention was held in the same city and was attended by most of the same delegates. It was under these circumstances that the party decided to join the Third International and to become the Chilean Communist party.

In the aftermath of these key shifts of policy and international alignment, the Railroad Federation and the Workers' Federation of Magallanes, both of which had participated in FOCH meetings as observers, now withdrew this form of endorsement, although they did not cease to communicate with the FOCH. Diaz Vera and others, who remained in the FOCH but agitated for a reversal of the Rancagua decisions, were eventually expelled from membership. Some of the Democrats and anarchists, and many of the anarchosyndicalists, appear to have re-

[50]*La Federación Obrera*, Dec. 26, 27, 1921.

[51]*El Socialista*, Dec. 28, 1921.

[52]Quoted from *La Nación*, Dec. 27, 1921. See also *ibid.*, Dec. 29, 1921.

[53]*Ibid.*, Dec. 30, 1921. The major decisions, principles, and laws adopted at Rancagua are reproduced in *La Federación Obrera*, Feb. 17, 1922.

[54]Simon, "Recabarren," pp. 172–173.

THE SOCIAL QUESTION

mained in the FOCH. This was really not so peculiar after all, since the communism of Recabarren and others of the older generation was not ideologically pure and since leftism in general was perhaps as much an emotional state of mind at that time as it was a matter of doctrine. The cohesive force of shared feelings of hostility toward others was for a few an even greater one than the divisive force of ideological disagreement. In the course of the 1920's, the FOCH did become a purer organization, but this was accomplished only after Recabarren's death and with the rise of a new and younger generation of Communist leaders. A symbol of this purification and also of the intimate relationship between the FOCH and the Communist party was the adoption in 1924 of a single paper, *Justicia,* to replace *El Socialista* and *La Federación Obrera* which were discontinued.

While acknowledging that the Rancagua policy of ideological conformity was not fully effective, it is pertinent to indicate that neither did it endure as a principle. Since the 1930's Chilean labor has most of the time been dominated by a single and ideologically diverse trade union center with no formal or official international affiliation. In the light of this history, Recabarren's move at Rancagua was a mistake. Despite the move, however, the FOCH in the early 1920's is said to have represented 80 percent of all organized workers in Chile, and total union membership has been estimated at more than a hundred thousand.[55]

While the FOCH represented many things to many workers it was not, even before 1921, the only trade union center which institutionalized conflict and nonconformity in society. When the FOCH went Marxist in 1919, a group of anarchist leaders, drawing on the tradition and the remnants of the old resistance society movement, immediately set about organizing a Chilean branch of the Industrial Workers of the World (IWW). Response to the IWW was quick and substantial in the port cities among the dock and maritime workers. Some bakers, masons, and shoe and leather workers also were recruited, and a total strength estimated variously at between 7,000 and 28,000 members was achieved in the 1920's. The IWW met stiff resistance from the govern-

[55]Robert J. Alexander, "The Labor and Socialist Movement of Chile," microfilm, Columbia University Library, 1941, pp. 63–64; "Membership of Trade Unions during the Years 1921 to 1926;" *International Labour Review,* September 1927, p. 394. Membership figures from the latter source actually range from 150,000 to 204,000 for the years involved, but they very probably greatly exaggerate union strength and include many mutual benefit society members. Our own suggestion of 100,000 is, nevertheless, entirely arbitrary.

111

ment and the courts and was divided internally on the issue of a united front with the FOCH. It did not outlive the 1920's, but anarchism itself, as a worker response to industrialism, remained the principal and most powerful alternative to Marxism until the end of the following decade.

VII

Why did the attitude of the new Chilean worker, perhaps a former *inquilino*, shift from one of respect and loyalty to the *hacendado* or concern for mutual benefit programs to revolutionary anarchism or socialism? Inflation? Miserable working and living conditions? The immigration of radical Italian and Spanish workers and the inflow of extremist literature? Recabarren's emotional problems? Capitalist exploitation and the class struggle? Or was the change an emotional response on the part of the newly independent industrial worker whom the rural aristocracy had not prepared for independence and whose dignity, independence, and responsibility as an individual were indeed denied by both the old and the new élites? The latter, which is part of the larger phenomenon of consensus, explains far more to this writer than the others, which are, at best, only symptoms of a deeper psychosocial conflict. Nothing about this particular shift in worker ideology was inevitable nor does it illustrate a dialectical pattern of class struggle.

The question of radicalism in the Chilean labor movement has never before been focused in this way, but individuals, at different times and under different circumstances of background and interest, have offered explanations which exemplify almost all the points of view implied in the preceding paragraph. Communist and socialist intellectuals, in particular, describe in great detail the nature, the volume, and the chronology of arrival of leftist literature in Chile, as though the mounting rebellion of the working class were, in some measure, a barren intellectual experience.[56] Non-leftists have also believed this, although they have not been proud of it and would rather have seen the flow shut off. One of them, a trade union leader, has very neatly explained that, when Marx and Bakunin split, the Latins fell heir to the latter and that books and immigrants from Spain, Italy, and France carried anarchist and anarchosyndicalist ideas to Latin America. "Identity of race, language, and temperament must be held responsible for this," he

[56]See, for example, Ramírez, *Historia del movimiento obrero en Chile*, pp. 141–148, 204–205 and César Jobet, *Ensayo crítico del desarrollo económico-social de Chile*, pp. 153–154.

added, "although it is language that has been chiefly responsible."[57] Had he been writing ten years later, he would have found predominantly socialist and communist labor movements in Latin America and the need for a new theory. Ross and Samuel Guy Inman also believed in the importation theory, and the former predicted that the opening of the Panama Canal would lessen Chile's isolation and "revolutionary working class ideas may quickly spread among her exploited and neglected masses."[58] Inman was even less ambiguous in stating that Latin American labor's preference for the "European model" rather than the "North American model" was due simply to greater contact with Europe. Before World War I, he pointed out, the influence of North American labor leaders in Latin America was practically nil, but

> European immigrants and propagandists, sent for that special purpose, began to plant ideas of organization and resistance in the docile minds of the Southerners [i.e., South Americans], whose only organization in the early days was of the mutual aid type. It was natural, then, that the patterns of German socialism or of Spanish-French syndicalism or anarchism were followed.[59]

Nothing could have been farther from the truth, for internal influences, and particularly élite attitudes, are much more significant than external influences in shaping the worker response to industrialization.[60] The conditions for worker revolt or adaptation to the industrial order are made at home, and if foreign models are successfully transplanted, it is because they fit these conditions in greater or lesser degree and not because they have created them.

Chilean Marxists have not explained the development of a revolutionary movement in their country with any imagination. They have taken the phenomenon for granted as the inevitable result of the unfolding of history, and their explanation is no more than the use of Marxian language to describe the economic and political events of the past.[61] Some other writers, however, have identified areas of analysis

[57]Santiago Iglesias, "Labor Organization in Latin America," *Current History*, vol. 26, September 1927, p. 930.

[58]Ross, *South of Panama*, p. 375.

[59]Samuel Guy Inman, *Latin America*, rev. ed. (New York: Harcourt, Brace and Company, 1942), p. 293.

[60]Chapter 3 "The Industrializing Élites and their Strategies," pp. 47–76 and Chapter 8 "The Workers: Impact and Response," pp. 193–233 of *Industrialism and Industrial Man* are particularly relevant to this point. See also John P. Windmuller, "External Influences on Labor Organizations in Underdeveloped Countries," *Industrial and Labor Relations Review*, vol. 16, July 1963, pp. 559–573.

[61]See Ramírez, *Historia del movimiento obrero en Chile* and César Jobet, *Ensayo crítico del dessarrollo económico-social de Chile*.

crucial to an understanding of the worker response to industrialization in Chile. Carlos Keller deals briefly but thoughtfully with the social question in his book, *The Eternal Chilean Crisis*. Writing in 1931, Keller looked back upon the genesis of a revolutionary labor and political movement as the consequence of clashing interests, emotions, and racial differences. The rural aristocracy and the capitalists, he said, were only on rare occasion concerned about the welfare of the workers and did not worry at all about their intellectual and moral development. The latter became embittered and delivered themselves to communism. "Their political attitude was, consequently, one of rebellion, that is to say, of negative tendency.... This movement acquired a violent character due to the racial differences between the low and the superior classes."[62] He attempted no explanation of élite attitudes and did not say what kind of intellectual and moral development the workers needed, but he was seemingly aware of some of the noneconomic (psychological and sociological) facets of the worker response.

A political writer of liberal tendency, Benjamin Vicuña Subercaseaux, fully appreciated the domestic origins of the social question in Chile. In 1908, many years before labor's swing to the left was completed, he admitted that "doctors of anarchism" had arrived in the country and had developed a following. But, he added, "if the people did not feel so much malaise and misery, if they were more respected and protected, they would not give in to the agitators and go out shooting." Chile had for centuries lived in a real patriarchy but industry was now changing this, making life more complicated, and the masses were becoming better informed. If justice and benevolence were again to flower in the hearts of employers and if the government were to pass and enforce labor legislation, then the people would feel like partners in a common task and would not seek emancipation through blood and fire. Yet the same writer could not accept the Democratic party as representative of a genuine worker rebellion and, as we shall see in Chapter 6, he could not concede to workers, their organizations, and leaders a full measure of respect and independence in the new industrial world.[63]

There are similar weaknesses in the analysis of Juan Enrique Concha who, as an intellectual representative of the aristocratic-Catholic élite, developed a long and closely reasoned proposal for solving the social question. His view, which we shall describe fully in the following chap-

[62]Keller, *La eterna crisis chilena*, pp. 25–26.

[63]Benjamín Vicuña Subercaseaux, *Socialismo revolucionario y la cuestión social en Europa y Chile* (Santiago, 1908), pp. 35–36, 235–238, 255.

ter and criticize in the concluding chapter, placed the social question in a psychological, religious, moral framework and relied essentially upon employer benevolence for solutions. While recognizing the salient importance of values and attitudes, Concha nevertheless turned to the past and to the *fundo* society for a paternal pattern of behavior he hoped one could reproduce in industry.

A most incisive comment on the radical mentality of the Chilean worker was made by an outside observer and student of the *hacienda* régime, George M. McBride. While he did not attempt a causal analysis in depth and while there may be a certain fatalism in his conclusions which this writer would find objectionable, it is apparent that he captured the spirit and understood some of the behavioral implications of the shift from *fundo* to factory or mine. Here are his views as expressed almost thirty years ago:

> Reds, communists, syndicalists, anarchists, nihilists, no one of these terms expresses too strongly the political tendencies of the typical Chilean "roto" [the worker or "ragged one"] when released from the restraint of an imposed authority, nor the utter destructiveness to be expected from the mass of this population. They have never been schooled in citizenship nor have they learned even the rudiments of civil responsibility. The only government they have known was that of the patrón imposed from above — mild and benevolent, to be sure, so long as they were completely submissive, but merciless if they undertook to assert even a measure of independence, either individually or *en masse*. No better school for radicals could be found than the Chile of the hacienda régime. The radical in politics is as much a product of the social organization in Chile and of the agrarian system which underlies it as is the aristocrat. He is just what might be expected from the training he has received. When emancipated economically from the hacienda, he joined neither of the historic parties (Liberal and Conservative) but swung far to the left and embraced the most radical doctrines. It was this element of the population that added its new-found strength to that of the liberals and the doctrinaire radicals and made a formidable party of opposition [i.e., the Liberal Alliance of 1920].[64]

This quotation implies an awareness of a superior-inferior relationship between *hacendado* and *inquilino* and the underdeveloped character of a peasant labor force which had learned only to obey. McBride also sensed the emotional origins of the problems these workers experienced when they were suddenly liberated by the pull of industry, found they could not understand or cope with the more adult world

[64]George M. McBride, *Chile: Land and Society* (New York: American Geographical Society, 1936), p. 211.

115

which confronted them in the cities and mining camps, and yet could not return to the rural *patrón* whose autocracy they now resented. Negative, violent, rebellious philosophies fitted their feelings. Their low cultural level made it impossible for them to appreciate the intellectual content and subtleties of anarchism, socialism, and communism.

Perhaps one of the greatest initial liberating experiences at work in this situation was the War of the Pacific. Thousands of soldiers and sailors were recruited from the countryside and their experience in and contribution to a successful war gave them a sense of ego and worth they would otherwise never have known and which they could not now sacrifice. After the war, they congregated in the cities and towns or went north to the nitrate *pampa*. For thousands of others, perhaps the offspring of *inquilinos*, a new life in industry was itself the primary liberating force. Many were awakened by the greater formal education available to them in the new public schools established after 1913.

VIII

Some legislative background is in order before going on, in the next two chapters, to the role of the intellectuals in the development of the Conservative and Liberal Alliance labor relations proposals. There were already a few, though relatively insignificant, legislative and other governmental achievements in the labor and social fields before the Conservatives presented the first comprehensive proposal in 1919. The passage of major legislation was in a limited sense, therefore, what one would have sooner or later expected, given several decades of congressional debate and the adoption of piecemeal reforms. Beginning in 1884, popular savings funds were set up in major urban communities, and in 1902 a law was passed regulating the sale of alcoholic beverages. In 1906 the first blue-collar housing law was adopted, and the following year Sunday was legally proclaimed a day of rest. Other laws required employers to provide chairs for white-collar employees in commercial establishments (1915), made employers liable for work accidents (1916), and stipulated that nurseries be provided for all enterprises employing more than fifty women workers (1917). Perhaps the most significant legal innovation in this period was a voluntary conciliation system which the Minister of the Interior decreed into existence in 1917. It was used with some degree of success in government efforts to resolve postwar strikes.

In addition to the above laws for the improvement of working and living conditions and labor relations (which were not, by the way, effectively enforced), the government also set up a Labor Office in the Ministry of Industry and Public Works (1907). Its job was to collect and publish statistics on the labor force, manpower requirements, wages and salaries, accidents, hours of work, and housing rentals. This was considered a service needed by both employers and the government and also a reliable source of information for the development of legislation. The Labor Office was handicapped from the start by a small budget, a small and untrained staff, and lack of cooperation from industry, but it did, nevertheless, manage to publish a bulletin of mixed quality on an irregular basis. Its contribution was that it developed, in the person of its director, a "labor expert" within the government who could be called upon in an emergency. This advantage was, as we shall see, fully exploited by President Alessandri in 1921.

As one might expect, the machinery of government came to reflect the new importance of the social question in more ways than the creation of the Labor Office. In 1906 the Chamber of Deputies set up a special Committee on Social Legislation, and after six years of continuous existence it was made a permanent standing committee. The Senate did not set up a special Committee on Social Legislation until 1920, and it continued to function as a special body for years before acquiring the status of a standing committee. The President of the Republic also named special committees in 1904, 1913, and 1919 to study and report on working conditions in the nitrate zone of the north, and each of these excursions resulted in the drafting of labor bills. None of them was, however, seriously backed by the Administration and none became law. Many individual members of the Congress also drafted and introduced labor bills, dealing primarily with working conditions rather than with labor relations, but only a few, which we have already identified, were debated and passed. The others dealt with such matters as the regulation of women and child labor, company stores, payment in cash rather than in tokens, minimum wages, and the eight-hour day. No union or strike bills were proposed in the period before 1919.

While there was a paucity of legislation and an incomplete and scattered number of labor bills, an intellectual ferment of considerable momentum, favorably disposed toward broad legislative treatment of social problems, had taken hold of university law professors and students and intellectuals in politics, business, and the journalistic field. In his admirable, well-documented study of *Chile and the United States, 1880–1962,* Pike has noted that "scarcely a reputable Chilean writer failed to indicate his awareness of the social problem that was

117

becoming increasingly acute during the parliamentary period." While it is true, as he concludes, that this literature failed "to stimulate amelioration of the conditions described,"[65] it was probably of some importance in the passage of the laws noted above. Moreover, and this is one of the themes of this study, the writings and political initiative of some intellectuals were amply reflected in the legal industrial relations system adopted in 1924.

The first intellectual voice to be raised on the social question actually anticipated the outpouring of the early 1900's by more than fifteen years. In 1884 Augusto Orrego Luco wrote a series of five articles on "La Cuestión Social en Chile" for *La Patria* of Valparaíso. Although in the light of later thinking on the subject his understanding of the sources of the social question appears naïve, his solutions included raising wages, improving health and sanitation, and changing the direct tax structure which, he said, unjustly burdened small shops and the working man. He warned that, if the social question were not given urgent attention, it could later on "require solutions of a harsh and violent character."[66]

Orrego Luco was one of those solitary figures of history who seem to appear ahead of their time and go unnoticed, perhaps for decades, before they are accorded some recognition. He won his due just five years ago when his articles were republished in the *Anales de la Universidad de Chile*.

The intellectuals who followed Orrego Luco in reflecting on the social question tended to fall into two camps, the aristocratic-Catholic élite and the middle-class élite. Each group was indispensable in the genesis of the labor proposals of the Conservative party and the Liberal Alliance.

[65]Pp. 103–104.

[66]Augusto Orrego Luco, "La Cuestión Social en Chile," a series of five articles originally published in *La Patria* of Valparaíso in 1884 and reproduced in *Anales de la Universidad de Chile*, vol. 119, Primero y segundo trimestres de 1961, nos. 121 y 122, pp. 43–55.

CHAPTER 5

The Conservative Project

and the Intellectuals

SEVEN Conservative party senators introduced a labor bill into the Senate on June 2, 1919. It consisted of three short titles and thirty-four articles dealing with working conditions, the legal union, and collective conflicts. This bill was the first major piece of proposed labor legislation to come before the Congress with the official backing of an entire party, and most of it eventually became law. Immediate concern in this chapter is first to describe the bill and then to investigate its intellectual origins. The latter will include a statement of its underlying philosophy and an evaluation of the part intellectuals played in the actual legislative development of the bill itself.

I

In essence the bill called for the improvement of working conditions, the establishment of the industrial or plant union (*sindicato industrial* or *sindicato de empresa*) for blue-collar workers, and the compulsory conciliation and arbitration of collective labor disputes. The first title on working conditions covered maximum hours, minimum wages, the form and place of wage payment, and women and child labor. It proposed a workweek of forty-eight hours and additional pay for any additional hours worked. A minimum wage, defined as "that necessary to sustain life," was prescribed and was to be fixed by zones in accordance with the special conditions to be found in each zone. Wage payment in tokens, script, or merchandise was prohibited and the act of wage payment could not take place in stores, canteens, or taverns. Free trade was declared in nitrate and other mining areas (an apparent move

119

against the monopoly position of the company store), and mining employers were given the authority to prohibit the sale of liquors, playing cards, and lottery tickets (but not wine).

Humane standards for the government of women and child labor, equal to or in advance of those found in more highly industrialized countries, were suggested. Children below twelve years of age were prohibited from working, night work and work in dangerous and unhealthful occupations were eliminated or closely regulated, provision was made for schooling minors, and expectant mothers were allowed forty days leave (without pay).

The Conservatives proposed in the second title of their bill that a legal union constitute all blue-collar workers above sixteen years of age in any manufacturing, mining, or transport establishment with more than twenty-five operatives. These unions would be created by the employer who was to register the names of all union members within thirty days after the effective date of the law. Unions so created were to bear the name of their plant and were to enjoy the rights to negotiate and enforce collective contracts, to represent individual workers, to represent workers collectively in conciliation and arbitration, and to develop a great variety of beneficial and cooperative programs. Each union was to elect a five-member board by secret, cumulative vote for an annual term. Workers with two consecutive years of service in the plant were to have two votes and one additional vote for each additional year of service. The board was to elect a president, a secretary, and a treasurer. Should the union not elect a board, or should the board not elect its officers, the board positions were to be filled by the five senior members of the plant. The union could pay its board members in whatever manner it might agree to by majority vote.

Unions were to derive part of their income from the employer who was to turn over to them annually a sum of up to 10 percent of his worker payroll, profits permitting and in the absence of any other profit-sharing arrangement voluntarily arrived at. Workers could by majority vote divide among themselves 50 percent of any monies so received, leaving 50 percent for the union itself. Union funds (dues, fines, interest, and employer contributions) were to be deposited in the nearest branch of the National Savings Bank and only the president and secretary of the union board, acting together, could withdraw them and only for purposes specified in the law. Financial transactions were to be made public from day to day in an appropriate place within the plant and were subject to "whatever other control measures good order might require."

In title three compulsory conciliation was prescribed and, in the event agreement was not reached at this stage, either party by simple request was permitted to take the dispute to arbitration. In the absence of such a request, the Conservative proposal recognized the possibility of a legal strike if voted by a majority of the workers in the plant. An arbitration award would, however, be binding and any worker who did not accept the award would have to leave the enterprise "without dismissal pay and losing all the advantages that organization brings him," namely a share of company profits. The employer could be fined for refusing to accept the award, but if he felt the award economically prejudicial to his operations, he could legally ignore it so long as he declared a lockout.

The Conservative bill allowed the President of the Republic to dissolve a legal union for violating the labor law or disturbing public order or engaging in activities contrary to the right to work. It said nothing about national unions or any form of union organization other than the local industrial or plant union.[1]

II

Why did the Conservative party produce a labor bill in 1919? What dislocations in society did they seek to remedy? Why did they feel socially secure in encouraging unions and such practices as conciliation and arbitration? The party itself never placed the labor bill within a larger system of thought, and one can imagine that individual members of the aristocratic-Catholic élite who accepted all or part of the bill did so for reasons which varied both in number and complexity. However, Catholic intellectuals had been concerned with the social question in Chile and had been explaining it and seeking solutions to it in terms of their own religious theology for many years before 1919. Interpreting the social question to their class as well as formulating a Catholic position with regard to its solution was certainly their first, although not their only or even most important, contribution. This was a task which only the intellectuals could perform, and their performance of it was a service both to their contemporaries, who needed an articulate view, and to later generations who sought, and still seek, a greater understanding of the deeper logic and intent of the Chilean labor code.

[1]Senado, *Boletín de las Sesiones Ordinarias en 1919*, pp. 42–46.

The intellectuals who elaborated the aristocratic-Catholic position on the social question in Chile took their inspiration from the doctrines of Christianity and especially from the encyclicals of Pope Leo XIII. They had one leader-theoretician, Juan Enrique Concha, who stood far above all the others in the depth of his analysis and in his perseverance through many years in seeking legislation and Catholic social action in the labor field. In 1898 Concha submitted to the Faculty of Law of the University of Chile the first thesis in the country on labor. Entitled *Worker Questions,* it offered an intellectually respectable and nearly complete system of social thought. Concha became a professor at the Catholic University and, after years of experience and a rounding-out and sharpening of his views, he reduced his fourteen "lessons" on the social question to writing and published them as a book under the title *Lectures on Social Economy.* Concha was a member of the National Society of Manufacturers, served briefly (1903–1905) as an officer of that organization, was active in the Conservative party for many years and became a member of its national executive committee, was elected to a Senate seat in 1919, and served on the Joint Committee for Social Legislation.

Many books were written in the pattern of Concha's pioneer effort. In 1904 Javier Diaz Lira contributed *Observations on the Social Question in Chile* and Marcos Gutiérrez Martínez wrote *The Worker Question and Property Rights.* Later came Eduardo Pantaleon Fontecilla's *Legislative and Political Reform and Our Social Question* (1907), Julio Vial Infante's *Labor Chambers* (1909), and in 1918 Bartolomé Palacios S., a political writer, added *The Conservative Party and the Radical Party Face to Face,* the only non-thesis in the list.

The Concha school of Christian democracy traced the origins of the social question to a breakdown of morality, and its solutions principally to the teachings of Christ as interpreted by the Roman Catholic Church. By the end of the nineteenth century, after more than thirty years of concern and study, the Church had taken a written position on the social question. This position was in large part a reaction to the philosophy of socialism presented by Marx in *Das Kapital.* Although Pope Leo XIII declared war on socialism very early in his reign and devoted much of his time thereafter to a rethinking of the social tenets of Catholicism, a synthesis of his views did not appear until 1891 in the famous encyclical, *Rerum Novarum.* Later, he refined and completed his definition of the Church's position on the social question.

Juan Enrique Concha and other Chileans analyzed labor-employer relationships in their country from the broad vista of morality and with a kind of cataclysmic philosophy of the downfall of modern industrial man, support for which they found in contemporary Chilean literature and in papal doctrine. To them the matter was not essentially an economic one whose solution, reduced to its simplest terms, was an increase in worker income. Neither was it essentially a question of legal right or justice which could be resolved by legislation or court decision. It was, as Concha explained, "...fundamentally a psychological, moral, and religious question, whose solution will be found, the world willing, only in the teaching of Christ, practiced by the individual and respected and supported by the State and by laws."[2]

The "natural order" of unity and harmony between unequal and conflicting interests had broken down in Chile. While the more obvious signs of trouble were strikes, demonstrations, and similar outbreaks, which arose in a limited field of economic activity and involved specific businessmen and groups of workers, the social question had much larger, more subtle, and more portentous dimensions. It was an attitude which pitted labor against the entire capitalist class, and then went yet another step and brought the proletariat into political conflict with the oligarchy. In Chile the Democratic party and, even more recently, the Socialist Workers' party were the political currents which had surfaced and, in the name of the proletariat, were contesting municipal and congressional elections in an effort to replace the existing leadership. When popular movements begin "to protest against the regimen of modern industry and to murmur about social injustices, abuses of the rich, and about lack of knowledge of any rights of the proletariat, we can then say...that we are in the presence of the Social Question."[3]

What had produced this critical state of affairs in Chile? What forces had changed the attitude of the working class from one of contentedness with their lot and deference toward their superiors to one of discontent and belligerency? What were the failings of the upper classes which contributed to the moral crisis?

With respect to the workers, three forces had recently and powerfully begun to affect their attitudes and habits. They were, first, the victims of antireligious propaganda in the public schools, the press, and the political arena. The consequent loss of religion was the greatest single cause of their change in outlook. Anticlericalism, the lay

[2]Concha, *Conferencias,* p. 221.
[3]*Ibid.,* pp. 127–128.

school, the Radical party were responsible. Second, the workers had been influenced by socialistic propaganda, whose principal political party source in Chile was disguised under the name "Democratic." Finally, the leading classes had not only forgotten but had completely abandoned the proletariat and no longer were concerned about their needs or their legitimate rights. Loss of religion took away the workers' attitude of resignation, democratic-socialist ideas generated pride, and the aloofness of the upper classes betokened an end of their affection and respect for the proletariat who in turn felt alone and unwanted.

The combined effect of these forces was to change the worker's attitude toward his job and his wage. In the past, he accepted work at the pay he was offered by a loving *patrón;* now he asked for more and more, always thought his pay low and unjust, and never considered the employer's financial condition.

What was the evidence of a moral downfall from the side of the upper classes? A prior question which troubled Concha and conditioned his response to the one just posed concerned the size and nature of the gulf between the ruling class and the "low class." The differences between the two classes in Chile were, he thought, extraordinarily great. Even visiting European professors, well acquainted with class divisions in their own countries, noted that Chile was a real aristocratic republic whose upper class dominated society through its learning, its wealth, and even its blood (though not in the legal sense of primogeniture, for example, which was abolished in Chile in the nineteenth century). The stark division of classes was observable everywhere — in the distribution of property, the lack of public schools, in the habits and way of living of the common people, in material things such as housing, and in the realm of politics and public life where the exercise of the suffrage and representation in the Congress both worked to the advantage of the élite and the perpetuation of their rulership.

With particular respect to the distribution of agricultural land, Concha said that less than 2 percent of the population owned all the farm acreage in the country. The inevitable result was the predominance of property owners over their workers "since the latter in reality have no ideas and are neither educated to have them nor enjoy the independence necessary to oppose the will of the *patrón.*"[4] In the past, farm workers simply voted as their *patrones* told them to. Now they were slowly awakening, but their votes could still be bought. Political power depended on money, and the Liberals and Conservatives vied

⁴*Ibid.,* pp. 108–111.

for the rural vote on this basis. While class structure was not therefore feudal, in the sense that special privileges and distinctions were conceded by law, there existed nevertheless a sharp separation of the rulers from the ruled. In Chile there was a *pueblo,* a common people, but there was no democracy.

In facing the role of the upper class in this system and their contribution to the social question, Concha was outwardly more concerned at the personal or attitudinal level than at the societal or structural level. The indisputable fact of extreme class differences in wealth and power did not buttress an argument for a social revolution but rather, as Concha saw it, imposed an even greater moral obligation on the wealthy and powerful to behave like Christians in their stewardship of society. To Concha, it was more a question of propriety and behavior, ethics or morality, than of changing the divine plan, although, as we shall see further on, he was not unwilling even to tinker with that.

There was a potent ruling class, then, and in the Catholic view, as interpreted by Concha, this was only the result of the working out of nature. The natural plan also included, however, a compassionate relationship between those at the top and those at the bottom, and this was the missing factor in the attitude assumed by the upper class in Chile toward the workers. That class was very charitable in dealing with abject misery and misfortune, but had developed no conscience whatever of the "social duty of Wealth" toward the thousands of poor who worked for a living. They made no contacts with the workers, were not interested in their economic problems. They even looked with disdain upon the study of social problems because they feared that social works on a large scale might awaken the proletariat and produce in them a dangerous "single-mindedness of thought." They preferred to believe that the *pueblo* was the same as it had always been.

At the level of the employers, Concha thought that Europeans treated their workers and domestic help with more respect and concern for their personal dignity than did Chileans. In Chile industrialists were obsessed with a get-rich-quick attitude which hindered the development of a social conscience and, together with their individualist economics, made then indifferent to the condition of their workers.

There was, therefore, real indolence on the part of the ruling class with regard to the commonweal. When social classes lived in permanent physical and spiritual isolation as they did in Chile, it was only natural that indifference, so akin to egotism, should possess those on top and that envy, so akin to hate, should consume those at the bottom. This was the heart of the social question.

What were the solutions? They fell into three major categories: social and industrial Stewardship *(Patronato)*; religious education; and social legislation. Only Juan Enrique Concha presented a meaningful analysis of the first, and his work, admirably done and perhaps an important contribution to the wider field of Catholic social thought, applied the teachings of the Church and its great theologians to the "social order of Wealth" and the social question in Chile. Although the goods of the earth were given to man in common, both private property and the accumulation of wealth by those favored in ability and industry were licit. A natural inequality of wealth distribution and a hierarchy of classes were to be expected, and indeed existed everywhere. Study of this phenomenon was called "Social Economy," a kind of divine science of the "social order of Wealth."

Christian social economy confirmed the obligation of the rich to distribute superfluous income among the needy and to perform certain social duties for the benefit of the less fortunate. There were only two motives for giving: simple justice in cases of extreme need, charity in all others.

The social obligations of wealth were not uniform but depended on whether wealth was anonymous or industrial. "Anonymous Wealth" came from interest alone and involved no physical participation in economic endeavor. "Industrial Wealth," on the other hand, came from profits in agriculture, mining, manufacturing, and commerce and was accumulated by active businessmen. The obligation to give superfluous income rested primarily upon the anonymous rich, who also had more time to practice "social Stewardship." In Chile, not just a handful but thousands of these rich should visit shops and factories and the shacks in which the poor lived to see how "they breathe, how they dress, how they sleep, and how they eat." The rich should talk with them, listen to their complaints, help them with their schools, circles, and mutual benefit societies, "make them see the absurdity of socialist utopias, and disabuse them of the false idea of economic equality by showing them there is a providential order which they must respect." It was not so much the gift of money that was needed as it was personal charity, the sacrifice of comforts, and the donation of time, thought, and learning. If the rich didn't go to the people, they would be leaving the field to the subversive elements who were sowing discontent and talking against the natural order of wealth in society. "The great duty of anonymous Wealth," concluded Concha, "is to personally associate with Poverty." Such a noble and tender display of concern "by the superior class for the inferior class" would convince the worker that a class struggle does not exist. The wealthy would be coming to him. He would learn once again to respect the social hierarchy. There would still be antipathy and perhaps even hate toward the individual employer, but collective antagonism of the working class toward general wealth would cease.

The primary obligation of "Industrial Wealth" was the payment of a "just wage." If the going wage *(salario corriente)* was not enough, in Pope Leo's words, "to sustain a frugal worker of good habits," then it should be supplemented by what Le Play called "the employer subsidy." The subsidy could be in specie or services, depending upon the circumstances of need, and should vary in amount depending upon the size of the worker's family. Should there be a conflict between payment of the subsidy and maintenance of the firm's liquidity, however, sound financial principles should rule.

Chilean employers had neglected the obligations "which they have as employers for their dependents." They practiced the immoral and anti-Christian principles of economic individualism developed by Adam Smith and Juan Bautista Say. Labor was not a commodity and the employer should not demand anything of his workers which violated their rights as human beings. Above all, the employer should keep uppermost in his mind "everything that attaches to his title of *Patrón.*" That word, meaning "of the father" *(de padre),* implicitly revealed the employer's responsibility to care for his workers.

There was no absolute freedom for children or women to labor in factories or for workers to suffer injuries on the job without obligation on the employer's part. Such an attitude was neither socialistic nor antiscientific. It was not socialistic for, if it were, Pope Leo would be the greatest socialist of all time. It was not antiscientific for Le Play, Perin, Dunoyer, and Stourm all taught that freedom alone was not enough; it was also necessary to reestablish "the economic precepts of the decalogue and, in the matter of relations between employers and workers, it was the hour to reconstitute Christian Stewardship." Only employers, and not laws, added Concha, could produce capital-labor harmony and create ties of affection and respect between "he who commands and he who obeys."[5]

Although religious instruction was the second important category of solutions to the social question, the conservative intellectuals spent little time writing about it. The issue of lay versus religious education

---

[5]The foregoing material on Catholic Stewardship comes from Concha's thesis and from his book of lectures, both of which have already been cited.

was debated and decided in 1913. A public school system was created, but private institutions were granted equal access to government financial support. In the process, however, the Church lost the children of the working class. Concha and others cried out against "atheistic" teaching disguised as "neutral, lay or scientific" and pled for a return to religious education, but they mainly shifted ground and emphasized a closer relationship with adult workers and the personal religious instruction inherent in the concept of social Stewardship.[6]

The followers of Concha believed that, in addition to social Stewardship and religious instruction, legislation had a role to play in the solution of the social question. Some of them thought this role a slight one, that social laws were essentially palliatives, and that countries with such laws still also had the social question. Yet unlike nineteenth century liberals who were still plentiful in Chile, they gave the state a supporting role in their redemptive scheme. Others, while holding to a moral emphasis, assigned a high priority to positive labor laws.

In any labor contract, the Catholic argument began, two matters stand out: one is the work done or the service rendered, the other is the worker himself. The first is material, the second moral. The labor contract clauses of the Civil Code were brief and did not protect the worker. They came from the slavery provisions of Roman law and from the Napoleonic Code which reflected the intransigent individualism of Rousseau. The Civil Code thus benefited the rich and contained little for the poor and the workers.

The status of workers before the law had to be changed because, until all employers learned to run their businesses like Christians, some outside force had to keep the heartless ones in line. Only the state could harmonize the contrary forces that operated within it. Social legislation was, therefore, needed to limit the rights and correct the abuses of selfish industrial Wealth and to protect the weak who would be oppressed by complete liberty. The state was a greater father who could teach wayward employers their duty toward their workers so that peace, order, and harmony could reign in the workplace, in industry, and in society.

Stewardship, religious education, and social legislation were the triumvirate solution of the Catholic intellectuals to the social question. Concha referred to members of his school as "social Catholics" and to

---

[6]See Concha, *Conferencias*, pp. 175–176; Marcos Gutiérrez Martínez, *La cuestión obrera i el derecho de propiedad* (Santiago: Imprenta Barcelona, 1904); and Partido Conservado, *La convención conservadora de 1895* (Santiago, 1895), pp. 24–35.

their program as "social Catholicism — the action of those imbued with the social and economic spirit of the Gospel."[7] Bartolomé Palacios S. used the term "CHRISTIAN DEMOCRACY," to distinguish the social reform Catholics from the socialists and from those conservatives who still believed in an exaggerated individualism.[8]

Social Catholicism, as explained above, posited a modern-day downfall of the classes in Chile. Although cynical, the philosophy as stated thus far was not fatalistic for it also posited redemption — in the sense of restoring the old order and its values. At this point of redemption, an important distinction is made in the roles of the workers, the state, and employers. Workers could apparently do little for themselves. The state could do something for the minority of un-Christian employers. The majority of good employers were the crucial element. They could redeem themselves and society as well by taking Christian care of their workers. They were not only obligated morally so to conduct their affairs (because of their superior station in life), however, but had to do so because workers were morally and physically incapable of taking the best care of themselves. Supporting evidence for this view is direct, as well as derived from Concha's emphasis upon the greater obligations of employers.

To illustrate the point of worker inferiority, Concha traced many cases of an apparently inadequate living standard not to low wages but rather to the consumption of a good wage in "pernicious drinking" and other immoralities. "Our people," he wrote, "are frankly drunken and alcoholism makes them quarrelsome and cruel"; they were, in addition, "unstable, uneconomical, wanderers by inheritance and choice with a broken and disorganized family life, proud and manly by race but poor workers."[9] Employers "are tangible beings, perfectly responsible, while workers and unions are not." The inferior class, those who obey, cannot rear responsible leaders on a national scale. The national union leaders already present in the country were professional agitators and parisites who were misleading and taking advantage of the workers.[10]

Agreeing with Concha, and even going beyond him in the sweeping nature of his view of worker immorality, was Javier Diaz Lira who blamed all the poverty and misery of the "low classes" on "the enor-

[7]Concha, *Conferencias*, p. 216.

[8]Bartolomé Palacios S., *El partido conservador y el partido radical frente a frente* (Santiago, 1918), pp. 39–52.

[9]Concha, *Conferencias*, pp. 154–155, 160.

[10]Senado, *Boletin de las Sesiones Extraordinarias en 1920–1921*, I, p. 346–349.

129

mous development of their vices" and the lack of moral habits like foresight and frugality.[11]

Not all Catholic writers were so harsh in judging the moral qualities of the working class. Eduardo Pantaleon Fontecilla, for example, pointed out that virtue required the attainment of a certain level of material well-being, and he did not believe Chilean workers had yet reached that level. Those who looked at the workers' economic plight partly or wholly as punishment for their own immorality were, he thought, mistaken.[12]

Nevertheless, the Concha view prevailed and is recognizable as the underlying spirit of the Conservative party labor bill. It was not only a natural derivation from his total system of thought but Concha found that it also fitted the antiworking class prejudices of narrow men in public and private life. While he may personally have preferred keeping a positive emphasis on employer responsibilities to developing a negative one on worker shortcomings (because of his deep and warm sympathy for the workers despite the grave faults he saw in them), in the Senate Concha was drawn toward a negative criticism of workers, their leaders, and their unions. This did not change the basic conception of his system of thought which, in any event, could only result in a labor relations system weighted heavily in favor of employer control. At the same time, however, it points up the important probability that some supporters of the Catholic view on the social question and labor legislation in reality supported only a part of this view; namely, that workers should be controlled by employers. Understandably, but to his discredit, Concha played into their hands.

Before going on to the legislative origins of the Conservative bill, we need to see the synthesis of its major parts with the tenets of social Catholicism. Improvement of working conditions and more humane and economically just treatment of working men, women, and children were derived from the employer's obligation, as father, to care for his workers. If he acted voluntarily, the obligation was moral; if he failed to act of his own will, the obligation, as in the case of the Conservative bill, became legislative.

The plant union and profit sharing came both from the employer's obligation to care for his workers and from the moral and character deficiencies of Chilean workers themselves. On the one hand, the em-

[11]Javier Díaz Lira, *Observaciones sobre la cuestión social en Chile* (Santiago: Imprenta Chile, 1904).

[12]Pantaleon, *La reforma legislativa y política y nuestra cuestión social,* pp. 28–29.

ployer was expected to set up an organization which would give him effective control of the "enterprise family" and encourage efficiency. He was also obliged to share enterprise earnings with those who helped produce them. On the other hand, the plant union was the lesser of union evils. Since workers could not govern themselves responsibly and tended to become the dupes of agitators, it followed that national unions and national union centers would maximize the danger from this source. A system of unconnected plant unions, dependent in the first and last analysis upon the *patrón*, would minimize this danger. Their officers would be the loyal older workers who had the largest number of votes and could use them, in a cumulative voting system, to elect one another. A share of the profits, in turn, gave employers additional leverage in dealing with union irresponsibles. If one member or the entire union refused a wage offer, profits could be withheld.

Finally, compulsory conciliation and arbitration at the request of either party would, in practice, assure greater equity in labor-employer relations by forcing irresponsible workers to come to an agreement. Such compulsion would operate upon and primarily affect the workers and their leaders. A voluntary system was out of the question because, while employers could exercise freedom responsibly, workers would respond only to a system of authority coupled with rewards and punishments. Forfeiture of a share of profits would be sufficient penalty to assure worker acceptance of awards. In addition, a compulsory dispute settlement procedure would cut the ground from under the agitators.

III

Juan Enrique Concha was, as we have seen, the outstanding Catholic intellectual authority on the social question. He was also, as we shall now see, the key figure within the Conservative party in the development and actual drafting of the 1919 labor bill.

Concha was an active member of the Conservative party from his youth and was elected to the Chamber of Deputies on the Conservative ticket around 1907. He served on the Chamber's special committee on labor and in that capacity fought constantly for labor and social reform measures. By 1918 he had become a vice-president of his party.

It has not been possible to reconstruct completely the historical development of the Conservative party's stand on the social question up to 1919 or to assess definitively Concha's influence in its evolution. Published party records are available only for the conventions of 1895 and 1918, although others may have been held in the intervening years.[13] At the earlier convention, the party adopted a platform which included a section entitled "Material, Economic, and Moral Improvement of the Working Class" and one delegate, by invitation of the party leadership, gave an address on the "Social Question" which showed an acute awareness of, and sympathy for, the content of *Rerum Novarum*.[14]

While the party's platform is of some importance and while Concha as a party member and Deputy certainly kept the social question alive as an issue of party policy, it is unquestionably more significant that in 1919 the Conservative party drafted a specific labor bill for presentation to the Congress and that Concha was the man of that hour. Most of the half dozen or so major political parties took a stand on the social question in the opening two decades of the century, but only two major labor bills (i.e., the Conservative and Liberal Alliance projects) were ever introduced into the Congress. What is more, only a portion of the memberships of the parties sponsoring these two bills actually stood behind them, a matter to be discussed in some detail later. The point to be made here is that the ranks thinned as commitment became more precise and took on a more personal meaning; those who remained in the fight for legislation were the leaders, and the intellectuals among them are the ones in whom we are most interested.

Two things about the 1918 convention of the Conservative party are outstanding. The first is that there was a sense of urgency among some of the delegates that the party should go beyond platform-type pronouncements on the social question and even beyond support for the generally accepted pieces of social legislation such as worker housing, accident bills, and Sunday rest. The party should commit itself on labor relations matters such as unions and collective bargaining, and then draw up bills and stand behind them in the Congress. The second outstanding aspect of the convention is that the party had the leadership capital available, in the person of Juan Enrique Concha, with which to exploit this unique situation. Why the Conservatives were willing to alter their course so dramatically in 1918 is pertinent to this study and we will examine this question at the appropriate time.

The reform atmosphere of the convention is indicated partly by the resolutions presented. Out of a total of 165 resolutions, 21 dealt with social and labor matters. Three of the latter proposed arbitration tri-

[13]For example, Guillermo Feliú Cruz refers to a 1901 convention of the party and briefly describes its platform on the social question. See his *1891–1924, Chile visto a través de Augustín Ross, ensayo de interpretación* (Santiago: Imprenta Pino, 1950), pp. 114–116.

[14]Partido Conservador, *La convención conservadora de 1895*, pp. 24–35, 49–50.

bunals, retirement and pension funds, and the written labor contract, respectively. Two others suggested that the convention name a special committee to study labor problems and projects.[15]

Concha was a member of the Platform Committee of the convention and was in charge of its "Social Action" content. He was also the convention's principal speaker on the social question. He took the initiative in both of these roles and urged the convention to accept, sincerely and frankly, the need for "ample and prudent social legislation." Because the Conservatives recognized natural inequality among men but also the duty of the strong to protect the weak, they had to demand state action to help fulfill their program.

Concha, therefore, asked the convention to endorse legislation on the following topics: protection of working women and children, accident and health standards for factories and shops, dismissal pay, a minimum just wage, limitation of working hours, permanent conciliation and arbitration courts, and "craft or blue-collar unions whose objectives would be to perfect the knowledge and improve the economic conditions of their members." Finally, and most important, he asked the convention to approve the designation of a "High Committee" of the party to study labor and laboring conditions in the various industries of the country and the situation of the middle class. This High Committee should report to a special assembly of the party to be held in Santiago in 1919 and its report should include "not only the results of its observations but also the legal measures and measures of a private nature" which the party ought to adopt.[16]

The convention voted favorably on both the "Social Action" platform and the High Committee, and the executive board of the party thereupon set about forming the committee. Party records indicate that the committee was named and began to meet by the end of the year. It consisted of at least nine members, among whom were representatives of industry, youth, probably labor, and others who came from an "at-large" category. One of the committeemen was Pedro Belisario Galvez, a journalist and newspaper director who was one of the first in Chile to write favorably on the social question from a Catholic

[15]"Convención Conservadora, 1918, resultado de la votación de las indicaciones propuestas en la Convención," Cartas, Santiago, 1918, Archivo del Partido Conservador.

[16]Partido Conservador, *Convención del partido conservador de 1918, actas,* Santiago, 1918, pp. 73–91, 280–284.

point of view.[17] Another, who presided over the meetings, was Juan Enrique Concha.[18]

Although the committee had a secretary, no minutes are known to be in existence and, probably for reasons of political strategy against party rivals, the committee released no news to the press. All we know is that the Conservative labor bill was written, approved by the party, and delivered to the secretariat of the Senate on May 20, 1919. At the time *El Mercurio* attributed to Concha "an important part" in drafting the bill.[19] Two years later the Conservative party stated flatly that Concha was its author.[20]

IV

What has been said thus far demonstrates that, as a politician, Concha engineered the party's commitment to a major labor bill in 1918 and 1919. But what was his contribution as an intellectual and what perhaps were the contributions of other Catholic writers to the specific content of the three titles of the bill? These are very difficult questions, for, in the nature of the media through which ideas are transferred, rarely can the truth be found in self-evident form. One cannot be sure, for example, of a causal relationship between the expression of the same idea at two different points in time. There are the added complications of the piecemeal development of an idea or its sudden crystallization. Moreover, in the case at hand there was nothing to prevent a Catholic writer from borrowing, in non-doctrinal areas, from intellectuals of the middle-class élite; they could even have borrowed from non-intellectuals among politicians, businessmen, or *latifundistas*. The pattern of idea transfer can thus be exceedingly intricate and complex and all that can be done here is to point to some interesting parallels between the content of the Conservative bill and earlier written records.

It should be further understood that the problem is not one of tracing ideas, like plant unionism or compulsory arbitration, to their original sources. This would take us abroad, to Europe principally, in all cases. In other words, the Conservative bill was not original in the

[17]See Ricardo Donoso, *Alessandri, agitador y demoledor* (México: Fondo de Cultura Económica, 1952), vol. 1, pp. 152–153 and Partido Conservador, *Convención del partido conservador de 1921, actas*, p. 298.

[18]See miscellaneous correspondence in Cartas, Santiago, 1918, Archivo del Partido Conservador.

[19]*El Mercurio*, May 21, 1919.

[20]Partido Conservador, *Convención del partido conservador de 1921, actas*, p. 223.

creative sense. It was original, however, in the selective and adaptive sense, in the kinds of ideas that were borrowed and the way they were put together. The problem is, therefore, to try to identify some of the sources within Chile which may have affected the content of the Conservative bill.

The task can be made more meaningful if we address ourselves not to the entire bill but rather to those parts or ideas which most distinguish it from the Liberal Alliance labor project. Many of the features of these two bills are similar, especially in the area of working conditions, and precedents for these features are numerous, not only in scholarly publications in Chile, but also in party platforms and in many individual bills presented to the Congress as early as 1900. In this category are, for example, payment of wages in legal tender, place of wage payment, sale of alcoholic beverages in the work area, conditions of minors and working women, and industrial hygiene. Such features as these in the Conservative bill cannot be ascribed to any single source. They had by 1918 become too much a part of the common political background.

Major points of difference between the two bills are with regard to maximum hours, minimum wages, unions, profit sharing, and conciliation and arbitration. The Conservative bill was less generous in its wage and hour provisions than the Liberal Alliance bill; it provided for compulsory plant unionism and the election of officers by cumulative vote, while the Liberal Alliance bill provided for voluntary craft unionism and the election of officers on a straight majority basis; the Conservative bill gave greater emphasis to profit sharing and allowed unions as well as individual workers to participate in profit-sharing plans; and, finally, it stipulated compulsory conciliation and arbitration at the request of either party, while the Liberal Alliance bill called for voluntary conciliation and voluntary arbitration. Where within the aristocratic-Catholic élite did the distinguishing features of the Conservative bill come from?

In its wage and hour provisions, the Conservative bill established the minimum wage for "workers who have agreed to remuneration in the use of land and pasture."[21] In other words it applied only to peasants and, even in this instance, was perhaps not intended to involve a minimum transaction in legal tender but rather may have been considered as a minimum concession of tillable land and animal pasture.

[21]Cámara de Senadores, *Boletín de las Sesiones Ordinarias en 1919,* "Proyecto de Ley," Título I, Artículo 8, pp. 42–46.

If this is true, the provision could better be described as a land redistribution scheme than as a minimum-wage guarantee. Concha's concern about the high concentration of land ownership could have led him to espouse such a measure. In any case, it is clear that the provision recognized only a limited application of the language of the minimum wage.

The maximum hours provisions of the bill were drawn as loosely as those dealing with wages. Forty-eight hours were first indicated as the weekly "duration" of "ordinary" work. Workers were allowed to "stipulate" longer hours, up to twelve a day, if they were paid "supplementary" wages. In "fortuitous" cases, even more than twelve hours could be worked "for an agreed upon remuneration." These are gaping loopholes and would seem to reveal lack of real conviction on the basic social and economic principles of a limited workweek.

There is no precise language in the writings of the intellectuals which antedates and is similar to the wage and hour provisions of the Conservative bill. At the same time, however, the general position that Concha took in his thesis (1898) on wage and hour legislation shows that, unless he later changed his mind, he was probably in full agreement with the spirit of these provisions and could well have put them in the bill himself. Concha wrote that, while the general idea of labor legislation was not socialistic, the minimum wage and the eight-hour day were socialistic and completely unworkable. "To pretend to fix a determined number of hours for all work," Concha said, "is as absurd as saying that all the stomachs in the world must receive the same amount of food." And again, "how can you fix a minimum daily wage for the same number of hours when there are some workers who do ten times as much in two hours as others do in eight or ten hours?" What the workers needed was neither high wages nor a determined number of work hours, both very relative matters, but rather they needed to work in a spirit of Christian fraternity. On the door of the workshop, at the mouth of the mine, at the gate of the cottage should be placed the inscription, symbolic of this Christian brotherhood, "Love One Another."[22]

On the subject of unionism, it should be pointed out that Concha developed what was very likely the first bill and may also have been the only bill prior to 1919 calling for a system of legal unions. No union bill, not even Concha's, was introduced into the Congress before 1919, however, so there is no question of legislative precedent for the union title of the Conservative bill. Concha's bill was a private one which

[22]Concha, *Cuestiones obreras*, pp. 77–116.

he included in his thesis. It consisted of thirteen articles whose regulatory and control features are quite similar to those of the Conservative bill and the Liberal Alliance project as well.[23]

Unfortunately, the Concha bill of 1898 does not contain even a hint as to the type of union organization he had in mind. The only other Catholic intellectual who wrote on union structure during our period was Eduardo Pantaleon Fontecilla. He mentioned the craft association (asociación profesional) briefly in his thesis and urged that it be given legal protection. His further comments indicate beyond a doubt that he used the word "craft" with full knowledge of its meaning, although there is no evidence in his thesis that he was making a deliberate or conscious choice between the craft form and some other form of union organization.[24]

It is perhaps significant that at the 1918 convention of the Conservative party Concha, in recommending legislation on unions, spoke of craft or worker unions (sindicatos profesionales u obreros). This choice of language could suggest that he had not yet made up his mind on the structural issue and/or that there were two points of view among interested convention delegates. An obrero or worker union can be construed as equivalent to a plant union because, as the Conservative bill later provided, only blue-collar workers (obreros) can belong to the plant union. A craft union, on the other hand, not only groups blue-collar workers by skills but also, in Chile, is the only permissible structure for white-collar workers. Craft or worker could therefore mean craft or plant. This seems a more likely explanation than that the two words were used imprecisely as alternate ways to describe some general unionism.

Plant or industrial unionism was neither prescribed nor recommended in Rerum Novarum, or in any other Catholic Church pronouncement on the social question, as preferable to a craft form of organization. The union clauses of the Conservative bill were not, therefore, inspired directly from the social doctrines of Catholicism. Actually, Pope Leo XIII never used the word "union" at all in the encyclical, Rerum Novarum, but elected a variety of more generic terms such as "association," "society," and "community." Moreover, he referred to associations "of workmen alone, or of workmen and employers together." It has been convincingly argued that the Pope's broad language resulted deliberately from his wish "not to seem to

[23]Ibid., pp. 38–49.
[24]Pantaleon, La reforma legislativa y política y nuestra cuestión social, pp. 48–50.

choose between the many types of organization entered upon by Catholics in the years before the encyclical, ratifying some and rejecting others."[25]

For approximately twenty years before the appearance of *Rerum Novarum,* Catholic writers espoused various types of organization, and each thought his scheme the best application of Christian principles to the work relationship. Some advocated a return to the craft guilds of the Middle Ages, others favored some modern form of corporate or joint worker-employer organization. In the latter case, there were those who preferred to base their scheme upon trades or crafts (Albert de Mun) and those who experimented with Christian factories (Léon Harmel).[26] Alfredo Barros Errázuriz, Professor of Civil Law at the Catholic University and one of the Senators who introduced the Conservative bill, wrote at length on the social question, knew the writings of Albert de Mun, and favored a corporate form of worker organization.[27] It is possible that Concha and others of the aristocratic-Catholic élite knew of these writings and were influenced by them.

The logic of social Catholicism as explained by Concha would appear to have favored the plant union over the craft union as the more appropriate unit for bringing into industry the harmony which, according to Catholic theology, was found everywhere in nature. Every plant had an employer or father but every craft or trade did not; the location of an enterprise was obvious, definite, and visible, while that of a trade might be vague and problematical; the exercise of authority in a system which exalted the employer would be easier and more expeditious in a plant than throughout a trade; finally, the workers needed help from the employer and protection from outside influences, and in both instances his needs could be met best in the physically close and administratively tight environment of a plant relationship.

It is also possible, however, that the Conservative option for an enterprise or plant union structure had a practical as well as an ideological basis. The aristocratic-Catholic élite was primarily a rural élite in control of the vast *latifundia* of the country. Their earliest and most meaningful contact with members of the working class was always in a rural setting — they as cultured, proud, and wealthy *patrones* and their workers as ignorant, unskilled, poor, and defenseless semiserfs.

[25]Jean-Yves Calvez, S. J. and Jacques Perrin, S. J., *The Church and Social Justice* (Chicago: Henry Regnery Company, 1961), pp. 381–383.

[26]*Ibid.,* pp. 403–405.

[27]Alfredo Barros Errázuriz, *El partido conservador* (Santiago: Imprenta Cervantes, 1917), p. 65.

Farms were huge, isolated, and self-sufficient. The only realistic unit was the individual farm. Indeed some members of this class might have found it difficult to comprehend a structure which divided their unlettered workers by trades or crafts; others would have objected to craft unionism on the grounds that it would turn "their" workers, who had always been loyal and obedient, toward outside leaders. Conservative industrialists who were the offspring of aristocratic families could also be expected to see the union problem in terms of their rural conditioning and background. Members of the Conservative High Committee of 1918–1919, other than or perhaps in addition to Concha, might therefore have had definite presumptions in favor of the plant union.

Allowing the union, as well as the individual union member, to receive a share of profits may be a unique Chilean contribution to labor relations. But whether a new or an old social invention at that time, it is logical that the aristocratic-Catholic élite should have given it a prominent place in their labor scheme. For, while they considered profit sharing a greater incentive to individual productive effort, they also looked upon it as an integral part of a general control system over workers. Control is obviously more effective if it can be exercised over the organization as well as over its individual members. By withholding or granting profits, employers could, as Juan Enrique Concha saw it, coerce the union into accepting decisions otherwise unacceptable to it. This did not proceed from a black heart or an evil mind, but was simply part of an internally consistent system for achieving harmony in industry under the moral guidance of the Christian employer.

No Catholic writer appears to have taken up, before the actual writing of the Conservative bill, the question of sharing profits with the union as distinct from its members. An explanation of its origins, beyond the logical one given above, is not, therefore, possible. However, two university students did write at length on the general subject of profit sharing and, even though one of them did not like the idea at all, both provided information and insights useful to anyone seeking to complete an employer-dominated industrial relations system. Rodolfo Marín Carmona (*Wages*, 1909) described profit sharing, with some exaggeration, as "a method invented by employers who do not wish to lose the position they occupy in the modern industrial world." Drawing upon the works of David F. Schloss (*Systems of Industrial Remuneration*) and Sedly Taylor (*Profit Sharing*), he reasoned that profit sharing was intended not only to increase production and profits but also to neutralize unions or prevent their establishment altogether. This was accomplished by making either "company unions" (*sindicatos amarillos,* literally "yellow unions") or no unions at all a condition precedent to the sharing of profits with workers.

Marín Carmona — and the socialists as well, he said — believed profit sharing to be a spoliation of the workers, and he accepted the conclusion, which he attributed to Gide, that it was precisely a means for legitimizing spoliation by causing the despoiled themselves to participate in it. Its practice and popularity were diminishing and this was due, as Gide again explained, to the disfavor with which all paternalistic schemes were beginning to be received. Employers and workers, instead of seeking out closer links, were trying to establish greater mutual independence.[28] Reading this thesis, a Chilean social Catholic would have little difficulty deciding how important profit sharing might be to his way of thinking.

Profit sharing was also a natural or logical complement to the industrial relations system devised by the Chilean aristocratic-Catholic élite. This was pointed out in 1914 by Pablo Sánchez Mira in his thesis also titled *Wages.* A mixed system of remuneration, part in wages and part in profits, appears to have had his unconditional acceptance, and he saw precedent for it in the share-cropping features of the *inquilino* system. The farm owner gave the *inquilino* land, seeds, and implements; in return, the *inquilino* turned over to him a part of the produce. Sánchez Mira realized that this practice was not exactly the same as profit sharing in industry but he thought that the principle, if not the specific form, was the same.[29] It is easy to see how he may have been articulating the views of many Conservatives and how he may have caused others to see for the first time the meaning and the potential of an industrial profit-sharing plan.

Two Catholic writers devoted all or most of their theses to conciliation and arbitration, and both agreed that machinery of this sort would solve social conflict and create the harmony which Leo XIII had said nature required. They also agreed that machinery should be permanent, but neither discussed the question of obligatory versus voluntary systems. However, one of these writers, Julio Vial Infante, seems to take the Belgian system of voluntary industry and labor councils *(Consejos de la Industria y del Trabajo)* as his preferred model and the other, Pantaleon, studied the voluntary institutions of several countries including Belgium, Germany, France, and Italy.[30]

[28]Rodolfo Marín Carmona, *El salario* (Santiago: Imprenta Bellavista, 1909).
[29]Pablo Sánchez Mira, *El salario* (Santiago: Imprenta Chile, 1914).
[30]Pantaleon, *La reforma legislativa y política y nuestra cuestión social,* pp. 53–75; Julio Vial Infante, *Las cámaras del trabajo* (Santiago: Imprenta Bellavista, 1909).

Other writers, whose politics, or ideology is not always self-evident, either stated a cryptic preference for obligatory dispute settlement or discussed, in more or less detail and more or less effectively, the relative merits of voluntary versus obligatory systems. Even though most of these latter writers opted for the voluntary form of dispute settlement, their thoughts on the social preconditions allowing for the success of obligatory systems (especially those of New Zealand and Australia) are relevant at this point. They may indeed have influenced the writing of the Conservative bill.

One of the first persons to propose the obligatory arbitration of strikes was Deputy Darío Sánchez Masenlli. He did so in a congressional speech in 1904, although he presented no bill to this effect and may have had in mind only an *ad hoc* arrangement.[31] Malaquías Concha, leader of the leftist Democratic party and member of the Liberal Alliance coalition, made a brief but favorable reference to obligatory arbitration in his 1907 thesis.[32]

Carlos Roberto González, who appears to have been a Radical, devoted half of his thesis on *Strikes* (1908) to a description of the conciliation and arbitration practices of several European countries, Canada, the United States, and New Zealand. He, like many others of his time, did not distinguish clearly between these two types of settlement and lapsed frequently into the use of the single term "arbitration" to describe both. He concluded that New Zealand was the only country in his sample which had adopted an obligatory system and, as a consequence of its operation, had enjoyed uninterrupted social peace for fourteen years. In spite of its "advantages," no other country had taken the system as a model, and his account of the reasons why is highly interesting. Only New Zealand, he said, had circumstances which favored obligatory arbitration. These circumstances were the smallness of the country, total unionization (as a result of laws making union membership obligatory), a geographic situation which freed the country from the competition of European labor, and the economic ability to satisfy in large part the aspirations of the workers. Why this rationale should have favored obligatory arbitration is an analytical point González did not raise, but equally important is the close similarity between what he saw as the prime features of an obligatory system and the major tenets of the Conservative party bill. González was not

[31]Cámara de Diputados, *Boletín de las Sesiones Ordinarias en 1903–1904*, p. 1520.
[32]Malaquías Concha, *Sobre la dictación de un código del trabajo y de la previsión social*.

141

himself impressed with any possible adaptation of the New Zealand experience to Chile, however, and with no further comment, concluded that "with respect to our country we must of course discard the idea of obligatory arbitration."[33]

Analysis useful to the Conservative point of view also comes from J. Zenteno Casanueva's thesis on *Various Aspects of Labor and Collective Conflicts* (1911), especially its two chapters on conciliation and arbitration. Casanueva reviewed Australia as well as New Zealand and the other countries treated by González, but his attention was primarily on the voluntary French system and his concern was to discover why this system had not worked well. This was due in part, he thought, to the absence of strong and responsible unions in France. Strong and responsible unions are the only guarantee in a voluntary system that workers will not strike while the court is sitting and will accept the court's award at the termination of the arbitral process. In the absence of strong unions, voluntary conciliation or arbitration tribunals will not have "any coercive means to force workers to fulfill their responsibilities." Employers can always be fined for failure to comply with an award because they have money, but the workers, unorganized or organized into weak unions, will not respond to fines because they have no, or inadequate, resources. Voluntary arbitration had worked effectively only in England, and success there was due in large measure to the trade unions which were strong and respectable bodies in both the moral and economic sense. Despite what he considered its limited practical success abroad, however, Casanueva, like González, also supported the voluntary model for Chile.[34]

While Casanueva was not a Conservative (as will become clear in the next chapter), his analysis, if given a reverse twist, becomes remarkably similar to Concha's. In other words, if workers are put in employer-dominated plant unions, they cannot become strong and this is desirable because otherwise their leaders would use their power irresponsibly; weak unions must, however, be forced to resolve their differences with employers, and one way to accomplish this is to get leverage through the granting or withholding of a share of profits; in this situation money will make them responsible.

A final thesis writer, Domingo M. Rocha *(Worker Questions,* 1916) also studied the French experience with conciliation and arbitration

[33]Carlos Roberto González, *Las huelgas* (Santiago: Imprenta Universitaria, 1908).

[34]J. Zenteno Casanueva, *Diversas consideraciones sobre el régimen del trabajo y los conflictos colectivos* (Santiago: Imprenta Moderna, 1911).

142

and his judgment was the same as that given by Casanueva. The French system had not produced the hoped-for results. Consequently, Gide and others were beginning to wonder whether it might not be advisable to alter it. This could take the form of substituting "if not obligatory arbitration, at least the attempt at conciliation."[35] One understands that Rocha was saying "at least the attempt at conciliation should be made compulsory," for that is the only way to give his comment meaning.

Disillusionment with voluntary methods, particularly the French model, may therefore have influenced the Conservatives in their search for a way to "solve" capital-labor conflict. They, like most Chileans of status, were close observers of the French scene and looked to France for intellectual and political leadership in many directions. Juan Enrique Concha in particular was a close student of Le Play and was also familiar with the writings of Gide, Leroy-Beaulieu, and others.

There is still, however, a practical and entirely Chilean phenomenon which may have borne significantly on the ultimate decision of the Conservatives to endorse obligatory dispute settlement machinery. That phenomenon is the centuries-long relationship between the owner of *latifundia* and his semiserfs, a relationship whose content and spirit were known by personal experience to many Conservatives, including Juan Enrique Concha. One does not negotiate (in the full meaning of that term) with those whom he considers his racial inferiors or with his children. One tells them both what is right and what to do, and is properly affronted when they question the system, thus showing lack of appreciation or respect. The master addresses his *inquilinos* with the familiar *"tu,"* a form also reserved for children or intimate friends, and the *inquilino* responds with the formal *"Usted"* or "thou." The good *inquilino* says, "Command me, Master" *(Mándeme, Patrón);* not "I disagree" or "I will do so if you will give me two more hectares of land." This authority system leads naturally to obligatory forms under the master's or employer's control. It is pertinent to note in this respect that the Conservative bill called for five-member boards of conciliation and arbitration, two members each to be named by the employer and the union, with the key fifth member to be named by the employer.

[35]Domingo M. Rocha S., *Cuestiones obreras* (Concepción: Imprenta Chile, 1916).

CHAPTER 6

The Liberal Alliance Project

and the Intellectuals

ARTURO Alessandri Palma, one of the truly great Presidents of Chile, was elected to office in June 1920. Exactly one year later, and in the name of the Liberal Alliance coalition which elected him, he presented to the Congress a long and ambitious labor code project. The project consisted of four "books" and more than six hundred articles dealing with such matters as working conditions, individual and collective labor contracts, unions and profit sharing, conciliation and arbitration, and social security. Like the Conservative party bill, most of this code project became part of the seven labor laws of 1924. After describing those features of the Liberal Alliance bill which are most pertinent to this study, we will discuss its origins, emphasizing the middle-class intellectuals and the degree and nature of their participation in the genesis of the bill.

I

The union (*sindicato profesional,* craft or professional union) proposed by the Liberal Alliance was defined as a local organization formed by either white- or blue-collar workers of the same craft or skill, or from similar or connected jobs. Its concern was to be "exclusively with the study, development, and legitimate defense of the common economic interests of its members." Unionism was restricted to the private sector; public employees were specifically denied the right to form or join unions.

Local unions of the same craft or skill were to have the right to form federations or confederations which, in turn, would also have the right to bargain collectively with employers and represent their members in conciliation and arbitration procedures. Both local and national unions were required to incorporate in order to win state protection and the local union needed twenty members as a minimum requirement. Incorporation procedure was described in the code and final authority for conferring or denying corporate status rested with the Executive. Membership in craft locals was to be entirely voluntary. Once in the union a member could withdraw at any time or could be voted out by his associates. Local union officers, whose number was not specified, had to be at least twenty-five years old, were to be elected by two-thirds of the "effective membership," and their terms of office could not exceed two years. Voting was on a unitary rather than a cumulative basis and each member had but one vote.

As to dissolution of a union, this could be accomplished by a three-fourths vote of the members at a special meeting attended by at least half of the union's voting members. The union could also be dissolved for infringing the labor law or regulations subsequently decreed by the President of the Republic, for non-acceptance of the decisions or awards of conciliation and arbitration boards, or when its membership fell below twenty. Finally, the President of the Republic or the Minister of the Interior could dissolve a local union for disturbing public order or for obstructing individual liberty, the right to work, or the rights of industry.

The Liberal Alliance code contained numerous provisions, in addition to those dealing with incorporation and dissolution, which set limits to or restrictions upon the scope of union rights and activities, imposed norms upon the conduct of union administrative affairs, and obligated unions to report regularly or upon request various types of information to the government. For example, the code listed under nine headings the general areas and specific provisions to be covered or contained in union statutes; forbade unions to acquire real property without the previous authorization of the President of the Republic; required express permission of the Executive for setting up union funds for mutual aid, retirement, or insurance purposes; stipulated that union property could not be attached; required unions to keep minutes, accounting books, books of correspondence, and a complete membership register; and stipulated that no reform of union statutes would be valid unless approved by the Executive. In addition, unions were required to communicate immediately to the Executive any change in the membership of the union board or in the location of union headquarters. They were also obligated to submit to the Executive monthly and annual reports on the number, nationality, and profession of union members, and an annual balance sheet. A final blanket requirement was that unions furnish the General Directorate of Labor whatever data that agency might request.

The profit-sharing scheme of the Liberal Alliance code was restricted to blue-collar workers with at least one year of seniority in certain, unspecified industries. Since craft unionism was voluntary there was no provision for subdividing profits on a union basis. The code also required all private corporations to share at least 10 percent of their stock with blue-collar workers who had more than one year of seniority in the corporation.

The code contained a long title on dispute settlement and strikes which proposed voluntary conciliation of all matters not resolved between the parties, voluntary arbitration of disputes not settled before conciliation boards, and the legal strike which could take place after failure of conciliation and the specific refusal of one or both parties to take the matter to arbitration. The nature of and procedure before conciliation and arbitration boards (which were permanent rather than *ad hoc*) were carefully spelled out.[1]

II

What is the significance of the above in terms of an élite analysis of industrial relations systems? Who were the middle-class intellectuals, what did they write on the social question, and how did their views differ from those of the aristocratic-Catholic élite? What basics were they, on the one hand, trying to preserve in their own inherited system of thought and what essentially were they willing to give up?

As had the aristocratic-Catholic intellectuals, so also the middle-class intellectuals first provided a philosophy, a reasoned justification for new social action. Their starting point was clearly not Catholicism, however, but rather nineteenth-century liberal thought, individualism, and open market concepts. Their task was to justify the amendment of traditional liberalism to permit state intervention in social and labor

[1]"Proyecto de Código del Trabajo y de la Previsión Social," *Folletos Varios*, Tomo I, Biblioteca del Congreso, Santiago, pp. 1–79.

matters. They borrowed not from papal encyclicals but from the writings of political economists of the liberal school like Paul Leroy-Beaulieu *(L'État Moderne et ses Fonctions)* and philsophers like Ludwig Stein *(La Question Social au Point de Vue Philosophique).*

The middle-class intellectuals lagged several years behind those of aristocratic-Catholic tendency in publishing their views on the social question. While Concha's first book dated from 1898, Jorge Errázuriz Tagle, the first of the Liberal Alliance group to make a solid contribution, did not complete his thesis until 1906. The same pattern of conservative headstart and liberal lag also characterized the parties of the two major élites with regard both to their initial attention to the social question and to their presentation many years later of concrete legislative proposals in this area. The circumstance of time would seem always to favor the older, entrenched, and more sophisticated élites everywhere, but, unlike the conservatives in Chile, those of other countries have not always wanted to or been able to exploit this apparent advantage.

It would be well to emphasize again at this point that the philosophic and geographic lines between the two élites, which are on the whole convenient for analytical purposes, do not always neatly or even appropriately apply to particular individuals. Some of the intellectuals who figure in this chapter on the Liberal Alliance (as political representative of the middle-class élite) had strong rural identifications and bear family names which are virtually synonymous with the aristocracy in Chile — for example, Jorge Errázuriz Tagle and Eliodoro Yáñez.

Indeed, Errázuriz Tagle could with some justification be discussed in either this chapter or the preceding one. He wrote his thesis in law on *The Historical Development of our Social Question* and, after graduating from the University of Chile in 1906, entered politics. As a Doctrinaire Liberal (the same Liberal party to which Alessandri belonged), he was for years identified with the Liberal Alliance. The Doctrinaire Liberals, however, split in the course of the 1920 presidential election, and Errázuriz Tagle appears at that point to have shifted his allegiance to the National Union, a coalition spearheaded by the Conservatives. On social legislation, his contribution began early, when he was still a Deputy, and continued until his untimely death in 1922. He was at one time chairman of the Committee on Social Legislation of the Chamber of Deputies and was also one of the young Liberals who persuaded their party to support the movement for social and labor reforms. Errázuriz Tagle ran for and won a Senate seat in 1919 and immediately became a member of the Senate's

Special Committee on Social Legislation, whose work was important to the later drafting of the Liberal Alliance labor code project. However, as a member of the Joint Committee on Social Legislation, the key congressional body in the development of labor legislation after 1921, he represented the National Union. Whether this political shift affected his labor views cannot be told from the record.

Benjamin Vicuña Subercaseaux, a political writer of Radical party affiliations, contributed a series of brilliant articles on the social question which appeared in *El Mercurio,* Chile's leading daily newspaper, during the years 1904–1907. These articles were published in book form in 1908 under the title *Revolutionary Socialism and the Social Question in Europe and Chile.* Arturo Fernández Pradel contributed a book on *The Social Tendencies of Liberalism* (1909), and a university professor and a poet-journalist attracted national attention with their descriptions of life in the nitrate *pampa.* The first of these was Alejandro Venegas, who wrote under the pseudonym of Dr. J. Valdés Canje. His book, *Sincerity, An Intimate Glimpse of Chile in 1910,* was a scourging exposé of working conditions in the nitrate mining camps. The second was Victor Domingo Silva who visited the nitrate camps in 1913 and then wrote a series of vigorous articles in the press of Iquique and Santiago in which he denounced the oligarchy of the north for their exploitation of nitrate labor. His articles also came out as a book which he called *Before Leaving, What I Saw and Heard in Tarapacá.* According to Ricardo Donoso, Silva's campaign led directly to the naming of the special parliamentary committee which investigated labor conditions in the north in 1913. Moreover, his press support of Alessandri as senator from Tarapacá in the 1915 campaign (due in part to his favorable impression of Alessandri as a social reformer) had "decisive influence" in Alessandri's triumph. Daniel Salcedo, a Valparaíso journalist, was likewise dedicated to social reform and played an important part in committing the Radical party to a reform position on the social question.[2]

Pedro Luis González, Professor Extraordinary of Social and Political Economy of the University of Chile and an early president of the Society for Factory Development, contributed his book on the *Labor Contract* (1912), perhaps the best statement of the middle-class position on labor in Chile. His work was followed by that of Jorge Gustavo Silva, *Political Liberalism,* which included an important section on lib-

[2]Donoso, *Alessandri,* vol. 1, p. 157–161, 164–167, 171, 176; Silva, *Nuestra evolución político-social,* pp. 77–83.

eralism and the social question. Tomás Ramírez Frías was a Professor of Law and member of the Liberal party who lectured frequently on the social question in this early period. He was later elected to the Senate and became one of the most active members of the Joint Committee on Social Legislation. Francisco Jorquera F., a Radical, wrote a thesis in 1913 on *Mining Labor in General and Particularly at Pirquen* and then went on to become a Deputy and a member of the Joint Committee. The outstanding representative of the liberal group toward the end of this period was Eliodoro Yáñez, a top leader of the Liberal party, founder and editor of *La Nación* which rapidly became one of the leading dailies of the country, president of the Society for Factory Development, member of the executive board of the National Agricultural Society, Senator, and chairman of the Joint Committee on Social Legislation. Yáñez said little that was new with respect to the social question, but his active support of social legislation was a symbol of the unmistakably heavy commitment of some of the powerful men of the business community and of government to an advanced position on the social and labor issues of the day.

No one among the liberal-radical intellectuals presented as complete an account of the liberal-democratic position as did Concha with regard to the conservative-paternalistic approach. Errázuriz Tagle's contribution was primarily in tracing the origins of the social question to the break-up of the feudal system and the growth of an industrial labor force and in exposing weaknesses in the arguments of those who believed there was not yet a social question in Chile. Benjamin Vicuña Subercaseaux dwelt on the need for a liberal solution as an alternative to extremism, particularly Marxian socialism. González, writing later and therefore from intellectually higher ground, was able to go on and apply liberal principles to the new world of industry and the phenomena of unions, strikes, and contracts. Yet the contributions of these men cannot with justice to any one of them be so clearly separated. Moreover, their works contain weaknesses and inconsistencies which, from the vantage point of the present, now seem obvious if not foolish. Yet, for reasons of greater clarity it would seem advisable first to present the liberal-democratic view of the labor problem as if it were indeed a single and internally consistent one. Some qualifications and refinements can then be introduced.

According to the liberal intellectuals, the social question in the modern sense began to develop in the later Middle Ages with the decline of feudalism and the growth of cities and emerged full-blown with the industrial revolution, the growth of factories, and the French

Revolution. These events brought a general malaise to the working masses, revealed a resistance to change among ruling classes, and, finally, demonstrated the ultimate triumph of justice and human rights. Although the interpretation that Marx gave to this history had sparked a general intellectual awakening, Marx himself was wrong in explaining the social question as one of the stomach. So also was M. Ziegler in believing it to be essentially a moral issue. Ludwig Stein had already called attention to the dangers of using such all-embracing and impressionistic explanations and had, in the historical development of the social question, seen it correctly as a complex of social ills which counseled restraint even in the use of the term *the* social question."

The social question had been present in Chile for a quarter of a century (i.e., since the early 1880's) — its most recent evidence, the strikes of 1903 and 1907. These armed clashes between workers and employers were not the artificial results of socialistic propaganda but, rather, were a response to real problems of the workplace. Wages were too low, misery was general and deep, workers were exploited and not treated as citizens with rights equal to those of the powerful and wealthy.

"Social liberalism," "political liberalism," or "liberal socialism," as the liberals variously called their philosophy, included four broad areas through which solution to the social problem would be found. The first was an extension of the area of state intervention in social legislation beyond the narrow limits set by orthodox liberalism — i.e., beyond women and child labor laws and the protection of adult male labor in hazardous industries. There were reasons of order, justice, and social utility for such an extension. It would, for example, help maintain social peace and avoid the grave consequences of strikes; it would be just, because in the absence of government protection a single worker was no match for an employer; and society would benefit from the greater production which the diminution of social strife would bring. It was in the public interest that legislation encourage close links between workers and their enterprises, and this could be done through profit sharing, cooperatives, and other measures.

While the state was assigned a greater role in the new liberalism, the major objective in an expansion of its influence was to provide workers with those basic rights and conditions which would permit them to work harmoniously with their employers in the joint resolution of difficulties. Employer acceptance of unions and the promotion of labor-management relations were therefore a second, and more far-reaching, area of concern to the liberals in their search for answers to the social question. Present labor contracts were individual, verbal, and vague in Chile and the need, they said, was for written collective agreements which would clearly lay down the rights and obligations of the parties and provide for the faithful execution of each one. The liberals recognized that even the "orthodox" economists were beginning to accept the collective agreement "because they consider it the expression of the principle of free association and as the means of limiting state action." With unions and collective bargaining "there is no need for the tutelage of the state in favor of the worker."[3]

Yet the liberals were aware that some employers in Chile did not want to have anything to do with unions, and some of the liberals themselves doubted that either the workers or their leaders were at that time capable of setting up serious, peaceful, and disciplined organizations. It was this ambivalence which seems to have led to detailed proposals for state control of unions in the Liberal Alliance project.

The generation of greater production and, thus, of wealth was considered to be not merely a consequence of any solution to the social problem but, in addition, one of the ways of solving it. This third area of liberal concern became somewhat more important as time went by, especially among those writers with business or employer affiliations, but it never received the same emphasis as protective legislation and certainly not as much emphasis as a present-day writer, steeped in development literature, might think it should have received. Yáñez probably reflected a general liberal-intellectual viewpoint when he stated, in support of industrial development, that "where production is abundant and arrives at low cost in the hands of the consumer the labor problem disappears or is related to causes other than the cost of living."[4] González went a tantalizing step further when he remarked that "all social problems turn on the new form of wealth distribution" but, instead of going on with an analysis of distribution and how wage or tax policy or social security legislation might effect changes, he returned immediately to the more comfortable area of production — "but," he said, "the fundamental basis of distribution is production. If there is no production, there is nothing with which to pay wages and salaries."[5] It is of course possible that in referring to "the new form of wealth distribution" he simply meant the wage system as such and did not intend to raise the matter of the redistribution of wealth.

[3]González, *El contrato del trabajo*, pp. 28–29.

[4]Eliodoro Yáñez, *Política de previsión y de trabajo* (Santiago: Empresa Editora Zig-Zag, 1920), p. 17.

[5]*Boletín de la Sociedad de Fomento Fabril*, vol. 38, February 1921, pp. 65–66.

Finally, the fourth general area in which the liberals sought redress for the ills of an emerging industrial society was education. A system of public schools, free of cost and of Catholic church control, had been a strong factor in the genesis of the anticlerical Radical party and was also advocated by many Liberal party leaders. Now the general diffusion of education could be bent to another purpose — providing the masses with the greater degree of general culture and sophistication required for living in a changing society, and providing the workers with the skills and training needed for industrial development and their own employment and advancement. The liberal-radical intellectuals therefore supported the establishment of technical-professional schools and apprenticeship programs as well as free public instruction.

Social liberalism was summarized by Vicuña Subercaseaux, aptly although incompletely, as

> a guarantee by the state of order and justice in the development of all human business and as that system which allows all those to advance who have the ability to do so, without crushing the weak, and which also constantly provides more public education so that every day there are more skillful people.[6]

While the above views of the liberal-minded intellectuals would seem to represent a logically consistent whole and a mature approach to labor questions even when judged against the standards of today, this was not always the case. Errázuriz Tagle, for all his recognition of the social question, was convinced that the Chilean worker was in some degree an inferior being. He referred to the "defects of the constituent races" of the working class and to their economic and moral vices "so deeply rooted that it seems impossible to destroy them."[7] Since he believed this was part of the reason why there was a social question in Chile, one wonders how sanguine were his hopes for change and how deep his faith in unions and conciliation. It is clear that he was not as outspoken as Enrique Mac-Iver who believed that, given the inferior character of Chilean workers, legislation would do no good. Yet the qualification he introduced was an important one and helps further to explain why the liberal-democratic position (i.e., the Liberal Alliance labor code proposal) was not "pure" and relied so heavily on the state for control and guidance of unions, their members, and leaders.

The views expressed by Benjamin Vicuña Subercaseaux on strikes and union leaders reinforce the impression that there were few intel-

---

[6]Vicuña Subercaseaux, *Socialismo revolucionario*, pp. 64–65.

[7]Jorge Errázuriz Tagle, *El desarrollo histórico de nuestra cuestión social* (Santiago: Imprenta Universitaria, 1906), pp. 38–40. See also, *El Mercurio*, April 19, 1919.

lectuals who could transfer to the field of industrial relations full faith in such liberal-democratic concepts as the free play of market forces, trust in the individual, social mobility, and the equality of a free citizenry. The Latin American countries had for several reasons, he said, long delayed in recognizing strikes as a legal weapon of the workers. Strikes in these countries had never been anything but agitations by malevolent men for no purpose but pillage. In Chile, workers went on strike because of agitators or because they succumbed to the pains of inequality or to primitive instincts. The strikes of 1905 and 1907 were the latest terrible examples. In such cases "repression by armed force has been good. Each time that such strikes occur energetic repression is advisable for reasons of social order and justice."[8]

He apparently lumped all leaders of the working class together as agitators or "labor bosses." Not all worker unrest was due to socialism; the really guilty ones were the labor bosses who interpreted socialism to the workers. These caudillos, whether called trade union leaders as in England or walking delegates as in the United States, almost never had the right attitude. They created conflicts "to satisfy personal rancor and passion and to get rich on the misery and blood of their fellow men." Sam Parks (an infamous labor racketeer at the turn of the century) was a typical American trade union leader, and there were many Sam Parkses in Chile which the press was not brave enough to unmask.[9]

Because they held the above views of economics and society, the middle-class group, like the aristocratic-Catholic élite, was faced with a paradox when the time came to translate philosophy into legislative action. If in the latter case the paradox was how to devise a moral industrial relations system which would force the parties, especially the workers, to act morally, in the former case it was how to devise a free industrial relations system and still maintain control over those (the unions) who could not be trusted with freedom. The conservatives relied upon compulsion and a system of rewards and punishments within a personal, family, and class view of society. The liberals relied upon voluntary institutions within a functional arrangement of economic endeavor and gave to the state that control over unions which the conservatives conceded to employers.

Those features of the Liberal Alliance project which were a genuine expression of the liberal emphasis upon freedom of association, free

[8]Vicuña Subercaseaux, Socialismo revolucionario, p. 187.

[9]Ibid., pp. 106–111. His information about Sam Parks was taken from an article by Ray Stannard Baker in McClure's Magazine which had been translated into Spanish and reproduced in Chile in the October 1904 issue of El Ferrocarril.

play of market forces, and voluntary decision making are easy to identify. First of all, the craft union was a voluntary organization — although one would have to argue that full freedom of association would have to permit a much broader range of structural selection, including the multicraft union, industrial union, and multi-industrial union. Moreover, related craft unions could federate and bargain as a single unit, and this not only recognized freedom of association but also indicated some willingness to let market and bargaining power determine the appropriate functional unit. Conciliation and arbitration were both voluntary processes available to the parties. The absence both of cumulative voting and of a scheme for placing union leadership in the hands of older workers might point to somewhat greater confidence in the individual than is evident in the Conservative bill.

Nevertheless, there were vastly significant limits to the recognition of liberal concepts in the Liberal Alliance project. If the authors of the bill had some respect for the individual unionist's responsibility and capacity to learn, they at the same time had mountainous doubts about unionists as an organized group. For this reason, they gave government the power of life and death over unions and their leadership, power that could be exercised at the will of the state and on any of a thousand different pretexts.

III

The origins of the Liberal Alliance project is a considerably more complex matter than that of the Conservative bill. It is more complex because there are several political parties involved and because there are more legislative precedents to trace, a larger number of intellectual contributors to study, and more external influences to identify. Moreover, the Liberal Alliance project is a comprehensive code of social and labor matters and it incorporates laws already in effect as well as proposed new legislation.

In approaching a study of the origins of the Liberal Alliance project, there are, as there were also in the case of the Conservative bill, two lines of analysis. The first is institutional and describes the political process which led to the development of the project. The second is intellectual and attempts to identify possible sources of the unique content of the project.

The Liberal Alliance was a coalition peculiar to the parliamentary period (1891–1924) in Chilean politics. The two major coalitions polarized around the Conservative party (National Union) and the Radical party (Liberal Alliance). Coalition politics tended to relax individual party discipline which, in turn, led to serious intra-party factionalism and to frequent and sometimes bewildering shifts and realignments among the subordinate parties of the coalitions. The Liberal party, for example, split into two groups, the Democratic Liberals lining up with the National Union, and the Doctrinaire Liberals, the larger of the two factions, joining the Liberal Alliance. There were loose elements in both Liberal wings who were often found in a coalition with which they would not normally be associated. The National party was consistently identified with the National Union but, like the two Liberal wings, it was not able to maintain perfect discipline, its members sometimes being found in the "wrong" coalition. The Democratic party usually supported the Liberal Alliance but, like the National party in the National Union, never had much to say in Liberal Alliance councils. The Socialist Workers' party was not counted in either camp but some of its congressional candidates did receive Liberal Alliance support in the 1921 elections. The Communist party, successor to the Socialist Workers' party, became after 1921 an out-and-out source of opposition to the major political groupings.

The volatile nature of coalition politics is immediately significant for three reasons. First, it points up the fact that the aristocratic-Catholic and middle-class élites cannot be related in a mutually exclusive or permanent way with the National Union and Liberal Alliance coalitions. While there is enough truth in such identifications to make them defensible and useful, they are in no sense absolute or inflexible. Second, there is the warning that an individual's loyalty or contribution to coalition programs, labor bills included, cannot necessarily be assumed from his party affiliations. Third, given the changing nature of alliances, it is important to know what major parties formed the Liberal Alliance in 1920, elected Alessandri, and perhaps supported his labor code project. These parties were the Radicals, still the largest group, the Doctrinaire Liberals (from whence came Alessandri), the Democrats, and a part of the Democratic Liberals. Concern is mainly with the first three groups because they were the largest and also because they were the regular constituents of the Liberal Alliance.

All three of these parties took up the study of the social question before 1921, said they recognized its existence in Chile, and went on record in favor of varying amounts and types of social and labor legislation. Intellectuals were sometimes key figures in moving party debate toward this issue and in drafting the party's platform stand on it. We will therefore review this aspect of party history in order to identify the intellectuals and to show their contributions.

The strategic gathering of the Radical party was in 1905. The platform committee of the party failed to reach agreement on the social question and two reports were brought before the convention. The majority report was written and defended by Valentín Letelier, Professor of Law and Rector of the University of Chile. Letelier responded to the growing middle-class and popular elements of the party which, fifteen years later, were to sweep Alessandri into the presidency. Although Letelier was by no means a Marxist, he was familiar with European socialism, especially developments within the socialist movement in Germany, and the Letelier bloc in the Radical party was known as the "socialist" tendency and its program as the "socialist" program. Letelier believed there were few cultivated nations which had not already legislated in the field of labor organization and working conditions and he wanted the Radicals to recognize "the social questions which were being aired in the country and to give them a place in the legal system."[10]

Letelier's opponent was Enrique Mac-Iver, owner of *latifundia* and defender of tradition. Jorge Gustavo Silva describes the convention confrontation as one between "individualist liberalism, defended by the golden voice of a great parliamentarian, and nascent 'socialism,' whose moving force was the sociological learning and doctrinal ardor of a great teacher."[11] Guillermo Feliú Cruz saw the battle as between "Manchesterian individualism and the socialism of the university chair. These were the principles of the two great men of Radicalism: Mac-Iver and Letelier."[12]

After a full week of heated debate, Letelier emerged victorious and the Radical party was thenceforward committed to seek "whatever laws and create whatever institutions necessary to put the destitute and the poor who work for a daily living on a footing of equality with the other social classes."[13] This was an ideological turning point for the Radical party, the major political force of the Liberal Alliance.

The Doctrinaire Liberal party took halting steps in the direction of a social reform position at its convention in 1907 but the more advanced elements of the party remained dissatisfied and the crisis came six years later. The party's 1907 statement was titled the "Worker Problem," and its equivocal spirit was manifest in the opening

[10]Feliú Cruz, *Chile visto a través de Agustín Ross*, pp. 123–124. See also Donoso, *Alessandri*, vol. 1, p. 155.

[11]Silva, *Nuestra evolución político-social*, pp. 77–83.

[12]Feliú Cruz, *Chile visto a través de Agustín Ross*, pp. 123–124.

[13]Quoted in Silva, *Nuestra evolución político-social*, pp. 77–83.

sentence which declared the party's intention "to establish labor legislation assuring rights to employers and workers and especially defining the employer's responsibility in cases of accidents attributable to him and defining the workers' responsibility when they prevent their comrades from exercising the right to work."[14]

The younger and more advanced elements of the party preferred to cast the platform in the broader mold of "Social Questions" and to commit the party unequivocally to positive legislation in benefit of the working classes. Leaders of this group were Jorge Errázuriz Tagle, Tomás Ramírez Frías, Manuel Rodríguez Pérez, and Jorge Gustavo Silva, all identified above as intellectuals of the middle-class élite.

These men monopolized the convention rostrum when the time came to debate the social plank and, after listening to their long, urgent, and sincere appeals for more popular action, the convention agreed to appoint a five-member committee to bring in a recommendation. Three of the committee members were Errázuriz Tagle, Ramírez Frías, and Rodríguez Pérez. Of the remaining two, one had moved the appointment of the committee and the other had submitted to the convention a proposed bill on first-aid in factories.

The committee suggested that the social plank be renamed "Social Questions" and that the convention agree to the general declaration that "within the existing order, social questions must be resolved as a matter of fundamental policy, not through charity but through social solidarity." Given this objective, it was therefore necessary "to establish an administrative and legal system which, without infringing the development of the individual, will establish on foundations of justice the well-being of the various social classes." The report then listed a number of "urgent matters" among which were retirement and social security funds for private white-collar workers, a "complete legislation" for blue-collar workers, and cooperatives. Minutes of the convention say the report was approved without change, and thus the Liberal party joined the ranks of those who, outwardly at least, stood for legislative action on the new social front.[15]

The Democratic party was founded in 1887 as a mildly socialistic party of the lower middle class and artisan groups and at its convention two years later hammered out a program which included three planks calling for social legislation. Beginning in 1900 the most outstanding

[14]Partido Liberal, *Acta, convención del partido liberal, 1907* (Santiago: Imprenta Barcelona, 1907), pp. 358–359.

[15]Partido Liberal, *Acta, tercera convención del partido liberal, 1913* (Santiago: Imprenta Barcelona, 1916), pp. 183–184, 201–224, 393–394.

of its founders, Malaquías Concha, sponsored separate bills on working conditions, industrial accidents, and security measures, none of
which however became law.[16] Concha also wrote a thesis on social security, and he was therefore a part of the intellectual reform movement
in the years of his association with the University of Chile.

In 1913 the Democratic party developed an "Economic Program"
which called for the establishment of a Ministry of Labor and Social
Security, recognition of "craft unions and associations," a general social
security program for all citizens (which would cover unemployment,
invalidity, old age, and death), the labor contract, and other subjects.
The party reached an accord with the Radicals in that same year which
laid out a social and labor legislation program and pledged both parties
to make common cause in the Congress to obtain its passage.[17] Specific
bills were not however drafted. In the years after 1913 Malaquías
Concha and the Democratic party tended to lose the initiative in the
social and labor field first to the Conservatives and then to the two
major partners in the Liberal Alliance, the Radicals and Doctrinaire
Liberals.

The Democratic Liberal party endorsed a number of measures to
ameliorate living conditions for the working classes at its 1896 convention, and in 1908 resolved to take steps toward the "regulation of
labor."[18] Again, however, the party sponsored no major labor or social
reform legislation.

So much then for the historical position of the Liberal Alliance
parties on the social question. What was taking place in these parties
on the eve of the election of Alessandri and the appearance of the Liberal Alliance code project? Were there events which led directly to the
drafting of the project, perhaps by a committee representative of the
several parties? Was the project really a Liberal Alliance project? Or
was it more the personal creation of Alessandri or someone else? As we
shall see, there would be some truth in an affirmative answer to each

[16]Feliú Cruz, Chile visto a través de Agustín Ross, pp. 126–132; for examples of
the labor bills introduced into the Congress by Deputy Malaquías Concha, see
Cámara de Diputados, Boletín de las Sesiones Extraordinarias en 1900, p. 552; 1901,
pp. 1335–1337.

[17]Partido Democrático, Nuevo programa y reglamento del partido democrático
aprobados por la convención ordinaria de 1913 (Santiago: Imprenta Central, 1915),
pp. 7–8; Feliú Cruz, Chile visto a través de Agustín Ross, pp. 130–132.

[18]Partido Liberal Democrático, Convención del partido liberal democrático, 1908,
Santiago, 1908, pp. 111, 115. See also, for background information on this party, José
A. Alfonso, Los partidos políticos de Chile (Santiago: Imprenta Esmeralda, [1902?]),
p. 30.

of these questions. The political events of 1918–1921 were complex and fraught with problems of an intercoalition, intracoalition, and intra-party nature. These events affected the genesis of labor legislation unequally, and no straight-line pattern of development is therefore observable.

After the congressional elections of March 1918, the Liberal Alliance was in control of both houses of Congress for the first time since the inauguration of the parliamentary system and coalition government in the 1890's. Under the circumstances, President Juan Luis Sanfuentes was forced to build his Cabinet around Liberal Alliance forces, although he was himself a representative of the National Union.

Social legislation had not been a campaign issue in the 1918 elections, and the victory of the Liberal Alliance has been interpreted simply as the result of a growing determination within the opposition political parties to break the decisive influence of the Conservatives. In other words, the Liberal Alliance parties sold the electorate on the bankruptcy of their political opponents and the need for a new régime in government.[19] Nevertheless, the conquest of congressional and ministerial power set new forces in motion within the Liberal Alliance and gave new urgency to the need to develop positive programs which would both assure the continued loyalty of the electorate and in addition prepare the Alliance for further conquest in the presidential election of 1920. Moreover, the Conservative party had responded to its defeat by taking a forward position on labor legislation and had appointed a High Committee to draft a comprehensive labor bill. As a consequence of both of these new pressures, the Liberal Alliance, operating as a government majority, began to draft labor legislation in 1919.

In April 1919 the Minister of the Interior appointed a Special Committee on Social Legislation to advise "the Ministry of the Interior on the drafting of several labor bills which the Government wanted to present to the Congress."[20] There appear to have been five members on the original committee, two each from the Liberal and Radical parties and one Democrat. Among the five were Tomás Ramírez Frías and Jorge Errázuriz Tagle. The Special Committee met about six times in May and drafting assignments were passed out to or assumed by its individual members. *El Mercurio* carried no news about the

[19]Donoso, *Alessandri*, vol. 1, pp. 208–209; *El Mercurio*, March 10, 1918. Before the 1918 elections, the Alliance controlled the Senate and the National Union controlled the Chamber of Deputies. *El Mercurio*, March 7, 1918.
[20]*Boletín de la Oficina del Trabajo*, no. 13, 1920, pp. 119–121.

Special Committee from June on, and, according to one source, the committee was formally dissolved late in July "for incidental reasons which it is not appropriate to go into here."[21]

The reasons for the Special Committee's early dissolution are no longer inappropriate for discussion and they were never incidental. Before taking them up, however, let us first examine the record and list the achievements of the Special Committee and, wherever possible, the authorship of the bills drafted. Bills calling for the establishment of a Ministry of Labor and Social Security, the eight-hour day, and the regulation of women workers and child labor were drafted by Tomás Ramírez Frías and Malaquías Concha, the lone Democrat on the Special Committee. All three of these bills were presented to the Congress during the summer of 1919. The Special Committee also endorsed bills on industrial accidents and wages which were already pending in the Congress. Finally, the Special Committee commissioned Errázuriz Tagle to draw up a bill which would establish "arbitral committees" to fix minimum wages for blue-collar workers and asked Tomás Ramírez Frías and Eugenio Frías Collao, head of the national Office of Labor, to draft a bill on unions.[22]

There is nothing to indicate that Errázuriz Tagle completed his assignment, but Ramírez Frías and Frías Collao did produce a craft union bill. The Special Committee did not discuss the bill before it ceased to function, however, and Ramírez Frías therefore sponsored the bill himself in the Chamber of Deputies. The Special Committee included conciliation and arbitration in its agenda, but the record does not show that that body subsequently acted on the subject. Nevertheless, it should be pointed out that the standing Committee on Social Legislation of the Chamber of Deputies, chaired by Errázuriz Tagle, did report out favorably in July a bill on conciliation and arbitration which had been pending in the committee for nine years.[23]

Within the very short span of only three months, therefore, the Liberal Alliance had considered nearly the whole gamut of social legislation and had endorsed, or developed itself, a wide range of projects. Yet the Special Committee was disbanded prematurely and the Liberal Alliance made no effort in 1919 to get any legislation through either the Chamber of Deputies or the Senate. What happened is a story of

[21]*Ibid.*
[22]*Ibid.; El Mercurio*, May 17, 20, 24, 27, 1919.
[23]*Boletín de la Oficina del Trabajo*, no. 13, 1920, pp. 119–121; *El Mercurio*, May 14, 15, 1919; Cámara de Diputados, *Boletín de las Sesiones Ordinarias en 1919*, pp. 1192–1195, 1967–1970.

the usual — intercoalition rivalry — and also of the unusual — the momentarily disastrous and nearly complete break-up of the Liberal Alliance. We will describe each of these developments only briefly.

By the time the Special Committee was set up in April, the Conservative party High Committee, in existence since December 1918, had probably already sketched the main outlines of its proposed labor legislation. The moves made by the Liberal Alliance were undoubtedly meant to save the situation by staking out the popular area of social legislation before the Conservatives were able to score. Even should the Conservatives present their bill first, the Liberal Alliance still controlled both Chambers of Congress and, for that reason, there would really be no need for alarm.

On May 20 the Conservative bill, signed by its seven-member Senate delegation, was delivered to the secretariat of the Senate and on June 2 it was taken up by that body for the first time. So the Liberal Alliance lost the first round, and the Conservatives could forever claim the honor of having made social legislation a serious congressional, as distinct from a personal or even party, issue. The Liberal Alliance moved to blunt the edge gained by the Conservatives by inviting two members of the opposition, one of them Juan Enrique Concha, to sit on the Special Committee.[24] Perhaps the hope was that this would lead to some kind of bi-coalition support for labor legislation in the Congress. However, events were moving fast within the Alliance itself and high-stake politics soon overshadowed labor bills and all other legislation as well.

The Liberal Alliance had shown signs of internal weakening just a few months after the 1918 elections. There were tensions between the Radicals and Liberals over the division of Cabinet posts, conflicts within the Radical party between the youth groups and the older and more conservative party members who received ministerial appointments, and a deep division in the Liberal party on the social question. Between the end of April and September 1919 the Radicals withdrew from the Liberal Alliance and the Liberal party split into two major groups, one of which respected and guarded the traditions while the other took an "advanced" or "reformistic" position on the social issues of the time. The latter group was the larger but it was itself divided by the personal rivalry between Arturo Alessandri and Eliodoro Yáñez, whose interests were now centered more on the presidential election of

[24]*Boletín de la Oficina del Trabajo*, no. 13, 1920, pp. 119–121; *El Mercurio,* May 15, 22, 1919.

1920 than on immediate legislation. The consequence of these strains was the shattering of the Liberal Alliance government and the loss of the Alliance majority in the Senate through the simple transfer of coalition allegiance. These were the "incidental" reasons for the demise of the Special Committee.

Political events continued to move on, however, and in late 1919 the Radicals, reform Liberals, and Democrats held separate conventions to define again their individual programs and objectives. At that time the Radicals confirmed their favorable stand on reform and called specifically for legislation to solve capital-labor difficulties, profit sharing, cooperative societies, and various matters of social security and economic well-being. The reform Liberals added to the 1913 Liberal program such pertinent things as the collective contract, social security provisions (which evidently were not to be limited in application to white-collar employees), "craft associations, unions, and federations," the right to strike and to lock out, and the incorporation of all these matters in a "Labor and Social Security Code." The Democrats pronounced in favor of permanent arbitration courts.[25]

In April 1920 the Liberal Alliance parties, having miraculously united, met in convention and, in addition to nominating Alessandri as their standard-bearer in the forthcoming elections, adopted a ten-point program. The several parties made it clear that they fully intended to maintain the "principles and purposes of their respective programs" but would at the same time do everything to provide their candidate with a parliamentary majority sufficient to pass the economic and social reforms of the Liberal Alliance platform, if he were elected President. Of the ten planks, one covered social legislation and it pledged the Alliance to solve immediately economic and social problems through the creation of a Ministry of Labor and Social Security and the passage of laws on the labor contract, social security, health and safety in the workplace, and labor dispute settlement.[26]

[25]Partido Radical, *Programa del partido radical* (Santiago: Editorial Numen, 1920), pp. 10–11; Partido Liberal, *Programa y estatuto orgánico del partido liberal, 1919* (Santiago: Imprenta Universo, 1921), pp. 17–18; Guillermo M. Bañados, *Avancemos* (Santiago: Imprenta La Universal, 1920), pp. 29–31.

The Radical party met again in 1921 and at that time called for permanent boards of conciliation and arbitration, a special law to benefit white-collar workers, and a "Labor Code." However, it is possible that the Liberal Alliance code project was in existence before the party met and that the party was therefore affected by the code rather than vice versa. See Partido Radical, *Estatuto; Programa; Programa Mínimo* (Santiago: Imprenta Artes y Letra, 1921), pp. 17–19, 27.

[26]The text of the Liberal Alliance program is reproduced in *El Mercurio*, April 25, 1920.

This program appears to resemble the minimum Radical platform of 1919, more than that of any other Alliance party, in its oblique reference to conciliation and arbitration machinery and in its failure to make specific provision for unions or for a code of labor laws. Also, while the program indicated general agreement among the parties as to certain broad areas of needed reform, it committed no one to a particular, detailed reform project in any of these areas. Furthermore, it openly preserved party independence. It is not unusual that the convention should have so limited the Alliance, but it is nevertheless important that this salient fact of limitation be pointed out.

The foregoing still leaves unexplained the source of the code project which Alessandri presented to the Congress in June 1921, one year after the Liberal Alliance convention. There was no drafting committee officially representative of the Alliance partners. Rather, Alessandri personally requested that Moisés Poblete Troncoso, a fellow Liberal, prepare a draft project. Both Poblete and Alessandri testify to this, although it is not clear whether Alessandri gave general instructions for a complete code or whether he left the nature and content of the draft project generally up to Poblete.[27]

Moisés Poblete Troncoso is one of the most widely known professors of labor law and one of the most prolific writers on social, labor, and political subjects in Latin America. As a student of the University of Chile's Faculty of Law and Political Sciences, he wrote a thesis on the legal status of illegitimate children which he completed in 1913. This book was followed by other publications on the problem of agricultural production in Chile (1919), social museums (1920), the parliamentary régime (1921), technical organizations of social policy (1923), and union organization (1926).[28] Since 1926 his scholarly production has been regular and substantial. In 1921 he became Professor Extraordinary of Social Economy in the University of Chile and later was named to the chair of Labor Law, a position he held until his retirement a few years ago.

Poblete was also an active member of the Liberal party. He attended

---

[27]Letter from Arturo Alessandri to Don Moisés Poblete Troncoso, Sept. 23, 1949; Moisés Poblete Troncoso, "Recent Advances in Labour Legislation in Latin America," *International Labour Review*, vol. 30, July 1934, p. 63. See also Walker Linares, *Nociones de derecho del trabajo,* p. 155.

[28]The Spanish titles of these works are: *La legislación sobre los hijos ilegítimos; El problema de la producción agrícola y la política agraria nacional; Museos sociales; Nuestro régimen parlamentario; Organismos técnicos de la política social;* and *La organización sindical en Chile y otros estudios sociales.*

both the 1913 and 1919 conventions of the party, and he was probably the author of the party's 1919 platform statement on the social question.[29] When the Liberal Alliance won the presidential election in 1920, Poblete was made director of the national Office of Labor.

Alessandri naturally turned to Poblete as a trusted party member, an intellectual of established reputation, and as a government expert to develop a labor and social security project. That the product of his labors was a code of four books and over six hundred articles bears witness to his diligence and to his ambition, although it must be kept in mind that his task had been greatly simplified by the work of the Special Committee of 1919. His job was essentially to make a uniform and internally consistent code out of the scattered bills, laws, and other documents, already in existence. Given both Poblete's remarkable energy and the meager staff resources of the Office of Labor, it is probably accurate to conclude that this physical job of putting the code together was carried out largely, if not entirely, by him.

To summarize up to this point then, it is fair to say that intellectuals played a significant role in the political genesis of the Liberal Alliance project. A rector of the University of Chile, Valentín Letelier, was pivotal in turning the Radical party into the popular reform currents gathering force in the early twentieth century; a small group of intellectuals spearheaded a similar shift in the Doctrinaire Liberal party; Errázuriz Tagle, Ramírez Frías, and Juan Enrique Concha were all members of the Special Committee of the Liberal Alliance; and, finally, Moisés Poblete Troncoso, university professor with large interests in the society around him, authored the Liberal Alliance code project.

IV

The intellectual origins of the Liberal Alliance project have now to be traced. Procedure will follow that developed for the Conservative bill; that is, analysis will be limited to a few distinguishing features of the project, such as its code proportions, the book on social security, the craft union as its structural model, and the voluntary nature of its conciliation and arbitration provisions.

Although there may have been others before him who mentioned the need for a labor code in Chile, Malaquías Concha was certainly the first to make a major and persuasive plea for such a code. His 1907 thesis was titled *On the Need for a Labor and Social Security Code*

[29]See Partido Liberal, *Acta, tercera convención del partido liberal, 1913*, p. 2 and Partido Liberal, *Programa y estatuto orgánico del partido liberal, 1919*, p. 4.

(*Código del Trabajo y de la Prevision Social*) which is the precise title Poblete gave to the Liberal Alliance project. For precedent Concha pointed to the French "Millerand Code" of 1901, the British Factory and Workshops Act of 1901, and to the "Industrial Codes" of Austria and Prussia. A Chilean labor code would, he said, include the labor references of the Civil, Commercial, and Mining Codes, a few individual laws, and new matters, primarily in the area of working conditions, which he considered appropriate.[30] In the same year Pantaleon also encouraged " the progressive formation of a General Labor Code" and enumerated many of the laws it should contain.[31]

One might think that comprehensive social security legislation would have been closely investigated in Chile before the drafting of the Liberal Alliance project, perhaps as a method of wealth redistribution or of achieving consensus in the industrialization process or as a simple matter of social justice. This was not the case, although there was much concern for particular aspects of social security such as work accidents and illnesses, factory hygiene and sanitation, and public asylums and hospitals.

Two or three writers made passing comments about the need for broadly conceived social security programs, but no one really exploited the subject. For example, Guillermo Rossel Silva remarked in 1906 that taking care of the sick and invalid was not enough and that "the solution is none other than worker security in whatever form. One or another of the systems adopted abroad would give the same or analogous results."[32] The next year Pantaleon wrote favorably about an obligatory social security program which would include insurance against sickness, invalidity, and old age for all workers and compensation to workers or their survivors in cases of industrial accident or death.[33] A third writer devoted his entire thesis to *Worker Security* (1908) but it was very short and did not go much beyond the field of accident legislation.[34] The social security book of the Liberal Alliance code project seems therefore to have been the work, in very large part, of Moisés Poblete Troncoso. He undoubtedly relied heavily on foreign precedent and experience, but, insofar as the borrowing and adapting

[30]Malaquías Concha, *Sobre la dictación de un código del trabajo y de la previsión social.*
[31]Pantaleon, *La reforma legislativa y política y nuestra cuestión social*, pp. 48–50.
[32]Rossel Silva, *De la necesidad de legislar sobre el trabajo*, pp. 33–38.
[33]Pantaleon, *La reforma legislativa y política y nuestra cuestión social*, pp. 48–50.
[34]Ernesto Munizaga O., *El seguro obrero* (Santiago: Imprenta Barcelona, 1908), 32 pp.

itself are concerned, this was apparently his contribution and not, to any significant degree, that of other Chileans.

The organization of workers by crafts into national as well as local unions was an idea the Liberal Alliance borrowed directly from French legislation (Waldeck-Rousseau Act, 1884). Poblete and many others have acknowledged this debt.[35] Few realize, however, that the high degree of freedom from state control which the French union enjoyed was not borrowed and that the establishment, functioning, and dissolution of the Chilean craft union were intimately linked to state regulation.

But who borrowed the craft union, and why did voluntary unionism appeal to those who borrowed and adapted? No debates on the relative merits of craft and plant unions are to be found in the literature and only one person explicitly framed his choice in terms of voluntary versus compulsory systems. In 1907 three writers made brief references to the French craft union and one of them, Pantaleon, urged that it be adopted in Chile.[36]

Eugenio Frías Collao, Poblete's predecessor in the national Office of Labor, provided the only detailed explanation of the French law of 1884, and he and Tomás Ramírez Frías appear to have been the major proponents of the craft union in Chile. Frías Collao presented a long and very favorable account of "Craft Association in France and Agricultural Unions" to an agricultural meeting in Concepción in 1914.[37] He also helped Ramírez Frías draft the union bill for the Special Committee in 1919. Ramírez Frías spoke to the question of compulsory versus voluntary organization when he presented the union bill to the Chamber of Deputies in August 1919, and he had no doubt but that compulsion would be "contrary to the freedom of association which our Constitution establishes." At the same time, he would not confer corporate status on a union only because it had freely organized; the dangers of this approach were, he said, self-evident. Rather, corporate status should be granted only in accordance with certain rules and regulations. His bill adopted "the latter temperament" which was the one

[35]For example, see Poblete, "Labor Organizations in Chile," *Monthly Labor Review*, vol. 28, February 1929, p. 83, and Aníbal Pincheira Oyarzún, *Sindicalismo* (Santiago: Nascimento, 1934), pp. 44–48, 86–93.

[36]Pantaleon, *La reforma legislativa y política y nuestra cuestión social*, pp. 48–50; Enrique Escala, *Sobre el contrato del trabajo*, Santiago, 1907, pp. 115–122; Malaquías Concha, *Sobre la dictación de un código del trabajo y de la previsión social*.

[37]Eugenio Frías Collao, "Anexos," *Boletín de la Oficina del Trabajo*, no. 10, 1915, pp. 1–43.

in greatest accord "with the spirit of our institutions and with our social behavior."[38]

The craft union title of the code project put together by Poblete is almost a verbatim copy of the Ramírez Frías bill. It is however somewhat longer, adding especially to the state regulatory and control features of the Ramírez Frías bill, and it also incorporates the innovations of the French Millerand Act of 1920.[39] We might also mention, incidentally, that the profit-sharing features of the Liberal Alliance code appear also to have been adapted from a French scheme set up in 1917.[40]

Solutions to social conflict, strikes, and other forms of industrial violence were of earlier and more urgent concern to writers and politicians than were such topics as unions and other aspects of labor-management relations. The major university theses had been written on conciliation and arbitration, and a voluntary system had been prepared and decreed into existence, even before the Conservative party set up its High Committee in 1918. Indeed, by 1910 the die had been cast and a bill developed which, with few modifications, eventually became the conciliation and arbitration title of the Liberal Alliance code project.

A member of the Radical party first proposed the legislative establishment of arbitration in 1903 shortly after the bloody and destructive events of the Valparaíso maritime strike. He presented no bill, however, and his Radical party membership does not necessarily mean that his views flowed along voluntary lines.[41] Enrique Escala wrote briefly on the French system of voluntary *ad hoc* arbitration in his 1907 thesis,[42] but it was Carlos Roberto González who produced the first serious study of conciliation and arbitration *(Strikes,* 1908) and took up the significant matter of compulsory versus voluntary systems. While there were advantages to both types, he thought that only one of them would work in a given country and that it was therefore academic to discuss the two with selection in mind. Internal circumstances

[38]Cámara de Diputados, *Boletín de las Sesiones Ordinarias en 1919,* p. 1966.
[39]For a comparison of these two union bills, see *ibid.,* pp. 1967–1970 and "Proyecto de Código del Trabajo y de la Previsión Social," *Folletos Varios,* Tomo I, pp. 41–51. One of the important innovations of the Millerand Act was the removal of restrictions on the holding of real property.
[40]J. Miguel Valdés Freire, *Acciones de trabajo* (Santiago: Imprenta Cervantes, 1922).
[41]Cámara de Diputados, *Boletín de las Sesiones Ordinarias en 1903,* pp. 312–313. The speaker at the time was Deputy Fidel Muñoz Díaz from La Serena.
[42]Escala, *Sobre el contrato del trabajo,* p. 129.

determined in advance what type would fit, and it was so obvious to him that for Chile this was the voluntary type that he made no further explanation. He simply endorsed "voluntary arbitration in a form analogous to that of England and Canada"[43] (which presumably means that he also preferred *ad hoc* to permanent machinery). Since González praised the Letelier triumph in the Radical convention of 1905, he may have been a member of that party.

A young Liberal, who rose rapidly and eventually reached the heights of power in his party and in the government, was the first to put a voluntary and *ad hoc* conciliation and arbitration scheme in the form of a legislative bill. Manuel Rivas Vicuña, member of a wealthy and respected family, was elected to the Chamber of Deputies in 1910 and introduced his bill the same year.[44] The bill was praised by Casanueva (1911) who thought that "voluntary arbitration squares better with our social-economic system and even with the spirit of our fundamental laws" than obligatory methods.[45] Although he did not refer to the Rivas Vicuña bill, Agustín Zegers Baeza (1911) also favored a voluntary conciliation system. To him, conciliation was "a delicate matter of social education which can be encouraged and facilitated but cannot be imposed."[46] Finally, Manuel Rodríguez Pérez, a young Liberal who fought for reform as a member of the party's 1913 Committee on Social Questions, wrote his thesis on *Conciliation and Arbi-*

[43]González, *Las huelgas*, pp. 25–50.

[44]For the text of the bill, see Cámara de Diputados, *Boletín de las Sesiones Ordinarias en 1910*, p. 1063. Manuel Rivas Vicuña was the author of the Liberal party's equivocal 1907 pronouncement on the worker problem, and he was probably the first chairman of the Chamber's permanent Committee on Social Legislation set up in 1912. He appears to have assumed the role of a moderator between the reformers who wanted to change the Liberal party's 1907 statement and those in the party who opposed such a change. He was appointed Minister of the Interior in 1913 and after that his interests became broader. He may have been a member of the Special Committee of 1919, but he subsequently fell out with Alessandri, set up the "electrolytic" Liberals, and took no part in the social and labor reform movement of the early 1920's. See Partido Liberal, *Acta, convención del partido liberal, 1907*, pp. 319–326; Cámara de Diputados, *Boletín de las Sesiones Ordinarias en 1912*, pp. 619, 1164; Partido Liberal, *Acta, tercera convención del partido liberal, 1913*, pp. 222–224; Cámara de Diputados, *Boletín de las Sesiones Ordinarias en 1913*, p. 540; *Boletín de la Oficina del Trabajo*, no. 13, 1920, pp. 119–1121; and Donoso, *Alessandri*, vol. 1, pp. 240, 244, 299, 367, 368.

[45]Casanueva, *Diversas consideraciones sobre el régimen del trabajo y los conflictos colectivos*, p. 56.

[46]Agustín Zegers Baeza, *Algunas ideas sobre el Estado y la cuestión social* (Santiago: Imprenta Chile, 1911), pp. 49–50.

tration in Strikes (1914) and approved the Rivas Vicuña bill which, he said, "establishes voluntary arbitration and sets up conciliation boards."[47]

In December 1917 Eliodoro Yáñez, Minister of the Interior in the Cabinet of President Sanfuentes, established by decree a system of conciliation and arbitration based upon and very similar to the one outlined in the Rivas Vicuña bill.[48] The Yáñez decree remained in effect for several years, and it was under the authority of this decree that the government intervened in the several serious strikes of the early postwar period.

The bill which Jorge Errázuriz Tagle and his Committee on Social Legislation of the Chamber of Deputies reported out in 1919 also preserved the voluntary and *ad hoc* features of the Rivas Vicuña scheme. It proposed in addition, however, that permanent factory councils of a bipartite nature be created in every factory or industrial center employing more than fifty operatives.[49] This bill, like the original Rivas Vicuña bill, was never debated on the floor of the Chamber or in the Senate. Yet it continued the lineage, and, as such, was a major influence on the labor program of the Liberal Alliance.

The more immediate origins of the conciliation and arbitration title of the Liberal Alliance code project are found in a proposal developed by the Office of Labor and made public in May 1920. This proposal introduced two important changes which Moisés Poblete Troncoso later incorporated in the Alessandri code. The first made dispute settlement a permanent rather than an *ad hoc* process and therefore required the establishment of permanent conciliation and arbitration boards. The second was provision for a national appelate board which would hear cases not resolved in the boards of first instance.[50] The Poblete code as presented to Alessandri and introduced into the Congress in 1921 thus called for voluntary conciliation and arbitration procedures and permanent boards of two instances. Although it did not copy the factory council feature of the Errázuriz Tagle bill, it did provide for "worker delegations" who were to attempt to work out an agreement directly with the employer before resorting to conciliation. Poblete

---

[47]Manuel Rodríguez Pérez, *La conciliación y el arbitraje en las huelgas* (Santiago: Imprenta Santiago, 1914).

[48]For the text of the Yáñez decree, see Decreto no. 4353, *Boletín de las Leyes y Decretos del Gobierno Sanfuentes.*

[49]Cámara de Diputados, *Boletín de las Sesiones Ordinarias en 1919*, pp. 1192–1195.

[50]The text of this bill was published in *El Mercurio*, May 28, June 1, 1920.

also added a section on strike procedure in the event all peaceful settlement efforts should fail.

It is now appropriate to indicate that the conciliation and arbitration law passed in 1924 was a composite of the two proposals of the Conservative party and the Liberal Alliance. Conciliation was made obligatory and arbitration was declared voluntary; boards were permanent, as advocated by both groups. The legislative triumph of obligatory conciliation perhaps represented a concession to the Conservatives and those of like views within the aristocratic-Catholic élite. The triumph was probably also a result of dissatisfaction with the inefficiency of the voluntary Yáñez boards.[51] Shortly before he became President, Alessandri himself is said to have spoken out for "obligatory arbitration,"[52] but it is doubtful that he spoke from deep personal conviction. That he supported the voluntary character of the Poblete code soon after his elevation to the presidency would seem to support such a conclusion. Experience with the functioning of the Yáñez boards may likewise have convinced Poblete and others in the Liberal Alliance camp that *ad hoc* procedures would not work and that permanent machinery was a necessity.

It is interesting to note, in conclusion, that none of the basic ideas of the Liberal Alliance code project was inspired directly by the draft conventions and recommendations of the International Labor Organization. This is explained in part by the fact that the ILO General Conference had met only twice before Alessandri presented the code project to the Congress and had acted upon only a few labor matters. Among these were the eight-hour day; working conditions of women, children, and young persons; unemployment; and working conditions in the maritime industry.[53] While ILO draft conventions and recommendations on these matters may have been of some technical help to Poblete in his development of the code project, the general areas of legislation which they covered had long since been marked out by Chilean scholars and politicians. Chile had already borrowed from the socially advanced

[51]Moisés Poblete Troncoso said of this decree in 1949: "In many cases it worked well, but in many others it was not effective because of its voluntary nature." Poblete, *El derecho del trabajo y la seguridad social en Chile* (Santiago: Editorial Jurídica, 1949), p. 67.

[52]See Alessandri's speech to the convention of the Liberal party on April 25, 1920 reproduced in Biblioteca América, Sección Chilena, *El Presidente Alessandri a través de sus discursos y actuación política* (Santiago: Imprenta Gutenberg, 1926), p. 1618.

[53]See League of Nations, *International Labour Conference, Proceedings, 1919* (Washington: G.P.O., 1919), pp. 256–264 and *ibid., 1920* (Geneva: ILO, 1920), pp. 501, 576, 579, 582.

nations of the world and was, in this sense, ahead of the ILO. Nevertheless, both Chile and the ILO found it to their advantage to say that the Liberal Alliance code was in conformity with and/or included the draft conventions and recommendations of the ILO. Alessandri, in particular, appreciated the political utility of making this identification. He assured the Congress in June 1921 that all civilized nations, without exception, had begun to pass laws based on the results of ILO conferences and that no country could therefore refuse to follow suit without losing honor and respect in the world community.[54]

[54]Cámara de Diputados, *Boletín de las Sesiones Ordinarias en 1921*, Anexo, pp. 3–5. See also "Labour Legislation Arising out of the International Labour Conference," *Official Bulletin of the International Labour Organization*, vol. 3, Feb. 16, 1921, p. 283.

CHAPTER 7

The Élite Opposition

THE SEVEN labor laws of September 1924 were not the result of debate and compromise on the Conservative and Liberal Alliance bills and the achievement of legislative consensus through the democratic process. A military junta, a most unusual rather than a usual phenomenon of Chilean politics, took over the government in that month and year and immediately forced the Congress, on pain of immediate dissolution, to pass the laws. The new industrial relations system and other reforms of the new Constitution of 1925 were subsequently worked into the fabric of politics and society through the instrument of the dictatorship of Colonel Carlos Ibañez del Campo (1927–1931), likewise an aberrant phenomenon in that usually democratic country. Although the crucial intervention of the military was not carried out in the name of any particular party or coalition or élite group, it opened the way for an eventual triumph of the middle class. This was accomplished, so far as control of the government is concerned, in 1925 by the reestablishment of the presidential system and the separation of church and state. While the presidential system did not end coalition government, it lessened the élite conflict between the Liberal Alliance and the National Union, and those two coalitions ceased altogether to exist. Powerful members of the aristocratic-Catholic élite, and some members of the middle class as well, could no longer rely upon a parliamentary system to guarantee government inaction and thus to protect their vested interests. The meaning of the military intervention was not so clear, however, in the first confused days and weeks after the coup as it was to become later. Thus, when the junta called upon Alessandri and the Congress to pass the labor laws, it did not specify the middle-class Liberal Alliance code, and the laws passed combined salient features of both the Conservative and Liberal Alliance proposals.

The élite conflict and the constitutional crisis which came to a head in 1924–1925 tend to conceal the fact that there was widespread and strong opposition to labor reform as such among members of both élites. There was opposition outside the Congress as well as inside it, and this general opposition was just as strong, or even stronger, in the years before Congress received the two major labor bills as it was after the bills had been developed. Indeed, as we shall see in a later chapter, opposition continued after the laws were passed. Their full implementation was consequently delayed for many years, even beyond the Ibañez dictatorship. Not until the Popular Front period of the late thirties did the system begin to function in a relatively complete way.

Before identifying the opposition to labor legislation, it would be well to indicate that Chilean writers have long been aware of the existence of such an opposition. Jorge Gustavo Silva takes up the matter briefly in his study of *Our Political-Social Evolution, 1900–1930*. After describing the attitudes of individual political parties and the two coalitions toward the social question, he concludes that "program-wise" all took a modern stand. However, he continues, between their words and their deeds was a great gulf, a gulf which separated "more or less sincerely professed ideals from the will to block, for reasons of personal selfishness and group interests, the realization of such ideals." While in public they pushed reforms and awoke great popular sentiment for them, in the secretariats of the congressional chambers and in the committees, social and labor bills were maneuvered to a standstill or were emasculated. There were many bills because no party wanted to be "less than the others" but, withal, general politics prevailed over the politics of social legislation. Perhaps, Silva concluded, what the sometimes corrosive pen of the Spaniard, Pio Baroja, once wrote of Chile still applied: "There is in Chile a political oligarchy; an oligarchy of appetites; an oligarchy of petulance, and, above all, of vanity, which treats the country as if it were a private fief."[1]

[1] Silva, *Nuestra evolución político-social*, pp. 77–83.

173

In 1920 when the Office of Labor released its conciliation and arbitration bill, *El Mercurio* remarked in a spirit of hopelessness that over the years many good bills had been written and presented to the Congress. And the paper queried, "what object is there to all these good bills if not a one is ever debated on the floor of Congress? What confidence can such beautiful declarations inspire among workers and businessmen if the years pass and everything remains mere words, bundles of papers filed in parliamentary secretariats?" The Office of Labor bill ran the risk of falling into the same bottomless pit with other bills, as if "every last drop of energy in the country had been spent in learned speeches and torrents of words" leaving nothing at all for the actual passage of laws.[2]

Many years after the revolutionary movement of 1924 Moisés Poblete Troncoso recalled that the Alessandri code project met the resistance of landholders, industrialists, and commercial people who dominated the Congress. The consequence was a military government and the sudden adoption by fiat of a complete industrial relations system.[3] Others have pointed vaguely and in Marxian terminology to "capitalist elements" in the Congress as the ones guilty of obstructing the democratic process.[4]

Concern in this chapter is to identify the élite opposition to labor reform in the pre-1924 period, describe its rationale, and evaluate its strength. The first section deals with an extreme form of opposition which denied there was any "social question" at all in Chile. Discussion then proceeds to the opposition as revealed in the activities and pronouncements of the political parties, the National Agricultural Society, the Catholic Church, the Society for Factory Development, and the Labor Association. Finally, although organized labor was not part of the power élite, it was part of the opposition to the élite industrial relations proposals, and this, perhaps to many readers unexpected, opposition is presented in Section VII. Some intellectuals also supported the opposition to social reform and they will be identified throughout the largely institutional sections of this chapter.

I

It would be inaccurate to characterize the opposition as either uniform in degree throughout the groups to be studied or as all-inclusive

[2]*El Mercurio*, May 29, 1920.

[3]Poblete, *El movimiento obrero latinoamericano*, p. 141.

[4]See, for example, Cora Carreño Ulloa, *El principio de la libertad sindical y la legislación chilena* (Santiago: Editorial Jurídica, 1952), p. 271.

with respect to the many areas of social and labor reform. A landowner, might find it possible to support some or even comprehensive labor legislation if it were to apply only to manufacturing and mining or to foreign-owned concerns, while he might be ferocious in his opposition if the same legislation were to apply to agriculture and commerce. A businessman might summarily reject unions, conciliation, and arbitration yet support some of the milder reforms (e.g., worker housing, factory sanitation, restrictions on the sale of liquor) for reasons of health, morals, or justice. There was an extreme form of opposition, however, which categorically denied the existence of the social question in Chile and any need at all to ameliorate working and living conditions or encourage closer and more systematic labor-management-government relationships.

In general, the opposition to social change was much less articulate than the forces which challenged the existing scheme of things. Indeed, one finds more complete and more consistent statements of the ideas and motivations of the opposition in the writings of the reformers than in the speeches and writings of the opposition itself. The reformers made constant references to "those who denied the social question" and explained some of their thinking, while the opponents of reform were more frequently content to express themselves through the choices they made, the votes they cast, the silence they maintained, or in the manipulation of parliamentary rules. A few of them were, however, intellectuals who defended the status quo and their writings will be cited in the section which follows.

The extremists in the opposition looked upon the social question as something that did not, and indeed could not, exist in Chile. It was a phenomenon of the older, worn-out societies of Europe, factory societies in the throes of death, tormented by violent clashes between workers and employers. Their test of a society in rapid decay was the presence of the minimum wage, which they apparently thought of as the lowest wage consistent with the maintenance of life and reproduction and as the nadir of a long secular decline in wages. As societies industrialized and grew older, the number of unskilled workers and the unemployed increased and the iron law of wages, which kept worker income at the minimum necessary to sustain life and allow reproduction, came to rule throughout society. The result was pauperism and the social question. The latter was thus found only in those older societies that had reached the maximum of human imperfection.

There could be no social question in Chile because Chile was a young and growing agricultural country with more jobs than job seek-

ers, wages above the minimum, vast unpopulated areas, and rich un-
tapped natural resources. The outbursts of labor violence in Chile
were accidents or were staged by agitators who, unrealistically, were
importing into the country the socialistic ideas of senile societies.
Unions, strikes, arbitration, collective contracts were the foolishness
of foreigners and their literature which had unfortunately impressed
some of the younger generation in Chile. Ideas from Spengler, Malthus,
Ricardo, and Marx can all be seen in the position of those who defended the status quo.

In addition, these men saw their world as one consisting only of
masters and servants, those who command and those who do, those
with rights and those with duties. The fundamental prejudice and injustice of such a dualistic system were not admissable by them; it was
the only world they knew, it had always been that way, and for them
it was right.[5]

The fantasy of Chilean youth, dynamism, hope, and economic well-
being relative to Europe tended to appear less real even to the most
adamant as the years passed and as Valparaíso was followed by Santiago,
Santiago by Iquique, as the Socialist Workers' party gave way to the
Communist party, and as the FOCH shifted from mutualism to the
Red International. Although events belied their rationale, they did not
cease to oppose social change.

II

As we have already seen, the Conservative party was among the first
to treat the social question favorably in its platform and the first to
propose a major labor reform bill. Nevertheless, that party sheltered
many who in the last analysis could not implement their vows. Indeed
a member of that party, Deputy Eulogio Díaz Sagredo, was one of the

[5]For a sample of the literature describing the rationale of those who denied the
social question, see Casanueva, *Diversas consideraciones sobre el régimen del trabajo
y los conflictos colectivos*, pp. 45–49; Emilio Castelar, *Legislación obrera* (Santiago:
Imprenta Cervantes, 1909); Errázuriz Tagle, *El desarrollo histórico de nuestra cuestión social*, pp. 21–28; Escala, *Sobre el contrato de trabajo*, pp. 131–133; González,
Las huelgas, p. 25; Hector Holley, *Las huelgas* (Santiago: Imprenta Aurora, 1905),
pp. 61–63, 142; Francisco Jorquera F., *Del trabajo minero en general y particularmente
del laboreo al Pirquen* (Concepción: Imprenta Moderna, 1913), p. 29; Pantaleon, *La
reforma legislativa y política y nuestra cuestión social*, pp. 26–27; Rossel Silva,
De la necesidad de legislar sobre el trabajo, p. 7; Fernando Sandoval Hurtado, *Ensayo
sobre la cuestión social en Chile* (Santiago: Imprenta Bellavista, 1913), pp. 6–24;
Jorge Gustavo Silva, *El liberalismo político* (Valparaíso: Imprenta Royal, 1914), p.
28; Vicuña Subercaseaux, *Socialismo revolucionario*, pp. 229–230, 258.

first to denounce partisans of labor reform and to deny the social question in Chile. Just after the Valparaíso strike in 1903 a Radical, Fidel Muñoz Rodríguez, proposed in the Chamber of Deputies that a special committee be named to study the worker problem and present a bill on arbitration, the labor contract, and other matters. Díaz Sagredo, who represented the agricultural province of Arauco, objected saying:

> Something unusual is happening here; we are being frightened by the worker question, a question which in reality...does not exist in Chile, because in truth it cannot be said that the worker problem or question which is the cause of so much worry in Europe has developed here....accidents like that of Valparaíso cannot reasonably be considered a manifestation of the existence of the social question of European societies.[6]

In rebuttal, Muñoz Rodríguez attacked Sagredo's position as that of the Conservative party itself and, while discount must be made for the partisan atmosphere of the Congress, there was a grain of truth to what he said. "The Conservative party or, more properly speaking, the Clerical party" he began, "cannot look with favor upon raising the veil of ignorance and misery which covers the working class of our country. The most they can do is extend the hand of Christian charity to the poor and the invalid." As a matter of doctrine they do not accept the workers "as their equals or as the free citizens of a Republic."[7]

Some of the most prestigious leaders of the National party, like the Conservative party a political representative of the aristocratic-Catholic élite, spoke out against the social question. Deputy Agustín Edwards supported a worker housing bill in 1903, although he explained that the only social-economic question in the country was that of a depreciating currency (which meant a loss in real wages and a rise in the price of imported articles of necessity). Unemployment, the social-economic problem of Europe, "does not exist nor can exist in a country like ours which has immense unpopulated areas and unexploited natural resources." One aspect of the "social problem" was, however, found everywhere regardless of the abundance of work or the low cost of living. That was "the human aspiration, the civilized aspiration, the aspiration of Christian charity to give the greatest measure of well-being to the greatest possible number of individuals." The housing bill was an expression of this aspiration and he therefore wanted to see it become law.[8]

---

[6]Cámara de Diputados, *Boletín de las Sesiones Ordinarias en 1903*, p. 338.
[7]*Ibid.*, p. 340.   [8]*Ibid.*, p. 329.

By 1910 Edward's position on this matter had changed, in form if not in essence. He was then a member of the national executive board of his party and, at its convention, declared that those who compared Chile with Europe and found there was no social problem in Chile were wrong. There was no unemployment or hunger or a "social question," but there were "social problems." Proof of this was in the labor movements of the large cities and the nitrate *pampa* where severe conflicts had occurred in recent years and military force had been used to bring them under control. These painful experiences had revealed to the skeptics the existence of "latent social ills." Those in commanding positions had in the past abandoned their duty to raise the moral level of the masses and to improve their material existence. At the same time, however, the state had helped the producers by cheapening the currency. Now it was time for the state to solve the worker problem by appropriate currency measures.[9] Apparently only his words had changed, not his mind.

A second top leader of the National party, Senator Antonio Varas, publicly rejected on the floor of the Senate the two major titles of the Conservative labor bill. He wanted industrial peace, he said, but the mere existence of permanent conciliation and arbitration machinery would increase rather than diminish labor disputes. Doubting also that plant unions would be agents of industrial harmony, he thought they might even become "the germs of discord'" which would ruin good employer-worker relations and hamper "the free development of our businesses at the very moment they show the greatest promise of growth."[10]

Juan Enrique Concha was the only outstanding member of the National Union coalition, who, in a real sense, dedicated a lifetime to the cause of the working class. Guillermo Feliú Cruz tells us that Concha's clear perception of the social question was "in disagreement with that of his fellow Conservatives."[11]

There is evidence in the writings of Concha himself that leads one to suspect that his standing among the party leaders of his day was not one of great prestige. Tame, or perhaps even reactionary, as his views may seem today, they were too advanced then for many Con-

[9]Partido Nacional, *Convención del partido nacional, 1910, actas* (Santiago: Imprenta Zig-Zag, 1911), pp. 76–78.

[10]Cámara del Senado, *Boletín de las Sesiones Extraordinarias en 1919–1920,* pp. 1013–1015.

[11]Feliú Cruz, *Chile visto a través de Agustín Ross,* p. 136.

servatives and for others of the aristocratic-Catholic élite. Concha lamented that many men of generous heart and recognized charity believed the social Catholics were socialists and their program socialistic. While this was not true, said Concha, it was true that many Catholics and many of the better educated and selfless men of public life in Chile were too individualistic and that there was much that was just in the aspirations of the populace and even of the socialists. He took special pains to make clear, however, that social Catholics respected the providential inequality of men and did not pretend that it could be abolished by law. They believed "almost absolutely" in private property, the only exception being expropriation for the public good. Socialism, he advised, wanted social leveling and the absorption of private property by the state. Yet he ventured to say on another occasion that the extreme concentration of rural landownership in Chile "can not and must not be considered something that will last indefinitely." Both his sensitivity to criticism and his sometimes defensive advocacy of labor and land reform are very likely measures of the discomfort he felt in his own political and social circles. In 1916 he admitted with regret that he lacked the prestige to bring about the serious and ample study of worker questions which he thought necessary.[12]

Concha ran for the office of Senator in a special election in April 1919, and it is significant, in terms of the general rural orientation of the Conservative party, that he ran in the urban province of Santiago. Furthermore, his victory was due in no small measure to the support he received from worker clubs and circles and from the Democratic party. Twelve worker organizations signed a letter favoring his candidacy. This letter, a copy of which was filed in the archives of the Conservative party, bears no greeting. However, internal analysis indicates that it was probably addressed to the president of the Democratic party. The worker representatives said they were not concerned about the party affiliation of whoever might be elected to fill the Senate vacancy so long as he could and wanted to serve the interests of working people. "We are perfectly well aware of the ideas and the political allegiance of Mr. Concha," they said, "but that is not important to workers who are only interested in having in the Congress those who will defend their cause." They asked, therefore, that the party proclaim Concha its candidate.[13]

[12]Concha, *Conferencias,* pp. 108–111, 203–210, 212–216, 230–231.
[13]See letter bearing twelve signatures the first of which is Manuel Gonzáles A. in Cartas, Santiago, 1919, Archivo del Partido Conservador.

After the election results were known, Guillermo Bañados, influential Democrat and Senator, telegraphed the Democratic party in Concepción that "the candidate who has the affection of all the Democrats in the province of Concepción has won by a large majority." He said that he and others in the party had lent their support "with the best will and enthusiasm for the triumph of Mr. Concha whose program fulfills the aspirations of the Democratic party."[14]

It seems almost certain, for the reasons and in light of the circumstances presented above, that the "social Catholicism" or "Christian Democracy" of the Concha school in Conservative ranks was a precurser of the movement which in the 1930's split the Conservative party and led to the establishment of the National Falange.[15] That group, now left of the political center and known as the Christian Democratic party, is one of the foremost proponents of labor and agrarian reform measures in Chile.

If there is some truth to all of this, then why did the Conservative party give preferential treatment to labor legislation at its 1918 convention and shortly thereafter approve the Concha bill? Did the party and the National Union as a whole really get behind this bill in the Congress? If not, what over-all political forces may have operated to discourage legislative action?

To answer the first question, the political atmosphere of late 1918 must be recreated. The Liberal Alliance had won the elections in March of that year, as we have seen, and controlled both houses of the Congress. This was the first time since the beginning of the parliamentary régime that the Liberal Alliance had won control of the government. The Alliance had controlled the Senate before but not the Chamber of Deputies, and therefore not the Ministry. The latent power of the Alliance, and especially of the Radical party, its chief party component, was thus dramatically revealed in 1918, and the political

[14]Telegram, Guillermo M. Bañados to Juan Pradenas Muñoz, April 1919, *ibid.*

[15]Halperin contends that two Jesuits priests (Fernando Vives del Solar and Jorge Fernández Pradel), working actively in unions and cooperatives and among Catholic University students in the second and third decades of the twentieth century, "created the climate and the specific conditions" that made the emergence of the National Falange possible. See Halperin, *Nationalism and Communism in Chile*, pp. 179–181. While their contribution may have been important, it is clear that in the opening decades of the century social reform ideas had already penetrated top levels of Conservative party leadership. Johnson has also noted that after 1891 a minority of "strongly Catholic elements with the approval of the Church began to dissociate themselves from the more reactionary segments within the Conservative Party." Johnson, *Political Change in Latin America*, p. 68.

right was stunned. As Donoso puts it, the Alliance victory caused such a "terrible impression" in the National Union that Sanfuentes even considered resigning the presidency. He was dissuaded by intimate advisers who thought he could play off one Alliance faction against another in making ministry appointments and thus gain some political advantage from adversity.[16]

Immediate loss of ministerial power was, however, only the first result of the 1918 elections so far as the Conservative party and the National Union were concerned. Even more ominous was the portent of losing the presidency in 1920. In the parliamentary system as it developed in Chile, presidents were often made at the ministerial level. The man who could put together a Cabinet was the power figure. He became Minister of the Interior, presided over the Cabinet, and, if he lasted long enough, grew quickly into presidential timber. What the Alliance won in 1918 was therefore not only control of the Ministry but a headstart in the presidential campaign two years hence. It is significant that Alessandri successfully organized the first Liberal Alliance Cabinet in 1918, beating out Eliodoro Yáñez who disputed the honor with him.

These were awful events for the Conservatives to witness because the Radicals were an anticlerical party fully and uncompromisingly committed to divorcing church and state and furthering a free, public, and lay system of education. The ideological clash with the Conservatives was head-on. The Radicals were more deliberately anti-Conservative than either the Democrats or the Socialist Workers' party, and their amazing success at the polls made their spectre a hundred times bigger and more frightening than that of both the leftist groups combined.

The Conservatives realized the danger in the situation and felt compelled to strengthen their electoral position through appeals to youth and the working class. Three months after the elections, the executive board of the party sent out a circular letter to all branches urging them to set up youth centers as one means of fighting the advance of radicalism. The board reasoned as follows:

> The alarming advance of Radicalism, in its tireless labor to take over all national institutions and to dominate the Republic unopposed, today has the support of all the other parties of the Alliance.
> To stop it in its effort to undermine everything sacred and respectable, it is paramount that our historic party, whose most outstanding characteristic is love of order and social peace, count absolutely on the enthusiastic and selfless participation of all its supporters.

[16]Donoso, *Alessandri*, Vol. I, p. 209.

To this effect, the Board wishes that in all the departmental head-quarters "Youth Centers" be established to second the actions of their respective departmental Directorates.[17]

In its call to the convention to take place in September 1918, the board again appealed for response and action on the basis of the consequences all would suffer should radicalism march on unopposed. Chilean radicalism was the same as the "socialist radicalism" of France, the board warned. The latter had persecuted religion, made enemies of capitalists and business men, established the system of "expropriating" wealth through high taxes, and damaged without piety the interests of the masses. If the Radicals took over the government completely in Chile, it would be even worse because they were less cultured and of baser passions than their French counterparts; they even refused to listen to their own leaders on the infrequent occasions when they spoke of moderation and prudence.[18]

At the convention itself, Juan Enrique Concha took up the Conservative-Radical clash before, and as a build-up to, his request for the appointment of a High Committee to draft a labor bill. Radicalism, he pointed out, was growing fast with little money and "socialist democracy" (probably a reference to the Democratic party) with even less; meanwhile, the Conservative party had become an electoral minority. The reason for this state of affairs was not that the Conservatives were a plutocratic, aristocratic, and oligarchic group, as some charged and more believed, but rather that religious and social hate were stronger in the country than the faith and social justice which dominated Conservative thinking. The believers among the people and those who respected social order were ignorant of the Conservative program, others mistakenly held the Conservatives to be unconcerned about the middle class, and the electoral masses lacked "convictions."[19]

Even while the general political climate readied the Conservative party for a definite break on the social issue, internal pressure came from the urban and worker elements of the party and from Concha, not from the rural stronghold of the *latifundista*. Resolutions on arbitration, unions, retirement and pension funds, the labor contract, and the High Committee came from the Santiago and Valparaíso delegations (representatives of the urban heart of the country) and from the party's labor representatives. As Concha began his speech on labor

[17]Circular dated July 5, 1918, Cartas, Santiago, Archivo del Partido Conservador.
[18]Rough ink draft of the convention call dated July 1918, *ibid.*
[19]Partido Conservador, *Convención del partido conservador de 1918, actas*, pp. 84–85.

legislation he said, "I enter upon this with no fear whatsoever" because our program "frankly interprets the legitimate aspirations of the worker whose authorized representatives we have listened to constantly"[20] which means that he probably *was* fearful of standing before the country's aristocracy to urge unionism upon them and that he needed to point to rank-and-file support for what he was about to request.

Political desperation undoubtedly explains why some Conservatives cocked a favorable ear, applauded warmly, and then cast a yea vote for his program. The same fate of circumstance also assured Concha a period of ascendancy in Conservative ranks as their much-needed expert on the social question. In addition, however, it is well to remember that a bill is only a bill under any circumstances, and that when a party is in the opposition and not in the government a bill can have little meaning indeed. Just how genuine or how insincere the Conservative party may have been in putting forth labor legislation is difficult to say, but for our purposes it is enough to know that there were those who opposed as well as those who favored the move.

Within a matter of weeks after the party took its labor bill to the Senate the Liberal Alliance disintegrated. Enough Liberals switched their coalition allegiance to give the National Union a clear majority in the upper chamber. Although the National Union majority changed somewhat in subsequent elections, that coalition retained control of the Senate until March 1924, or for five long years. Yet Juan Enrique Concha was the only Senator who really fought for the Conservative bill in the Congress, and the most the Senate itself ever did was to pass its innocuous first title, dealing with working conditions. Calling a bluff sometimes reveals a bluff; this was apparently one of those times.

Incongruous as it may seem, one of the things which changed the political picture and which may have made the Conservatives feel a little less desperate was the election of Alessandri. His election meant in the first place that, for the Conservatives, another political battle had been lost and that, for them, the political value of an advanced position on the labor question had temporarily declined or changed in its nature. The Liberal Alliance had the Chamber, the Ministry, and the presidency all in its power. However, the margin of his victory was very slim and he did not win over the Senate until too late. The second meaning of these events was therefore that the National Union and the forces in society which it represented were still safe, even if one

---

[20]*Ibid.*, pp. 87–88.

assumes for the moment that the Liberal Alliance was united behind Alessandri. The Liberal Alliance for all of its radicalism did not turn out to be radical at all because, for all of its power, it was powerless. While the middle class had apparently won a great electoral victory, it had not completely unseated the landed oligarchy. The office of President was weak and Congress strong in the parliamentary régime, and National Union control of the Senate gave that group virtual veto power over the affairs of state. Moreover, events were to prove soon after 1920 that the Liberal Alliance itself was divided on the social question and that Alessandri could not control his labor project even in the Chamber of Deputies. This circumstance was also undoubtedly of great comfort to those members of both élites who frowned on any major social advance.

Despite the "beautiful declarations" of the Liberal and Radical parties, they likewise had influential members whose dedication to the individualist ethic was unshakeable. They could no more accept Leroy-Beaulieu than some Conservatives could accept Pope Leo XIII. Guillermo Feliú Cruz says of the Liberals that "not a few of them denied the existence of a social question" and that Deputy Manuel Rivas Vicuña created "no little alarm among his fellow Liberals" in 1910 when he presented his conciliation bill. The latter bill, he says, was a "novelty" at the time precisely because it had come from a Liberal.[21]

The Liberal party's platform change of 1913 identified a dissident group with such strong anti-feelings on the social question that it joined a splinter movement six years later. One of its members was Senator Luis Claro Solar, of patrician lineage and from the rich Acon-cagua valley of central Chile. Senator Claro Solar did not believe the Liberal party's grudging recognition of the "worker problem" in 1907 had become archaic and he feared that to change or expand it would be to accept socialism.[22]

Cleavage in the Radical party was not so great that it ever resulted in an open break or division as it did in the Liberal party, but it was there nevertheless and the "anti" faction was eminently respectable and powerful. Enrique Escala, a thesis writer, was so impressed by the strength of the opposition that he looked upon the apparent triumph of Letelier and the "socialist" bloc with merciless scorn. Unfortunately,

[21]Feliú Cruz, *Chile visto a través de Agustín Ross*, pp. 132–133.
[22]Partido Liberal, *Acta, tercera convención del partido liberal, 1913*, pp. 219–221. For the remarks of other delegates at the convention who also opposed changing the party's social platform, see *ibid.*, pp. 206–207, 209.

he said, the party's 1905 program was nothing more than propaganda. "In a country of *caciques* like ours, the parliamentary delegation of the Radical party is composed of a few more or less ignorant oligarchs who lack completely any inclination to improve the working class."[23] While this is too cynical an observation in its general sweep, it is an acute one in suggesting there is an important distinction between the party as a whole and its much smaller congressional delegation. It is obviously more difficult to implement policy in a competitive arena like the Congress than it is to develop policy in the politically homogenous atmosphere of a party convention. A Congressman is also a much more powerful success figure than most party members and his ties to the leadership élite of the country may be closer and more direct than those of the general party membership. Moreover, it is important to know what side of a party issue is represented, or better represented, in the Congress than another. Letelier, chief protagonist of social reform in the Radical party in the opening decade of the century, was not a member of the Congress. Enrique Mac-Iver, leader of the opposition, was and he remained there until 1922 when he died.

Although Mac-Iver's influence in the Radical party probably declined as party membership bulged and its congressional delegation shot up, he always retained power and a respectable following. At the 1920 convention of the Liberal Alliance, for example, he was one of three candidates for the presidential nomination. He also always fought hard against the expansion of government and never relinquished his belief that labor legislation was futile and inadvisable. His speech in the Senate against Title I of the Conservative bill in 1921 is a classic statement of the views of the élite opposition to social reform in Chile. In this regard, it is to be noted that Mac-Iver, although a Radical and supporter of the Liberal Alliance, was also a great *hacendado* whose values were perhaps likened more to those of the aristocratic-Catholic élite than to those of the middle class. As the following excerpt from the speech indicates, Mac-Iver believed that the Chilean worker, a mestizo, was by nature lazy, that Chile needed to put forth more effort rather than to pass an eight-hour law that would, as he saw it, limit productive work, and that legislation could not reduce labor-management strife:

> What concerns me is what we are in Chile, not what happens in Germany, France, or England, but what we Chileans are, descendents of the Spanish and the indigenous race. Our propensity, is it work or

[23]Escala, *Sobre el contrato de trabajo*, p. 135.

idleness? I have heard it said that our worker, our people, that we are workers. I see, Mr. President [of the Senate], — I don't know if my view is erroneous, — that we are not workers; — only a most indispensable need makes us dedicate ourselves to work. I see, besides, — I don't know whether I am mistaken or not, — that the intensity of our work is very low, that the intensity of our work scarcely reaches the limited effort a man expends when he does the most insignificant thing. If I were to judge with a certain liberty of language what we are, I would say that we are a lazy people, a people without an affinity for work, a people which flees from work. The country is profoundly weakened by this defect in our make-up. That we are worth more than the indigenous peoples of the interior of Bolivia, of Peru, or of Colombia, cannot be doubted; in comparison with the inhabitants of those countries, our people are workers, without any doubt.

So what we need is not to stimulate a non-working habit in order to conserve the individual, but to stimulate the individual to work.

. . . .

The persistence of this certain biological state of our working class [laziness] does not derive from the country, or from the nature of the country, nor does it come from an economic or social situation which expresses itself in this way; it comes from defects or if you wish from a quality. The worker doesn't rise, he doesn't prosper because he doesn't make the effort that he must make.

. . . .

Why then this fixing of the hours of work? Because socialist or non-socialist books tell us to do it? Because laws have been passed in Europe and America with this objective?

But among us such a need does not exist. I do not ask whether these laws are necessary in Europe or in America where they have been promulgated, but I do say that we do not need them.

This law [the Conservative bill] is born only of the spirit of imitation. Others did it, let's do it also, for reasons that are not reasons for us.

. . . .

It is an error to believe that with laws...social disorders, strikes, lack of work, shortcomings in the fulfilment of duty, immoralities in work itself are going to be prevented. Nothing like that is going to be avoided with laws like this.

Nations that have passed them, suffer the same difficulties in modern industrial life as we.

. . . .

I do not like to do this; but I want though in any case to give my opinion and I must say that this sort of thing leads to nothing but the stimulation of idleness. It will only contribute to making bigger the biggest social ill of Chile, which for me is not alcoholism; it isn't even that unfortunate illness, whose name can be said in a Chamber of Congress just as it is said everywhere. It is not syphilis: it is idleness.

. . . .

Work hurts no one; the intensity of work is not as far as I am concerned an explanation for the degeneration of a race. Work is useful; it is, above all, ennobling. I would like to see my country more noble for its ten or twelve hours of daily work than to see it, following modern and biological theory, accept the eight hours of which this bill speaks.[24]

The Liberal Alliance controlled the Chamber of Deputies during the entire period of Alessandri's Administration and controlled the Senate from March 1924 until the military intervened in September. Notwithstanding these clearly favorable political circumstances, no serious debate ever took place on the floor of either the Chamber or the Senate with regard to any major aspect of the Liberal Alliance code project. Some useful committee discussion has been recorded, especially the work of the Joint Committee on Social Legislation, but for the most part even the committees made little headway. The genuine support that Alessandri and others brought to the reform program was not broad enough to overcome the opposition, strong in both élites and in both political coalitions, and the inherent weaknesses of the parliamentary régime.

III

A good part of the opposition came from the rural aristocracy, the wealthy and cultured *hacendados* who looked to Europe for intellectual stimulation, lived like medieval barons on their broad estates, and treated their *inquilinos* like children from the day they were born until the day they died. The very concept of labor relations was antipathetic to their way of life, a challenge, a threat, a revolt which implied an end to special status and high privilege.

Perhaps the most representative institution of this rural élite, other than the *fundo* itself, was the National Agricultural Society (SNA). The record left by this organization is not so complete or definite in content as one might like, but it is enlightening. The monthly journal of the SNA carried a summary of the minutes of its executive board meetings as well as editorials, by-lines, and articles, and these are rich sources of information.

The Society discussed the worker or social question more frequently, in more detail, and more openly in the earlier years of our period, when it was not yet a national issue, than in the later years when it was. This is an interesting phenomenon, made all the more so by the fact that it also describes what took place in the Society for Factory Develop-

[24]Senado, *Boletín de las Sesiones Extraordinarias en 1920–1921*, I, pp. 509, 511.

ment. Only a partial explanation suggests itself and this will be presented later.

The National Agricultural Society took up the "worker question" for the first time in 1907 just before the Iquique tragedy. Immediately thereafter the SNA discussed it again at length, softening its attitude considerably, and then with only two or three exceptions did not return to the matter until 1919. In its first effort the SNA declared that the celebration of May 1 and "too frequent resort to strikes" were unjustifiable and out of place in Chile. They were the revolutionary socialist and anarchist practices of Europe and were not proper in Chile because the Chilean working class was better off than the middle class and even better off than a portion of the upper class. How then could the workers legitimately protest anything or show irritation or hate the other classes? They simply copied May Day because they saw everybody else copying whatever came from Europe, or they were led into it by "criminal and destructive advisers." Any educated person would support their desire for equitable and cordial relations with capital but only if this desire was sought "in a spirit of mutual cooperation, tranquility, and order and by fair and legitimate routes."[25]

After a strike had broken out on the railroads in May 1907 the Society criticized the railroad company for not having taken any measures to prevent or minimize the effects of the strike. It had not even taken the "elementary precaution of eliminating from its shops those pernicious elements who upset worker tranquility and are the permanent cause of disorder and anarchy." The strike was brought on by subversives and professional agitators who "today slip into the unions to anarchize and exploit them."[26]

Urban workers were the sources of violence and evil in the country. They set themselves up in societies or clubs, held meetings, called strikes, and generally made news through their turbulent activities. The rural worker, on the other hand, was more peaceful and passive and provided less for the police and the courts to do.[27]

The SNA reacted to the dreadful events of Iquique with compassion and there were signs of greater understanding and a resolve to improve the social and legal system. Yet many of its old attitudes remained and the Society did not act on the good intentions it announced. The strike

[25]"La Cuestión Obrera en Chile," *Boletín de la Sociedad Nacional de Agricultura*, vol. 38, May 15, 1907, pp. 278–281.

[26]*Ibid.*, vol. 38, June 15, 1907, pp. 349–351.

[27]*Ibid.*, vol. 38, July 15, 1907, pp. 415–417.

at Iquique, the Society's journal began, was not a local or isolated event but another deplorable explosion of deep social unrest to which the leading classes had seemingly closed their eyes. It was no longer possible, or prudent, or patriotic to continue denying the evidence. The social question existed in Chile and "we believe the hour has come to face it resolutely in order to prevent widespread disasters of incalculable consequences. To be obstinate in seeing nothing, doing nothing, remedying nothing, is the same as throwing more fuel on the fire."

Even though the SNA continued to feel that the workers were relatively well off, it admitted that many strikes occurred in the better-paid industries and areas and that this was a genuine sign of worker discontent — along with emigration and internal migration. The simple fact was that the worker felt badly "because he suffers privations, because his existence is arid and painful, and because he wants to improve his condition."

While strikes pointed to just desires for reform, they were nevertheless the wrong way to express discontent and were the work of perverse agitators. "There are in the cities gangs of malefactors of the worst sort, roving idlers, exploiters of the people who make their living out of disorder and revolt. They are not, properly speaking, socialists, or anarchists, or anything; they are roguish idlers who always begin by organizing what they call resistance societies whose principal objective is to provide them with the funds they need in order to live without working....they are the fomenters of every uprising because social peace would be their ruin." They also contaminated the rural workers who lived within their reach. Good rural workers were good for the same reason that good indians were good — they had no contact with outsiders.

If unions, strikes, the development of union leadership, and formalization of labor relations were apparently not only not solutions to the social question but aggravators of it, what kinds of solutions were there? The journal listed six: (1) cheap hygienic homes, (2) family development, (3) hobbies and moral and physical culture, (4) encouragement of private saving, (5) counseling services, and (6) reduction of social distances by contact with the people and through raising their economic standards. Workers who participated in these things "feel well, and do not take part in strikes or join the rebels against the social order."[28]

[28]*Ibid.*, vol. 39, Jan. 15, 1908, pp. 1–9; Feb. 15, 1908, pp. 67–75.

A few years later when the SNA returned to the social question its outlook had apparently narrowed. Order, morality, and social welfare would be guaranteed if the worker but had his own home and his own plot of ground. He would cease definitely to be a source of social upheaval and the instrument and victim of plotters. The 1906 workers' housing law was a step in the right direction and it should be extended to rural workers.[29]

The Society was roundly criticized in 1911 by one of Santiago's leading daily newspapers for not doing anything about the improvement of rural labor conditions. The paper charged that the way work was carried on in the *fundos* was "simply monstrous and unworthy of a civilized country." The Society was offended and, while granting that the condition of the farm worker was bad, denied that the landowner had anything to do with it. The worker was not a "serf" inhumanly exploited by a "feudal lord," and he himself and the government were the ones responsible for his plight. He drank and the government did not enforce the law on alcoholic beverages. The government likewise did not maintain order in rural areas and theft was consequently so common that no worker dared buy any furniture or personal belongings for his home, and that was why he had none. Moreover, the *patrón* was now the one who had to submit to the demands of the worker, and not the other way around as it used to be. Since labor was scarce, the worker imposed the amount of his wages, and his impositions were neither very intelligent nor very justifiable.[30]

A strike of railroad switchmen and brakemen in 1913 brought the Society back completely to its pre-Iquique position of adamant and uncompromising opposition to unions and union leaders. The railroad men struck for higher wages and payment in gold as insurance against the continued erosion of real income. The SNA reaction was that, while strikes were all right if they had just cause, if they respected the right of those who wanted to work to continue to do so, and if they were a last resort measure, the railroad strike did not qualify under any of these tests. The inflation of which the strike leaders complained affected all workers and all classes, and hurt employers as much or more than any other group. *All* railroad workers had told their employers that they disapproved of the strike and wanted to work, but they were forced to strike anyhow for fear of reprisals from their leaders. This strike was therefore like all the others before it — the work of "pernicious

[29]*Ibid.*, vol. 42, March 15, 1911, pp. 132–134.
[30]*Ibid.*, vol. 42, May 15, 1911, pp. 268–271.

elements who exercise a strange influence over the people, elements who generally are not the product of our own soil." They were neither workers nor Chileans and they did not support strikes to improve working conditions but to create the disorder and anarchy which would justify their position as union leaders and keep them from having to work and earn an honest living. It was therefore time to give the government the authority to deal with this "invasion of human refuse, cast out by the police of other countries. . . . The freedom which is invoked to protect this social gangrene is not recognized in any enlightened nation."[31] The government did enact a "residence" law which permitted the deportation of undesirable aliens, but very little use appears to have been made of it.

In 1919 it was reported to the executive board of the SNA that *inquilinos* of the Catemu region were setting up unions and demanding concessions from *fundo* owners, apparently with the help and encouragement of the Catemu miners. The Society considered the situation grave and the *inquilinos* impertinent, and was pleased to know that the *patrones* were taking effective measures to combat the development.[32] Isolated disturbances and union activity in the countryside continued, however, especially on *fundos* close to the cities and towns where FOCH affiliates were active. The Society feared that unless something was done the *inquilinos* would sooner or later all be organized into the FOCH and would be calling strikes and demanding wage increases. It was distressing that they wanted higher wages because this would only raise prices to the consumers, and it was likewise distressing that the *esprit de corps* of the *inquilinos* was being directed against the *patrón* "who is their companion and associate in work." Some factories in Santiago had had to close because of the excessive economic demands of workers and the same thing would happen on the farms unless *fundo* owners themselves organized and took the initiative. They should organize by zones and then take measures necessary to prevent their *inquilinos* from setting up unions. Wages, job rates, and conditions should be standardized from farm to farm and this would take the incentive out of organization. Unorganized *inquilinos* in one farm would no longer have to have a union in order to win the better conditions they saw elsewhere. Credit and marketing cooperatives, clean homes, and both primary and adult education should also be provided. If

[31]*Ibid.*, vol. 44, Dec. 15, 1913, pp. 733–736.
[32]"Acta de la Sesión del Directorio del 17 de Noviembre de 1919," *El Agricultor*, May 1920.

the farm owners acted with benevolence, morality, and charity, they could avoid making any basic changes in the traditional relationship between themselves and their *inquilinos*.[33]

It is likely that the renewed interest of the SNA in the labor problem was the result not only of *inquilino* unrest but also of the national attention focused on the problem by the Conservative party and the Liberal Alliance. In April 1921 the executive board of the SNA invited Juan Enrique Concha to meet with it to discuss agricultural unions. The minutes of this meeting suggest that Concha urged action to halt FOCH inroads in rural areas and thus prevent the growth of a class struggle type of unionism. He spoke well of *inquilino* organizations of a mutual benefit and cooperative nature and of the individual written labor contract. This was much weaker than the relevant provisions of the Conservative bill which allowed for collective relations, the collective contract, and conciliation and arbitration. Concha's presentation to the Society may have been the result of a deliberate effort on his part to adapt the ideal to the narrower views of an *hacendado* audience. It may also have come from a realization that the Senate defeat of the stronger sections of the Conservative bill, which had occurred just two weeks before his meeting with the Society, required a new approach. In any case, the executive board agreed after listening to Concha that unions should be formed for cooperative, athletic, and moral purposes and that the individual written contract should be instituted. All *fundo* owners should unite to keep out militant unions, prevent strikes, and blacklist the agitators.[34]

Shortly after Alessandri announced the Liberal Alliance code project in June 1921, the SNA appointed a committee to meet with him to explain its views on the labor question. The committee was instructed to tell him that the Society was sponsoring its own "associations" to further the welfare of the workers and their families and that there was not a single outstanding conflict or disagreement in the country between *patrones* and *inquilinos*. For these reasons, there was no need for state-authorized unions or for conciliation and arbitration boards. The National Agricultural Society was engaged in satisfying in every measure the aspirations of the *inquilinos*.[35] From this date on little of importance appeared in the Society's journal with respect to labor legis-

[33]M. Correa Pastene, "La Sindicalización de los Labriegos," *ibid.*, January 1921, p. 1; M. Correa Pastene, "Necesidad de Unificar los Salarios," *ibid.*, February 1921, p. 1.

[34]"Acta de la Sesión del Directorio del 25 de Abril de 1921," *ibid.*, July 1921.

[35]"Acta de la Sesión del Directorio del 30 de Mayo de 1921," *ibid.*, October 1921.

lation. A committee was appointed to study the Alessandri code project, and in 1922 the Society petitioned the Chamber of Deputies to exclude agriculture from the coverage of the white-collar bill which had been added to the legislative program of the Liberal Alliance.[36]

IV

The *Diario Ilustrado*, owned by the Catholic Church (the Archbishopric of Santiago) and a group of Conservative party individuals, was recognized as the paper which spoke for the Church in Chile during the period under study. Certainly no fundamental issue, inimical to the interests of the Church or contrary to the views of the hierarchy, was propagated in the paper. The editorial comment of this paper is our source for learning the attitude of the Church toward labor legislation.

The best measure of the Church's position on labor reform is in the way it received the Conservative bill. The social Catholic proponents of that bill drew principally upon the papal encyclicals for authority and considered labor legislation an important Christian solution to the social question. If, in view of this, the Catholic Church opposed the Conservative bill, then it would certainly not approve of legislation emanating from any other source, such, for example, as the Liberal Alliance. The Conservative bill is therefore a proper choice for the acid test.

First of all, it must be noted that not until the Conservative bill had been developed did the *Diario Ilustrado* show any interest or concern for labor questions. It was not a part of the intellectual movement for reform within the aristocratic-Catholic élite and did not expound upon *Rerum Novarum*, or attempt to develop, or lead or encourage others to develop, a positive Catholic point of view on the social question in Chile. The paper was of course fully aware of this and gave two reasons in explanation of its lack of concern. First, the paper believed that social legislation was peculiar to the advanced, industrial economies of the world and that the Chilean economy simply did not yet qualify as advanced and industrial. There were only two exceptions to this, the paper pointed out, and these were the nitrate and copper industries (which, the writer adds, were also foreign-owned and controlled). Since labor legislation was useful principally in dealing with problems which had their origins in industrialization, the

[36]"Acta de la Sesión del Directorio del 1 de Agosto de 1921," *ibid.*, December 1921; *ibid.*, August 1922.

paper had no need to be interested and "in this sense we could afford to wait." Second, there were other reforms, more fundamental and more urgent than social legislation, for the improvement of the welfare of the working classes. These were stabilization of the currency, tax reform, and obligatory primary education. They had to precede other social laws. "We have wanted briefly to record these points," said the *Diario Ilustrado*, "before the public authorities enter fully into the study of so-called social legislation."[37]

Nevertheless, the paper admitted that some changes had taken place in the country which justified some alteration of its previous stand. The reasons for no action given above were still controlling, but it was true that the social question in Chile had sharpened since the end of the war in Europe. Prices were higher and life was harder because of the scarcity of consumer goods. Moreover, there was now in Chile "a movement of opinion" which favored social legislation, and Chile had joined the League of Nations which likewise supported labor laws. Some laws should therefore be passed. Why? — because to do so would prevent others from charging that "we are not doing anything in benefit of the popular classes" and that "our social legislation is backward relative to that of the principal countries of the world." Still "we must not forget the special conditions of work in our country or imitate blindly. . . . The state must intervene in labor questions but in a practical, educated, and prudent way."[38]

Where might the country begin? With the establishment of a labor ministry "the organization in charge of studying, preparing, and applying whatever laws we want to pass."[39] This editorial was written three weeks before the Conservative bill arrived in the Senate. Did the paper hope that its suggestion on procedure would cause the party to reconsider its bill and make a fresh start at the less ambitious level of ministry development?

On the day the Conservative bill was made public, the *Diario Ilustrado* printed it in full and remarked that it was "interesting" and included most of the modern concepts of social legislation. The paper did not doubt that the project "will be enthusiastically received by the worker element."[40]

A week later the paper began to editorialize on the content of the bill and in three separate editorials covered its three titles. First, work-

[37]*El Diario Ilustrado*, May 23, 27, 1919.
[38]*Ibid.*
[39]*Ibid.*, May 1, 1919.
[40]*Ibid.*, May 21, 1919.

ing conditions. The paper said that it approved the eight-hour day but suggested rather sweeping exceptions to such approval. (The reader is reminded that the provision in the bill itself was loosely drawn and susceptible to emasculation by interpretation.) The eight-hour day was all right for the good, sober workers who came to work every day, but the custom in Chile was to drink so heavily on the weekends that many workers regularly missed work on Monday. They had to work more than eight hours a day during the five remaining days in order to get their job done. "We would therefore make many exceptions to the eight-hour day and would leave it for jobs of a certain nature." Legislation on the work of women and children was acceptable in principle but the Conservative bill was not flexible enough. Children should be permitted to do light work because the country was short of labor, and employers should not be asked to furnish schools for the children of workers. The minimum wage was not "in any way" practical. It would limit demand for labor if fixed too high and would therefore cause unemployment or it would be laughed at by employers. If fixed too low, it would benefit no one. In a crisis period "a low wage is better than none."[41]

In many countries of the world, began the editorial on unions, worker organizations are considered the solution to the social question, and even in Chile "there is confidence in unionism to the point of stimulating it and almost making it obligatory rather than regulating it in a prudent way." "Perhaps" it was advisable to stimulate the limited associations of the workers of each enterprise, as the Conservative bill proposed, but who could prevent plant unions from setting up federations and who could really predict what the future "spirit" of these organizations would be? Would this spirit be prudent and conservative or one of blind resistance and revolution? Questions like these must be asked in order to moderate the enthusiasms of those who propose union formulas. "Let us recognize unions and accept them when they come forth spontaneously and with just and legitimate objectives; but let us not stimulate them artificially through the power of law."[42]

Forcing the employer to share profits with the union also went too far. Justification for the measure was not evident. Obligatory profit sharing might in the final analysis only harm the worker by causing the employer to seek redress through a wage reduction.[43]

[41]*Ibid.*, May 28, 1919.
[42]*Ibid.*, May 29, June 17, 1919.
[43]*Ibid.*, May 29, 1919.

The paper discussed title three of the bill under the heading "obligatory arbitration," which it considered excessive and premature for Chile. Compulsory arbitration was exceptional in the world and there was no way of knowing whether it would ever be put into general practice. Sometimes the parties to a conflict had to reject it, either because it might ruin the firm, in the case of the employer, or because it would compromise economic interests too much, in the case of workers. Finally, the enforcement features of the arbitration clause (fines) were ill-advised because "the nature of things cannot be forced." The *Diario Ilustrado* closed its commentary on the Conservative bill saying that the observations it had made did not take from the bill either its merit or its day in court. "It may be the best basis of discussion for the important questions it treats."[44]

An interesting footnote to the church-labor question comes from the Conservative party. In a biographical sketch of Juan Enrique Concha, the party mentioned that Cardinal Gibbons had enthusiastically praised his labor bill. There was no mention of any similar praise coming from a member of the Chilean hierarchy.[45]

A great deal about the Catholic Church's position on the labor question can be understood when it is recognized that until 1925 Catholicism was the official state religion. This meant that crucial appointments at the top of the hierarchy were made only with the approval of the government. The government, in turn, was, until the later years of our period, largely the National Union coalition and particularly the Conservative party. In addition, the Catholic Church was a large landholder in its own right and had a direct vested interest in preserving the existing society and its social arrangements. The Church's natural alliance was with the aristocratic *hacendados* and, as part of them, it could be expected to share their limitations and imperfections. It is enlightening to note that the Church opposed the publication of *Rerum Novarum* in Chile and that Spanish translations of this key social encyclical had to be brought into the country from Argentina.[46] With

---

[44]*Ibid.*

[45]Partido Conservador, *Convención del partido conservador de 1921, actas,* p. 223.

[46]Conversation with Bishop Mark G. McGrath, February 1966, Cornell University. It is equally enlightening to note that the *Diario Ilustrado* refused in the 1930's to publish the social encyclical *Quadragéssimo Anno.* Its director, Luis Silva Silva, believed the refusal was necessary "to free the Church from the imprudent pronouncements of the Popes." See Henry A. Landsberger y Fernando Canitrot, *Iglesia, intelectuales y campesinos; la huelga de Molina* (Santiago: Editorial del Pacífico, 1966), capítulo VI "La Doctrina Social de la Iglesia y el Problema Laboral," p. 46.

the severance of official church-state relations in 1925 and the sale of most of the Church's lands since 1928, the latter has acquired a more liberal and progressive outlook on social and reform matters.

V

The Society for Factory Development (SFF) took an earlier and more positive interest in social legislation than did the National Agricultural Society, and it in fact deserves a great deal of credit for the passage of the pre-1924 laws on worker housing, alcoholism, Sunday rest, and industrial accidents and the law which created the Office of Labor. Yet, however progressive we may wish to classify the SFF on these matters, the same cannot be said for its labor relations position, which differed little from that of the SNA.

The Society was set up in 1883 and almost from the start encouraged the improvement of vocational training, the establishment of technical schools, and the construction of decent housing for workers. It produced a voluminous study of worker housing and a housing bill both of which were useful in developing the 1906 housing law.[47]

The Industry Committee of the Chamber of Deputies asked the SFF for its opinion of Malaquías Concha's 1901 bill which covered the employment of children and women, factory sanitation and hygiene, safety and accidents, the ten-hour day, Sunday rest, and inspection. The SFF responded by appointing a two-member committee to study the bill and report its findings to the executive board. One of these men was Juan Enrique Concha. (He joined the SFF in 1902, was elected a member of the executive board in 1903, and resigned two years later with the explanation that he had no time to attend board meetings.[48]) The only provision of the bill which the committee rejected outright was the ten-hour day which it said was favored only by socialists and would in any case violate the right to work. The SFF accepted the Committee's report, with the exception of its favorable response to Sunday rest, and sent the Chamber's Industry Committee a revised bill.

[47]See Pedro Luis González, *50 años de labor de la Sociedad de Fomento Fabril* (Santiago: Imprenta Universo, 1933), pp. 3–4, 29–30; "Acta de la Sesión del Consejo Directivo del 30 Junio 1900," *Boletín de la Sociedad de Fomento Fabril,* vol. 17, June 1, 1900, p. 237; *Boletín de la Sociedad de Fomento Fabril,* vol. 21, April 1, 1904, pp. 113–114; and Cámara de Diputados, *Boletín de las Sesiones Ordinarias en 1903,* p. 344.

[48]"Actas de las Sesiónes del Consejo Directivo del 6 de Enero 1903 y 19 de Julio 1905," *Boletín de la Sociedad de Fomento Fabril,* vol. 20, Feb. 1, 1903, p. 75, vol. 22, Sept. 1, 1905, p. 587.

The SFF later supported the 1907 Sunday rest law and, at the request of the government, wrote the by-laws for it. The only other subject of the Malaquías Concha bill to become law before 1924 was its safety and accident title, and the SFF also endorsed this piece of legislation.[49]

The Society cooperated with the Ministry of Industry and Public Works in launching the Office of Labor in 1907, favored tightening the law on the sale of alcoholic beverages, and proposed legislation on the labor contract "in its various forms" and on social security. With regard to social security, the Society printed a communication from Germany which indicated that obligatory social security there had not damaged business; rather, production had increased from year to year "due in good part to the healthy condition of the workers."[50]

Much of the relatively progressive image reflected by the SFF in these years is due to the work and the personality of Pedro Luis González. He was president of the Society for a number of years (1906–1912) and, equally if not more important, was the editor of its monthly journal for almost the entire period of our study. He taught Social and Political Economy as a Professor Extraordinary of the University of Chile and wrote a prize-winning study of the *Labor Contract*. His editorials supported all, and are the original source of many, of the legislative endorsements made by the SFF. It was González, for example, who as editor called for both state social security and labor contract laws. He later authored an SFF memorandum to the President on "political economy" which repeated his concern for the above, and other, social and labor reform measures.[51]

[49]"Acta de la Sesión del Consejo Directivo del 10 de Septiembre 1902," *ibid.*, vol. 19, Oct. 1, 1902, p. 401; "Informe de los Señores Concha y Quezada," *ibid.*, vol. 20, Jan. 1, 1903, pp. 25–27; "Legislación del Trabajo," *ibid.*, vol. 20, July 1, 1903, pp. 217–218; Carta, Sociedad de Fomento Fabril a la Comisión de Industria, *ibid.*, vol. 20, July 1, 1903, pp. 243–246; "Actas de las Sesiones del Consejo Directivo del 3 y 10 de Junio 1903," *ibid.*, vol. 20, July 1, 1903, pp. 249–250; Carta, Sociedad de Fomento Fabril al Señor Ministro de Industria, 17 Diciembre 1907, *ibid.*, vol. 25, Jan. 1, 1908, pp. 55–56; *ibid.*, vol. 26, Feb. 1, 1909, pp. 73–76; *ibid.*, vol. 30, Dec. 1, 1913, pp. 1109–1115; and "Acta de la Sesión del Consejo Directivo del 22 de Junio 1915," *ibid.*, vol. 32, July 1915, p. 502.

[50]Marcial Martínez, "Ley sobre Alcoholes," *ibid.*, vol. 19, June 1, 1902, pp. 203–205; Carta, Eduardo Guerrero V. al Ministro de Industria y Obras Públicas, 21 Noviembre 1906, *ibid.*, vol. 23, p. 773; "Acta de la Sesión del Consejo Directivo del 20 de Noviembre 1906," *ibid.*, vol. 23, p. 783; *ibid.*, vol. 27, Sept. 1, 1910, p. 561; and "Los Beneficios del Seguro Social Obligatorio," *ibid.*, vol. 30, May 1, 1913, pp. 416–418.

[51]Sociedad de Fomento Fabril, *Memorandum sobre política económica* (Santiago: Empresa Zig-Zag, 1916).

While in his book González urged collective labor-management relations, he never, as editor of the SFF journal, wrote about unions, the collective contract, the strike, or dispute settlement. An insight into his apparently different behavior as editor may be drawn from the statement in his book that Chilean employers did not want to have anything to do with unions.[52] The SFF seems therefore to have taken an enlightened and self-interested stand on the range of practical matters like housing and safety which, properly enforced (and they were not), could have improved both worker well-being and production. Leadership or interest stopped at the point where change would have meant a self-imposed sharing of power with organized workers. Even though this appears to be an accurate analysis of the SFF as an organization, there were unusual persons like González and Eliodoro Yáñez (who was president of the Society during 1918–1925) who were willing to make some change in power relationships in the larger social interest.

The costly and violent strikes and demonstrations of the post-World War I years faced the SFF with a challenge more serious in nature and magnitude than any it had faced before. Although the written record leaves much to be desired, it seems certain that these events split the SFF, the more conservative elements leaving and setting up the "Labor Association" to fight independent unions and "solve" capital-labor difficulties. The size of this withdrawal from the SFF cannot be precisely figured, but it appears to have been large. The SFF itself followed a more reasonable line of conduct and supported much, though not all, of the Liberal Alliance labor program.

At the January 1919 meeting of the executive board of the SFF several members expressed concern over the growing frequency of strikes and the "excessive" wage demands of the unions. They thought that tariff protection and stabilization of international exchange were ways of dealing with the crisis. At the suggestion of González and Yáñez, the board agreed to communicate to the government the SFF's "specific ideas and the urgent need for solving these questions before they take on greater seriousness."[53]

This was not the kind of response which several members of the board wanted to see the SFF make, however, and they laid their cards on the table at the July meeting. Unions were creating severe problems, said one delegate, because they struck from firm to firm and

[52]González, El contrato del trabajo, pp. 28–29.
[53]"Acta de la Sesión del Consejo Directivo del 7 de Enero 1919." Boletín de la Sociedad de Fomento Fabril, vol. 36, January 1919, pp. 61–62.

forced all employers to grant the same concessions. He wanted the SFF to take the initiative and organize employers by industry "in order to harmonize relations with workers." Another member added that the police might be used to protect workers who didn't want to strike, although it would be difficult to do since strikers followed workers right into their homes to keep them from working. Others were not persuaded that the SFF should make such a move, for they believed that it would only bring upon them the hate of the workers. While employers had every right to organize to improve production and working conditions, as they did in many countries, it was inadvisable to do so "in order to draw up the battle lines against the workers." It was the government's responsibility to pass the kinds of laws that would harmonize worker-employer relations. Debate did not continue to a showdown at this meeting, but it was agreed that the SFF should write to the "Argentine Industrial Union" and get a copy of the strike bill that organization had prepared.[54]

When debate was resumed later in the year it had shifted ground and attention was placed, so far as the minutes reveal, exclusively on a legislative solution to the ceaseless round of strikes. Business should demand that an arbitration court be set up "to resolve the difficulties between employers and workers." When the further suggestion was made that an "Assembly of Businessmen" should be called to study the worker problem, it was accepted and an organizing committee was appointed.[55]

In the minds of some board members, obligatory arbitration offered a complete and final solution to industrial conflict. This is implicit in the language quoted above, and explicit in remarks made at a subsequent session of the board. At this session, and before the Assembly of Businessmen convened in 1920, the Yáñez decree on conciliation and arbitration was declared ineffective in disposing of conflict because it rested upon the voluntary consent of both parties. What Chile needed was obligatory arbitration which would "put an end to the influence of the subversive ideas which characterize European labor movements."[56]

[54]"Acta de la Sesión del Consejo Directivo del 11 de Julio 1919," *ibid.*, vol. 36, July 1919, p. 469.

[55]"Actas de las Sesiones del Consejo Directivo del 7 y 14 de Noviembre 1919," *ibid.*, vol. 36, November 1919, p. 734.

[56]"Acta de la Sesión del Consejo Directivo del 9 de Abril 1920," *ibid.*, vol. 37, April 1920, p. 234.

The Assembly of Businessmen, whose attendance was not reported, reached eighty-six "conclusions" on subjects ranging from the tariff, money, transportation, and communication to "social matters." Only three of these, the social ones, had any direct connection with labor. This would seem to indicate that many businessmen at the Assembly may have considered strikes, union demands, and wage concessions more as a pretext for demanding their own favorable treatment, in the form of higher tariffs and the like, than as issues in their own right. Yet the "social matters" they discussed were not unimportant. They agreed to ask the Liberal Alliance government to designate a committee to draft a "Labor and Social Security Code," recommended that the Congress legislate on "forced labor," and "insisted" that a "Ministry of Labor and Social Security" and a labor inspection service be established immediately.[57]

Endorsement of a labor and social security code probably reflects in some degree the influence that Yáñez brought to bear as SFF president and as a major figure in the Liberal Alliance. That Alessandri did not later appoint a committee to develop the code may have been a mark of the personal rivalry between the two men. The social matters with which the Assembly identified are, however, more significant for what they left out than for what they included. Curious indeed that nothing was agreed upon, or if agreed upon considered too incidental for treatment as a separate conclusion, in the area of arbitration. No evident consensus either with respect to unions, maximum hours, minimum wages, collective contracts, and the other "difficult" issues.

Like the National Agricultural Society, the Society for Factory Development became silent on labor matters after 1921. It appointed a committee to study the Liberal Alliance code but never published its views. In September 1924 the Society's journal printed the law on unions, but without commentary.[58]

VI

The Labor Association was founded in September 1921, nine months after the SFF's Assembly of Businessmen and only three months after the Liberal Alliance had released its code. Its announced objective was "to coordinate and to concentrate the action of its affiliates in all

[57]"Asamblea de Industriales, Conclusiones Aprobadas," *ibid.*, vol. 38, February 1921, pp. 67–73.
[58]"Acta de la Sesión del Consejo Directivo del 9 de Septiembre 1921," *ibid.*, vol. 38, September 1921, p. 532; *ibid.*, vol. 41, September 1924, pp. 643–647.

matters related to work and affecting the natural and legitimate development of industry, agriculture, and commerce." It would support anything tending "to harmonize the legitimate interests of capital and labor."[59] The statutes of the Association pointed to the following benefits employers could expect to derive from membership: (1) defense of their interests through associated effort, propaganda, and the study of problems effecting labor; (2) maintenance of an Association-wide blacklist which would permit the hiring only of those blue-collar and white-collar workers whose reliability was guaranteed in advance; (3) immediate "mediation" in case of conflict; and (4) representation of their interests before the public authorities.[60]

The Association said it recognized that a lone worker had no power and that he had to associate with others. But this had to be done in accordance with the law and for the noble objective of improving conditions through justice and equity. Mutual benefit activities were permissible within this concept; presenting demands to employers was not.[61]

Membership in the Labor Association was open to agricultural organizations and individuals as well as to representatives of industry and commerce. According to its own figures, which may be inflated, there were 78 affiliated firms in 1922, 1,075 in 1923 (employing 110,000 workers), and 1,122 in 1924 (employing 127,390 workers). If these data are only half true, the organization was of fair size. The Agrarian Union, with 604 farm owners, joined in a body, and the president of the Association in 1924 was Ricardo Lyon, a wealthy and well-known *hacendado*.[62]

The inspiration for the founding of the Association may have come from disaffected elements in the SFF. It was modeled after the Argentine Industrial Union which had interested some SFF members in 1919.[63] Only one member of the executive board of the SFF resigned during this period ("for private reasons," he said), but with the data available it has not been possible to trace his subsequent course.[64] More

[59]"La Asociación del Trabajo de Chile," *Horizontes Nuevos*, Nov. 22, 1924, p. 3.
[60]Poblete, *La organización sindical en Chile y otros estudios sociales*, pp. 53–54.
[61]"La Solución Directa y el Derecho de Asociación," *Horizontes Nuevos*, May 13, 1922, p. 1.
[62]*Ibid.*, Sept. 18, 1923, pp. 4–5; Aug. 23, 1924, p. 5; Nov. 22, 1924, p. 3; Dec. 6, 1924, p. 7.
[63]Poblete, *La organización sindical en Chile y otros estudios sociales*, p. 53.
[64]"Acta de la Sesión del Consejo Directivo del 3 de Diciembre 1920," *Boletín de la Sociedad de Fomento Fabril*, vol. 37, December 1920, p. 751.

important, however, in suggesting its possible SFF lineage is the interest Yáñez showed in the organization and his fear lest it provoke industrial warfare. As editor of *La Nación*, he reported that the Labor Association was a group representing businessmen who wanted to consolidate their action opposite labor. "Certainly," he added, "it is not advisable that capitalists arm themselves for war, thus contributing to the undermining of society." Public authority was responsible for enforcing the rights of all citizens, and public authority also understood that the freedom of some extended only so far as the rights of others began. The destructive work which some misguided spirits were undertaking was "profoundly censurable" and all necessary measures should be adopted "to assure social tranquility and to avoid the undermining of our institutions."[65]

The FOCH thought that all the capitalists in Chile belonged to the Labor Association and that its objective was to fight the FOCH itself and to stop the growth of real unions by setting up "yellow" or company-controlled organizations and combating strikes. The FOCH came into possession of a letter allegedly sent by the secretary-general of the Association to an affiliated member which advised as follows: "You have a perfect right to prevent within your private property whatever act that may be contrary to your interests, and on this principle of right you may base your action." The Association's first major field campaign was against the coal miners during their 1922 strike.[66]

Although the evidence presented above is meager, it would seem to suggest that the Labor Association was on principle opposed to any positive labor legislation which would recognize or encourage genuine collective practices between labor and management. The Association's specific declarations on the subject of labor legislation tend to support this conclusion. Before the passage of the labor laws in 1924, the Association printed only one legal article, a criticism of profit sharing, in its paper. It must be left to the employer, the Association argued, to give, if he wishes, a percentage of his profits to those workers who have worked hardest and most efficiently. Only the employer knows how business is going and whether or not he can afford to share profits. Besides, workers prefer a high and steady wage to a system which would never permit them to know how much they were going to receive.[67]

[65]*La Nación*, Dec. 17, 1921.
[66]*La Federación Obrera*, Feb. 19, 21, March 27, 1922.
[67]*Horizontes Nuevos*, Sept. 29, Oct. 6, 1923.

The reaction of the Association to the laws after they were passed was equivocal but, at the same time, generally unfavorable and counseled repeal. One writer in the Association's paper applauded the "good spirit" of the laws, but then added that businessmen had not been consulted, that the laws had been passed precipitously, and that they would therefore be a dead letter. Opinion, as expressed in the paper, was divided on the social security law, opposed the accident and white-collar laws and called for their repeal, and indicated that dispute settlement would not be effective since arbitration had not been made obligatory. There was no comment at all on the union law or the labor contract.[68]

While the Labor Association was not founded for the avowed purpose of opposing the labor reform movement in the Congress, its stated objectives, its large membership, and its activities would all seem to qualify it as an important part of the élite opposition to a new industrial relations system. Its position was both more extreme and more negative than that of either the SNA or the SFF and its presence probably accounts for the slackening interest in labor matters of both the SNA and the SFF after 1921. The hostile spirits of both organizations apparently joined the Labor Association.

VII

Organized labor can also be considered part of the opposition to the élite industrial relations proposals. It is doubtful that, even had labor supported reform legislation, this would have made much difference in the Congress because blue-collar workers were not yet organized to exercise political pressure effectively. Nevertheless, the opposition of the FOCH can be introduced at this point to indicate the breadth of opposition and also as background for labor's attitude toward the laws after 1924 (the subject of Chapter 9, "Unanticipated Consequences").

To say that organized labor opposed the élite industrial relations proposals is somewhat misleading because it portrays a definiteness and clarity of policy that did not really exist. The published record of FOCH convention proceedings and the content of labor and political journals do not indicate that the FOCH ever debated or discussed the élite proposals or declared against them. This could lead one to believe that the organization simply had no faith in "bourgeois" parliaments and their laws, and indeed its leaders and news media often said so.

[68]*Ibid.*, June 27, 1925, Dec. 13, 1924, Nov. 1, 1924, Dec. 6, 1924, Nov. 8, 1924, Nov. 12, 1924, Nov. 15, 1924, Jan. 31, 1925.

Notwithstanding this fact, however, the FOCH was closely allied to the Socialist Workers' party and later the Communist party, its leaders ran for political office and some of them won seats in the Congress, it developed a labor reform bill of its own and submitted this bill to President Alessandri and the Congress, and its congressional representatives frequently sought government aid for particular groups of workers. The confusion may in part be explained by the popularity Alessandri enjoyed among workers and a consequent reluctance on the part of Recabarren and others to jeopardize their own following by attacking him and the Liberal Alliance code proposal. It was also due, however, to the general emotional state of leftism in Chile at the time, a lack of structural separation of doctrinal differences, and, particularly, a failure to agree upon a legislative policy. The leadership of Recabarren left much to be desired. He was indecisive, uncooperative, a dreamer. He acted like a democrat, thought like a utopian, and talked and organized like a revolutionary.

In one of his congressional campaign speeches in February 1921, Recabarren told his worker audience that he would not go to the Chamber of Deputies to pass labor laws and that he was sure they would not want him to or expect him to:

> We, the workers, now know that the social problem cannot be resolved by laws, for the bourgeoisie will never permit laws benefiting the people and if any were passed, they would not respect them.
>
> If Socialist representatives were to go to Congress to contribute to the passing of new laws, they would not go to obtain the true liberty we need nor to obtain real benefits for the working class.
>
> Any law apparently beneficial that a Socialist deputy might obtain would be of no use to the people, because they have never been of benefit. They contribute instead to strengthen the capitalist system and they postpone and retard genuine popular emancipation, because they arouse hopes in the people which can never be translated into social welfare.

It was nevertheless necessary to have a true representative of the working class in the Congress so that he could expose "the entire uselessness of bourgeois laws" and speak the voice of the common people "who groan under the disgraceful slavery and merciless exploitation of the capitalists."[69] *El Socialista* thought that both Recabarren and Santiago Labarca, a Radical deputy who identified with the FOCH, considered politics useless and the pastime of the incompetent and the venal.[70]

[69] See Simon, "Recabarren," pp. 79–181 and *El Socialista*, Feb. 10, 1921.
[70] *El Socialista*, April 1, 1921.

At the same time, however, the national executive board of the FOCH drew up a fifteen-article labor bill, or "Contract of Industrial Socialization," which it sent to President Alessandri and later to the Chamber Committee on Social Legislation. The bill reflected ideas that Recabarren had long and sincerely espoused. It was also supported by *El Socialista,* which declared that the Chilean Congress could do nothing more monumental than to pass the bill and thus hand over to workers and employers the solution of the social question and capital-labor relations.[71] The stated objective of the FOCH bill was to promote economic and social peace through joint worker-employer administration of the enterprise and the equal sharing of profits. The bill proposed that the government require the employer and the workers of every company employing at least ten persons to sign an "industrial socialization contract" under the terms of which the parties would contribute capital and labor, respectively, for the development of production and would agree to share profits. Such a contract would be administered by a bipartite council of employer and worker representatives. The council would fix wages and hours, rule on hiring practices, sanitation, and conditions under which workers would acquire or forfeit profit-sharing rights, and would determine anything else necessary to the fulfillment of the contract. Grievances concerning the application or interpretation of the contract would be resolved in a system of five bipartite arbitration courts located in key cities of the country.[72] The industrial socialization contract posited faith in "bourgeois" government. It was visionary, utopian, anarchistic, and democratic.

Recabarren became a member of the Chamber Committee on Social Legislation charged with the study of the Liberal Alliance code project. He attended its meetings at first, was apparently hurt because the committee did not discuss the FOCH bill, and then, along with several other members, ceased altogether to support the work of the committee. The Rancagua convention of the FOCH did not debate either of the two élite industrial relations projects but did question the congressional behavior of Recabarren. He had introduced a bill on behalf of the railroad workers which called for the establishment of a bipartite railroad administrative commission. Some FOCH delegates expressed the view that the bill, if passed, would result in "collaboration with a capitalist régime" and that such a thing would be anomalous in view

[71]*Ibid.,* July 25, 1921.
[72]*El Despertar,* March 1, 5, 1921, *La Federación Obrera,* Oct. 1, 1921, and *El Socialista,* July 25, 1921.

of the FOCH's pending affiliation to the Red International of Labor Unions. Recabarren defended his action with the explanation that workers would constitute a commission majority in his proposal; the plan would therefore not involve collaboration and would, on the contrary, provide good training for union leaders who one day would have to run the railroad enterprise alone.[73]

At the party gathering which followed the FOCH convention and set up the Communist party, there was lengthy discussion of what the parliamentary role of the party was to be. All delegates who spoke to the question were anxious to avoid the charge of "collaborationism" or "reformism" but were not prepared to agree on what the specific and permissible area of parliamentary activity should be. The convention finally voted a motion, put by Recabarren, which referred the matter to the party's executive committee.[74]

A clear statement of legislative policy, which allowed Communist party representatives in the Congress to support and propose laws favorable to revolutionary objectives and oppose or reject all others, was not agreed upon until after Recabarren's suicide in 1924 and the rise of a new and younger group of Communist leaders. In the interim, the anarchist element in the FOCH remained large and influential and Recabarren himself showed little leadership ability in the Congress. When the white-collar bill was being debated in 1922, he refused to participate in the voting, remarking that he had no faith that such a bill could achieve positive results. A year later, after his return from Soviet Russia, he voted against the holding of special sessions in the Chamber to debate the labor contract bill. When the voting began he took to his feet and protested saying, "This is music, and nothing else!"[75]

[73]*La Federación Obrera*, Jan. 1, 1922.
[74]*El Socialista*, Jan. 12, 1922.
[75]Cámara de Diputados, Boletín de las Sesiones Ordinarias en 1922, vol. 2, pp. 1413–1415; Cámara de Diputados, *Boletín de las Sesiones Extraordinarias en 1923–1924*, pp. 103–104.

CHAPTER 8

Crisis in the Congress

OUTRIGHT opposition to social reform, competition between the reform views of the Liberal Alliance and the National Union, and, above all, the unresolved élite struggle (symbolized most dramatically by the continued existence of an ineffectual parliamentary system of government) led inexorably to crisis. The effect of these three forces can be fully observed and studied in the Congress where they, almost inseparably, frustrated debate and action on labor legislation. The task in this chapter is to tell the story of the congressional crisis in four vignettes: the Conservative bill in the Senate, the Liberal Alliance project in the Chamber of Deputies, the Joint Committee on Social Legislation, and, finally and briefly, the military intervention.

I

The Conservative bill was assigned to the Senate Committee on Legislation and Justice for study shortly after its introduction in 1919. Since the Liberal, Radical, National, and Democratic parties as well as the Conservative party had members on this committee, it was to be expected that differences of opinion would be aired. Indeed, a majority of the committee could agree only on Title I which treated working conditions. The members split three ways on Title II (the legal union) and Title III (conciliation and arbitration) and submitted three reports to the Senate in January 1920 when they completed their work. The first, signed by Senators Enrique Mac-Iver (Radical) and Arturo Alessandri (Liberal) proposed that the Senate accept the project for debate in its original form. The second submitted by Senators Alfredo Barros Errázuriz (Conservative), and Malaquías Concha (Democrat) recommended two minor changes, one of which made the National Savings Bank a partner in the administration of union funds. The third came from National party leader Antonio Varas who rejected Titles II and III entirely.[1] The record of Senate debates does not indicate that that body made a formal decision among the three reports, and the project therefore remained in its original form.

The negative attitude of Senator Varas was probably symbolic of the views of many other Senators on labor legislation, but it must also be remembered that 1920 was an election year. Conventions and campaigning distracted from the law-making process, but there was also the larger question of who would win the office of President and the impact this would have on the urgency for labor legislation and the kind of system to be proposed. Under the circumstances, it could not be expected that the Senate would take expeditious action on the labor bill. To do so would commit the National Union majority in that body to a position it might regret should Luis Barros Borgoño, candidate of the National Union, emerge the victor. Also, since the Senate would not be renewed (in part) until the following year, the National Union could afford to play a waiting game, confident that there would be time in the extraordinary session (October 1 to May 1, 1920) to take up important matters.

Thus, during the regular session of 1920 (May 1 to October 1), no progress was made in the Senate on the labor bill. Two efforts to open floor debate in July and August failed. On September 2 Senator Juan Enrique Concha refused to make further speeches on the need for legislation for, he said, "I have the impression that the project lacks favorable atmosphere in this room." Senator Carlos Aldunate Solar, a signer of the bill, added that for very respectable reasons many Senators, perhaps half of the Senate, did not consider the moment opportune for discussion of the matter. On the other hand, Senator Malaquías Concha felt that labor legislation as a general subject did not have "bad atmosphere" among his colleagues and was sure to be debated eventually. On September 2 the Senate formally suspended

[1]Senado, *Boletín de las Sesiones Extraordinarias en 1919–20*, pp. 1013–1015.

further debate on the bill for the remainder of the regular session but agreed to name a special committee to study it in the interim before the 1921 session.[2]

The announcement of Alessandri's election just as the regular session ended caused some National Union leaders to give more importance to the bill than they had contemplated giving it. Perhaps they saw immediate Senate action on the Conservative bill as a bargaining tool which would enable them to get a better law, to their way of thinking, than the "radical" Liberal Alliance would propose. In any case the Senate, rather than appoint a special committee to study the bill as had been agreed, resumed debate on it in November when the extraordinary session began. Debate continued until the end of that session in April 1921, at which time Title I was approved as a separate project and sent to the Chamber of Deputies. This was a revealing sequence of events and in it and in the opinions expressed in the debates themselves there was evidence of the narrow limit to which many leading politicians would go, even with "safe" sponsorship, toward reform of the relationship among labor, management, and the government. This evidence must have caused acute observers to despair or rejoice, depending upon their outlook, at the negative prospects indicated for any general labor reform in the near future.

In accordance with custom, the Senate first debated the labor bill in general, approved it in principle, and then proceeded to debate each title and article in detail. Senators Juan Enrique Concha and Malaquías Concha occupied most of the time spent on debating the bill in general. Juan Enrique Concha admitted that some of his colleagues thought the minimum-wage proposal somewhat advanced, that it would endanger some industries, but he was not disposed to retreat in his support of it. If certain enterprises could not pay a wage which would enable the worker to buy sufficient food and live in relative comfort, then Concha thought such enterprises should close their doors. Supply and demand economics had to be revised by the minimum-wage principle, a principle which dated from the encyclical *Rerum Novarum* and was then reaffirmed, he said, in the Washington and London conferences of the International Labor Organization and the Versailles Peace Treaty. Concha also noted that some Senators thought the title on legal unionism to be revolutionary while others, taking an opposite point of view, had labeled it reactionary. He spoke at length about

[2]Senado, *Boletín de las Sesiones Ordinarias en 1920*, p. 339–340, 656–659, 858–859, 942–943, 1148.

labor agitators and the power they wielded over the masses and the economy.[3]

Malaquías Concha supported the general principle of legislating in the labor field, and he approached the subject as a partisan of the Liberal Alliance and with much sympathy for the worker and the union. In his view, employers in Chile generally were backward, still handled workers as slaves were handled in earlier days, and blamed all strikes on "agitators." He told the assembled Senators that he thought these agitators were necessary and were an asset to the labor movement. They were more intelligent and better informed than most workers and taught the latter their rights. He therefore did not share the slogan "we must fight the agitators," and he charged that those who did were nothing more than agitators for their own cause. The remedy was not to be found "in persecuting the agitators but in identifying the just demands of the workers in order to see if it is possible, within the limits of company earnings, to give them a better wage."[4]

Conservative Senator Barros Errázuriz countered that the strikes which had occurred during 1920 had generally been promoted by agitators. Zenón Torrealba, a Democrat who is said to have been the first workingman elected to the Chilean Senate, believed there were labor leaders who deliberately sought to stir up trouble but that they were only a small minority. Workers generally elected their leaders from among the more capable, those they knew and trusted, and not from among those who were strangers to the enterprise and to their problems and grievances. So many times, he complained, he had heard it said that Chilean workers were a turbulent, radical lot, by nature at odds with their station. This was wrong. It was not their nature that made them unhappy and disposed to strike, but low wages. Conflicts would continue so long as wages did not permit the working class a decent living standard.[5]

On November 11 the Senate began to debate Title I. Representatives of agriculture and commerce objected in principle to Senate consideration of this type of legislation, especially maximum hours and minimum-wage provisions, on the grounds that such legislation would injure the economy, was contrary to natural economic laws, and was unnecessary in Chile. The reformers, on the other hand, while supporting the title in principle, argued that it should be more tightly

[3]Senado, *Boletín de las Sesiones Extraordinarias en 1920–21,* I, pp. 343–349.
[4]*Ibid.,* I, pp. 492, 495.
[5]*Ibid.,* I, pp. 496, 498.

drawn in order to assure that it would really provide effective protection to the working class.

Enrique Mac-Iver was a spokesman of the first group and it was at this point that he made his classic refutation of the limited workday and censured the Chilean worker for his lack of industry and initiative. Those who wanted to reduce his hours of work were, he said, foolishly copying the laws of Europe and, if they were successful in having them passed in Chile, the result would be to make a bad situation incredibly worse. Replying to the remarks of Senator Mac-Iver, Malaquías Concha declared that Title I was not a mere imitation of laws passed in other countries. Such laws were not the result of whim or a desire to copy what others had done but were the realistic and necessary response of a society to its industrial growth and to the new social and economic problems which this growth carried along with it.[6]

The first day of debate therefore revealed a serious difference of opinion on the fundamentals of Title I and, perhaps partly for this reason, debate was not resumed until mid-December. In the interim a compromise was worked out: the bill would be passed with some changes in wording designed to strengthen it but it would not be applied to commerce and agriculture. The bill was amended to accord with this understanding, and it was then quickly approved in two succeeding sessions.[7]

In January 1921 the Senate proceeded to debate Title II. The first article, which said that blue-collar workers "shall be free to associate for legitimate ends" was approved unanimously. However, the Senate was unable to move beyond this point in its treatment of labor legislation for lack of adequate support either from the extreme right or the left. A majority of the extreme right was flatly opposed to any legislation at all which would set up a system of legal unionism. The left considered the Senate project too closely identified with employer aims and some of them believed better legislation might be obtained in the new Alessandri Administration. Therefore when debate moved on to the second article of Title II Malaquías Concha took the offensive against it and the plant union in general. With his speech Senate consideration of labor legislation during the special session came to an abrupt end.

Concha's analysis of the union proposal is interesting in itself and also provides a useful prologue to the congressional debate which con-

<hr />

[6]*Ibid.,* I, pp. 514–518, 621–625.
[7]*Ibid.,* I, pp. 501–503, 876–882, 979–988, 1035–1039; II, pp. 1128–1131.

tinued later in the year. Concha declared that the first and second articles were in diametric opposition and that their difference was so fundamental that he could not visualize an acceptable compromise. Wholeheartedly accepting the concept of free association of the first article, he could not reconcile this with the stipulation in Article 2 that a worker association "shall constitute through the ministry of the law all blue-collar workers more than sixteen years of age...," etc. In his opinion this language would impose upon workers a state obligation to organize whether they wanted to or not and would thus breach the principle of free unionism. Workers should have the right to organize, and if they chose to exercise that right, then, and only then, should the law fix certain norms for the government of their union.

Although free versus obligatory unionism was his major concern, Concha also pointed out that encouraging unions to set up social funds based upon joint worker-employer contributions would tend to tie the worker to the plant. He would not be able to quit work without surrendering the benefits that he himself had helped to accumulate. Requiring that unions incorporate was also a serious weakness of the proposal, for everyone knew that the Civil Code established several grounds for canceling the corporate status of an institution. Once this status was lost, the entire union membership would have to forfeit all benefits which had accrued to them through the union's special funds.

All of this caused Concha to conclude that the project would benefit the employer at the expense of the worker. It was "unjust, arbitrary, despotic, and tends to establish the domination of one social class over the other." Why, he asked, were not equal obligations imposed upon employers? If they too were required to organize "in such and such a way" and to invest their funds for certain specified objectives he would agree to the legislation. Various worker groups had told him, he said, that they considered Title II "a snare set for them." There was no hurry to pass such legislation, he advised, and it should therefore be carefully studied.[8]

The Senate project was not discussed again until April when it was formally agreed to suspend further debate on Titles II and III. The Senate voted to send Title I to the Chamber as an independent project. Shortly after the Senate reconvened in regular session in May 1921 Alessandri presented his own labor code project to the Congress. The Senate bill was not revived until the end of the year when a joint committee was appointed to study labor legislation.

[8]*Ibid.*, II, pp. 1195–120.

II

The popular vote in the 1920 presidential election was close, so close that the electoral college delayed for three months in completing its study of returns and announcing the result. The college conceded victory to Alessandri by the slim margin of five votes (179 to 174).[9]

Alessandri was inaugurated in December but, since the entire Chamber and one-third of the Senate were to be renewed in March 1921, he made few legislative moves until after that key event. Before the March elections, the National Union had an overwhelming majority in the Senate (about 86 percent) and the Liberal Alliance narrowly controlled the Chamber (about 55 percent). The elections did not change the situation in the Chamber but did reduce the National Union margin in the Senate to 60 percent. Over-all, the results did not greatly improve the difficult position of the Liberal Alliance in the Congress and, what is more, within the Alliance there was a shift of power toward the Radicals. Of sixty-six Liberal Alliance Deputies, thirty-nine were Radicals while the Alessandri Liberals accounted for only twelve. The Democrats also had twelve which gave them a degree of influence to which they had not been accustomed. In the Senate the Radicals and Alessandri Liberals each had six seats and the Democrats three.[10]

With one Chamber against him, a weakening of his own party in the Liberal Alliance, and a close victory himself in the presidential election, Alessandri did not face an encouraging prospect on the eve of the struggle for social reform. Despite these unenviable political circumstances, he sent the ambitious code project to the Congress soon after it convened in June, and indications are that he considered it priority legislation. His strategy called first for an effort to establish a joint committee of Deputies and Senators to study and report to both Houses on the project. He probably saw little difficulty in getting Chamber cooperation in this respect because the Liberal Alliance had won a majority of seats in that body and, in addition, the Chamber had not studied the project which originated in the Senate and was not committed to any specific labor legislation. The Senate, on the other hand,

[9]Arturo Alessandri Palma, *Recuerdos de gobierno* (Santiago: Editorial Universitaria, 1952), vol. 1, pp. 45, 53–54. The electoral college was then composed of 354 electors appointed from and representing the 72 departments in Chile.

[10]*El Mercurio*, June 3, 1920, March 7, 9, 1921. In 1921 there were 37 Senators, 15 of whom were members of the Liberal Alliance and 22 belonged to the National Union. In the Chamber there were 119 Deputies divided as follows: Liberal Alliance 66, National Union 49, and 4 independents (2 of whom were Socialists).

had preserved its National Union majority and was familiar with a project presumably more acceptable to it than the Alessandri code.

It is therefore doubtful that Alessandri had much hope of obtaining Senate approval for joint consideration of his project. If such approval could be had, however, it would be a blow to the project of the Conservative party and at the same time would facilitate immensely the early consideration of his code in the Congress. Failing in this objective, Alessandri would not immediately propose that a joint committee consider the Senate project as well as his own because this would give an advantage to the Senate project on two counts: first, the Chamber had not yet approved the Alessandri code and this would weaken the hand of the Deputy representatives on a joint committee; second, the Senate was the more prestigious body and it had had labor legislation under consideration for almost two years. Alessandri, if defeated in the first round, would then try to push his project through the Chamber before approaching the Senate again and proposing joint consideration of both projects. In this case his code would gain a tactical advantage if the Chamber voted it quickly. Delay in the Chamber could only favor the Senate project.

In late June Senator Ramón Briones Luco, at Alessandri's request, moved that the Senate invite the Chamber to form a joint committee to study and report on the President's code project. Briones, a Radical from the province of Tarapacá, had just been elected to the Senate the previous March. He had had Alessandri's support and was indeed filling the vacancy created in the Senate by Alessandri's election to the office of President. In making his motion he assured his colleagues that the FOCH was not subversive and should be distinguished in this respect from other organizations in the country. If Briones' sponsorship of the motion, in the first place, and his FOCH comment, in the second place, seem to put him solidly behind the Liberal Alliance and in favor of a most generous appraisal of the labor situation, this was at least not to be the case for long. In less than two months he would be aiding the Conservatives in turning out Alessandri's first Ministry and a year later he would openly support the Conservative rather than the Alessandri project. In June he was apparently discharging a political debt.

Briones' motion lost by a two to one margin (15 to 7). A roll call was not taken but seven Senators spoke against and three in favor of the motion. All those who spoke in favor were partisans of the Liberal Alliance or *aliancistas* (Briones, Héctor Arancibia Lazo, a Radical, and

Abraham Gatica, a Liberal) but so also were three of the seven who voted no (Malaquías Concha, Enrique Mac-Iver, and Enrique Zañartu), thus indicating a major breach in Senate *aliancista* ranks in the very first test of Administration labor policy.[11] The negative vote of Malaquías Concha was predictable to anyone who had followed events of the preceding six months. Concha gambled his political career for a post in a predominantly National Union Ministry in 1920 and when Alessandri won the presidency Concha paid the political consequences. He (Concha) found that he had limited his usefulness to the Liberal Alliance. When Alessandri by-passed him and appointed another Democrat to his first Cabinet, Concha was probably offended, and for this reason chose not to support the Liberal Alliance in his vote. The explanation of Mac-Iver's negative vote is undoubtedly that he did not wish to concede labor legislation the privileged position of joint committee discussion. The opposition of Zañartu, a Democratic Liberal who identified with the Liberal Alliance rather than the National Union, was only a preview of the division in the Liberal Alliance vote on reform legislation.

The forces of the National Union, on the other hand, spoke uniformly against the motion, but this did not necessarily indicate that they approved of the Senate bill or indeed of any labor legislation at all.

Four days after this initial setback, Alessandri sent his Minister of the Interior to the Chamber with the urgent request that that body activate its Committee on Social Legislation and give immediate attention to the labor code. The committee was composed of seven members of the Liberal Alliance, four of the National Union, and one, Recabarren, who was shortly to become a founder of the Communist party in Chile. Perhaps in deference to the Democratic party's long interest in labor legislation, one of its members, Luis Correa Ramírez, was named chairman.[12]

The political situation within the committee was difficult from the

---

[11]Senado, *Boletín de las Sesiones Ordinarias en 1921*, p. 333. Senado, *Boletín de las Sesiones Extraordinarias en 1921-1922*, Vol. I, p. 595. The other four Senators who voted against the motion were Joaquín Echeñique, a Conservative, Guillermo Rivera, a *liberal unionista*, Héctor Zañartu, a *liberal democrático unionista*, and Luis Claro Solar, a *liberal unionista*.

[12]The other members of the committee were José Ramon Herrera Lira (Conservative), Tito V. Lisoni *(liberal democrático unionista)*, Ismael Edwards Matte *(liberal unionista)*, Santiago Labarca (Radical), Jaime Larráin (Conservative), Francisco Jorquera (Radical), Juan Pradenas (Democrat), Rafael Torreblanca (Radical), Tomás Ramírez Frías *(liberal aliancista)*, and Ernesto Escobar (Radical).

beginning and the resultant delay caused the Minister of the Interior to return to the Chamber in early July to repeat the President's request. On this occasion the President of the Chamber suggested that a special committee might be set up to study the labor code project, but various Deputies protested that the Committee on Social Legislation was made up of capable people who could properly handle the matter.

The committee was eventually activated but made little headway. By the end of September thirty meetings had been called but only eleven were held. Although illness and temporary absence from Santiago accounted for some of the difficulties of the committee, it was crippled by differences within *aliancista* ranks, obstructionist tactics of the National Union, and a boycott practiced by Luis Emilio Recabarren. As to the first point, Conservative Deputy D. Ramón Herrera Lira charged, partly tongue in cheek, that the Liberal Alliance was entirely to blame for the committee's failure to meet more often. He pointed out that the committee could session with a quorum of only four members, while the Liberal Alliance alone had seven representatives on the committee. Never, he said, did more than four Liberal Alliance supporters attend a session, frequently it was unable to session at all for lack of a quorum, and on several occasions he was the only committee member to show up. He concluded that the Liberal Alliance which "says it holds the people in such high esteem does not attend committee sessions."[13]

Herrera Lira was exaggerating only slightly. Juan Pradenas, a Democrat, attended only two sessions. Rafael Torreblanca, a Radical, was present at only one. Pradenas explains that he was in Concepción part of the time and ill the rest. Most significantly he adds, however, that his party had little influence in the Liberal Alliance and had received no benefits from it. The only party to benefit, he claimed, was the Liberal party which was monopolizing the Ministry.[14] National Union propaganda had in 1920 tried carefully to sow doubt in the minds of Democrats about their recognition in the Liberal Alliance should Alessandri win, and this propaganda had evidently had some effect. Along with the conduct of Malaquías Concha, the Pradenas complaint seems to show that some members of the Democratic party were, for reasons of general political strategy, withholding their support from the legis-

[13]Cámara de Diputados, *Boletín de las Sesiones Extraordinarias en 1921–1922*, vol. 1, pp. 498–499.
[14]*Ibid.*, pp. 466–468.

lative program of the President. By the end of the year many Democrats were openly questioning whether the party ought to remain in the Liberal Alliance, and, when the matter was voted at the party's convention, those who favored staying in carried the day by only twenty votes (67 to 47).[15]

It is not so clear, but yet it is creditable, that Torreblanca may also have stayed away for higher political reasons. The Radicals had enjoyed a clear triumph in the March 1921 elections and, in spite of this show of increased strength, had not been favored with greater Cabinet representation. A Radical, Briones, helped topple the Ministry in August and the Radicals thereupon gained an additional ministerial post, but, for highly complicated political reasons which we cannot here venture to explain, the new Ministry lasted only a few short weeks and the Radicals refused to accept a single seat in its successor. Not until March 1922 did the Radicals compose their differences with Alessandri and rejoin the Cabinet.

However, another Radical Deputy, Francisco Jorquera, whose longstanding intellectual interest in labor was at least equal to his party loyalty, did take his assignment on the committee seriously. He blamed the National Union, and specifically Herrera Lira, for the committee's failure to do more than it did, charging that Herrera Lira consistently refused to wait longer than the legal fifteen minutes after posted meeting time for a quorum to be established. Despite these difficulties, Jorquera believed that the committee had made progress and indeed he went so far as to say that it met more often and did more work than any other Chamber committee. The committee had decided from the start to treat the code project in parts rather than as a whole, he explained, and had already sent to the Chamber floor the sections on collective conflicts, the craft union, and work accidents. The section on accidents had been approved by the Chamber and was pending in the Senate.[16]

There is undoubtedly some truth to Jorquera's charges of National Union obstructionism. Deputy Ismael Edwards Matte, a Liberal who supported the National Union, frankly admitted on the Chamber floor that he could not properly study the Alessandri code project even if he were given an entire year. He supports Jorquera's information that

[15]Guillermo M. Bañados, *La última convención del partido democrático* (Santiago: Imprenta Universal, 1922), pp. 73–76.

[16]Cámara de Diputados, *Boletín de las Sesiones Extraordinarias en 1921–1922*, vol. 1, pp. 779–781.

the committee declined to study and report out the project as a whole, as Alessandri had asked, and decided to treat it in sections.[17]

In addition to all of the political and personal matters described above which operated against and, in themselves may have prevented, favorable action by the Committee on Social Legislation, there was also some feeling, in and outside the Congress, that a labor code was not vital legislation, and that the Administration should address itself to more fundamental problems such as the crisis in the nitrate industry.[18]

Alessandri himself, while explaining that several of those most interested in the code were traveling about the country, indicated in late September that he was not at all satisfied with the committee's work. Its lack of progress was not justified in any way. He therefore proposed that henceforward the committee meet in the President's office. If the committee refused to do so, the result would clearly place responsibility where it belonged. His only obligation, he said, was to take the initiative in proposing legislation and the Congress was responsible from that point on.[19] This suggestion brought forth the charge in some quarters that Alessandri had exceeded the powers of the executive office in making the request in the first place and that, if the committee were to accept it and carry out its functions in the *Moneda* (presidential palace), this would amount to a usurpation by the executive of congressional authority. Conservative party Deputy, Jaime Larraín, immediately handed in his resignation from the committee.

Jorquera tells us that Alessandri was willing to accept only a unanimous decision of the committee to meet in the *Moneda* and that, although the committee did not decline the invitation, neither did it arrive at a unanimous decision. Having failed therefore to get the committee to meet with him, Alessandri then proposed that he be permitted to meet with the committee. This was declined also, Deputy Ismael Edwards Matte explaining later that it would have been beneath the dignity of his office had the President "descended" to the committee's place of meeting and deliberated shoulder to shoulder with its members. A few days later Alessandri charged that the National Union members of the committee were those who were obstructing work on the code project and that they were playing politics in disregard of

[17]*Ibid.*, pp. 682–686.
[18]Summary of a presidential press conference published in *La Federación Obrera*, Sept. 29, 1921.
[19]*Ibid.*

national interests.[20] The work of the committee evidently came to a complete standstill in October when the Chamber voted (27–24) in favor of postponing debate on the collective conflicts' section of the project, which had, as Jorquera correctly stated, been reported out by the committee.[21]

In mid-November a move got under way to replace the Committee on Social Legislation with a special committee whose responsibility would include only the study of the labor code project, not social legislation in general. This was the same procedure the president of the Chamber had suggested the preceding July, but now it was put in the form of an official motion by four Deputies (two Democrats, a Radical, and a Socialist), who with some generosity might be considered to have all been *aliancistas* but, in any case, none of whom was a National Union member or *unionista*. The motion was defeated thirty-one to seventeen, the opposition arguing that such a move would be an open censure of the Committee on Social Legislation and a gratuitous insult to its membership.[22] A substitute motion was then offered by three Liberals and a Democrat, all *aliancistas,* proposing that the special committee be set up, that the Chamber invite the Senate to designate a similar committee, and that these committees jointly consider not only the Alessandri code project but all other social legislation pending at that moment in either Chamber. This development undoubtedly meant that the high command of the Liberal Alliance had, looking back over months of near fruitless activity in the Chamber of Deputies, decided to seek compromise with the National Union on social legislation. It meant specifically that the President would be willing to see the Conservative bill thrown into the ring and that he would take his chances with a Senate committee certain to contain a National Union majority.

The motion was approved in the Chamber by a thirty-eight to nine vote. As an immediate consequence, five Deputies resigned from the Committee on Social Legislation, explaining their action before their colleagues solely on the ground that the committee was now a useless decoration.[23] This abrupt action by representatives of both the Liberal Alliance (two) and the National Union (three) apparently indicates that top Liberal Alliance and National Union strategists probably had

[20]Cámara de Diputados, *Boletín de las Sesiones Extraordinarias en 1921–1922,* vol. 1, pp. 682–686, 780–781.
[21]*Ibid.,* pp. 32–33.
[22]*Ibid.,* pp. 463, 498–499.
[23]*Ibid.,* pp. 394, 437–438, 682–687, 691, 731, 741, 769, 773, 783.

not come to an agreement on joint consideration of social legislation in advance of the introduction of the Chamber motion. If they had, news of such an agreement had not yet been communicated to their followers.

In accordance with the Chamber vote, the Senate was officially invited to help set up a joint committee. Ismael Tocornal, a Liberal *unionista* who had become Minister of the Interior in November in Alessandri's fourth Cabinet shakeup, addressed the Senate in the name of the government and indicated the urgent need for legislation based on the results of the Washington and Geneva conferences of the ILO. Since Chile shared the ideals of the Versailles Treaty, the Republic was, he said, obligated to so legislate. The Senate agreed to the idea of a joint committee and by the end of December each Chamber had designated seven committee representatives.

On the Chamber of Deputies' delegation were five *aliancistas* and two *unionistas;* the Senate group was composed of four *unionistas* and three followers of Alessandri. Thus, should a straight political vote be obtained in the Joint Committee with all present and voting, the Liberal Alliance stood to win eight–six. However, among the political partisans of the Liberal Alliance in the Senate group were Eliodoro Yáñez and Ramón Briones Luco. Yáñez did not see eye to eye with Alessandri on social questions and preferred some of the features of the Conservative bill to those of the Liberal Alliance project.[24] Briones had no strong personal convictions on social legislation and was subject to the influence of his more conservative colleagues. Two Democrats, a Deputy and a Senator (president of his party and one whom Alessandri years before had called a "shameless" character) also sat on the Joint Committee and their votes were not necessarily predictable. The apparent advantage for the Liberal Alliance was not therefore real and the Joint Committee was to be the scene of a long and difficult, and not very successful, struggle.

III

At its very first meeting in December 1921 the Joint Committee elected its officers and made several decisions on procedural questions which were to affect the nature of its work greatly. Senator Eliodoro

[24]As early as August 1920 Yáñez proposed that a joint congressional committee be set up to handle labor legislation. The Conservative bill was the only piece of legislation then pending in the Senate, and joint consideration would clearly have been a concession to it. See *La Nación,* August 15, 1920.

Yáñez became chairman and Deputy Ismael Edwards Matte vice-chairman of the committee. Senator Yáñez had not participated actively in earlier Senate debate on the Conservative party bill and his views on labor legislation were not a matter of public record. Surely, however, his position was known to his intimate friends and fellow Congressmen as a positive but conservative one. He did not oppose legislation in this field as did Enrique Mac-Iver and Antonio Varas nor did he go so far along the liberal path as did Alessandri. He rather liked the plant union scheme and yet he was obviously subject to more pressure from the Liberal Alliance than was any Conservative party Senator. Since the chairman of the Joint Committee was bound to be a Senator rather than a Deputy, Yáñez was under all the circumstances an acceptable choice from the Administration's standpoint. Perhaps Guillermo Bañados, a Democratic Senator, would have been better, but he, like Ramón Briones Luco, was a newcomer to the upper chamber and was not therefore in line for a committee chairmanship. Ismael Edwards Matte, an unequivocal supporter of the National Union, swung the balance so far as the committee directorship is concerned toward the Conservative bill. Had the vice-chairman been an *aliancista* the reverse would have been the case, at least on the surface and at that moment, given the lack of definition of Yáñez's position. Even so, the Liberal Alliance probably considered itself somewhat better off than it would have been with a Conservative as chairman and an *aliancista* as vice-chairman.

The Joint Committee adopted a quorum of five and agreed, as the Chamber Committee had previously done, to discuss and dispatch separately the various subjects before it. One suspects that this was not a mere procedural decision which favored separate laws as against a code, even less that it revealed a consensus of urgency in favor of passing individual labor laws as they came out of the committee rather than waiting for approval of an entire code. Rather, the strategy would allow some things to be shelved and others to be approved as the tug of party politics and individual opinion dictated, just as had already happened during consideration of the Conservative project when the labor contract, the least controversial of its three titles, was the only one to clear the Senate barrier.

Of more than usual importance was the committee's decision not to invite employers and workers to testify. The committee explained that past experience indicated that such procedure would not result in any useful information or opinions. It was willing, however, to submit to

222

the public a list of the subjects to be treated by the committee and to invite written comments upon them. Edwards Matte advised the committee that he already had three copies of the Liberal Alliance code annotated with the observations of the Nitrate Company of Antofagasta, the Society of Tierra del Fuego, and the Society of Plasterers.

Unfortunately, there is no record of any opinions the committee may have received or of the annotated codes to which Edwards Matte referred. It is virtually certain, however, that the committee was informed of the attitudes of the Society for Factory Development, the National Agricultural Society, and the Labor Association. Each of these organizations had sympathetic and, in some cases, prominent spokesmen on the committee or in the Congress. The Executive Council of the Society for Factory Development agreed in September 1921 to consult with some of the Society members about the Liberal Alliance code project and, with their comments in mind, to review the project in detail.[25] It is quite likely that this was done and that the Joint Committee had some kind of report on the project from the Society. The National Agricultural Society in August 1921 charged its Committee on Legislation with responsibility for studying the Alessandri code. Eliodoro Yáñez and Enrique Zañartu were two of the four members of this committee.[26] It is probable that the Joint Committee of the Congress knew that employer opinion was deeply divided on the matter of social and labor legislation, some opposing and others favoring it in all or in part, and that favorable opinion was in turn sharply split between the Liberal Alliance and Conservative party proposals.

As for the labor point of view, the FOCH had presented its project to Alessandri in March 1921 and to the Chamber Committee on Social Legislation later in the year.[27] This document was undoubtedly placed in the files of the Joint Committee and committee members were thus aware that accommodation of views on labor legislation with the FOCH would be beyond all presumption. Significant changes were coming within the FOCH itself and it was difficult to predict what the Communist line on such legislation would be. By philosophical definition the anarchists of the IWW took a negative position on any legislation and, if they had been invited to testify before the Joint Committee, they

---

[25]"Actas de las Sesiones del Consejo Directivo," *Boletín de las Sociedad de Fomento Fabril,* vol. 38, September 1921, p. 532.

[26]"Acta de la Sesión del Directorio del 1 de Agosto de 1921," *El Agricultor,* December 1921.

[27]*La Federación Obrera,* Oct. 1, 1921.

either would not have come at all or would have made no constructive contribution.

The Joint Committee's deliberate refusal to schedule outside witnesses has, therefore, as the above implies, a number of explanations. The committee probably already had written opinions from some important organizations. Some members favored the Liberal Alliance and the Conservative party projects, but strong anti-views were not represented and it could be assumed that the committee wanted to keep it that way. Finally, the committee's decision on this matter of procedure may have been in some degree a confession of failure, an admission that differences within the committee were in themselves great enough without introducing complications and that, in all, the task facing the committee was so impossible and untimely that a minimum effort, and no more, should be expended.

The Joint Committee ended its first day of deliberation by agreeing to discuss the labor contract first. It instructed Senator Yáñez to draw up a complete list of all the subjects to be handled by the committee and to deliver this to the next meeting.[28]

Yáñez listed eleven projects, nine of which dealt with protective labor matters, social security, health and medical programs, and cooperatives. The other two were the labor contract and conciliation and arbitration courts. The list included nothing on unions; conciliation and arbitration occupied last place; and, as already indicated, the labor contract was first. Ramírez Frías wanted to change the list and put conciliation and arbitration first, which he considered of greatest urgency. Edwards Matte thought this was logical but doubted it would work because, as he explained the situation, the committee had no basis upon which to resolve the subjects raised by Ramírez Frías, while they did have the Senate-approved project on the labor contract as well as that section of the Alessandri code which also dealt with the labor contract. No changes were made following this brief exchange of divergent views. The committee proceeded to invite Moisés Poblete Troncoso, head of the Labor Office, to participate in its deliberations and work began on the labor contract in January.[29]

The Joint Committee completed its study of the labor contract in July 1922 and at its next session in August, with no explanation, began to discuss the subject of union organizations, which had not even fig-

[28]Congreso Nacional, *Actas de la Comisión Mixta de Legislación Social* (Santiago [1923?]), Sección I, pp. 3–5.

[29]*Ibid.*, Sección I, pp. 6–9.

ured in the original Yáñez list. The committee was immediately faced with the fundamental problem of whether to use as the basis of discussion, the craft union proposal, the plant union proposal, or a "free association" bill presented by *aliancista* Deputy Ramírez Frías. The latter bill clearly favored the craft union and was patterned closely after the Liberal Alliance project, but in stipulating freedom of association it also permitted the formation of voluntary plant unions. The Ramírez Frías concept of freedom of association was thus a limited one (freedom to choose between two types of legal unions) and the intent of the bill was not, in fact, to achieve freedom of association in the union field at all. It was designed to put teeth in the Liberal Alliance bill by taking away from the plant union its obligatory membership feature, a change which Ramírez Frías thought the *unionistas* might somehow accept. If compromise between the two major proposals were to become the goal of the Joint Committee, then the advantage would fall to one side or the other depending on whether membership should, so far as the law was concerned, remain obligatory in the plant union or be made voluntary as Ramírez Frías proposed. A closed shop, guaranteed by law to all plant unions upon their formation, would limit the organizing potential of the craft unions. The Ramírez Frías bill thus permitted freedom of association in the sense that it would allow two union types to start out on an equal footing, the outcome to be determined by the relative merits of these unions and their functional strengths and weaknesses in the Chilean environment. Nevertheless, the term "freedom of association" was often used by each side in subsequent debate in the Joint Committee as a cloak for concealing its bid for advantage.

At this opening session Senator Yáñez moved that the Conservative project be adopted as the departure point of discussion. His only interest in so moving, he affirmed, was to expedite the committee's work. Since, as he contended, the Senate had already approved the Conservative bill and the committee would therefore not have to analyze it so carefully, time could be saved. Ramírez Frías disagreed with this procedure and suggested that before any project was adopted the committee should first make a decision among the obligatory plant union, the craft union, or freedom of association. Structure and freedom were the major points at difference among the projects, he explained, and a decision in this area would at the same time identify the project with which to begin. Luis Undurraga, a Conservative, while saying that he was willing to go along with the Ramírez Frías motion, preferred to wait until Senators Ramón Briones Luco and Juan Enrique Concha "who have special interest in this matter" were present. It was so agreed.[30]

At the next session of the committee, debate began on the relative merits of the plant union, craft union, and freedom of association. Senator Concha defended the Conservative project arguing that it did not violate the constitutional guarantee of freedom of association because, in addition to the obligatory plant union, it also allowed the free association of workers outside the workplace. The project as a whole inspired order and harmony for it rested upon the concept of solidarity between labor and capital. The other two projects were in diametric opposition to this concept, resting instead upon the idea of class struggle.

Deputy Santiago Labarca, a Radical and *aliancista,* agreed with Concha's analysis but he did not accept its inferred conclusion. He believed that union structure in Chile should correspond to, and facilitate the expression of, the true feeling of the masses. Class struggle unionism, which he identified with craft principles, would, he said, be more realistic than capital-labor solidarity. The achievement of harmony would be failure because it would signify the division and weakening of the working class. As far as Ramírez Frías was concerned, the Senate project violated freedom of association and he thought it also violated the worker's sense of independence due to its paternalistic character. The Senators were proposing to give all the benefits of association to the legal plant union and none to free associations; the result would be conflict and animosity between the two union types. Moisés Poblete Troncoso opposed the Conservative project for the same reasons and told the Joint Committee that all the other countries of the world respected freedom of association.

When a vote was taken on the Yáñez motion to use the Conservative bill as the basis of discussion, the motion carried seven to four. The dissenters were all *aliancistas* (Labarca, Ramírez Frías, Luis Correa Ramírez, a Democrat, and Francisco Jorquera, a Radical); two *aliancistas* (Yáñez and Briones) joined five *unionistas* in the yea vote.[31] Had the *aliancistas* voted as a block, they would have won six to five. Nevertheless, it should not be supposed that this was an important defeat or victory for either side. In the aftermath a stalemate was to be reached, the sides so evenly matched that both of the union bills were

[30]*Ibid.,* Sección III, pp. 3–4.
[31]*Ibid.,* Sección III, pp. 5–9.

finally accepted by the committee and integrated, almost verbatim, into a single union bill.

Although Senators Yáñez and Jorge Errázuriz Tagle, a Liberal *unionista*, claimed, after Allesandri had been elected and had submitted his code project to the Chamber of Deputies, that the Senate had approved the entire Conservative project and sent it to the Chamber,[32] the record of Senate debate does not indicate that this was in fact accomplished. Yet the Senate bill as submitted to the Joint Committee in 1922 did differ in some respects from the bill as originally proposed in the Senate. One might conclude that, after Alessandri presented his more liberal proposal in June, the National Union, still in control of the Senate, may have decided without resorting to formal action that it would be advisable to improve and to back the Conservative project rather than run any risks by leaving the field clear for the Liberal Alliance proposal. At any rate, the changes made in the Conservative project were not fundamental. For example, federations (or meetings of two or more local unions) were now allowed but only to facilitate health and sanitation projects, retirement schemes, and the formation of cooperatives.[33]

The Joint Committee held regular sessions on the union issue from August 1922 until February 1923. By the middle of December, however, the main lines of a compromise were worked out which enabled the committee to proceed to draw up a single bill. This bill was essentially the same as the present union sections of the Labor Code, for it preserved both the craft union and the plant union. The organizational distinction between white- and blue-collar workers in Chile thus has its origins in the two élite proposals and the different labor philosophies they represented. The discussion which took place within the Joint Committee in arriving at the compromise is basic to a proper understanding of present union forms and problems.

Much of the work of the committee involved the interpretation and amendment of the first two articles of the Conservative project. The first article was the one which supporters of the Conservative project cited as permitting blue-collar workers to organize in free associations outside the plant. The second article made union membership obligatory for all blue-collar workers in any plant with more than twenty-five operatives. The free association would in law have none of the func-

[32]Senado, *Boletín de las Sesiones Extraordinarias en 1921–1922*, vol. 1, pp. 549–550, 598.
[33]*Actas de la Comision Mixta*, Sección III, pp. 9–15.

tions or ends of the plant union. The latter would therefore monopolize collective bargaining, conciliation, and other rights. The objective of the partisans of the craft union and the white-collar worker's right to organize was to introduce such changes in these two articles as would guarantee freedom of choice and equality of legal rights for the two union types. The essential question was, by what procedure does the obligatory plant union get set up?

Senator Briones opened the contest within the committee by explaining that, if there was silence among the workers at the time a plant union was about to be set up, arrangements would proceed and such a union would in fact be established. Presumably, although he did not say so, the key actor would be the employer. If there was a "show of opinion" against the plant union, however, then the workers, freely associated, could bargain with the employer over their working conditions. Both Jorquera and Ramírez Frías objected to this procedure and said that the only way to resolve the committee's difference of opinion would be to give the free union the same rights in the law itself as those granted to the plant union; i.e., the right to make demands upon employers, the right of access to government conciliation machinery, and the like. The plant union, they said, was presumed to exist not because of any positive decision in its favor but because of the absence of a negative decision. Briones answered that "the simple entrance of the worker into the factory is an expression of his desire to form part of its legal union." Ramírez Frías rejected the latter analysis completely, saying that one of the most outstanding aspects of the capital-labor struggle was employer resistance to free unions. For this reason the worker, under the Conservative proposal, would have to choose between two equally undesirable alternatives: join the plant union and continue in his job or set up a free association and consequently face discharge and misery. This choice was not an acceptable one. While it was necessary to supervise the formation and functioning of unions, workers should not be required to organize or not to organize in a set way. He seconded Jorquera's modification of Article 1.

At this point in the debate, an apparent stalemate having been reached, Moisés Poblete Troncoso suggested that the committee go on to Article 3 and return to the first two articles at a later date. He also proposed that fifteen of the administrative and procedural articles of the Liberal Alliance project be added to the Conservative bill. Yáñez believed that these fifteen articles did not affect the essence of the Conservative bill and the committee thereupon approved both of Poblete's motions.[34]

For the next two months the committee discussed and approved Articles 3-13 of the Conservative bill without touching the basic difference which still existed among the members. In the middle of December, however, Article 14 came up for discussion and it concerned the annual election of officers in the "plant." To Juan Enrique Concha it was now evident that the matter could be put off no longer and that a decision was necessary "regarding the social criterion which must serve as the basis for the project under study." It was necessary to determine who could decide against the plant union, how many contrary votes would suffice, and when this should be done. Briones immediately spoke to the point indicating that a simple majority vote of the operatives in the plant could destroy the presumption of will in favor of the plant union. After Ramírez Frías repeated his concern over the fate of the craft union under such a system, Briones explained that the employer would not necessarily prefer that his workers organize in plant unions because the latter imposed upon capital a series of gravamens and responsibilities.

Yáñez then brought before the committee a three article rewrite of the original two articles of the Conservative bill which made it even clearer that the plant union alone would be assured legally protected bargaining and other rights. The committee accepted the Yáñez rewrite as the new basis for discussion, but Ramírez Frías quickly countered with a move that his own project be substituted. Juan Enrique Concha's reaction was that to pass laws on free unions like those proposed by Ramírez Frías would in itself amount to an infringement of freedom of association for, no matter how or whether or not you defined these unions, they were already a manifestation of the freedom of association guaranteed in the Constitution. You could regulate them regarding their duties but you could not set specific standards for their creation. They must be allowed full freedom to organize and incorporate in accordance with provisions of the law already in effect. Ramírez Frías answered that to facilitate the organization of craft unions would not impair the concept of freedom of association. Indeed, one could not separate completely the craft union from the plant union because they pursued the same end of improving the conditions of the working class. He could see no other basis for distinguishing between them except that of profit sharing.

[34]*Ibid.*, Sección III, pp. 16-31.

Senator Yáñez was not willing to go all the way on the craft union and proposed instead that Articles 1, 2, and 6 of the Ramírez Frías project (1 defined the craft union, 2 forbade public workers to form unions, and 6 prohibited the craft union from doing anything which would impair individual liberty, the right to work, or the rights of industry) be accepted and that the Conservative bill then be discussed in detail. To clarify the matter once and for all before going any further with any project, Labarca moved that the committee make a clear decision whether it was going to propose legislation on free unions or on plant unions. After more than three months of debate on this point there was little new to be said, however, and, perhaps giving in to sheer weariness, the committee agreed then and there to include both unions in its recommendations to the Congress. From this point on there was no question that the outcome of the Joint Committee's work would be some combination of craft and plant unionism, but it was yet not certain which, if either, of the two unions would be given legal advantage over the other.

The question of relative legal advantage was resolved when the committee decided, after lengthy debate, that membership in the plant union should definitely be obligatory for all blue-collar workers. What this kind of security meant when proclaimed and enforced by the state was that the plant union would also have priority over the craft union with regard to bargaining and other rights. The government could not logically force workers to join unions and then allow other voluntary organizations to take over their functions.

The vote on the above question was seven to two, with interesting arguments on both sides. Senator Concha and Deputies Irarrázaval, Edwards Matte, and Undurraga, all *unionistas,* spoke for compulsion, Concha saying that this was "the only way of arriving at the solution of labor conflicts." The Deputies saw compulsion in this case as beneficial to the worker; he was being forced to do something good for himself and this was not objectionable. Compulsory plant unionism would benefit and protect the worker just as did legislation on worker health, welfare, and safety, on the labor of women and children, and on the length of the working day. Ramírez Frías was against compulsion as a matter of principle and he believed the obligatory plant union would violate the Constitutional guarantee of freedom of association. Although he did not like the compulsory union, Labarca voted for it anyway, his presumption and hope being that in the ensuing competition with the craft union the former, even though compulsory, would still be defeated.[35]

With the above matter settled, the Joint Committee turned to a full consideration of the craft union. The committee used the Ramírez Frías rather than the Alessandri proposal as the basis of discussion, but this, with one exception to be noted below, no longer had any special significance. Agreement upon compulsory membership for the plant union had shorn the Ramírez Frías project of its salient principle and left it nothing more than a copy of the code project. The committee expressed itself in favor of Articles 1, 2, and 6 of the Ramírez Frías project and agreed to examine the rest of it article by article. This was done very quickly and the changes introduced were few and of minor importance.[36]

Early in January 1922 Moisés Poblete Troncoso and the committee secretary brought in a draft of the combined projects which consisted of two titles: Title I, "The Craft Union," Title II, "The Industrial Union" (i.e., plant union). The first thing done, at the suggestion of Senator Yáñez, was to reverse the order of the titles. The committee then went over the project as a whole and made a number of final changes, most of them minor.

As to the craft union, the committee made only one significant change. It will be remembered that the union title of the Liberal Alliance bill conceded to the craft union jurisdiction over only one craft or occupation. The Ramírez Frías bill, on the other hand, which the committee was now using, allowed a local union to include members of more than one craft. At the suggestion of Poblete and with the approval of Ramírez Frías, the committee reverted to the original and more limited single-craft structure. The action was evidently prompted by opposition within the committee to the strong national craft union with bargaining rights. To save the national union, Poblete and Ramírez Frías were willing to give up the multicraft feature of the Ramírez Frías bill and accept monocraft unionism. This explanation was not made at the time, but its accuracy seems plausible, given Yáñez's admission that he was against national unions "especially when they are allowed to defend the economic interests of their members."[37]

In terminating its work regarding labor organizations, the Joint Committee made applicable to the plant union eleven of the articles

[35]Ibid., Sección III, pp. 34–62.
[36]Ibid., Sección III, pp. 72–79.
[37]Ibid., Sección III, pp. 90–91.

which subjected the craft union to minute state regulation and control. Thus the plant union, which previously had been tied almost exclusively to the employer, was now delivered into the hands of the state as well. This was a very important change for it meant that the organization of a plant union would not depend upon the will and the initiative of the employer and, in addition, it obviously meant that, once constituted, the plant union would theoretically have two masters.[38]

On February 21, 1923 the Joint Committee sent the union project to the Senate and to the Chamber. Deputy Ramírez Frías was the only committee member who declined to support the final bill. He could not, he said, force workers to join unions against their own free will. He thought the plant union would convert workers into the *inquilinos* of the factory employer and that, while this would have been all right during the Middle Ages, circumstances had since changed. Neither, he warned, would profit sharing bring an end to socioeconomic conflict as others assumed it would. Ramírez Frías later introduced his own project directly into the Chamber of Deputies but it was never debated.[39]

After the Joint Committee reported out the union bill, it was to take up the subject of conciliation and arbitration but the minutes of any sessions that may have been held on this matter after February 1923 were never published. In his annual message of June 1, 1924 Alessandri remarked that the Joint Committee was advancing in its study of the conciliation and arbitration project but, in any case, the latter was not reported out by the committee before the collapse of the Alessandri government in September.[40] The Joint Committee does not therefore appear to have done any effective work after completion of the union project.

IV

If the work of the Joint Committee was not such as to excite either envy or admiration, the record of the Congress was even less so. Neither the labor contract nor the union bill, the only items reported out by the Joint Committee, was ever debated on the floor of either Chamber. What little had been possible in the bi-coalition Joint Com-

[38]*Ibid.*, Sección II, pp. 80–113.

[39]Cámara de Diputados, *Boletín de las Sesiones Ordinarias en 1924*, vol. 1, pp. 30–34.

[40]Editorial Ginebra, *Legislación social de América* (Santiago: Editorial Ginebra [1937?]), vol. 1, pp. *18, 21*.

mittee appointed for the deliberate purpose of effecting compromise was entirely out of the question in the Senate, still loyal to the National Union, or in the lower Chamber, still flying the Liberal Alliance banner. Besides, the Senate became addicted to turning out Alessandri's Cabinets, which either Chamber could do by the simple device of an unfavorable vote on a major Administration measure. All told, eighteen Cabinets paraded briefly but with lively step across the political scene from the time of Alessandri's election until his resignation in September 1924. The conflict between the President and the Senate had already become dangerously acute by late 1923, and Alessandri tells us that at that time a great many people were insisting that he declare a dictatorship and close the Congress.[41]

While Alessandri may not in any case have been the "dictator type," two considerations encouraged him to turn a deaf ear to more impatient elements. The first and most important was that new congressional elections were coming in March 1924 and he counted on making Liberal Alliance control of government complete at that time by winning over the Senate. This victory would, he thought, end four years of political and governmental chaos by giving him the total support he needed to enact his program. Second, he hoped that bi-coalition support of an Administration measure to provide Congressmen with salaries would assure passage of the measure early in the year. If passed, it would encourage a different breed of politician to seek office in the coming elections — more responsible, more patriotic, and more loyal men who would help him put across social and constitutional reforms.

According to Alessandri, the ministerial representatives of the National Union (there were two in the Cabinet in January 1924) and all the political parties were agreed upon the need for a congressional salary system and signed a "pact" to this effect.[42] Alessandri thereupon submitted a salary bill to the Congress. It was passed by the lower Chamber, evidently before the March elections, but not by the Senate.

As the President had hoped, the Liberal Alliance swept the elections and stood in unchallenged control of the government. In his message to the new Congress in June, Alessandri, with what degree of confidence we cannot say, asked for sweeping constitutional reforms intended to correct the major abuses of the parliamentary system and strengthen the office of the President. Among other things, he wanted the Senate deprived of its then existing right to vote lack of confidence in the

[41]Alessandri, *Recuerdos de gobierno*, I, p. 373.
[42]*Ibid.*, pp. 306–308.

Ministry; he wanted every ministerial appointment to be ratified by the province or department from which the appointee came; and he wanted the congressional salary measure enacted into law.

What followed in the crucial months from June to September was a sordid repetition, on perhaps an even bolder and more shameless scale, of what had transpired during all the preceding years of Alessandri's Administration. And not all of it was due to the National Union. Alessandri himself had inadvisably and unnecessarily (the Liberal Alliance would probably have triumphed in any case) used the army to influence the outcome of the elections in some areas in March, and the recriminations in the Congress were legion. Most of its time was wasted arguing election results. When the Congress eventually went on to other things, it took up the salary bill, leaving more urgent fiscal matters unattended to, and then found that the January "pact" was meaningless. For one thing the National Union, and some Liberal Alliance politicians as well, had discovered that it was procedurally unconstitutional for the new Congress to approve the bill and, for another, some Congressmen of both coalitions refused to do anything else until the salary bill was passed. Pressure from the latter source only made the opposition more vigorous and determined, and the Senate was forced to resort to special sessions on the salary measure.

Thus, contrary to Alessandri's expectations, the principal difficulty was apparently not a politically divided Congress but the parliamentary system itself. "The evil," he recalled later, "was deeper than I believed. Parliamentary tyranny became stronger and more irresponsible. . . . The diseased craving among Congressmen for a ministerial seat was aggravated, became formidibly intense, and finally ended in collective degeneration."[43]

The spectacle of the Congress interminably wrangling over its own pay after decades of near governmental paralysis finally forced the enormously patient Chilean army into action. As we shall see, however, its motivations were not entirely patriotic. On the evening of September 2, fifty or more uniformed army officers, mostly lieutenants and captains, walked into the Senate gallery. The great enjoyable political game was over. Within nine days a military junta would take official control of the government and then make preparations for a constitutional convention and an end to the parliamentary system.

[43]From an undated letter to an unnamed person reproduced in Biblioteca América, Sección Chilena, *El Presidente Alessandri*, pp. 277–278.

Those intervening nine days are immensely important to this story of the labor laws. Much of what happened is clear; why it happened as it did is not so clear. According to some accounts, the army acted on its own initiative and as the interpreter of the popular will in favor of long-postponed reforms. Others, while agreeing that the army acted independently, add that many officers had become convinced by the noisy debate over congressional salaries that, if resources for such a purpose were available, they should share in the government's largesse. One scholar carries this point so far as to conclude that all the reform demands of the army officers were but a cover for their own desire to have higher salaries. This does not, however, explain why a military junta was formed and, after its salary demands were met, took over the government, arranged for a constitutional convention, and did not depart the scene until the following year. Nor does it explain the continuing military interest in government in the 1920's and the eventual rise of dictator Ibañez, an army colonel. Emilio Rodríguez Mendoza wrote a book about the revolt of the military in which he tried to prove that the whole thing was planned by Alessandri who advised the army on how and when it should act and what reforms it should demand. Alessandri himself swears that he knew "nothing, absolutely nothing" about the revolt, and he charges, on the other hand, that the National Union did everything within its power to get control of the movement, turn it against him, and force him to resign.[44]

Alessandri and his ministers first determined to discipline the officers severely who appeared in the Senate gallery, but, upon learning that the entire army was behind the show of force, Alessandri invited high-ranking officers to meet with him in the *Moneda*. They came on September 5 and presented him with a list of eleven demands, one of which was for the immediate passage of the labor code. "Upon hearing such a thing," Alessandri confided years later to Moisés Poblete Troncoso, "I thought to myself that perhaps the time had arrived to get out of the Congress the laws they had resisted for four years." He decided then and there to play along with the rebels and they, in turn, promised

[44]See Alessandri, *Recuerdos de gobierno*, pp. 306–308, 328, 374, 412, 425; Robert J. Alexander, *Prophets of the Revolution* (New York: The Macmillan Co., 1962), p. 54; Luis Galdames, *Historia de Chile*, décimotercera edición (Santiago: Empresa Editora Zig-Zag, 1952), pp. 540–543; Emilio Rodríguez Mendoza, *El golpe de estado de 1924* (Santiago: Editorial Ercilla, 1938); and Juan Tapia Carvajal, *Legislación del trabajo en Chile, algunos antecedentes históricos* (Santiago: La Gratitud Nacional, 1937).

they would return to their barracks when their demands had been met.[45]

The following day Alessandri announced the formation of a new Cabinet headed by General Luis Altamirano. Members of the Cabinet contacted the presidents of both Chambers of the Congress and told them that Alessandri wanted their cooperation in dispatching several legislative matters. The Congress met on September 8 and by nightfall had passed, individually rather than in the form of a code, seven labor laws. Included among these were all the major subjects of both the Conservative bill and the Liberal Alliance project, as well as the white-collar bill which had been introduced into the lower Chamber in 1922. Later the same night the Council of State, presided over by Alessandri, convened and approved the laws.[46]

But that did not end the military revolt. By that time a military junta was functioning and, far from ordering the troops back to their barracks, called upon Alessandri to dissolve the Congress. Believing that this request fatally compromised his authority as President, Alessandri resigned and took refuge in the United States Embassy. Although his resignation was rejected by the Senate, the Chamber of Deputies, and the Junta, he did not reconsider and shortly thereafter fled the country. The military junta took formal control of the government on September 11 and did not relinquish it until the following year when Alessandri was persuaded to return from voluntary exile to complete his term. Although he resigned again before his term was up, he remained in office long enough in 1925 to engineer the adoption of a new Constitution which returned Chile to the presidential system.

V

The most obvious and most compelling reason why labor reforms were not effected by constitutional means during 1919–1924 is that the long-standing conflict between the aristocratic-Catholic and the

[45]Carta, Alessandri a Poblete, 30 Noviembre 1929, reproduced in Poblete, *El derecho del trabajo y la seguridad social en Chile*, pp. 23–24. See also *Justicia*, Sept. 7, 1924.

[46]*El Mercurio*, Sept. 7, 9, 1924; *El Diario Ilustrado*, Sept. 8, 1924. These two papers do not agree as to the number or subjects of the legislative demands served upon the Congress through the intermediary of the Cabinet. Moreover, *El Mercurio* lists no labor laws at all and *El Diario Illustrado* lists only conciliation and arbitration. This is most interesting and, along with the controversy regarding the role of Alessandri and the military, suggests that detailed study of the events of 1924 would be most useful.

middle-class élites was approaching its day of reckoning. The parliamentary system was on the verge of collapse. Even in its earlier, if not much better, days there were times when legislative action was a rarity. Voting the budget, among the most essential functions of the Congress, sometimes waited until political exhaustion waylaid the players of both coalitions or until a day's further delay would have brought national economic disaster. The 18 Cabinets of Alessandri's Administration (up to his resignation in September 1924) only continued the parade at a little faster pace than for other years. Over the period 1886–1924 there were 121 Cabinets, or an average of more than 3 Cabinets a year for 39 years. It would not be reasonable to expect a stellar legislative performance in any field under such circumstances.

Alessandri himself clearly came to see the larger élite conflict, evidenced in the parliamentary system, as his chief adversary when, after March 1924, a political "full house" for the Liberal Alliance failed to produce legislative results. It was to the correction of this basic social and constitutional flaw that he, the military, and the country at large repaired in the months succeeding the September *coup*. The Constitution adopted in 1925 substituted a strong Executive for the parliamentary system.

The parliamentary system was not, however, the only really important obstacle to labor legislation. Inability to compromise the reform ideas of the two coalitions was a second significant factor. Eliodoro Yáñez, as early as 1920, saw joint congressional consideration of all labor legislation as a strategically necessary procedure.[47] That Alessandri did not from the beginning choose this route and that he tried first to get his own bill through the lower Chamber, may have made compromise more difficult to achieve. In any case, the record clearly shows that the Joint Committee, of bi-coalition membership and generally favorable to basic labor legislation, worked for months on the union issue alone and then proposed a bill which did little more than put together, unchanged, the separate Conservative and Liberal Alliance proposals. A basic philosophical difference, centering upon freedom versus the use of compulsion, appears to have divided committee members. The Liberal Alliance wanted free association and voluntary dispute settlement; the National Union wanted a tighter system which they could control and which would end capital-labor conflict.

Even had there been effective governmental machinery and a disposition to compromise in the Joint Committee, it is questionable whether

[47] *La Nación*, August 15, 1920.

any, and even more questionable whether all, of the labor bills would have been democratically enacted. As we have seen, the opposition was formidable. It came in varying degrees from rural landowners, industrial and commercial employers, the Catholic Church, sectors of the political parties, and even from organized labor. The wonder is not that the Congress did not legislate but that anyone, the army included, should have felt there was a universal demand and a political need for a complete, even sophisticated in some respects, industrial relations system.

Who wanted it other than the intellectuals? Perhaps a few astute politicians like Alessandri,[48] a few astute businessmen in the Society for Factory Development, and a few leftists like Malaquías Concha and Zenon Torrealba. Nearly everyone else had only selective interests, if any at all, in the labor legislation field. Many of them would have supported the individual written labor contract, or an amendment to the accident law, or a Ministry of Labor; some would have voted for arbitration of a "solve the labor problem forever" type; only a handful really wanted unions. The only persons who organized on their own behalf and sought direct benefits in labor legislation were those of the lower middle class and the government bureaucracy. Through their Federation of the Middle Class and the Radical party, they brought pressure to bear — but not for the whole gamut of labor proposals. Their interests were primarily in a white-collar labor contract bill, social security, and a Labor and Social Security Ministry.

There is unfortunately little to say with regard to a positive show of opposition in the Congress. To what degree this was due to the constitutional crisis, which overshadowed legislation, or to the successful maneuvering of the opposition itself in bottling up the labor bills is difficult to say. The only floor debate and vote came in the Senate in

---

[48]Pike has argued (*Chile and the United States 1880–1962*, p. 171) that Alessandri did not really want social reform and that his failure to get it was due fundamentally to his own lack of conviction. Thus: "Alessandri and the majority of those who backed him were in accord with the Conservatives in the belief that the old system was still fundamentally viable and that the basic patterns of social and political hierarchy and stratification could be preserved." The writer believes that Alessandri's record on the labor code, as presented in this chapter, permits a somewhat more favorable interpretation. Other writers appear to share a more generous view of Alessandri's role and the key importance of constitutional and political factors in explaining the failures of Alessandri's administration. See, for example, Alexander, *Labor Relations in Argentina, Brazil, and Chile*, pp. 242–243, 255, 267; Alexander, *Communism in Latin America*, p. 178; Halperin, *Nationalism and Communism in Chile*, p. 30; and Johnson, *Political Change in Latin America*, pp. 69–70.

1921. A majority of that Chamber were at that time against the union, conciliation, and arbitration features of the Conservative bill and so voted. In addition to this, one can assume that the decision made by committees in both Chambers to treat labor legislation piece by piece rather than as a whole sprung from opposition to a system or code and reflected selective interests. Even the Radical party, which certainly was the most popular party of the time, came to appreciate the uphill nature of the battle for labor reforms. In 1923 the party agreed that its congressional delegation should push for the labor code but quickly added that if they should encounter "insoluble difficulties" they should then try to get only three laws: one on conciliation and arbitration, another for white-collar workers, and a final one on the protection of women workers and minors.[49]

Chile's enactment by military fiat of all labor legislation pending in the Congress in 1924 was an accident of history. Alessandri found sudden and unexpected support from the military junta with which he cooperated, going down himself in the aftermath. Why he allowed significant parts of the Conservative bill (obligatory industrial unionism and compulsory conciliation, especially) to become law, as well as the Liberal Alliance project, is not clear. Perhaps time alone and the urgent need to satisfy the military were the ruling factors. There may not have been time to disentangle the two projects. Perhaps Alessandri was not fully aware of the degree to which the union sections, in particular, of the two bills had become unified in the course of the Joint Committee's work. Perhaps, since the military eventually showed a middle-class bias, the junta erroneously assumed in September 1924 that all pending social legislation was part of the Alessandri Administration and the Liberal Alliance program. Perhaps, too, the swift positive action on social legislation simply proves the larger point that the parliamentary system and the church-state question were the more fundamental issues of the élite conflict. Despite their significant differences, the two élite labor proposals agreed that the major objective was to prolong authoritarianism and not to take genuine strides toward a pluralistic society through encouragement of free unions. Therefore, enactment of both proposals could not, in the broad sense, do any harm to the present society. However, speculation on the motivation of the military and the reaction of Alessandri is no substitute

[49]Partido Radical, *Memoria de la mesa directiva de la junta central radical* (Santiago: Editorial Minerva, 1923), pp. 6–7.

for deeper research. The role social legislation played in the intervention and subsequent behavior of the military needs more careful study.

That the enactment of the laws in 1924 was an historical accident reminds us, as we all need to be reminded now and then, that the best theories of human conduct and institutional behavior sometimes fall far short of explaining reality. Because we do not fully understand these moments, we rationalize them as the "exceptions" to the "rule."

PART III

CHAPTER 9

Unanticipated Consequences

IN ONE sense, the really decisive evidence of this study remains to be presented. A major thesis is that there was no consensus for labor reform in Chile and that the industrial relations system owed its birth largely to the intellectuals and the military. If the thesis is correct, then enactment of the system did not create consensus and, under these circumstances, the system could not have become immediately operative. In truth, as this chapter endeavors to show, it did not. Formidable employer opposition, a strong division of opinion within the established "free" labor movement with regard to legal unionism, and alternating periods of government inaction, confusion, and strong-arm enforcement methods combined to delay for many years the achievement of some success in the implementation of the 1924 laws. In fact, not until the unification of the labor movement in 1936 and the election victory of the Popular Front government two years later did development of the legal industrial relations system take on a real and lasting momentum. The interesting events of these years (1924–1938), including the violence and the travail which were both inevitable consequences of the use of force in 1924 and also the price paid for the eventual achievement of a functioning system of industrial relations, are sketched in this chapter.

242

UNANTICIPATED CONSEQUENCES

I

The key labor organization in the 1920's was, as we have seen, the Federation of Chilean Workers (FOCH). The FOCH represented the Marxist left which, as communism or socialism, continues to the present day to dominate the country's organized blue-collar workers. The position the FOCH took with respect to the labor laws was, in the unfolding of history, to remain unchanged as that of the labor majority. That position was opportunistic; the FOCH went along in general with the new system, accepting most but rejecting other aspects of the laws. The only labor organization to reject the laws in a body was the Industrial Workers of the World (IWW), and the only labor organization to accept both their content and their ideology was a newly formed Confederation of White Trade-Unions, a Catholic group. The anarchist unions of IWW descent have been a persistent, though in the last two decades or so a declining, force in the general union picture in Chile. They are the so-called "free" or "independent" unions who have coined the terms "yellow" and "collaborationist" to describe the legal unions.[1] The Catholic or Christian unions have existed only sporadically since 1925, although their strength appears to have been growing in recent years. The Confederation of White Trade-Unions did not prosper.[2]

As a Deputy, Recabarren hindered more than he helped the development of labor legislation, and when the army took over in September 1924 he was much more concerned about the revolutionary significance of the proposed constitutional assembly than about the labor laws. Fundamental policy differences had already developed between himself and other leaders of the FOCH and the Communist party, and these differences now became greatly exacerbated. The National Executive Board of the FOCH and the Communist party took an extremely cautious wait-and-see position,[3] while Recabarren affirmed in *Justicia* that the proletariat was in full agreement with the idea of a constitutional assembly, that they were living through a "revolutionary moment," and that if the constitutional assembly were to be free and open

[1] For the IWW's statement of its position during the military intervention of September 1924, see *Justicia*, Feb. 13, 1927.
[2] Poblete describes the Confederation of White Trade-Unions as an organization collaborating with the state in its social politics. See Poblete, *La organización sindical en Chile y otros estudios sociales* (Santiago: Imprenta Ramón Brias, 1926), p. 56. See also United States Department of Labor, Bureau of Labor Statistics, *Bulletin 461*, pp. 22–41.
[3] *Justicia*, Sept. 7, 8, 1924.

243

the proletariat would be in the majority. He had no illusions, he said, about the chances of erecting a "communist or anarchist" republic but "we must work to develop the resources with which to set one up later."[4] At an extraordinary convention of the Communist party four "younger generation" members were elected to the National Executive Council, and they wanted the party to ask Recabarren to disavow his *Justicia* article and to remind him that the council was the only authorized spokesman for the party. The convention rebuked neither Recabarren nor his foes.[5] It is likely that this challenge to his leadership of the working class, and his failure to win re-election to the Chamber in March, added to a growing despondency which finally overcame him and caused him to take his own life in December 1924.[6]

It is also likely that the challenge to Recabarren concerned the labor laws as well as grander political strategy and the constitutional assembly. Just two weeks before the tragedy of Recabarren's death, Luis V. Cruz, who had served with him as a Communist Deputy in the lower Chamber and had followed his congressional leadership of the party, began a series of seven articles in *Justicia* in which he urged qualified acceptance of the labor laws. His interpretation of them was from the "revolutionary point of view," he announced, and accorded with concepts approved at the first congress of the Red International of Labor Unions. His first article faced the issue squarely in its title: "Must We Ask for Repeal of the Recently Enacted Labor Code?" Cruz revealed that members of the party and the FOCH were agreed only upon one thing, the need to fight capitalism, and that they disagreed on how it should be done and what weapons should be used. While disagreement was due not to ideological differences but to a "lack of revolutionary understanding," it could nevertheless be fatal and should be debated forthrightly. He and those who agreed with him had to

---

[4]*Ibid.*, Sept. 13, 1924.

[5]*Ibid.*, Oct. 22, 1924.

[6]Some observers have explained Recabarren's suicide as the consequence of his disillusionment with the Soviet Union. Fanny Simon has denied this, saying that he was discouraged about the situation in his own country. The FOCH was growing smaller, the Communist Deputies had failed to win re-election in March, the military had taken over, and finally, she says, the Communist party itself was becoming a tool of the intellectuals. Fanny Simon, "Recabarren," pp. 226–227. Alexander notes that at the time many Chileans believed he had been assassinated by the Junta "because they were afraid of his influence with the workers." Alexander discounts the notion, agreeing that Recabarren's emotional instability drove him to suicide. See Alexander, *Communism in Latin America,* p. 179.

demonstrate to our comrades that we must squeeze from the laws the greatest benefits possible, so as to build up a superior revolutionary potential. We will also show up as an absurdity the idea put forth by some comrades and central organizations of asking for their repeal or of paying no attention to them...which would seem to indicate misunderstanding of our revolutionary point of view.[7]

There were three ways of looking at social legislation, only one of which was correct from the revolutionary standpoint. Reformists believed that social legislation was an end in itself, that through it capitalism would be changed. Anarchists repudiated all laws. Communists looked upon social laws in a capitalist society as the revolutionary conquests of the proletariat. The bourgeoisie respond to a revolutionary movement by passing laws:

It is, then, the proletariat, without asking for it, without demanding it, with only its organizing activities, which causes the bourgeoisie to legislate with the notion that it is satisfying innumerable social needs.[8]

Despite Cruz's propaganda campaign, a division of opinion continued to plague the FOCH. Some of its affiliates, who seemed to be following "Recabarrenism" or the example of the IWW, petitioned FOCH leaders to work for repeal of the laws. They argued that the laws had not been debated or voted on in either Chamber of the Congress, that they had been passed by a *de facto* government and were therefore unconstitutional, and that the workers did not have to recognize them. They argued further that revolutionary unionists should not on principle concede to the government any right to regulate labor, and they feared that such laws would convert the unions into reformist organizations. Workingmen should put all their energy into the forthcoming constitutional convention. Cruz labeled their views "pure anarchism, absurd, and prejudicial to the working class." If the workers had the strength to accomplish repeal, he pointed out, they could just as easily suppress capitalism altogether and be done with it. Carlos Contreras Labarca, a fellow Communist and future leader of substantial reputation, agreed. In his opinion the FOCH should not reject the laws out of hand but rather should study them closely and "to the extent they agree with some of our aspirations or immediate demands, we should take advantage of them IN ORDER TO PERSEVERE IN THE CLASS STRUGGLE." He accepted the opposition's point that the workers had not been consulted in the passage of the laws and were therefore not obligated to respect them. But he con-

[7] *Justicia*, Nov. 24, 26, 1924.
[8] *Ibid.*, Nov. 27, 28, Dec. 3, 4, 5, 1924.

sidered this flaw as equivalent to the concession of an option which the workers could exercise at their own discretion, rejecting some laws and accepting those that squared with their interests. In doing so, they would in any case only be following the example set for them by the capitalist class which "accepts and respects the law exclusively when it is advantageous to do so; the law is for that class only a snare for catching incautious workers or a cloak which conceals their real strategy, and nothing more." "Why," Labarca asked, "should the wage-earning class behave any differently?"[9] A series of additional articles promised from the opposition[10] never made their appearance in *Justicia*, and this probably indicates that the Communist successors to Recabarren had, by the spring of 1925, consolidated their position in the FOCH hierarchy.

Differences of opinion continued to agitate the rank and file, however, and the debate was resolved, for the time being and for a majority within the FOCH, at its December convention. At that time the Communist position was adopted after a long discussion in the course of which reformist as well as anarchist alternatives were offered and supported. The winning policy stated that the FOCH would not allow itself to be deceived either by the mirage of reformism or by the intransigence of an antipolitical stand which could only serve the interests of the employer. The FOCH must, without losing sight of the ultimate goal of achieving power for the working class, "use all the social legislation of the capitalist state to fight capitalism itself." The FOCH would therefore work for the implementation or the repeal of laws in accordance with the desires of the working class and the dictates of its long-term objectives.[11]

The only law the convention voted to repeal was the one providing for a national social security program. Although they did not say so, some of the delegates probably feared that such a program might satisfy the needs of many workers and might thus weaken their interest in an ultimate goal of revolution. Others believed, and said so, that the law only intended to take money out of the worker's pocket and deliver it to the government which was in a chronic state of "economic agony." *Justicia* later printed several articles calling for repeal of the law, but the campaign was evidently soon forgotten.[12] Luis V. Cruz believed that many politicians wanted the white-collar law only so they could

[9]*Ibid.*, April 5, 8, 9, 1925.
[10]*Ibid.*, April 5, 1925.
[11]*Ibid.*, Dec. 23, 24, 27, 29, 1925.
[12]*Ibid.*, Jan. 31, Feb. 7, 11, 14, April 23, 1926.

246

put the middle class in conflict with the working class, but he did not advocate repeal.[13]

For two basic reasons, the Communist-led majority favored the union law. In the first place, they might with proper government enforcement of the law be able to extend their influence into areas where organization was weak or nonexistent and, second, they were attracted by the financial potential of profit sharing in the plant union scheme. This does not mean that all leaders who considered themselves Marxists or Communists accepted the law or that all who said they accepted them were as convinced of the correctness of the "line" as was Cruz. Something approaching unanimity in this respect was not achieved until 1936 when free unions and legal unions were brought together in the Confederation of Chilean Workers.

Indeed, the actual experiences of trying to organize plant unions during the politically unstable years of 1925–1927 undoubtedly dampened rather than stimulated the ardor of those who sought to use the labor laws within the larger framework of their revolutionary aims. Immediately thereafter, with the advent of dictator Ibañez in 1927, the radical left was driven from the union scene and legal unions were set up under close government surveillance. Under these circumstances, the FOCH clearly became hostile to the government system, but its hostility was not so much an expression of opposition to the labor laws as such as it was an expression of anger that the laws were being used to destroy FOCH organization and membership. The nature and intent of FOCH and Communist attitudes toward the legal industrial relations system in the years after 1924 have not heretofore been fully appreciated by other observers.[14]

[13]*Ibid.,* June 19, 1926.

[14]For example, Alexander's unqualified statement that Communist labor leaders and the FOCH fought the new labor laws clearly overstates the negative reaction, does not mention the favorable, opportunistic line developed by Cruz in *Justicia,* and ignores the positive action of the FOCH 1925 convention. Alexander has written as follows on this point: "Meanwhile the Communists were conducting a campaign throughout the country against governmental registration of trade unions. Legalization and registration of the unions were among the measures provided for in the legislation passed in September, 1924, but it was not until the reinstallation of Alessandri in January, 1925, that the government took active steps to have the unions register under the law.

"The Communists feared that the registration of unions would result in their falling under the government's political control, thus undermining the position of the Communists, who until that time had dominated the labor movement. It was not until the middle 1930's that the Communists allowed unions under their

While routing the leftists of the labor movement and erecting large numbers of legal unions, Ibañez also codified the labor laws at the end of his régime in 1931. After he was driven from office, constitutional government was restored and competition returned to the labor and political fields. As the forces of popular front government then began to gather, the stage was set for the unification of the labor movement referred to above. The full acceptance of the legal system of labor relations which this unification symbolized has endured. Structural unity itself, in the sense of the uninterrupted existence of a single major trade union center, has not, but, to the extent that union rivalry and structural separateness has occurred, it has taken place largely within the legal system. There are still free unions, but, while they were in the majority for several years after 1924, today they are few in number and of little political or economic significance. A closer examination of the period from the time of the passage of the labor laws until the popular front era can now be undertaken.

What happened when FOCH leaders and others first tried to organize unions in 1925? What was the reaction of employers and the government when they were faced with an organizing spirit not based on a desire for harmony, mutual understanding, and cooperation with employers but borne on the wings of revolution? The *Diario Ilustrado* had predicted the possibility of such a dilemma many years before, but perhaps for many the reality of it was largely unanticipated. Nor was a revolutionary spirit the only unanticipated consequence of passage of the laws. Labor organizers showed a preference for the plant union which in the Conservative bill and in congressional debate had been proposed and touted as the agent *par excellence* of harmony in industry. Moisés Poblete Troncoso even continued to believe this of the plant union after the first wave of organizing had gotten under way. He noted "an appreciable movement in favor of the new social laws especially the industrial union [i.e., the plant union] which eliminates

---

control to seek government registration. In 1925 the Communists fought bitterly the activities of the government commissions sent out by Alessandri to encourage union registration throughout the country.

"The Party not only opposed the union registration law, but most of the other measures which had been passed in September, 1924, and which Alessandri attempted to put into execution in 1925. It was particularly active in agitating against the two laws which established Social Security Funds for manual workers and white-collar workers." Alexander, *Communism in Latin America*, p. 180. See also, Alexander, *Labor Relations in Argentina, Brazil, and Chile*, pp. 255–256.

from industry the free and semirevolutionary union."[15] There was of course no intrinsic relationship between free or legal unions and labor ideology, at least so long as the government played a neutral role. Many FOCH leaders had realized this immediately.

Some employers, particularly in the south of Chile, accepted unions as inevitable and perhaps a few even encouraged their establishment. Over-all, however, the reaction of business was negative and was expressed in open warfare against union organizers, as in the nitrate *pampa*, or in more subtle moves to undercut organizing campaigns as in Valparaíso, Concepción, and elsewhere. Government implementation and enforcement of the laws were slow, only partial, and carried out in the general atmosphere of confusion and instability which characterized the era. After all, the laws were not self-explanatory, nor were they self-enforcing. The job of interpretation and enforcement in a country largely inexperienced in such matters and with the special communications problem imposed by its three-thousand-mile length was bound to be slow and to lead to confusion. Lack of trained personnel as labor inspectors, government chairmen of conciliation boards, and middle-level labor ministry officials was a part of this larger problem of implementation. Moreover, there was the perennial dilemma of finance. Forced passage of the laws did not make up for the absence of budgetary planning. Where were salaries and other administrative expenses to come from and who was to pay the costs of a nationwide system of conciliation boards? All this apart from the political question as to whether the government wanted to encourage communist-led workers to set up legal unions.

How prompt and energetic was the government in setting up industrial relations machinery? In the first place, it must be understood that Chilean laws, like laws in other countries with a Roman legal background, are not operative until the executive provides their "regulations" (the details of how they are to be implemented) through the decree system. It may take several decrees to regulate a single law if it contains subject matter already legislated upon and regulated in a broader or more general context. No part of the union law was regulated until November 1925 and then only the union incorporation procedure was detailed.[16] Most of the rest of the law was not regulated

[15]Poblete, *La organización sindical en Chile y otros estudios sociales*, p. 76.

[16]Decreto No. 2736 del Ministerio de Justicia promulgado en el *Diario Oficial* el 25 de Noviembre de 1925. Incorporation procedure was amended by Decreto No. 498 del 17 de Marzo de 1930.

until 1929,[17] and effective protection against discharge for union officers and candidates for union office (fuero sindical) was apparently not provided until May 1931.[18]

The conciliation and arbitration law was regulated in June 1925, and the regulating decree indicated the jurisdiction and seat of each of the ten general boards to be established, and identified nitrates and mining as two industries which should have their own special conciliation boards. These boards should be created as funds were available and "when their creation is considered necessary." The decree advised that the proposed budget included funds for four boards.[19] Although information may not be complete, it appears that only one board was set up before the advent of Ibañez. This board had jurisdiction in the two provinces of Santiago and O'Higgins and had its seat in the capital city of Santiago.[20] The government's intention actually was for a time to establish not one but two sets of conciliation boards, one for the blue-collar and another for the white-collar workers. A third set of worker housing boards also existed, at least on paper. These three sets of boards were consolidated into a single system of "Labor Tribunals" at the beginning of the Ibañez Administration.[21] With the adoption of the Labor Code in 1931 a separate system of conciliation boards, this time serving both blue- and white-collar workers, was again established, and this is the system as it operates at present. Data are lacking, but it appears that most of the regular and special conciliation boards presently operating were not created or did not begin to function until the mid-1930's and after. The 1931 code also provided for a system of labor courts to interpret and enforce both the labor laws and the individual and collective contracts agreed to under these laws. Prior to 1931 interpretation was handled by the Executive and enforced through presidential and ministerial decrees. Such an arrangement was inefficient and failed to satisfy minimum requirements with respect either to the volume of business to be transacted or to the expedition needed.

The kind and degree of government implementation described above

[17]Decreto No. 2148 del Ministerio de Bienestar Social promulgado en el Diario Oficial el 31 de Diciembre de 1928.

[18]Decreto No. 178 del Ministerio de Bienestar Social promulgado en el Diario Oficial el 28 de Mayo de 1931. The regulations for the union content of the Labor Code (i.e., Book III of the code) were consolidated in Decreto No. 642 del 3 de Noviembre de 1936.

[19]Decreto No. 303 promulgado en el Diario Oficial el 23 de Junio de 1925.

[20]Decreto No. 801 promulgado en el Diario Oficial el 13 de Septiembre de 1926.

[21]See Decreto No. 2,100 promulgado en el Diario Oficial el 5 de Enero de 1928.

meant essentially that, in the period before 1931, legal unions could be set up with little difficulty if the government gave its encouragement or took the initiative in the process and if employers did not fight too hard. The incorporation procedure was there. Once set up, however, there was little guarantee of either a long or secure or effective existence. Officers could be discharged with relative ease, until 1929 the nature and permissible limits of all union functions were vague, and the signing of collective agreements was virtually impossible in the absence of compulsory conciliation machinery.

In the nitrate *pampa*, FOCH organizing efforts were stopped dead in their tracks, and employers, with the cooperation of the national police force *(carabineros)*, appear to have broken up newly formed industrial unions before they were able to achieve government recognition as legally incorporated bodies. FOCH leaders and Communist party Deputies said that immediately after unions were first set up in 1925 their officers were arrested, charged with subverting public order and fomenting civil war, convicted, and ordered to leave the *pampa*. All union members were discharged. "In this way," said Communist Deputy Pedro Reyes, "you can understand why unions in the *pampa* are a failure. There is fear. Union presidents, secretaries, and treasurers have been taken from their homes at night and made to walk through the immensity of the *pampa*."[22] At La Coruña the army was called in to restore order during a strike, and several sources have estimated the number of nitrate workers "massacred" in this process at between 59 and 3,000.[23]

In December 1925, at the FOCH convention, several delegates indicated that "persecution" of workers and unions continued in the nitrate zone and that the labor laws had not changed the situation in this respect. It was just like the pre-1924 period. The legal industrial unions were a failure because "the same authorities charged with guaranteeing the formation of such unions are the first to destroy them and persecute their militant members." Meetings were broken up by the *carabineros* on the ground that the workers were discussing questions outside the permissible area conceded in the law, and employers were trying to erect industrial unions with "yellow elements" in control. Workers could not, however, abandon the industrial unions because to do so

[22]*Justicia,* April 10, 19, 1926.
[23]Arnold Roller, "White Terror in Liberal Chile," *Nation,* vol. 121, Oct. 14, 1925, pp. 415–416; *American Labor Year Book,* 1925, p. 400; César Jobet, *Ensayo crítico del desarrollo económico-social de Chile,* p. 172.

would be to surrender and to allow employers to turn the unions into fascist organizations.[24] Difficulties persisted, the FOCH charging that nitrate companies only laughed at the union law because it had not been regulated and that not a single collective agreement was signed because of the government's failure to provide compulsory conciliation machinery.[25]

Elsewhere, among non-communist workers, the scene was a little brighter. In Valparaíso and Viña del Mar, government labor inspectors took the initiative and went from factory to factory encouraging the workers to organize. At one point about ten unions had been established among sugar refinery workers and in textile and bed factories. This was disconcerting to the communists and they made it clear they would not themselves organize under such circumstances. One of their congressional spokesmen said:

> We are told that the spirit of the Government, upon passing these laws, was to be able to regulate and establish understanding between employers and workers; but the communist bloc is convinced that this is impossible and although we may be told that we are only emotionally defending our doctrines, no one can tell us that the so-called social laws have had any practical result. The people have lost because of you [government authorities] who have smothered every hope of their betterment through legislation so wisely passed.[26]

Flour workers were organized in Concepción but the tramway workers of that city were unable to overcome employer opposition and were forced to sign individual contracts.[27]

Organizing results up to the time Ibañez took over the presidency in July 1927 were poor. Government figures indicate that only three industrial unions received a share of company profits in 1926 and only five in 1927. Even if there were ten times as many unions in all as there were those that shared in profits, the number would still be very small. The meager results obtained up to 1927 can be indirectly verified by jumping ahead for a moment and looking at the more complete organizing data for later years. In 1929, the earliest year for which a total industrial union figure is available, there were only 61 such unions; and in 1932, which is the earliest year for which both craft and industrial union data are available, there were 168 industrial unions and 253 craft unions with a total membership of about 55,000.

[24]*Justicia*, Dec. 24, 26, 30, 1925.
[25]*Ibid.*, April 16, May 7, 23, 1926.
[26]*Ibid.*, April 23, 28, 1926.
[27]*Ibid.*, April 8, 1926.

Since the economically active population then numbered some 1,500,-000 persons, it becomes clear that legal unionism was still largely a nascent force.[28]

II

Ibañez was installed in office after an election in which he was the only candidate and after a long pre-election period during which he had exercised *de facto* control of the government, first as Minister of War and later as Minister of the Interior. His rise to power was followed closely and anxiously by the FOCH and the Communist party who noted a growing fascist spirit in government and announced in February 1927 their intention to create anti-fascist committees in every factory, mine, town, and city in the country. Their duty would be to "denounce the leaders responsible for the anti-worker movement" and to demand that the country's economic and financial crisis be solved at the expense of the bourgeoisie.[29] The government, determined not to permit the dissemination of any revolutionary or subversive propaganda, closed down the leftist *Justicia* and inaugurated a general anti-radical campaign that effectively destroyed both Marxist and anarchist labor organizations. Free unions disappeared or went underground and only legal unions under non-Marxist leadership were encouraged in their activities. Even the latter were not left alone, but, rather, were used for political purposes. A fascist or corporate union structure was not introduced, however.

Before he created his own legal union movement, Ibañez gave serious consideration to the abolition of the plant or industrial union as a structural type. He was undoubtedly influenced strongly in this direction by events of the preceding two years and the FOCH's adoption of this union as the best expression of the revolutionary aims of the working class. He was also impressed, however, by a document published by the International Labor Organization which revealed that the Communist party of the Soviet Union had endorsed worker plant committees as revolutionary bodies. He therefore appointed a special committee to study and propose reforms in several of the labor laws. The committee was said to represent workers as well as "capital," and one of its members was named by the Society for Factory Development.[30]

[28]Morris y Oyaneder, *Afiliación y finanzas sindicales en Chile, 1932–1959,* Tabla I, p. 18, Tabla VI, p. 45.

[29]*Justicia,* Feb. 13, 1927.

[30]*Boletín de la Sociedad de Fomento Fabril,* vol. 45, June 1928, p. 350, October 1928, p. 641.

253

The committee reported in April 1929 and recommended that the plant union be discontinued and that only craft unionism be accepted in the legal system because, argued the committee, industrial unions had not brought the results expected of them. Authors of the union law had believed that plant unionism would orient employers and workers toward goals of mutual cooperation and prevent the class struggle. If these noble ends had been achieved, the plant union would be "something like a patriarchal institution," but it was, on the contrary, "a permanent factor of disorganization and perturbation in the work order" and had something in common with the factory committees of the Bolshevik Revolution. The plant union potential in Chile, in terms of number, was very great because there were many small enterprises in the country and a union could be set up in every one that employed more than twenty-five workers. This meant, moreover, that there would eventually be many more union leaders in the country than there would be under a craft union system. Since union leaders were customarily professional agitators anyway, why create more of them than absolutely necessary and why make the job of finding any good ones at all more hopeless by enlarging the volume of demand? The committee concluded that the activities of the industrial union, far from being beneficial or inducing peace, had been destructive of good order. The industrial union was "the seed of discord in the workshop, and what is more, it represents the petty and sterile struggle between employers and small groups of workers which. . .is the bitterest, most annoying and most harmful of all."[31]

Ibañez did not accept the committee's recommendation. That he did not may be explained in part by the argument in rebuttal offered by the employer and worker representatives of the government's Social Security Council. Their view, published in a separate document, was that the plant union was not a Russian invention and had no similarity at all to the worker committees which took over factories during the Bolshevik Revolution. With the mechanization of industry and the concentration of production, the industrial union had simply become the most useful and realistic union type, and the craft union was no longer as valid as it was when hand methods predominated.[32]

There is little doubt, however, but that Ibañez was persuaded to keep the industrial union mainly because he was confident of his own

[31]Comisión de Reformas de las Leyes Sociales, *La legislación social* (Santiago: Imprenta la Nación, 1929), pp. 91–96.

[32]Julio Green Ortega y Segundo Correa Osorio, *Observaciones al anteproyecto de reforma de la legislación social* (Santiago: Imprenta Artes y Letras, 1929), pp. 28–34.

ability to control it. In the regulations which he decreed for the union law on December 31, 1928, the area of control and supervision staked out for the government was broad, and the qualifications established for union membership and leadership were exacting. The regulating decree declared in the first instance that all legal unions were to be institutions of mutual collaboration among the factors which contribute to production, and, consequently, "all organizations whose procedures handicap discipline and order in work will be considered contrary to the spirit and standards of the law." Government officials were given the right to preside over union meetings and to know about "all the activities unions engage in." No one could belong to a union who in the opinion of the authorities was a subversive or was "harmful to the social order." Neither could "vagabonds" or "persons who do not work or who dedicate themselves to activities the authorities consider dangerous" become members of legal unions. Eight qualifications for the officer positions of the industrial union were laid down, one of which established a year's residence in the province or region where the enterprise was located as a prerequisite for officer candidacy and another of which denied an elective position to anyone convicted of a crime or misdemeanor or tried for any crime for which the law assigned corporal punishment. All existing unions were required to conform to the content of the decree within sixty days.[33]

It was largely with the authority of the above decree that Ibañez eliminated radicalism, for the time being, from the labor movement and developed a "kept" movement of his own. The essential policies and objectives of the Ibañez Administration in the labor field were threefold: (1) to destroy by force the leftist leadership and orientation of the labor movement, (2) to eliminate free unions and consolidate and encourage the expansion of the legal union system, and (3) to develop the working class as a political force for the perpetuation of Ibañez in office and as a guarantee of the continuation of the "revolutionary" movement of September 1924. While, as some observers have claimed, Ibañez may have been influenced in his approach to government by the example of Italian fascism, the practical results he achieved in the labor field bore only a superficial resemblance to the intricate and organizationally sophisticated union and political structure of the corporate state. His labor movement was largely a political movement, amorphous and weak, with none of the discipline, the zip, or the polish of Mussolini's black shirts and totally lacking in anything

[33]See Artículos 3, 7, 10, 12 y 17 del Decreto No. 2148 del 31 de Diciembre de 1928.

even faintly resembling the hierarchy of centralized labor and management structures characteristic of fascism. He preserved the legal system of 1924 with its reliance upon the local union and plant-level relationships. His implementation of the system emphasized the growth of unions as a source of political support for the government, and it does not appear that he did anything to build up the economic and dispute-settlement aspects of labor relations.

To permit the development of an obedient political labor movement, Ibáñez had not only to regulate the union law but also to amend the electoral law. This he did, extending to any political, social, or economic organization the right to participate in elections and present candidates for Senate and Chamber of Deputy vacancies. With this groundwork completed he was ready to move ahead, and with encouragement from the *Moneda* a group of workingmen met in December 1929 and founded the "Republican Confederation for Civic Action of Blue- and White-Collar Workers" (CRAC). They announced that the work of national reconstruction initiated by the "revolutionary" movement of September 5, 1924 had revealed the need for vigorous civic action which would rally around the fundamental principles of that movement. This new force had to be free of contamination from those political groups which "destroyed the prestige of national institutions and depressed the public conscience." It could rest only upon working people and those who encouraged them in their aspirations and feelings. The founding group declared its complete and fervent loyalty to the President of the Republic, "one of the most worthy of all popular leaders who have consecrated themselves to the glory of the fatherland and have opened to the hosts of labor the fertile roads of social dignity and political advancement." In that historic moment of the Republic he stood out as the "Great Worker of National Glory." The group declared that, in addition to lending him its political support, it would strive to maintain and to perfect the social laws.[34]

The principal organizations behind the founding of CRAC were the Workers Social Congress (a confederation of mutual benefit societies), the Union of Private White-Collar Workers (a federation of legal craft unions), and a group of about fifteen blue-collar plant and craft unions, the largest number of which represented copper and coal workers.[35]

[34]The program of the CRAC is printed in *La Nación*, Dec. 16, 1929. See also, *ibid.*, Dec. 19, 1929.

[35]A list of the founding unions was published in *ibid.*, Dec. 16, 18, 1929.

Ibañez provided the CRAC with a headquarters building in Santiago, and the CRAC established links with its local affiliates through a provincial committee system. In 1930 and 1931 the CRAC ran its own candidates in a number of congressional elections, but their showing was generally poor and the traditional parties, with the exception of the Communist organization, lost little of their appeal and electoral support.[36] That the political movement never caught on was undoubtedly a decisive factor in the overthrow of Ibañez in July 1931. With him went the CRAC.

While the CRAC failed as a political force during the Ibañez régime, it enjoyed successes in other directions, and the general legacy of the years of dictatorship had positive as well as negative content so far as labor and political matters are concerned. The labor policy of Ibañez should be remembered for its achievement of preserving and buttressing the legal union system. It is not clear that the system would have survived, given the growing opposition to the FOCH and to plant unions, had Ibañez not decided to make it part of the apparatus of his government. The legal unions which formed part of CRAC, and there must have been around three hundred of them by 1931, survived the overthrow of Ibañez and the disappearance of CRAC and went on to become the accepted and overwhelmingly predominant integers of the Chilean labor movement. That Ibañez went so far as he did in destroying their independence was deplorable, but that he accepted and protected them as part of the social and constitutional reform movement of the twenties was, in the light of history, constructive. A second outstanding achievement of Ibañez and the CRAC was the expansion and codification of the labor laws, completed just two months before the "Great Worker" lost his job. Finally, it is to be noted that when democratic government was restored, the politically inclined labor movement was no longer so much the creature of the Communist party as it was in the pre-Ibañez era. A new Socialist party was set up in 1933, many of the legal unions were attracted to that party, and it quickly became and has remained a major force in working-class politics. The Ibañez interlude and the Communist reverses attributable to it may have been an object lesson which encouraged some people to seek a safer outlet in the Socialist party for the expression of their discontent.

[36]For the results of some of the congressional elections of these years, see *ibid.*, Nov. 12, 17, 1930, April 31, 1931.

III

With the fall of Ibañez, political instability returned and for a year and a half democracy and constitutional government hung in the balance. The climax came with the installation of a short-lived "Socialist Republic" in mid-1932, and the shock of this episode seemed to restore a degree of political faith and unity and national sobriety which the country had not known for many years. Presidential elections were held; Arturo Alessandri Palma won his second term and re-entered the *Moneda* in January 1933. He served out the entire term and in 1938 passed on the reigns of government to Pedro Aguirre Cerda and the Popular Front.

The end of dictatorship also meant the rebirth of competition in the labor movement. The FOCH emerged from the underground and rapidly regained membership strength, although it probably had far fewer members than the one hundred thousand attributed to it[37] and never recovered the prestige or the following it had enjoyed before Ibañez. With the memory of the CRAC and the fate of legal unions still fresh in their minds, many FOCH leaders (the followers of Elías Lafertte) were now wary of the legal system and of government and appear to have relied upon the free union as their organizing unit. They were especially strong in the nitrate, copper, and coal-mining areas. An ineffectual Communist minority (the followers of Manuel Hidalgo) split their efforts between the legal unions and anarchist organizations. As a result, the legal unions, after several years of political independence and economic and legislative orientation, were, as we shall soon see in greater detail, captured by the Socialists.[38] The anarchists also regrouped for what was to be their last major bid for a leadership position in the labor movement. Battered by the dictatorship, strategically weakened by the proclamation of legal unionism in 1924, and their individualist philosophy outmoded by the collectivist ideas of a growing factory population, they had little chance of success. Nevertheless, in October 1931 they all got together, created what they called the "General Confederation of Labor" (CGT), and announced their opposition to the FOCH and to legal unionism. It is said that there were ten thousand of them and that they grew by 50 percent in the course of a few years, but these figures are probably too generous.[39]

[37]See Editorial Ginebra, *Legislación social de América*, p. 212.
[38]See Alexander, *Labor Relations in Argentina, Brazil, and Chile*, p. 257.
[39]Editorial Ginebra, *Legislación social de América*, pp. 218, 220 and Julio César Jobet, *Luis E. Recabarren* (Santiago: Prensa Latinoamericana, 1955), pp. 150–152.

Just as many company unions in the United States transformed themselves into strong independent trade unions after the passage of the Wagner Act, so also the "kept" legal unions of Ibañez became the core of independent unionism in Chile in the 1930's. They were the new force, the new vitality of the labor movement which set the tone and direction of labor events. Ibañez had not federated them by industries or by crafts but had simply placed them in a loose confederation with intermediate provincial committees. They regrouped, after the dissolution of CRAC, into two similar confederations, one for Santiago and the other evidently taking the rest of the country as its jurisdiction. A Confederation of Industrial Unions of Santiago was organized in November 1931 to promote legal unionism and to improve the blue-collar provisions of the labor laws. To judge from the content of its statutes and its journal, *El Sindicalista,* it was purely a union organization which accepted the existing society and was not a socialist organization, as socialist writers have claimed. Since the Socialist party was not formed until 1933, it was not likely in any case that the Confederation would have adopted a socialist platform. The Confederation was aware, it said, that "there are no men or citizens capable of changing the way of living of the present society, and it is therefore necessary to expand and to defend legal unionism." It would pursue no political objectives but would study and develop among its affiliated unions cooperative, mutual benefit, and social security programs. The Confederation claimed thirty affiliated unions and ten thousand members in 1931. The following year it invited the craft unions of Santiago to join, and by mid-1933 its roster included fifty-four unions and some thirty thousand members.[40]

In April 1932 a National Federation of Unions and Labor Organizations of Chile was formed which accepted both legal and free unions into membership. Like the Confederation of Industrial Unions of Santiago, its affiliates were local rather than national unions, and their strength has been set at some fifty thousand members. Membership of these two organizations thus totaled eighty thousand and this is very close to the legal union membership figures released by the government in 1933 and 1934.[41]

A merger of the two groups was effected in 1934 and the new organization, called the National Confederation of Unions of Chile (CNSC),

[40]For the statutes and other information about the Confederation, see *El Sindicalista,* May 1, Sept. 15, 1933; *Libertad,* Nov. 28, 1931; and *Crónica,* December 1931.

[41]See *Rumbos,* August 1939, p. 16.

adopted a socialist platform, proposed abolition of the present society and the creation of "a new economic régime with a higher social morality and based on the collective or common ownership of the instruments of production and exchange."[42] The Socialists had clearly, by this time, decided to capture the legal unions as their means of gaining a voice within the labor movement and had successfully controlled the merger convention. Their next move was to try to outmaneuver political rivals by taking the initiative and bringing to a head the growing sentiment for general labor unity among those elements which favored a popular front position. The CNSC therefore called a labor unity convention to meet in Valparaíso in 1935 for the purpose of founding a "Grand Trade Union Center for All Chilean Workers." While this effort failed, the Socialist party and the legal unions had by that time and by the boldness of that act established themselves as a force that could not be ignored by the older segments of the labor movement.

By the middle of the decade two major movements which had started on parallel and independent courses, one Chilean and the other international, were converging to form a new synthesis of structure and content, if not of ideology, in the Chilean labor movement. The first was the legal union system, consolidated by Ibañez, taken over largely by the Socialists, and represented by the National Confederation of Unions of Chile. The second was the political Popular Front movement engineered largely by international communism to check the growth of fascism in Europe. In Chile, as in many countries, the Popular Front had no strong fascist movement to fight (indeed, Chilean Fascists briefly supported the Popular Front!) but found ready acceptance nevertheless as part of the world-wide trend to the left during the depression decade. In Chile the atmosphere was made especially favorable by the years of dictatorship and by the second Alessandri Administration which was generally rightist in both political leadership and program. The Popular Front bid for power in Chile was made by the Radical, Socialist, and Communist parties who organized for this purpose in 1936, looking to the presidential elections two years hence as their first major test of strength. The accomplishment of unity on the party level would not have been effective if competition had continued among the unions, principally the CNSC under socialist control and the FOCH dominated by the Communists. Moreover, the political unity of all "democratic" forces, including the Communist

[42]Quoted from its declaration of principles in *Legislación social de América*, p. 214.

party, coupled with their bid for power through the election process, involved a commitment to the present society which made continued communist opposition to legal unionism a theoretically untenable position. The Communists had once again to accept legal unionism both because of the logic of their Popular Front position and as an inevitable practical result of cooperating with the Socialists. This does not mean, however, that they did, or had to, immediately convert their own free unions into legal ones. For the more cautious among them, at least, that could wait until 1938 and the outcome of the presidential election. A Popular Front victory would mean a government friendly to the working class and would wipe away the last defensible trace of major opposition or hostility to the legal industrial relations system.

As early as December 1934, the Communist *Frente Unico* called for a "united front of the working masses" and while, as we have seen, the Socialists would have preferred at that time to unite the labor movement under their own leadership through the CNSC, they eventually supported labor unity under Popular Front auspices. This was made easier by the entrance of the Radicals into the Popular Front, the nomination of a Radical candidate for the presidency, and the Communists' decision, for tactical reasons, not to accept Cabinet representation in a Popular Front government if Aguirre Cerda were elected.[43] Whatever resistance to a political Popular Front and to labor unity remained was destroyed by government suppression of a railroad strike in 1936. Just a few months after the subsequent launching of the political Popular Front, socialist and communist labor leaders responded by setting up a new blue-collar trade union center which they called the Confederation of Workers of Chile (CTCH).

Leaders at the unity convention explained that the principal differences among the delegates concerned whether the new organization's structure should be based upon industries and whether legal unions should be allowed to participate in it. The answer the convention gave to the latter question was a foregone conclusion, although some unionists from both the FOCH and the anarchist CGT, which was represented there, resisted an accommodation with legal unionism. The convention declared that both free and legal unions were to be accepted within the CTCH and that "in accordance with the state of organiza-

[43]According to Alexander, the Communist party policy in Chile was the same in this respect as Communist policy in Europe: "They were part of the Front so they could take credit for its successes, but they were not part of the government, so they could deny any connection with its failures." Alexander, *Labor Relations in Argentina, Brazil, and Chile*, pp. 258–259.

tion, national industrial unions might be formed with both free and legal local union affiliates."[44] The CGT decided not to give up its separate identity by merging into the CTCH, but the CTCH nevertheless was the first central organization to bring together on a large scale both free (FOCH) and legal (CNSC) trade unions.

With the accomplishment of unity and especially with the triumph of the Popular Front candidate in 1938, legal unionism for the first time broke out of the general confusion, suspicion, and hostility which had held it back for over a decade, and forged rapidly ahead to become, numerically, the heart and center of the labor movement. As Alexander explains,

> President Aguirre Cerda threw all of his government's prestige behind the labor movement, with the result that important employers who had hitherto either refused absolutely to recognize unions or had maintained company-dominated workers organizations within their plants came to terms with the legitimate labor movement. These included the coal-mine operatives, many textile plants, and other important employers.[45]

Consequently, legal unions, which had moved from zero members in 1924 to 55,000 in 1932 and 87,000 in 1936, added 30,000 in 1937 alone, 9,000 in 1938, and 47,000 in 1939. By 1941 there were almost 210,000 workers in state-recognized industrial and craft unions. While these figures are somewhat inflated, they unmistakably mark the sharp upward trend of the legal union system. The membership crest was not reached until the mid-1950's, but the success of the system, gauged only against the criterion of its overwhelming acceptance by the workers, dates from the Popular Front era.[46]

The Popular Front, it should be mentioned incidentally, was fatally weakened and soon collapsed as a consequence of the Nazi-Soviet Pact. The Socialists, who had a majority in the CTCH, grew so rapidly in the country at large that they could not consolidate their gains in the institutional sense, their leaders fell to quarreling among themselves as well as with the Communists, and in a few years they lost their majority position. The CTCH itself remained intact until 1946 when the split was formalized and separate socialist-led and communist-led cen-

[44]Quoted from the conclusions of the convention in Confederación de Trabajadores de Chile, *Acuerdos del congreso constituyente 1936*, Santiago, sin fecha, pp. 25, 29. For further information about the issues and decisions of the convention, see *Legislación social de América*, pp. 215–216, 220.

[45]Alexander, *Organized Labor in Latin America*, p. 94.

[46]Membership data are from Morris y Oyaneder, *Afiliación y finanzas sindicales en Chile, 1932–1959*, Tabla II, p. 20.

ters were set up. Unity and a political alliance of the Socialists and Communists were reestablished in 1953 when the present Single Central of Chilean Workers (CUT) was organized.

The political and union events of the 1930's did not transpire in an industrial relations vacuum. The employers were still organized but, interestingly and significantly, not into an antiunion front, such as the old Labor Association of Chile, but into the Employer Union of Commerce and Industry (UPCIC) which accepted the Labor Code and sought only to represent employer interests in its implementation and amendment. The UPCIC, which dates from 1932, planned to stimulate the formation of legal employer unions, which the code also permitted, as the organizational basis it considered appropriate for the effective representation of employer interests within the legal industrial relations system.[47] The organizational plan did not prosper (e.g., there is no national group of legal employer unions today), but the UPCIC did for a number of years speak out on labor matters.

One of the most conspicuous, if not most lasting, new developments in labor relations for which the UPCIC merits some credit was the establishment in 1934 of a tripartite Superior Labor Council. This was the peak of the pyramid, as visualized by the UPCIC, whose base was to be made up of legal employer unions and legal worker unions. The Superior Labor Council was to keep the Labor Code under permanent study, hear minimum-wage appeals, serve as the classifying board for blue-and white-collar jobs, and be the arbitrator of collective labor conflicts not settled in the conciliation process. The Superior Labor Council functioned for a few years, was never an outstanding success, and was finally abolished in 1948. There is some suggestion of the corporate approach in the grand scheme of the council pyramid, but it would be inaccurate to say that that pyramid followed the fascist model.

More lasting, and in that sense more significant, changes in the labor law, due in part to the activities of the UPCIC, concerned such things as the job tenure of union leaders, legal holidays, the constitution of conciliation boards, and strikes. Job protection after the termination of union office was reduced from one year to six months, the number of holidays was reduced, employer associations were allowed to participate in the nomination of employer representatives to the conciliation boards, and strikes were more closely regulated. The UPCIC worked

[47]For information concerning the founding of UPCIC and its program, see *La Nación*, Sept. 11, 13, 1932; *El Mercurio*, Sept. 11, 1932; "Leyes y Código del Trabajo," *Industria y Comercio*, September 1932, pp. 132–133.

effectively during the Alessandri Administration, and it was especially active in 1936 when the government amended and consolidated (Decree No. 642) all the regulations dealing with Book III of the Labor Code (unions, incorporation, profit sharing, job protection of union leaders, and the establishment of national unions which were now regulated for the first time). With this important legislative job done, the UPCIC had less reason to continue its activities, and, finally, the triumph of the Popular Front severed the close ties it had developed with the *Moneda*.[48]

By the close of the 1930's both unions and employers had accepted the legal industrial relations system and the government had fully regulated the Labor Code. With a friendly administration in the *Moneda*, labor faced the prospect of a new era of organizational growth and political prestige. The great problem continued to be that employers and the government (even the Popular Front since it was really dominated by the Radical party) accepted the legal industrial relations system for reasons totally at odds with those for which the socialist and communist blue-collar majority accepted it. The former saw it as a mechanism for organizing protest and achieving greater justice within an evolutionary society. The latter saw it as a capitalist subterfuge to be used and manipulated by the workers for the greater end of revolutionary upheaval.

[48] The UPCIC's monthly bulletin, *Boletín Mensual de la Unión Patronal de la Industria y del Comercio de Chile*, carried regular accounts of the organization's legislative and other activities during 1932–1937.

CHAPTER 10

Conclusion

IN THE introduction to this book three major themes were identified, namely, (1) that an understanding of the present industrial relations system in Chile can be greatly enriched through study of its historical origins, particularly the values, attitudes, and motivations of those who framed the system; (2) that intellectuals, including students, were more important in developing the industrial relations system than perhaps Chileans themselves realize, and certainly more important than intellectuals from the more advanced Western countries might suspect; and (3) that the industrial relations system did not mend or prevent consensus loss in Chile and the ideological alienation from the power élite of socially significant groups of the working class. In the first three chapters descriptive and theoretical material pertinent to the development of each of these themes was presented, and the elaboration of each has continued, with variations in persistency, depth, and success, too, no doubt, up to this point. The intention now is to summarize the intellectual theme (Section I), present an analytical summary, in synthesis, of themes one and three (Section II), and, finally, bring together a few thoughts of other observers on the present consensual state of the classes in Chile (Section III).

265

I

The reader will recall that there was no important group of revolutionary intellectuals in Chile until the 1930's, several years after the industrial relations system had been established in the law. The intellectuals of this study were practically all non-violent democrats. They identified with both the aristocratic-Catholic élite and with the middle-class élite (more with the latter than with the former, however), and did therefore constitute a "floating" or non-class element, as Mannheim, Kerr, and others have noted. Moreover, there were within both of these élites intellectuals who opposed, as well as intellectuals who favored, social and labor reforms. They split on the social question just as the élites as a whole split. Yet the proportion of intellectuals among those who favored reforms was much higher than the proportion of intellectuals among those who opposed reforms. In the former group the intellectuals were among the preponderant leaders; in the latter they were dependent allies of the preponderant leaders.

How did they lead? Contrary to the behavior observed elsewhere by writers like Shumpeter, the intellectuals in Chile did not join forces with the organized labor movement (essentially the FOCH) to propagandize or to erect a labor party (the Socialist Workers' party was the creature of Recabarren and the FOCH). Many of them feared the genuine unions and part of their interest in reform was to eliminate radicalism by setting up new unions under employer or state control. The FOCH reciprocated their antagonism and refused to support the movement for labor legislation.

The intellectuals led in essentially two ways: (1) as politically minded intellectuals who spoke and wrote on the social question and translated and adapted the labor relations laws of other countries, and (2) as politicians who committed their parties to a reform position, drafted labor bills, and worked for the passage of labor legislation in the Congress. In the former group are the journalists, the seventy-odd thesis writers, and individual businessmen and political writers like Pedro Luis González and Benjamin Vicuña Subercaseaux. In the latter group are persons like Valentín Letelier, Juan Enrique Concha, Moisés Poblete Troncoso, and Tómas Ramírez Frías. Intellectuals were not the only reform leaders, however. There were many progressive politicians, men of business, and others who encouraged or initiated legislative action in the labor field. Surely one of the most outstanding of these men was Arturo Alessandri Palma.

How important was their leadership? It is difficult to imagine that, if there had been no intellectuals, and particularly no political activists among them, Chile could have enacted a complete industrial relations system in 1924. As Guillermo Feliú Cruz has said, the "atmosphere" for the "solution of a truly significant problem, the social question, was created in the university." Although the theses were not distributed as widely as might have been desirable, they nevertheless contained "the foundations of a positive legal system."[1] Let us add that they were deposited in key and accessible places like the Library of Congress and the National Library. Would the Conservatives have drafted a bill covering all the "difficult" areas, if it had not been for Juan Enrique Concha? Very probably the answer is no, and the Conservative case is perhaps the clearest of all in exemplifying a preponderant intellectual role. The direct participation of intellectuals in the development of the Liberal Alliance project was less impressive because in this case they (Poblete, Ramírez Frías, Jorge Errázuriz Tagle, Francisco Jorquera) had to share honors with others (Manuel Rivas Vicuña, Malaquías Concha, and Alessandri, for example). They nevertheless performed as co-stars rather than as bit actors.

While it would be untrue to say that the labor bills pending in the Congress in 1924 were there *only* because of the intellectuals, they probably would not have been there, or would have been there in vastly different form, had the intellectuals not made their contribution. Furthermore, the role of the intellectuals is much more significant than it would have been had the Congress passed the laws democratically. The opposition to labor legislation from the more persistent élite elements and other disruptive forces was so strong that the military stepped in and forced the Congress to act. So in Chile one can say that, because of the political crisis of 1924, the intellectuals and the military leaders, in effect, combined to create and enact an industrial relations system.

Quite apart from the special crisis role of the intellectuals, however, they were generally strong actors even in the non-crisis pre-1924 period in the genesis of protest literature and social legislation. In this respect, they confirmed the traditional view of the intellectual in Latin America and departed from the behavior of the modern intellectual in the United States, Canada, and parts of Europe. There is, to be sure, some evidence of the capturing and using of intellectuals by both Chilean élites; some intellectuals seemed more like allies or followers or servants than leaders or protesters. Such were particularly those who

---

[1]Feliú Cruz, *Chile visto a través de Agustín Ross,* p. 136.

opposed the recognition of new social rights and who took their cue from the powerful men of the old school like Enrique Mac-Iver, Agustín Edwards, and Antonio Varas. It would also appear to describe Juan Enrique Concha at one special moment in his lifetime of concern about the social question—1918, when the Conservatives needed him badly. On the whole and throughout most of the period, however, the intellectuals were protesters and politicians who tried to persuade change and even to accomplish it themselves. There is something of the role of the philosopher-king in their activities, for some of them combined writing and teaching with active political careers as Deputies, Senators, and government appointees. In the case of Poblete, even when his role in the Joint Committee was formally stamped as that of "expert" from the Office of Labor, he participated in debate, made motions, and acted like a regular committee member. That he did so is probably because the committee, and in effect society, accorded him superior status as an intellectual and expected him to lead as well as to advise.

II

The legal industrial relations system did not immediately and still has not restored normative consensus to Chile. This is evident particularly in the broad spectrum of ideologies effectively represented at the polls by the major political parties of the country and in the alienation of the CUT-controlled labor movement from the government and the present power élite. Since the intellectuals and men of public life who were alarmed by the "social question" hoped to eliminate extremist philosophies and worker-based political opposition through social and labor legislation, one must conclude that these hopes have not been realized. Despite disappointing political results, however, the industrial relations system has functioned with at least minimum effectiveness in the narrower economic and administrative range of its concern—i.e., minimum wages, vital salaries, conflict resolution, encouragement of unions, plant-level relations, and the like. This is a seeming paradox to which the writer has called attention.

That there was and remains an absence of consensus in the industrial relations system only reflects a more general absence of consensus in Chilean society as a whole. The industrial relations system is not an independent phenomenon which can be studied apart from the larger society, particularly its élite groups. The system as developed more than forty years ago was not, therefore, the expression of an emerging industrial society in consensus but, rather, was an effort to preserve many of the values of a traditional society in the initial stages of disintegration. Intellectuals of both the aristocratic-Catholic and middle-class élites looked with disdain upon the early anarchist unions and thought of union leaders generally as professional agitators and parasites. They, and many of the others who wanted to do something about the social question, thought of definitive "solutions" and controls, not of concessions and accommodation to new social forces. If the workers could be provided decent homes, safe and sanitary working conditions, and the opportunity to worship on Sunday, and if upper-class men and women would visit them and see that their children received medical care and clothing, then they would be happy. They would not strike or be influenced by radical talk in the shop or factory. Workers should be encouraged to join new legal unions primarily as a control measure to be held in the hands of either the employer or the state. Conflict should be prevented by compulsory settlement of disagreements. These statements fit the views of the aristocratic-Catholic élite much better than they do those of the middle class. The craft union and voluntary conciliation conceded a degree of independence and dignity to the working class not found in the Conservative bill, yet the Liberal Alliance bill at the same time regulated the craft union in the most minute detail. Strategic predominance of aristocratic-Catholic views is to be judged by the legislative triumph of the industrial union (winning obligatory status as compared with the voluntary nature of the craft union) and by the enactment of compulsory conciliation.

It would probably not distort the facts to say that, for many of the proponents of social and labor legislation, any unions, any leaders, any political parties, or any programs not under their control would have constituted a challenge which they probably could not, in good faith, have accepted and could not, least of all, have encouraged. Many of the leading elements of Chilean society, particularly the landowners and their allies, had an authoritarian, and in some cases a tyrannical, view of their role opposite the masses. To say that they were the victims of a class arrangement and a social inflexibility passed on to them by their forefathers is partly true. The Spanish conquerors of Chile and the whites who followed them did not establish an egalitarian society in which the Indian and the mestizo had all the rights and the opportunities of the immigrants and the creoles. The whites took over the land and the Indians and their mestizo offspring worked it for them.

Class was immediately frozen and institutionalized in the structure of the *fundo* and the *inquilino* system. This was the way the whites and the creoles wanted it. This is the way most of them continued to want it two hundred and fifty years later.

It is not suggested here that it would have been possible or advisable for them to have suddenly established completely free unions and an unregulated industrial relations system. Had this been done, the result would surely have been chaotic, given the paternal-tyrannical tendency of the Chilean employer at that time and the explosive potential of the freed and unsophisticated *inquilino*. However, preparations for an eventual shift of social power and a better educated and more responsible citizenry could have been begun long before, and, lacking that, the élites of the early twentieth century could have recognized the social question not as a rebellion to be quelled and then controlled forever but as the raucous voice of new social forces, to be trained and eventually set free. With the advantage of hindsight, it is now possible to see that they erred not so much in the form they gave to the industrial relations system as in the heavy authoritarian and paternalistic spirit they breathed into it.

Social Catholicism, as developed principally by Juan Enrique Concha, contained great truths and also great fallacies as a guide to social action. Concha correctly observed that many upper-class leaders feared even to study social problems because they thought that to do so might "awaken" the proletariat. These leaders were the most insecure of all, felt a deep need to have a dependent class permanently subjected to their authority, and were emotionally unwilling to encourage change. He also correctly saw the bond between *patrón* and *inquilino* as the success factor in the life of the *fundo*. In recognizing psychology, morality, and religion as the principal areas of solution to the social question, he touched upon the critical media but greatly overemphasized morality and Catholic doctrine and did not really understand psychology. He was also apparently misled by some of the language of religion and religious theology ("children of God" and "the providential inequality of man," for example) in his conception of workers as the "children of the employer" and as the constituents of an "inferior class."

Concha's scheme was essentially static, as was the rural society which reared him. The employer, he said, was by definition the father of all workers. Workers were inferior members of society who could not be expected to assume adult burdens. The fact that they felt alone and

270

unwanted, an acute observation on Concha's part, could be remedied most effectively by the employer's reassumption of his moral obligation to take care of them, an invalid conclusion—at least in the long-run or as an ultimate social response to industrialization. Economic individualism on the employer's part is not wrong if the rights and the dignity of workers are also recognized and if the state assumes its proper role of promoting the best interests of society at large. "Class," "inferiority," "inequality" are not terms that can portray absolute or permanent values within industrializing (i.e., egalitarian) societies. Concha's interpretation of a "moral breakdown" was misleading because it concealed his desire to restore the old order, and it also erroneously implied that the upper classes were consciously aware of wrongdoing in their treatment of the new working class. Concha, in continuing to look upon the emerging industrial workers as *inquilinos* who wanted and needed the employer's compassionate leadership, was only saying that he wanted to preserve the Chile he knew. He, and all those in the aristocratic-Catholic élite for whom he so eloquently spoke, wanted and needed to believe in their own inherent superiority. There was nothing objective or scientific to support the belief, and it could have been changed to something else by their decision to do so.

When Juan Enrique Concha tried to explain the worker downfall he thought he observed, he again betrayed the egotism of his system. It was loss of religion, socialist propaganda, and upper-class neglect which caused workers to complain about conditions and to support leftist political parties. Workers to him were thus the pawns of others (agitators, priests, employers) who could do something for them or against them. So deeply submerged in a centuries-long tradition of centralized authority and *fundo* psychology that he could not liberate his thinking, he was unable to see or to concede to workers a separate ego.

The conceptual framework of the middle-class élite was less encumbered in general than that of the aristocratic-Catholic élite, as developed principally by Juan Enrique Concha, though it did suffer from some of the same blocks. Middle-class intellectuals were, for example, able to see workers as citizens with equal rights, and they considered the fulfillment of these rights as a condition which would permit them, the workers, to deal harmoniously with employers. They also supported free public education as the purveyor of the greater sophistication they recognized as a requirement for living in a changing society. There was, nevertheless, an ambivalence in their attitude which, in the final analysis, did not allow them to trust the working class with the freedom in which they so fervently believed for themselves. They provided the craft unions with an exacting father — the state — and admitted no desire ultimately to grant them and their members greater independence and therefore heavier responsibilities. If more of the spirit of the Liberal Alliance project had triumphed in 1924 and less that of the Conservative bill, time might eventually have brought somewhat greater equity and responsibility to labor relations than have actually resulted. However, the larger fact remains that the two élites found more to unite than to divide themselves opposite the working classes and their representatives.

Until the 1930's when intellectuals became leftists in large numbers, Chile's anarchism, socialism, and communism all appear to have been overwhelmingly emotional and worker movements. While such movements can be the most explosive of all, they may also be less stable than mature movements based upon ideological conviction. In the opinion of this writer, the reestablishment of consensus in Chilean society would have been easier to accomplish before the 1930's than it has become since that time.

The selfish, class approach to the content and machinery of industrial relations, particularly with regard to the aristocratic-Catholic élite, meant that there was little consensus in the structure of the industrial relations system proposed and finally adopted in 1924. This, in turn, only reflected the lack of consensus in society at large, a result which had been in the making since the latter part of the nineteenth century. The break-up of the two-party system, party proliferation during the parliamentary régime, and the formation of parties with a narrow, working-class base altered social stability. Developments in the political sphere were paralleled by a dramatic shift from mutualism to a medley of anarchist, socialist, communist, and Catholic unions and worker associations. By the 1920's the main labor organization (FOCH) was under firm communist leadership.

The élite desire to control, subject, and keep the workers subordinate was obvious to the blue-collar working class. They therefore accepted the industrial relations system in form but not in spirit and tried to turn it to their own purposes. During the Ibañez interlude, an attempt was made to correct the situation by ridding the labor movement of its radical leaders, but this was an attack upon the symptoms of the disease and not its cause. The disease remained and the symptoms promptly returned when Ibañez was forced out of office.

There are today many workers, particularly of the white-collar class, whose political allegiance runs along Radical and Christian-Democratic lines, who largely accept the industrial relations system. Undoubtedly, some plant unions have fulfilled the fondest hopes of the legislators of two generations ago. They are apolitical, are run by the most "trustworthy" workers, and cause no trouble to anyone. There are others formed only for the purpose of sharing in the profits. Some are set up by labor inspectors for political reasons and show little vitality of any kind. Many of the craft unions, which a few legislators thought would become the stentorian voice of the working class, are weak and therefore easily disorganized or controlled by employers. They are weak because membership in them is voluntary and because in the white-collar unions, which are perhaps their largest variety, members of management affiliate and often occupy elective offices. Moreover, a very impressive proportion of local union leaders and management representatives in the principal urban centers of Chile indicate strong acceptance of one another and a desire to rely on bargaining and the Labor Code for resolution of their differences.

Despite all that has been said in the preceding paragraph, however, the fact remains that revolutionary Socialists and Communists have been very successful in retaining the political loyalty of large segments of the blue-collar workers and in capturing and using the labor relations machinery to further their goals. Indeed, the single most impressive and most consistent feature of the Chilean labor movement during the last half-century has been its left extremism. Presently, the CUT and most of its strong affiliated national unions are run by socialist and communist officers. Their influence over the unionized workers is probably greater than it is over the larger, non-union sector (Frei won heavy majorities in the cities in the 1964 presidential election), but there is little question that they are a strong, divisive, and strategic force in politics and the labor movement.

III

The fundamental social conflict which besets Chile today, the origins of which have been traced in this study, is of critical concern throughout the hemisphere. Concern is all the more anxious because those who watch are aware that the drama unfolds within the context of deep respect for political democracy and constitutional procedures.

Recognizing that the values which sustain democratic government are seemingly well institutionalized in Chile, D'Antonio suggests that the main difficulty lies in "educational, economic, and status relationships" whose values have remained those of a landed aristocracy. The bleak outlook is, therefore, that "Chile's days of crisis, uncertainty, and travail remain, like so many of her neighbors', in the future and not in the past."[2] Pike also contends that the continuing, critical social situation has its explanation in the failure to modify or surrender "a set of values associated with a rapidly disappearing way of life" whose cardinal feature is "a sociopolitical structure based on paternalism and on the perpetual existence of a participating, privileged minority that is served by a nonparticipating, nonprivileged majority."[3]

No one is better qualified than Eduardo Frei to interpret the state of social health in contemporary Chile, and he too sees the critical danger in an absence of shared values suited to a modernizing nation. Anyone willing to face reality will see, he declares, "that there are no common motives that move all the sectors of the people. We can almost affirm the contrary. It is enough for one social group to favor an idea to evoke suspiciousness, if not open antagonism toward it, among the other groups." It is not therefore enough to talk about "our democratic régime"; it is even more crucial, Frei urges, that the "internal proletariat" of Chile be fully integrated into national life on a basis of equality with other, heretofore more privileged, groups. Nor is it only a matter of economics—of more houses, more potable water, and more schools; the spirit of paternalism, of *noblesse oblige,* the class structure, and second-class citizenship for the masses must be changed. The essence of Chile's crisis, as seen by Eduardo Frei, "is that the people no longer want to follow and be the object of history; they want to be the subject of history."[4]

The superior-inferior complex of many of Chile's privileged people (including middle-class leaders, for to a considerable degree they have adopted the values of those above rather than of those below them) continues to be at the heart of the consensual problem in Chile today,

---

[2]D'Antonio, "Democracy and Religion in Latin America," chap. 13, p. 246, in D'Antonio and Pike, eds., *Religion, Revolution, and Reform.*

[3]Pike, *Chile and the United States,* p. xxi.

[4]See Eduardo Frei Montalva, "Catholic Social Justice, Democracy and Pluralism," pp. 214–217, in Fredrick B. Pike, ed., *The Conflict between Church and State in Latin America* (New York: Alfred A. Knopf, 1964), and Frei, "Paternalism, Pluralism, and Christian Democratic Reform Movements in Latin America," chap. 1, pp 37–39, in D'Antonio and Pike, eds., *Religion, Revolution, and Reform;* also p. 119.

just as it explains much of the consensus loss of several generations ago. That it frequently takes on the character of a purely racial matter will shock no one who has walked the streets and roamed the valleys, mountains, and desert areas of that fair land and looked her people in the eye. Indian blood runs high the farther down the social scale you go, and some Chileans hold it responsible for all the country's ills. One of the best known of Chilean university professors of labor law is the author of a textbook on labor law which has gone through five editions and which teaches university students that the inferior quality of the Chilean worker is a major obstacle to the solution of the social question. "The common people," he writes, "are still too indigenous [i.e., too Indian] and need a greater mixture of European blood to give them thriftiness, seriousness, honesty, hygienic habits, etc.; it is indispensible, then, that we stimulate immigration to improve the race, increase production and consumption, and raise the human level of our people."[5] Real cultural unity, i.e., consensus, will return to Chile only as entirely contrary values become part of the national consciousness—only, that is, as Chilean leaders come to respect the dignity and the equality of every human soul within their borders. An ever greater development of each individual in society, which requires a constant sharing of power with others and a mature empathy, is the social capital which permits sustained social, economic, and political progress.

The political repercussions of value conflict in Chile are still very strong and very important. Despite his pronounced feeling that Salvador Allende's election defeat in 1964 was also a defeat for the Marxist message, Ernst Halperin asserts that the result might have been different had either one of two things happened—i.e., had the FRAP run a more colorful and more persuasive candidate or had the Cuban missile crisis not occurred or been terminated in defeat for the United States. In the latter case, the Marxists would either have won the presidency or come so close to victory "as to enable them to sabotage the normal functioning of democracy."[6] Although other astute scholars also recognize the strength of democratic traditions in Chile, they are careful not to speak of a guaranteed democratic future and hedge their commentary with such qualifiers as "short of a victory

[5]See Francisco Walker Linares, *Nociones elementales de derecho del trabajo,* quinta edición refundida (Santiago: Editorial Nascimento, 1957), pp. 45–46. Such racist views are said to be commonplace in Chile. See, for example, Pike, *Chile and the United States,* pp. 289–293.

[6]Halperin, *Nationalism and Communism in Chile,* pp. 223, 239.

of the ideological extremes" and "barring the setting aside of democratic processes."[7]

Just a few months before he became President of Chile, Frei pointedly warned the American public that the Marxist left in Chile, especially the Communist party, represented the challenge of "another civilization, another system of life, another interpretation of man. That is why the political challenge in our country is a total challenge." Even the program of the Christian Democratic party, he admitted, made the quest for political power in Chile entirely different from elections in the United States. Christian Democracy posited not slight variations of policy but "a change in the entire social structure, requiring new orientations for family, education, state, and man."[8] Perhaps Allende's defeat was a telling blow to Marxism; it may mark the end of a leftist threat, through victory in a presidential election, to the democratic route of modernization. We cannot yet be sure. Whatever that verdict, however, it is much too early still to know whether Christian Democracy will make the kind of progress toward a pluralistic society which will end ideological division in Chile.

[7]See, for example, Johnson, *Political Change in Latin America*, pp. 91–92 and Silvert, *Conflict Society*, p. 75.

[8]Frei, "Paternalism, Pluralism, and Christian Democratic Reform Movements in Latin America," pp. 36–37, 119.

Bibliography

THIS bibliography is intended to serve two purposes. In the first place, it will allow the reader to make an easy assessment of the kinds and general quality of materials used in the study. This could be accomplished through a careful reading of the footnotes but only at a greater cost in time, considerable repetition, and a generous dose of boredom. Second, the bibliography will be a useful guide to those interested in a deeper understanding of the origins of the legal system of industrial relations in Chile or some particular aspect of it. All known publication information is provided for each entry, which should facilitate library request or, in limited cases, purchase or some other form of acquisition.

The listing does not include nearly all of the materials that the author read or consulted in the course of his research. Only those materials found most useful and actually cited at least once in the foregoing pages are included here. The bibliography is, therefore, not exhaustive but is rather selective, with respect to the subject matter of this book. By the same token, it falls even much shorter of being exhaustive with respect to broad areas like the social question, labor legislation, immigration, the labor movement, or economic development which have been touched upon lightly or explored only as background to the narrower emphasis upon the role of élites and intellectuals in the genesis of the industrial relations system in Chile.

BIBLIOGRAPHY

Materials considered worthy of identification here are entered only once under one of the following headings: Government Documents, Archival Material and Student Papers, Newspapers and Journals, Proceedings of Private Organizations, Periodical Literature, and Books and Pamphlets. Government documents consist essentially of the record of debates of the Chilean Congress. The archives of the Conservative party are the only archival source which yielded important unpublished papers. The author combed the files of several newspapers and journals, covering periods of up to twenty-eight years, and only these extensive searches are listed. Many other similar sources, which provided only a citation or two in this book, have been omitted from the bibliography.

Fortunately, the official proceedings of the executive body or the general organizational meeting of a number of political parties, employer associations, and unions were accessible. These proceedings vary in kind, detail, and quality and are really not complete stenographic records. Party convention proceedings are generally more complete than employer or union organization proceedings, but this quality advantage is offset by the sad fact that, during the years covered by this study, the political parties appear to have celebrated only a few of the conventions they normally should have. On the other hand, the executive council of the Society for Factory Development met quite frequently and the minutes of these meetings are reproduced in the official organ of the Society. Only one union convention record is listed in the section on proceedings, but it must be explained that several others have been reported in installments in union or party newspapers at convention time. For example, the major decisions adopted at the 1921 Rancagua convention of the FOCH were faithfully reproduced in *La Federación Obrera*. Indeed, reliance upon the newspaper in general as a publication medium in Chile (and in Latin America as a whole) seems to be greater than in other areas of the world which have achieved a highly differentiated communications system.

A great many of the books listed in the bibliography are university student theses, and they have been a rich primary source for this study of the intellectuals and the labor laws of 1924. They are cited primarily in Chapter 5, "The Conservative Party and the Intellectuals," and in Chapter 6, "The Liberal Alliance Project and the Intellectuals." Political party proceedings are used in the same two chapters. Proceedings and periodical literature, particularly minutes and articles from the journals of the Society for Factory Development and the National Agricultural Society, figure importantly in Chapter 7, "The Élite Opposition." Government documents (congressional debates, bills, decrees, and laws) are basic sources for Chapters 5 and 6 and, very especially, for Chapter 8, "Crisis in the Congress," and Chapter 9, "Unanticipated Consequences."

A wide range of materials have gone into Chapters 1–4 ("Chile Today: Ideological Division and the Industrial Relations System," "The Intellectuals," "Consensus," and "The Social Question") and Chapter 9, "Unanticipated Consequences," which reflects an especially heavy reliance on union and party newspapers.

As to physical location, the bulk of the materials in this bibliography were consulted in Chile in the Congressional Library, the National Archives, the National Library, and the Library of the Faculty of Juridical Sciences.

GOVERNMENT DOCUMENTS

Congreso Nacional. *Actas de la Comisión Mixta de Legislación Social.* Santiago, [1923?].

—————. Cámara de Diputados. *Boletín de las Sesiones Extraordinarias.* 1900–1924.

—————. Cámara de Diputados. *Boletín de las Sesiones Ordinarias.* 1903–1924.

—————. Cámara del Senado. *Boletín de las Sesiones Extraordinarias.* 1919–1922.

—————. Cámara del Senado. *Boletín de las Sesiones Ordinarias.* 1919–1921.

Diario Oficial. 1925–1936. Source for the texts of many decrees and other laws used in this study.

League of Nations. *International Labour Conference, Proceedings.* 1919–1920.

"Proyecto de Código del Trabajo y de la Previsión Social." *Folletos Varios,* Tomo I, Biblioteca del Congreso, Santiago.

United States Department of Labor. Bureau of Labor Statistics. Bulletin 461.

ARCHIVAL MATERIAL AND STUDENT PAPERS

Archives of the Conservative Party of Chile. Letters, reports, and resolutions from 1895 to 1924.

Bullemore, Mabel. "Departamento Sindical del Partido Radical." Student paper, 1961.

González Labbe, Fernando. "El Departamento Sindical del Partido Demócrata Cristiano." Student paper, 1961.

Morgado Valenzuela, Emilio. "Departamentos Sindicales de Seis Partidos Políticos Chilenos." Student paper, 1964.

BIBLIOGRAPHY

NEWSPAPERS AND JOURNALS

Boletín Mensual de la Unión Patronal de la Industria y del Comercio de Chile. 1932–1937.

Boletín de la Oficina del Trabajo. 1910–1921.

Boletín de la Sociedad de Fomento Fabril. 1900–1928.

Boletín de la Sociedad Nacional de Agricultura. 1900–1920.

Diario Oficial. 1925–1936.

El Agricultor. 1920–1922.

El Despertar. 1921.

El Diario Ilustrado. 1919–1924.

Horizontes Nuevos. 1922–1925.

Justicia. 1924–1927.

La Federación Obrera. 1921–1922.

La Nación. 1919–1932.

PROCEEDINGS OF PRIVATE ORGANIZATIONS

Actas del Consejo Directivo de la Sociedad de Fomento Fabril, 1900–1924. *Boletín de la Sociedad de Fomento Fabril.*

Actas del Directorio de la Sociedad Nacional de Agricultura, 1919–1921. *El Agricultor.*

"Asamblea de Industriales, Conclusiones Aprobadas." *Boletín de la Sociedad de Fomento Fabril,* vol. 38, February 1921, pp. 67–73.

Confederación de Trabajadores de Chile. *Acuerdos del congreso constituyente 1936.* Santiago, sin fecha.

Partido Conservador. *La convención conservadora de 1895.* Santiago, 1895.

―――――. *Convención del partido conservador de 1918, actas.* Santiago, 1918.

―――――. *Convención del partido conservador de 1921, actas.* Santiago, 1921.

Partido Democrático. *Nuevo programa y reglamento del partido democrático aprobados por la convención ordinaria de 1913.* Santiago: Imprenta Central, 1915.

Partido Liberal. *Acta, convención del partido liberal, 1907.* Santiago: Imprenta Barcelona, 1907.

―――――. *Acta, tercera convención del partido liberal, 1913.* Santiago: Imprenta Barcelona, 1916.

―――――. *Program y estatuto orgánico del partido liberal, 1919.* Santiago: Imprenta Universo, 1921.

Partido Liberal Democrático. *Convención del partido liberal democrático. 1908.* Santiago, 1908.

Partido Nacional. *Convención del partido nacional, 1910, actas.* Santiago: Imprenta Zig-Zag, 1911.

Partido Radical. *Estatuto; Programa; Programa mínimo.* Santiago: Imprenta Artes y Letra, 1921.

―――――. *Memoria de la mesa directiva de la junta central radical.* Santiago: Editorial Minerva, 1923.

―――――. *Program del partido radical.* Santiago: Editorial Numen, 1920.

BIBLIOGRAPHY

PERIODICAL LITERATURE

"La Asociación del Trabajo de Chile," *Horizontes Nuevos,* Nov. 22, 1924, p. 3.

Ballesteros, Marto A. and Tom E. Davis. "The Growth of Output and Employment in Basic Sectors of the Chilean Economy, 1908–1957." *Economic Development and Cultural Change,* vol. 11, January 1963, pp. 152–176.

"Los Beneficios del Seguro Social Obligatorio." *Boletín de la Sociedad de Fomento Fabril,* vol. 30, 1 de Mayo, 1913, pp. 416–418.

"Carta, Eduardo Guerrero V. al Ministro de Industria y Obras Públicas, 21 Noviembre 1906." *Boletín de la Sociedad de Fomento Fabril,* vol. 23, p. 773.

"Carta, Sociedad de Fomento Fabril a la Comisión de Industria." *Boletín de la Sociedad de Fomento Fabril,* vol. 20, 1 de Julio, 1903, pp. 243–246.

"Carta, Sociedad de Fomento Fabril al Señor Ministro de Industria, 17 Diciembre 1907." *Boletín de la Sociedad de Fomento Fabril,* vol. 25, 1 de Enero, 1908, pp. 55–56.

"Chile." *Current History,* vol. 13, March 1921, p. 545.

Correa Pastene, M. "Necesidad de Unificar los Salarios." *El Agricultor,* Febrero 1921, p. 1.

———. "La Sindicalización de los Labriegos." *El Agricultor,* Enero 1921, p. 1.

"La Cuestión Obrera en Chile." *Boletín de la Sociedad Nacional de Agricultura,* vol. 38, 15 de Junio, 1907, pp. 349–351.

"La Cuestión Obrera en Chile." *Boletín de la Sociedad Nacional de Agricultura,* vol. 38, 15 de Julio, 1907, pp. 415–417.

"La Cuestión Obrera en Chile." *Boletín de la Sociedad Nacional de Agricultura,* vol. 38, 15 de Mayo, 1907, pp. 278–281.

"La Cuestión Obrera en Chile." *Boletín de la Sociedad Nacional de Agricultura,* vol. 39, 15 de Enero, 1908, pp. 1–9.

"La Cuestión Obrera en Chile." *Boletín de la Sociedad Nacional de Agricultura,* vol. 39, 15 de Febrero, 1908, pp. 67–75.

"La Cuestión Obrera en Chile." *Boletín de la Sociedad Nacional de Agricultura,* vol. 42, 15 de Marzo, 1911, pp. 132–134.

"La Cuestión Obrera en Chile." *Boletín de la Sociedad Nacional de Agricultura,* vol. 42, 15 de Mayo, 1911, pp. 268–271.

"La Cuestión Obrera en Chile." *Boletín de la Sociedad Nacional de Agricultura,* vol. 44, 15 de Diciembre, 1913, pp. 733–736.

D'Antonia, William. "Community Leadership in an Economic Crisis: Testing Ground for Ideological Cleavage." *American Journal of Sociology,* vol. 71, May 1966, pp. 688–700.

Davis, Tom E. "Eight Decades of Inflation in Chile, 1879–1959, A Political Interpretation." *The Journal of Political Economy,* vol. 71, August 1963, pp. 389–397.

Frías Collao, Eugenio. "Anexos." *Boletín de la Oficina del Trabajo,* no. 10, 1915, pp. 1–43.

BIBLIOGRAPHY

Iglesias, Santiago. "Labor Organization in Latin America." *Current History*, vol. 26, September 1927, p. 930.

"Informe de los Señores Concha y Quezada." *Boletín de la Sociedad de Fomento Fabril*, vol. 20, 1 de Enero, 1903, pp. 25–27.

"Labor Legislation Arising out of the International Labour Conference." *Official Bulletin of the International Labour Organization*, vol. 3, Feb. 16, 1921, p. 283.

Landsberger, Henry A., Manuel Barrera, and Abel Toro. "The Chilean Labor Union Leader: A Preliminary Report on His Background and Attitudes." *Industrial and Labor Relations Review*, vol. 17, April 1964, pp. 399–420.

Laughlin, J. Lawrence. "The Strike at Iquique." *The Journal of Political Economy*, vol. 17, January–December 1909, p. 643.

"Legislación del Trabajo." *Boletín de la Sociedad de Fomento Fabril*, vol. 20, 1 de Julio, 1903, pp. 217–218.

"Leyes y Código del Trabajo." *Industria y Comercio*, Septiembre 1932, pp. 132–133.

Lipset, Seymour Martin. "Some Social Requisites of Democracy: Economic Development and Political Legitimacy." *American Political Science Review*, vol. 53, March 1949, pp. 69–105.

Martínez, Marcial. "Ley sobre Alcoholes." *Boletín de la Sociedad de Fomento Fabril*, vol. 19, 1 de Junio, 1902, p. 203–205.

Mejía Valera, José. "Los Sindicatos como Grupos de Presión." *Revista de Sociología* (Universidad Nacional Mayor de San Marcos), vol. 1, no. 1, (Julio-Diciembre 1964), pp. 5–21.

"Membership of Trade Unions during the Years 1921 to 1926." *International Labour Review*, September 1927, p. 394.

Michels, Roberto. "Some Reflections on the Sociological Character of Political Parties." *American Political Science Review*, vol. 21, November 1927, pp. 753–772.

Montenegro, Ernesto. "Chile's First Middle-Class President." *Current History*, vol. 13, December 1920, pp. 400–401.

Morris, James O. "Consensus, Ideology and Labor Relations." *Journal of Inter-American Studies*, vol. 7, July 1965, pp. 301–315.

Moulian, Tomás. "La Conducta de la Clase 'Alta' Chilena." *Panoramas*, vol. 3, Mayo-Junio 1965, pp. 55–61.

Orrego Luco, Augusto. "La Cuestión Social en Chile." *Anales de la Universidad de Chile*, vol. 119, primero y segundo trimestres de 1961, nos. 121 y 122, pp. 43–45.

Poblete Troncoso, Moisés. "Labor Organizations in Chile." *Monthly Labor Review*, vol. 28, February 1929, pp. 83–88.

————. "Recent Advances in Labour Legislation in Latin America." *International Labour Review*, vol. 30, July 1934, p. 63.

Portuando, José A. "Los Intelectuales y la Revolución." *Cuba Socialista*, vol. 4, Junio 1964, pp. 51–64.

Roller, Arnold. "White Terror in Liberal Chile." *Nation,* vol. 121, Oct. 14, 1925, pp. 415–416.

Shils, Edward. "The Intellectuals in the Political Development of the New States." *World Politics,* vol. 12, April 1960, pp. 329–368.

"La Sociedad durante 30 Años." *Boletín de la Sociedad de Fomento Fabril,* vol. 30, 1 de Octubre, 1913, p. 919.

"La Solución Directa y el Derecho de Asociación." *Horizontes Nuevos,* 13 de Mayo, 1922, p. 1.

"South America III: Chile." *Fortune,* vol. 17, May 1938, pp. 75–76, 154.

Windmuller, John P. "External Influences on Labor Organizations in Underdeveloped Countries." *Industrial and Labor Relations Review,* vol. 16, July 1963, pp. 559–573.

————. "Model Industrial Relations Systems." *Proceedings of the Sixteenth Annual Meeting of the Industrial Relations Research Association,* Boston, Mass., Dec. 27, 28, 1963, pp. 62–75.

Wirth, Louis. "Consensus and Mass Communication." *American Sociological Review,* vol. 13, February 1948, pp. 1–15.

BOOKS AND PAMPLETS

Alba, Víctor. *Historia del movimiento obrero en América Latina.* México: Libreros Mexicanos Unidos, 1964.

Alesandri Palma, Arturo. *Recuerdos de gobierno.* Vol. I. Santiago: Editorial Universitaria, 1952.

Alexander, Robert J. *Communism in Latin America.* New Brunswick: Rutgers University Press, 1957.

————. *Labor Relations in Argentina, Brazil, and Chile.* New York: McGraw-Hill, 1962.

————. "The Labor and Socialist Movement of Chile." Microfilm, Columbia University Library, 1941.

————. *Organized Labor in Latin America.* New York: The Free Press, 1965.

————. *Prophets of the Revolution.* New York: The Macmillan Co., 1962.

Alfonso, José A. *Los partidos políticos de Chile.* Santiago: Imprenta Esmeralda, [1902?].

Almond, Gabriel A. and Sidney Verba. *The Civic Culture: Political Attitudes and Democracy in Five Nations.* Princeton, N. J.: Princeton University Press, 1963.

Armstrong Verdugo, Alberto. *Las huelgas en Chile en 1962: su magnitud y causas.* Tésis. Santiago: Universidad de Chile, 1964.

————. *El proceso de negociación colectiva en Chile.* Santiago: INSORA, 1964.

Arriagada Contreras, Daniel. *El contrato de trabajo.* Santiago: Imprenta Nacional, 1920.

Bañados, Guillermo M. *Avancemos.* Santiago: Imprenta La Universal, 1920.

—————. *La última convención del partido democrático.* Santiago: Imprenta Universal, 1922.

Barría Serón, Jorge. *Trayectoria y estructura del movimiento sindical chileno, 1946–1962.* Santiago: INSORA, 1963.

Barros Errázuriz, Alfredo. *El partido conservador.* Santiago: Imprenta Cervantes, 1917.

Bendix, Reinhard. *Work and Authority in Industry.* New York: John Wiley and Sons, Inc., 1956.

Bernales Zañartu, Moisés. *Estudio sobre la legislación del trabajo.* Santiago: Imprenta Claret, 1913.

Biblioteca América, Sección Chilena. *El Presidente Alessandri a través de sus discursos y actuación política.* Santiago: Imprenta Gutenberg, 1926.

Blasier, Stewart Cole. "The Cuban and Chilean Communist Parties." Ann Arbor: University Microfilms, 1956.

Briones, Guillermo and José Mejía Valera. *El obrero industrial.* Lima: Instituto de Investigaciones Sociológicas, Universidad Nacional Mayor de San Marcos, 1964.

Calvez, Jean-Yves, S. J. and Jacques Perrin, S. J. *The Church and Social Justice.* Chicago: Henry Regnery Company, 1961.

Carr, Edward Hallet. *What Is History?* New York: Alfred A. Knopf, 1962.

Carreño Ulloa, Cora. *El principio de la libertad sindical y la legislación chilena.* Santiago: Editorial Jurídica, 1952.

Castelar, Emilio. *Legislación obrera.* Santiago: Imprenta Cervantes, 1909.

Choron, Jacques. *Death and Western Thought.* New York: Collier Books, 1963.

—————. *Modern Man and Mortality.* New York: The Macmillan Company, 1964.

Comisión de Reformas de las Leyes Sociales. *La legislación social.* Santiago: Imprenta la Nación, 1929.

Concha, Juan Enrique. *Conferencias sobre economia social.* Santiago: Imprenta Chile, 1918.

—————. *Cuestiones obreras.* Santiago: Imprenta Barcelona, 1899.

Concha S., Luis Malaquías. *Sobre la dictación de un código del trabajo y de la previsión social.* Santiago: Imprenta Cervantes, 1907.

Cook, Alice H. *An Introduction to Japanese Trade Unionism.* Ithaca, N. Y.: New York State School of Industrial and Labor Relations, Cornell University, 1966.

D'Antonio, William V. and Howard J. Ehrlich, eds. *Power and Democracy in America.* Notre Dame, Ind.: University of Notre Dame Press, 1961.

D'Antonio, William V. and Fredrick B. Pike, eds. *Religion, Revolution and Reform: New Forces for Change in Latin America.* New York: Frederick A. Praeger, 1964.

de Huszar, George B., ed. *The Intellectuals.* Illinois: The Free Press of Glencoe, 1960.

Díaz Lira, Javier. *Observaciones sobre la cuestión social en Chile.* Santiago: Imprenta Chile, 1904.

Donoso, Ricardo. *Alessandri, agitador y demoledor.* Vol. I. México: Fondo de Cultura Económica, 1952.

Dunlop, John T. *Industrial Relations Systems.* New York: Henry Holt and Company, 1958.

Dynes, Russell R., Alfred C. Clarke, Simon Dinitz, and Iwao Ishino. *Social Problems: Dissensus and Deviation in an Industrial Society.* New York: Oxford University Press, 1964.

Ebenstein, William. *Today's ISMS.* 4th ed. Englewood Cliffs, N. J.: Prentice-Hall, Inc., 1964.

Editorial Ginebra. *Legislación social de América.* Vol. I. Santiago: Editorial Ginebra [1937?].

Eliade, Mircea. *The Myth of the Eternal Return.* New York: Pantheon Books, Inc., 1949.

Erlijman, J. *La función social de los intelectuales.* Buenos Aires: Editorial Bibliográfica Omeba, 1962.

Errázuriz Tagle, Jorge. *El desarrollo histórico de nuestra cuestión social.* Santiago: Imprenta Universitaria, 1906.

Escala, Enrique. *Sobre el contrato del trabajo.* Santiago, 1907.

Feifel, Herman, ed. *The Meaning of Death.* New York: McGraw-Hill, 1959.

Feliú Cruz, Guillermo. *1891–1924, Chile visto a través de Agustín Ross, ensayo de interpretación.* Santiago: Imprenta Pino, 1950.

Fetter, Frank W. *Monetary Inflation in Chile.* Princeton: Princeton University Press, 1931.

Galdames, Luis. *Historia de Chile.* Décimotercera edición. Santiago: Empresa Editora Zig-Zag, 1952.

Galenson, Walter. *Why the American Labor Movement Is Not Socialist.* Reprint no. 168. Institute of Industrial Relations, University of California (Berkeley), 1961.

González, Carlos Roberto. *Las huelgas.* Santiago: Imprenta Universitaria, 1908.

González, Pedro Luis. *Chile industrial.* Santiago: Imprenta Universo, 1921.

—————. *50 años de labor de la Sociedad de Fomento Fabril.* Santiago: Imprenta Universo, 1933.

—————. *El contrato del trabajo.* Santiago: Imprenta Universo, 1912.

Green Ortega, Julio y Segundo Correa Osorio. *Observaciones al anteproyecto de reforma de la legislación social.* Santiago: Imprenta Artes y Letras, 1929.

Gutiérrez Martínez, Marcos. *La cuestión obrera i el derecho de propiedad.* Santiago: Imprenta Barcelona, 1904.

Hagen, Everett E. *On the Theory of Social Change: How Economic Growth Begins.* Homewood, Ill.: The Dorsey Press, Inc., 1962.

Halperin, Ernst. *Nationalism and Communism in Chile.* Cambridge, Mass.: M.I.T. Press, 1965.

BIBLIOGRAPHY

Hermansen Vergara, Robinson. *El problema social y la enseñanza del derecho.* Santiago: Imprenta Barcelona, 1907.

Hirschman, Albert O. *Journeys toward Progress.* New York: The Twentieth Century Fund, 1963.

Holley, Héctor. *Las huelgas.* Santiago: Imprenta Aurora, 1905.

Inman, Samuel Guy. *Latin America.* Rev. ed. New York: Harcourt, Brace and Company, 1942.

Jobet, Julio César. *Ensayo crítico del desarrollo económico-social de Chile.* Santiago: Editorial Universitaria, 1955.

————. *Luis E. Recabarren.* Santiago: Prensa Latinoamericana, 1955.

Johnson, John W., ed. *Continuity and Change in Latin America.* Stanford: Stanford University Press, 1964.

————. *Political Change in Latin America: The Emergence of the Middle Sectors.* Stanford: Stanford University Press, 1958.

Jorquera F., Francisco. *Del trabajo minero en general y particularmente del laboreo al pirquen.* Concepción: Imprenta Moderna, 1913.

Kahler, Erich. *The Meaning of History.* New York: George Braziller, 1964.

Keller R., Carlos. *La eterna crisis chilena.* Santiago, 1931.

Kerr, Clark John T. Dunlop, Frederick H. Harbison, and Charles A. Myers. *Industrialism and Industrial Man.* Cambridge: Harvard University Press, 1960.

Lagos V., Tulio. *Bosquejo histórico del movimiento obrero en Chile.* Santiago, 1947.

Landsberger, Henry A. y Fernando Canitrot. *Iglesia, intelectuales y campesinos: la huelga de Molina.* Santiago: Editorial del Pacífico, 1966.

Landsberger, Henry A. y Raúl Dastres M. *La situación actual y el pensamiento del administrador de presonal chileno.* Santiago: INSORA, 1964.

Lipset, Seymour Martin. *The First New Nation: The United States in Historical and Comparative Perspective.* New York: Basic Books, Inc., 1963.

————. *Political Man: The Social Bases of Politics.* New York: Doubleday and Company, 1960.

MacGaffey, Wyatt and Clifford R. Barnett. *Cuba, Its People, Its Society, Its Culture.* New Haven, Conn.: Hraf Press, 1962.

McBride, George M. *Chile: Land and Society.* New York: American Geographical Society, 1936.

Maitland, Francis J. G. *Chile: Its Land and People.* London: Francis Griffiths, 1914.

Marín Carmona, Rodolfo. *El salario.* Santiago: Imprenta Bellavista, 1909.

Mendoza Diez, Alvaro. *La revolución de los profesionales e intelectuales en Latinoamerica.* México: Universidad Nacional Autónoma, 1962.

Millen, Bruce H. *The Political Role of Labor in Developing Countries.* Washington: The Brookings Institution, 1963.

Mills, C. Wright. *The Power Élite.* New York: Oxford University Press, 1956.

————. *White Collar.* New York: Oxford University Press, 1951.

BIBLIOGRAPHY

Monsen, Jr., R. Joseph and Mark W. Cannon. *The Makers of Public Policy: American Power Groups and their Ideologies.* New York: McGraw-Hill, 1965.

Morris, James O. y Roberto Oyaneder C. *Afiliación y finanzas sindicales en Chile, 1932–1959.* Santiago: Universidad de Chile, 1962.

Munizaga O., Ernesto. *El seguro obrero.* Santiago: Imprenta Barcelona, 1908.

Needler, Martin C. *Latin American Politics in Perspective.* Princeton: Princeton University Press, 1963.

Neufeld, Maurice F. *Poor Countries and Authoritarian Rule.* Ithaca, N. Y.: New York State School of Industrial and Labor Relations, 1965.

Palacios S., Bartolomé. *El partido conservador y el partido radical frente a frente.* Santiago, 1918.

Pantaleon Fontecilla, Eduardo. *La reforma legislativa y política y nuestra cuestión social.* Santiago: Imprenta Chile, 1907.

Parada Zapata, Teodorindo. *Algunas consideraciones sobre inmigración.* Santiago: Imprenta El Globo, 1913.

Paz, Octavio. *The Labyrinth of Solitude: Life and Thought in Mexico.* Translated by Lysander Kemp. New York: Grove Press, 1961.

Pike, Fredrick B. *Chile and the United States.* Notre Dame, Ind.: University of Notre Dame Press, 1963.

————, ed. *Freedom and Reform in Latin America.* Notre Dame, Ind.: University of Notre Dame Press, 1959.

Pincheira Oyarzún, Anibal. *Sindicalismo.* Santiago: Nascimento, 1934.

Poblete Troncoso, Moisés. *El derecho del trabajo y la seguridad social en Chile.* Santiago: Editorial Jurídica, 1949.

————. *El movimiento obrero latinoamericano.* México: Fondo de Cultura Económica, 1946.

————. *La organización sindical en Chile y otros estudios sociales.* Santiago: Imprenta Ramón Brias, 1926.

Rama, Carlos M. *Los intelectuales y la política.* Montevideo: Ediciones Nuestro Tiempo, 1962.

Ramírez Necochea, Hernan. *Historia del movimiento obrero en Chile, siglo XIX.* Santiago: Talleres Gráficos Santaro, 1956.

Rand School of Social Science. *The American Labor Year Book, 1916 and 1925.* New York: The Rand School of Social Science, 1916, 1925.

Rocha S., Domingo M. *Cuestiones obreras.* Concepción: Imprenta Chile, 1916.

Rodríguez Mendoza, Emilio. *El golpe de estado de 1924.* Santiago: Editorial Ercilla, 1938.

Rodríguez Pérez, Manuel. *La conciliación y el arbitraje en las huelgas.* Santiago: Imprenta Santiago, 1914.

Ross, Arthur M. and Paul T. Hartman. *Changing Patterns of Industrial Conflict.* New York: John Wiley and Sons, Inc., 1960.

Ross, Edward A. *South of Panama.* New York: Century, 1915.

Rossel Silva, Guillermo. *De la necesidad de legislar sobre el trabajo*. Santiago: Imprenta Cervantes, 1906.

Sánchez Mira, Pablo. *El salario*. Santiago: Imprenta Chile, 1914.

Sandoval Hurtado, Fernando. *Ensayo sobre la cuestión social en Chile*. Santiago: Imprenta Bellavista, 1913.

Sanhueza, Gabriel. *Santiago Arcos, comunista, millonario y calavera*. Santiago: Editorial del Pacífico, 1956.

Silva, Jorge Gustavo. *El liberalismo político*. Valparaíso: Imprenta Royal, 1914.

————. *Nuestra evolución político-social (1900–1930)*. Santiago: Imprenta Nascimento, 1931.

Silvert, Kalman H. *Chile: Yesterday and Today*. New York: Holt, Rinehart and Winston, 1965.

————. *The Conflict Society: Reaction and Revolution in Latin America*. New Orleans: The Hauser Press, 1961.

Simon, Fanny. "Recabarren." Unpublished book manuscript.

Sociedad de Fomento Fabril. *Memorandum sobre política económica*. Santiago: Empresa Zig-Zag, 1916.

Stevenson, John Reese. *The Chilean Popular Front*. Philadelphia: University of Pennsylvania Press, 1942.

Tapia Carvajal, Juan. *Legislación del trabajo en Chile, algunos antecedentes históricos*. Santiago: La Gratitud Nacional, 1937.

Valdés Canje, J. (pseudonym used by Alejandro Venegas). *Cartas al Excelentísmo Señor Don Pedro Montt*. Valparaíso, 1909.

Valdés Freire, J. Miguel. *Acciones de trabajo*. Santiago: Imprenta Cervantes, 1922.

Vial Infante, Julio. *Las cámaras del trabajo*. Santiago: Imprenta Bellavista, 1909.

Vicuña Subercaseaux, Benjamín. *Socialismo revolucionario y la cuestión social en Europa y Chile*. Santiago, 1908.

Walker Linares, Francisco. *Nociones elementales de derecho del trabajo*. Quinta edición refundida. Santiago: Editorial Nascimento, 1957.

Williams, Robin M., Jr. *American Society: A Sociological Interpretation*. 2nd ed. rev. New York: Alfred A. Knopf, 1960.

Yáñez, Eliodoro. *Política de previsión y de trabajo*. Santiago: Empresa Editora Zig-Zag, 1920.

Zegers Baeza, Agustín. *Algunas ideas sobre el Estado y la cuestión social*. Santiago: Imprenta Chile, 1911.

Zenteno Casanueva, J. *Diversas consideraciones sobre el régimen del trabajo y los conflictos colectivos*. Santiago: Imprenta Moderna, 1911.

Index